Studies in Relational Grammar 1

Studies in

Edited by
David M. Perlmutter

Relational Grammar 1

The University of Chicago Press

Chicago and London

DAVID M. PERLMUTTER is professor of linguistics at the University of California, San Diego. He is the author of numerous articles and books, including *Deep and Surface Structure Constraints in Syntax* and (with Scott Soames) *Syntactic Argumentation and the Structure of English*.

The University of Chicago Press, Chicago 60637
The University of Chicago Press, Ltd., London

5 4 3 2 1   83 84 85 86 87 88 89

Library of Congress Cataloging in Publication Data
Main entry under title:

Studies in relational grammar.

   Includes index.
   1. Relational grammar—Addresses, essays, lectures.
I. Perlmutter, David M.
PS158.6.S76   415   82–6945
ISBN 0–226–66050–8   AACR2

Contents

Acknowledgments

The names of some of the people who contributed to this volume appear neither in the table of contents nor in the acknowledgments for individual papers. These include Charles Jackson, who went over the edited manuscript, making many changes and corrections, William Davies, who prepared the index and helped with the proofreading, Jeanne Gibson, who edited one of the papers, and Inci Özkaragöz, who helped with the proofreading.

Introduction

The emergence of relational grammar (RG) in the 1970s was a direct challenge to some of the most basic assumptions of syntactic theory. Structuralist and transformational grammar (TG) shared the assumption that clause structure can be represented in terms of linear order and dominance relations among the elements of a clause. TG added transformations such as Passive, Subject Raising, WH-Movement, etc., conceived of as operations moving constituents from one position in a phrase marker to another. But TG retained the structuralist conception of clause structure in terms of linear order and dominance. RG challenged this assumption by showing that there are significant generalizations, both cross-linguistic and language-internal, that can be captured in terms of grammatical relations but not in terms of phrase structure configurations or morphological case. To capture such generalizations, it is necessary to abandon the structuralist-transformational approach and represent clause structure in terms of grammatical relations.

Since the inception of RG, a number of 'surfacist' frameworks have been proposed which posit only one syntactic level (extensionally close to the final level in RG). Some have adopted relational representations of clause structure, at least in part. Some posit a level of semantic, thematic, or other 'deep' relations, but they differ from RG in not positing purely *syntactic* notions such as subject, direct object, and indirect object at more than one level.

RG thus makes two basic claims that distinguish it from other current syntactic frameworks:

(1) a. The grammatical relations needed for individual grammars and for cross-linguistic generalizations cannot be defined in terms

The editor is indebted to Peter Cole, William Davies, Gilles Fauconnier, and especially Sandra Chung and Carol Rosen for comments on earlier drafts of this introduction.

of other notions, but must be taken as primitive notions of syntactic theory.

b. It is necessary to posit distinct syntactic (i.e., nonsemantic, nonthematic) levels.

Some other frameworks deny one of these claims and some deny both. RG is the only current framework that makes both claims.

The papers in this volume support these claims. The cross-linguistic and language-internal generalizations they bring to light are achieved through the use of primitive grammatical relations and distinct syntactic levels. The results are therefore a challenge to frameworks that reject these constructs.

Two of the papers in Part One show some of the first generalizations undetected in phrase structure or morphological terms which became apparent in terms of grammatical relations.

Perlmutter and Postal's paper "The Relational Succession Law" (RSL), written in 1972, antedates the development of RG. Written in a transformational framework, RSL points out a relationally based generalization governing raising rules in natural languages. The same generalization is then shown to hold for ascension out of nonclausal nominals in Malagasy—a degree of generality not previously attained. The existence of such cross-linguistic regularities in terms of grammatical relations is one of the motivations for a relationally based theory of clause structure.

"Toward a Universal Characterization of Passivization" (UCP) argues that the devices used in structuralist and transformational grammar are unable to give an adequate cross-linguistic account of passivization. Passivization cannot be characterized in terms of movement (as in TG), case marking, or verbal morphology. Once clause structure is conceived of in terms of grammatical relations, however, passives in the languages examined all have something in common. UCP proposes a universal characterization of passivization in terms of grammatical relations, arguing that the word order and case patterns in active and passive clauses in various languages are predictable from grammatical relations plus independent word order and case marking rules of the languages in question. The idea that passivization involves movement of nominals is seen to be an illusion created by the fact that actives and passives have different grammatical relations, resulting in different word orders for actives and passives in many languages.

These ideas made it possible to see the fundamental distinction between Passive, Dative Movement, Raising, etc., on the one hand, and Question Movement, Relativization, and Topicalization, on the other: the rules in the first class are promotions of nominals to one of the three 'term' relations: subject, direct object, or indirect object, while the rules in the second class do not involve nominals assuming term relations. This distinction holds not only internal to English, but cross-linguistically. Similarly, conditions on Equi controllers, Equi victims, and the antecedents of reflexives were seen to operate in terms of grammatical relations rather than phrase structure configurations. Verb agreement, case marking, and linear order were seen to be predictable from grammatical relations in individual languages. The various phenomena characterizable in terms of grammatical relations are independent of linear order and phrase structure configurations.

The TG tradition had fostered two related ideas about grammatical relations: the idea that they are relevant only at the level of deep structure and the idea that they can be defined in terms of phrase structure configurations. These ideas are related because (as pointed out in the Afterword to RSL) the definitions of grammatical relations proposed in TG do not work for derived structures, even in English. Further, the range of cross-linguistic variation in word order and case patterns makes it impossible to give cross-linguistically viable definitions of grammatical relations in terms of phrase structure configurations or case. Grammatical relations must be considered to be primitive notions and must figure in syntactic representations. UCP therefore introduced relational networks (RNs), which represent the grammatical relations that elements of a sentence bear to each other and the syntactic level(s) at which those relations hold. While RNs also reconstruct constituency relations, the role of grammatical relations in RNs makes RNs fundamentally different from the phrase structure conceptions of clause structure shared by structuralist and transformational grammar.

The RG conception of clause structure, based on taking grammatical relations as primitive notions and positing distinct syntactic levels, has had significant consequences in a number of areas.

First, it has made it possible to formulate laws of grammar such as those in "Some Proposed Laws of Basic Clause Structure" (SPL), which would not be statable without the cross-linguistically viable notions of grammatical relations obtained by making them primitives of the theory. These laws also presuppose distinct syntactic levels.

Another cross-linguistic regularity in terms of grammatical relations can be seen in causative constructions. In many languages differing in word order and case patterns, the final subject (1) of finally intransitive complements is the direct object (2) of the causative, while the final 1 of finally transitive complements is the indirect object (3) of the causative. This regularity cannot be captured without cross-linguistically viable notions of '1', '2', '3', 'transitive', and 'intransitive'. Frameworks that attempt to define grammatical relations in terms of other notions instead of taking them as primitives have not been able to give cross-linguistically adequate definitions of these five notions. Definitions of the 3-relation in terms of other concepts have not even been attempted.

Viewing grammatical constructions in terms of grammatical relations enables one to see that the same constructions recur across languages, despite differences in morphology and word order. For example, the papers in this volume by Chung, Aissen, and Allen and Frantz show the advancement of 3s to 2 in Indonesian, an SVO language, Tzotzil, a VOS language, and Southern Tiwa, which has relatively free word order. In the same vein, diverse languages have been shown to have advancements to 1, 2, and 3, the same class of demotions (Inversion, Antipassive, and 2-3 Retreat), relationally based ascensions (raising constructions and Possessor Ascension), Clause Union, and dummy constructions. Thus, the relational conception of clause structure has led to the discovery that natural language clause structures are limited to four types: revaluations (advancements and retreats), ascensions, Clause Union, and dummy constructions.

Indeed, the relational conception of clause structure has proved to be the most effective approach to date to the problem posed by the apparent diversity of natural language clause structures. One needs the right concepts to account for them all, without undue proliferation of theoretical apparatus. In bringing out previously undetected cross-linguistic similarities, the relational conception of clause structure reduces the number of structures that linguistic theory must posit. This strongly suggests that grammatical relations and syntactic levels are the right concepts for reducing the apparent diversity of natural language clause structures to a small number.

The theoretical constructs developed in RG yield insight into the structure of individual languages, making it possible to understand phenomena which would otherwise be mysterious. For example, Southern Tiwa, a Tanoan language of New Mexico, has a complex system of verbal prefixes marking agreement with various nominals in the clause. As Allen and Frantz show, once 3-2 Advancement is recognized, the prefixes are seen to agree not only with the final nuclear terms (1 and 2) of the clause, but also with the initial 2. With 3-2 Advancement and distinct syntactic levels, the problem is solved. In a similar vein, Aissen shows that 3-2 Advancement is needed to understand the suffix -*be* in Tzotzil. Aissen and Perlmutter show that positing Clause Union in Spanish constructions with certain verbs governing Equi or Subject Raising explains patterns of clitic placement that would otherwise be mysterious, and correctly predicts complement dependents to behave like matrix clause dependents with respect to

Reflexive Passive, Object Raising, and causative constructions.

Relational and transformational accounts of certain Indonesian data are contrasted in Chung's paper. Chung confronts the question of how a grammar of Indonesian is to state rules referring to direct objects. She shows that having rules refer to the notion 'NP in immediate postverbal position', as was traditional in TG, would work in certain cases, but not where that NP is, in relational terms, a chômeur. This is evidence not only for the concept of chômeurs, but also for grammar construction and syntactic representation in terms of grammatical relations rather than phrase structure. Chung's demonstration of the inadequacy of an account based on linear position is echoed by Aissen and Perlmutter's argument that the word order in Czech, Jacaltec, and Quechua makes it impossible for a transformational account in terms of adjunction or restructuring to mimic the relational idea of Clause Union.

Several papers in this volume bear on the adequacy of certain RG theoretical constructs. For example, it has been claimed in effect that data from Kinyarwanda violate the Stratal Uniqueness Law in SPL. Dryer's paper addresses this issue, arguing that an analysis conforming to the Stratal Uniqueness Law is superior to one that violates it. This issue is also discussed in SPL. Bell's paper is a contribution to syntactic typology that bears on the cross-linguistic adequacy of the notion of subject. This notion has been claimed to be inapplicable to Philippine languages. Since these languages do differ from more familiar languages in certain respects, the question is how to characterize the differences. Bell's proposal for Cebuano localizes the differences in two places. She argues first, that nominals bearing any of a number of different grammatical relations can advance to 1, and second, that only an *initial* 1 can serve as the antecedent for Equi and reflexives. In other respects, Cebuano is like other attested languages. Bell concludes that the various laws and principles of RG, though logically independent, support a straightforward and consistent analysis of the Cebuano data in which the notion of subject plays a key role.

A theoretical innovation of RG is the chômeur relation, which has no antecedents either in traditional grammar or in modern theories. Of all the grammatical relations posited in RG, the chômeur relation is the clearest example of a relation that cannot be defined in terms of phrase structure configurations, morphological case, or semantic or thematic notions. Further, a construct equivalent to the chômeur relation cannot be incorporated into a framework that posits only one syntactic level. Evidence for the chômeur relation is therefore evidence both for the primitive nature of grammatical relations and for distinct syntactic levels. Chung's paper provides such evidence. In Indonesian, the chômeur in the Passive construction appears as object of the preposition *oleh,* while that in the 3-2 Advancement construction has no case or prepositional marking. Chung shows that chômeurs behave as a class distinct both from terms (1s, 2s, and 3s) and obliques with respect to Quantifier Shift. Since this generalization is unstatable in terms of phrase structure configurations, morphological case, or semantic or thematic notions, and since it requires distinct syntactic levels, it provides evidence not only for the chômeur relation, but also for the relational conception of clause structure.

The 1970s saw far-reaching changes in TG and the emergence of a number of alternative frameworks, many of which have yet to be evaluated in the light of data from the less familiar languages. The papers in this volume provide solutions in relational terms to a wide range of empirical problems that other frameworks have not yet confronted. The fact that more than one nominal in Kinyarwanda clauses can behave like an object, discussed in Dryer's paper and in §8 of SPL, ostensibly violates principles of certain frameworks. So does the fact that in Niuean, as Seiter shows, both 1s and 2s can raise. Many other frameworks have not yet proposed analyses of Philippine languages that account for Bell's Cebuano data. Aissen's 3-2 Advancement analysis of Tzotzil, which has no final 3s, is incompatible with some frameworks' claims. The data and solutions in this volume provide material that alternative theories of clause structure must come to terms with.

The solutions presented here are all the more interesting because many alternative frameworks explicitly reject the types of devices on which these solutions rely. For example, advocates of surfacist theories claiming that one syntactic level is sufficient must show that those theories' accounts of the phenomena discussed here do not entail loss of generality. How do they account for verb agreement in Southern Tiwa without complicating the grammar or unduly broadening the class of agreement systems that linguistic theory must recognize? How do they deal with Seiter's arguments that the raised nominal in Niuean cannot be an initial dependent of the matrix clause? Since they lack the notion of chômeur (which relies on distinct syntactic levels), how can they exploit Chung's generalization about Quantifier Shift in Indonesian?

In all these cases, the relational solutions proposed here provide a standard against which other frameworks' solutions must be judged.

Since the papers in this volume were written at different times, they show to differing degrees the influence of the transformational framework out of which RG developed. One can see a development from the transformational framework of RSL to the later papers which adopt syntactic representations in terms of RNs. In between lie studies like

Chung's, where phenomena are treated directly in terms of grammatical relations, but no explicit notation is yet available. Chung's paper also reflects the early RG conception of the class of grammatical relations as consisting basically of the subject, direct object, and indirect object relations. In that framework, a chômeur was a nominal that had 'lost' its grammatical relation. The conception of chômage as a grammatical relation (the chômeur relation), like syntactic representation in terms of RNs, was introduced in UCP.

The papers in this volume also differ with respect to whether they assume a derivational framework, with rules converting structures into other structures. For the concerns of this volume, the issue of derivations does not play a significant role.

In Part One, the three papers by Perlmutter and Postal introduce the basic framework. Dryer's paper complements the discussion of Kinyarwanda in §8 of SPL. Part Two consists of four papers on advancements. The papers in Part Three deal with ascension and Clause Union.

The reader unfamiliar with RG should probably begin with UCP and RSL, which presuppose no previous knowledge of the framework. From there, one may proceed to some of the empirical papers written in relatively familiar (in most cases, derivational) terms: Chung's, Aissen's, Allen and Frantz's, Aissen and Perlmutter's, and Seiter's. Alternatively, one may go directly from UCP and RSL to §§1–7 of SPL, which state some basic laws in terms of RNs, perhaps following that with Bell's paper, which uses RNs extensively. While Dryer's paper can be read at any point, the discussion of Kinyarwanda in §8 of SPL is probably best reserved for relatively late in the sequence. It is devoted primarily to the methodological issues that arise when language-particular data conflict with a set of proposed universals.

The papers in this volume give some of the basic motivations for RG and illustrate its application to a variety of languages. Together with the papers in *Studies in Relational Grammar* 2, they show how a small number of simple ideas has provided successful accounts of data in a wide range of languages, incorporating both language-internal and cross-linguistic generalizations not statable in terms of the phrase structure representations shared by structuralist and transformational grammar, or the single-level representations used by recent surfacist theories. RG's achievements support its basic claims that syntactic theory needs both grammatical relations as theoretical primitives and distinct syntactic levels.

Part 1

1 Toward a Universal Characterization of Passivization   (I)

David M. Perlmutter and Paul M. Postal

p. 37

1   Introduction

This paper has two goals: to offer an introductory, relatively informal characterization of 'passivization' in language-independent terms and to draw some implications of this characterization for the nature of grammatical rules and linguistic structure in general.

Any adequate theory of language must be able to achieve the first goal. There exists a vast literature on the most diverse languages making use of concepts such as 'passive', 'passive voice', and 'passivization'. While the phenomena in particular languages referred to in these terms are usually described as having language-particular and idiosyncratic features, what is striking about the descriptions in the literature is the fact that in using such concepts they appeal to a universal underlying reality of some sort. The nature of this universal underlying reality, however, is not specified. We maintain that no grammatical theory can be considered adequate unless it is able to give these notions substantive content. In this paper we take initial steps toward achieving this goal.[1]

2.1   A Characterization in Terms of Word Order

Consider first an active-passive pair in English:

(1) a.   Louise reviewed that book.
     b.   That book was reviewed by Louise.

Since the appearance of Chomsky 1957, which proposed that the relation between active sentences and the 'corresponding' passives be treated by means of a transformation, a number of different proposals

Perlmutter's work has been supported in part by the National Science Foundation through Grant No. BNS 76-00764 to the Massachusetts Institute of Technology. An earlier version of this paper appeared in *Proceedings of the Third Annual Meeting of the Berkeley Linguistics Society.*

3

have been made as to how such a transformation should be stated. The following structural descriptions have all been proposed at one time or another:

(2) a. X – NP – V – NP – Y
 b. X – NP – V – (Prep) – NP – Y
 c. X – NP – V X – NP – Y

Under these proposals, Passive applies to any string that satisfies the structural description, which requires an NP immediately followed by a verb, followed by another NP. The structural descriptions in (2) differ with respect to what, if anything, may intervene between the verb and the second NP. But they agree that the class of structures to which Passive applies in English is characterized in terms of 'NP immediately followed by a verb followed by NP.'

There have also been a number of different proposals concerning the structural change effected by the passive transformation. These have differed as to whether the preposition *by,* the auxiliary verb *be,* and the participial morphology on the verb are inserted by the passive transformation, are already present in deep structures, or are accounted for by separate transformations. Common to the structural changes under various different proposals, however, are postposing of the preverbal NP and preposing of the postverbal NP. Proposals have differed with respect to whether these two operations are performed by a single transformation or two separate transformations.

Despite a great deal of variety in detail, then, most advocates of a passive transformation have agreed that:

(3) a. Passive in English applies to strings in which an NP, Verb, and NP occur in that order.
 b. Passivization involves postposing of the preverbal NP and preposing of the postverbal NP.[2]

Given such attempts to characterize passivization in English in terms of the linear order of elements, one might attempt to generalize this approach and characterize passivization in general in such terms. It is easy to see, however, that a statement of passivization along the lines of (3) cannot provide a universal account of the phenomenon. Because different languages have different characteristic word orders, neither structural descriptions like those in (2), summarized in (3a), nor a structural change like that in (3b) could possibly be universal.

Consider the following active-passive pair in Turkish:

(4) a. Hasan bavulu   açtɨ.
     Hasan suitcase-ACC open-PAST
     'Hasan opened the suitcase.'

b. Bavul   (Hasan tarafından) açıldı.[3]
suitcase-NOM (by Hasan)   open-PASS/PAST
'The suitcase was opened (by Hasan).'

How Passive would have to be formulated as a transformation for Turkish[4] is not fully clear. But it is at least evident that none of the structural descriptions in (2) can characterize Turkish Passive simply because the verb in Turkish is clause-final.[5]

A theory of language that requires statement of passivization in terms of a transformational structural description will not only have distinct rules for English and Turkish but will require a distinct rule for each language where the order of relevant constituents is different. Malagasy, where the verb is initial and the subject is normally in final position (see Keenan 1972), has active-passive pairs like:

(5) a. Nividy ny vary ho an'ny ankizy ny vehivavy.
bought the rice for the   children the woman
'The woman bought the rice for the children.'
  b. Novidin'   ny vehivavy ho an'ny ankizy ny vary.
bought-PASS the woman   for the   children the rice
'The rice was bought for the children by the woman.'

To state Passive in Malagasy as a transformation, a structural description something like the following would be necessary:

(6)   V – NP – X – NP

The structural change would have to permute the two NPs.[6] Passivization in Malagasy would thus be distinct from passivization in both English and Turkish.

Similarly, consider an active-passive pair in Nitinaht, a Wakashan language of British Columbia discussed in Klokeid 1975:

(7) a. Ch'ixwat-saʔap ʔa (ox) bowach ʔaq ʔoyoq Ralph.
frighten   AUX CASE deer   the CASE Ralph
'The deer frightened Ralph.'
  b. Ch'ixwat-saʔab't ʔa (ox) Ralph ʔoxwit   bowach ʔaq.
frighten-PASS   AUX CASE Ralph CASE-PASS deer   the
'Ralph was frightened by the deer.'

Nitinaht has VSO clause order. Thus a transformational statement of Passive in Nitinaht would yield a rule distinct from those in English, Turkish, and Malagasy.

In addition to yielding distinct Passive rules for different languages, an approach to passivization in terms of linear order, preposing, etc., is inadequate in another respect. Such ideas cannot even provide a gross account of the most superficial facts internal to the grammars of certain languages. First, there are languages in which the order of constituents in 'corresponding' actives and passives does not differ. Two such languages are cited in §7. Second, a theory that attempts to formulate passivization in terms of preposing and postposing will not yield natural accounts of passivization in languages with a word order free enough to eliminate motivation for positing a fixed 'underlying' order of constituents.

We have thus argued that attempts to state passivization transformationally require recognition of at least as many distinct passivization rules as there are different possible characteristic orders of relevant constituents in human clause structures. This is a consequence of the fact that the statement of a grammatical phenomenon in transformational terms *requires* reference to the linear order of elements. The failure of a transformational account of Passive to provide an adequate universal characterization is then a special case of the impossibility of a universal characterization of passivization in terms of the notions of linear order, 'preposing', and 'postposing'. Passivization is a phenomenon of natural language that is independent of linear order.

2.2   A Characterization in Terms of Case

In languages such as Latin and Russian, an active sentence and its 'corresponding' passive exhibit the same nominals with different case markings.

(8) Latin:
    a. Magister   puerōs   laudat.
        teacher-NOM boys-ACC praise-3SG
        'The teacher praises the boys.'
    b. Puerī   ā magistrō   laudantur.
        boys-NOM by teacher-ABL praise-PASS-3PL
        'The boys are praised by the teacher.'

(9) Russian:
    a. Car'   soslal Puškina.
        czar-NOM exiled Pushkin-ACC
        'The czar exiled Pushkin.'
    b. Puškin   byl soslan carem.
        Pushkin-NOM was exiled czar-INSTR
        'Pushkin was exiled by the czar.'

In both Latin and Russian, the nominal that is in the accusative case in the active sentence is in the nominative in the 'corresponding' passive. The nominal that is in the nominative case in the active sentence is marked differently in the 'corresponding' passives in the two languages. In Russian, it is in the instrumental case, while in Latin it is in the ablative case, accompanied by the preposition *ā*. Since Latin and Russian differ with respect to the marking in passive clauses of the nominal that is nominative in active clauses, a universal characterization of passivization in terms of case would have to focus on what is the same in these two languages, namely:

(10)   The nominal that is in the accusative case in an active clause is in the nominative in the 'corresponding' passive clause.

However, obviously no statement like (10) can even begin to serve as a basis for a universal characterization of passivization, for several reasons. First, (10) makes use of concepts like 'nominative' and 'accusative', which stand in exactly as much need of universal characterization as passivization itself. Second, there are vast numbers of languages like English (barring marginal pronominal phenomena) and Indonesian, in which the relevant 'corresponding' nominals have no case marking at all. Consider Indonesian:

(11) a.   Dokter itu me-meriksa   saya.
          doctor the TRANS-examine I
          'The doctor examined me.'
     b.   Saya di-periksa   oleh dokter itu.
          I   PASS-examine by   doctor the
          'I was examined by the doctor.'

The only difference in nominal marking between an active sentence and the 'corresponding' passive in Indonesian is the fact that one nominal in the passive is accompanied by the preposition *oleh*. Third, there are languages like West Greenlandic Eskimo manifesting both passivization and an ergative type case-marking system. As the following examples from Rischel 1975 illustrate, in such cases the 'corresponding' nominals can be in the absolute case in both active and passive:

(12) a.   Gimmi-p miiraq   kii-va-a.
          dog-ERG child-ABS bite-3SG-3SG
          'The dog bit the child.'
     b.   Miiraq   gimmi-mik kii-tsip-puq.
          child-ABS dog-INSTR bite-PASS-3SG
          'A child has been bitten by the/a dog.'

Since Eskimo has no accusative case at all in any sense, any characterization like (10) would fail for Eskimo even if it could be given a sound universal basis. Finally, there are languages in which nominals are marked with case but where the case marking of 'corresponding' nominals in active and passive is *exactly the same.* Basque, as described by Lafitte (1962), is of this type:

(13) a. Piarresek egin du etchea.
Peter-ERG make has house-ABS
'Peter made the house.'

b. Piarresek egina da etchea.
Peter-ERG made is house-ABS
'The house was made by Peter.'

In both the active and passive, *etchea* is in the absolutive case and *Piarresek* is in the ergative. Yet the two sentences differ in structure. While (13a) is transitive, (13b) is superficially intransitive, as evidenced by the auxiliary *da*, a form of *izan* 'be' used with intransitives (contrasting with the use of *ukan* 'have' in transitive clauses [see Postal 1977]), and by the fact that *Piarresek* does not trigger agreement in (13b).[7] The fact that case marking in (13a–b) is the same, however, reveals the hopeless inadequacy of a universal characterization of passivization in terms of case.

2.3 A Characterization in Terms of Verbal Morphology

In all the languages considered so far, active sentences differ from the corresponding passives in terms of verbal morphology. Typically, passive verbal morphology involves either a passive marker of some kind (prefix, suffix, or infix), or a participial or other nonfinite form of the verb plus a so-called auxiliary verb. This could suggest the possibility of characterizing passivization universally in terms of passive verbal morphology, with the differences in word order and case marking associated with passivization in some languages taken as a derivative effect.

However, such an attempt also obviously cannot get off the ground. First, there is no language-independent notion of 'passive morphology', that is, no way to independently theoretically pick out certain morphological properties in some languages as 'passive' rather than 'active'. Second, even if this fundamental problem could be overcome, there are languages in which a passive clause does not differ from the 'corresponding' active in verbal morphology..

Mandarin Chinese is such a language, as indicated by the following active-passive pair cited in Cummins 1976:

(14) a. Zhù lǎoshī   píyè-le   wǒ-de kǎoshì.
Zhu professor mark-ASP my   test
'Professor Zhu marked my test.'

b. Wǒ-de kǎoshì bèi Zhù lǎoshī   píyè-le.
my   test by Zhu professor mark-ASP
'My test was marked by Professor Zhu.'

While the active and the corresponding passive differ in word order and in the appearance of the preposition *bèi* in the passive, there is no difference between active and passive verbal morphology (*píyè-le*).

Achenese, studied by Lawler (1977), is another language where actives and passives do not differ in verbal morphology:

(15) a. Gɔpnyan ka   gɨ-cɔm lón.
         she   PERF kiss   I
         'She (already) kissed me.'

     b. Lón ka   gɨ-cɔm lé-gɔpnyan.
         I   PERF   kiss   by-she
         'I've (already) been kissed by her.'

In Achenese, actives and passives differ in word order and in the appearance of *lé* in the passive. But verbal forms are identical in 'corresponding' active and passive. Thus passivization can in no way be given a universal characterization in terms of verbal morphology.

3   Two Universals of Passivization

The fact that passivization cannot be given a universal characterization in terms of case, verbal morphology, or the linear order of elements does not mean that it cannot be characterized in language-independent terms. On the contrary, this result only shows that those notions are not the right ones for specifying grammatical rules like Passive. We claim that there are two universals of passivization underlying the data considered so far and that in order to explicate these it is necessary to appeal to, inter alia, such largely traditional (if unexplicated) relational notions as 'subject of' and 'direct object of'. This requires making a basic universal assumption about the nature of clause structure, which can be stated very informally as follows:

(16)   A clause consists of a network of grammatical relations. Among these relations are 'subject of', 'direct object of', and 'indirect object of'.

Once this assumption is made, the two universals of passivization referred to stand out rather clearly:

(17)   A direct object of an active clause is the (superficial) subject of the 'corresponding' passive.

(18)   The subject of an active clause is neither the (superficial) subject nor the (superficial) direct object of the 'corresponding' passive.[8]

Universals (17) and (18) taken together have the following consequence:[9]

(19)   In the absence of another rule permitting some further nominal to be direct object of the clause, a passive clause is a (superficially) intransitive clause.

If (17–18) are correct, then a direct object of an active clause is the subject of an *intransitive* clause in the 'corresponding' passive. We will now briefly sketch how this accounts for much of the data in §2, postponing further discussion to §6.2.

Consider first the data on case marking in passives in §2.2. The fact that the direct object of an active clause is in the nominative case in the 'corresponding' passive in Latin and Russian follows from the fact that the nominative is the case used for (superficial) subjects in those languages, i.e., subjects of active transitive and intransitive clauses. The fact that in Eskimo and Basque the direct object of an active clause is in the absolutive case in the 'corresponding' passive follows from the fact that the absolutive case is used for the subjects of *in*transitive clauses in those languages. The fact that in English, Indonesian, Mandarin Chinese, and Achenese the direct object of an active clause has no case or prepositional marking in the 'corresponding' passive follows from the fact that superficial subjects have no case or prepositional marking in those languages. Nothing has yet been said about the marking of the subject of an active clause in the 'corresponding' passive. This is dealt with in §6.2. The marking in passive clauses of the nominal that is the direct object in the 'corresponding' actives, however, has been shown to follow automatically from (17) and (18) plus the independently existing case-marking rules of the languages in question.

Now consider the data on word order in §2.1. If a direct object of an active sentence is the subject of the 'corresponding' passive, then it should stand in the same position in a passive clause as do the subjects of other superficially intransitive clauses in languages where the order of elements is not free. And this is in fact the case. Thus in English, Indonesian, Mandarin Chinese, and Achenese, where the subject is normally clause-initial, the direct object of the 'corresponding' active is normally in clause-initial position in the passive. In Malagasy, where subjects are clause-final, the direct objects of actives are likewise clause-final in the 'corresponding' passives. And in Nitinaht, where subjects immediately follow verbs, the direct object of an active immediately follows the verb in the 'corresponding' passive. All of this follows automatically from (17).

While we claim that (17–18) are universals of passivization, it does not follow that they are necessarily part of the rule Passive itself. It is necessary to sort out what in (17–18) is due to Passive itself and what to other universals of language that interact with it. We confront this problem in §6.

Our proposal that (17–18) are universals of passivization entails that (17–18) are characteristic of passivization in every language manifesting this phenomenon. This means that (17–18) must find expression internal to the grammar of each such language. This is possible only if clause structure in human languages is characterized in terms of the notions that make it possible to state (17–18)—that is, in terms of such relations as 'subject of', and 'direct object of'. In other words, in order to state (17–18), it is necessary to make assumption (16) both in universal grammar and in the grammars of particular languages. In §4, we sketch roughly and informally the way we conceive of and represent clause structures relationally.

4   On the Representation of Clause Structure

Our basic claim is that the structure of sentences, and also of clauses, which we will focus on here, consists of an object we will call a 'relational network' (RN). An RN is, formally, a graph-theoretic object involving as primitives three types of entities: 'nodes', which represent linguistic elements of all sorts, 'relational signs', which represent grammatical relations between elements, and 'coordinates', which represent distinct levels at which relations hold. Nodes are of two types, 'terminal' and 'nonterminal'. Terminal nodes represent substantive linguistic elements, including morphophonemic forms of morphemes. Nonterminal nodes represent more abstract elements such as clauses, phrases, and the like. Nonterminal nodes can be identified with positive integers. Relational signs can be thought of, informally, as the names of grammatical relations. Coordinates are also just numbers (distinct from nonterminal nodes). We can represent them as $c_1 \ldots c_n$. Unlike the set of nonterminal nodes, the set of coordinates is finite, in fact, quite small.

In terms of these three types of primitives, one can formally define the basic building blocks of RNs, which are called 'arcs'. Informally, an arc involves an ordered pair of nodes (a 'first' or 'dependent' node and a 'second' or 'governor' node) associated with exactly *one* relational sign and with a nonnull sequence of coordinates. Thus one particular arc might be the following, represented in two equivalent notations:

(20) a. $[1(45,666) \langle c_1 c_2 \rangle]$ b. 666

$$1 \mid c_1 c_2$$

45

If 1 is the name of the subject relation, 666 is a clause node and 45 a nominal node,[10] then the arc in (20) expresses the fact that the node 45 bears the subject relation to the clause node 666 at the c_1 and c_2

levels. Formally, a full RN is simply a set of arcs like that in (20).

Let us suppose now that we wish to represent in terms of arcs the entire linguistic structure of some clause, say that in:

(21)   Naomi gave that book to me.

We would then have to make explicit every node in such a clause and every relation between those nodes. This would involve all the nodes relevant to the syntactic, semantic, morphological, and phonological structure of the clause.

We are obviously not in a position to attempt this at this stage of our understanding. Consequently, we ignore all logical representations, and the relations of all elements to anything but clause nodes. This means, inter alia, that we artificially compress all those sub-RNs involving, for example, nominals, into single nodes. Thus, in representing (21), we would treat *that book* as a single node, ignoring for discursive purposes the obvious fact that it has internal structure. With this in mind, we can now represent the clause in (21) as follows:

(22)

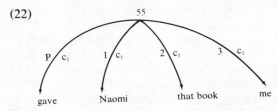

Given that 1, 2, 3, and P are the relational signs which name the respective grammatical relations 'subject', 'direct object', 'indirect object', and 'predicate', (22) indicates that (21) involves a clause with three nominal dependents and one predicate dependent, with the nominals bearing the 'subject', 'direct object', and 'indirect object' relations. Among the other simplifications in (22) is the fact that verbal tense and agreement are ignored, as is the relation of linear precedence holding between some nodes.

Before continuing, we should stress that we are not dealing here with the important question of how primitive relations like 1, 2, 3, and so on, are given an empirical interpretation. This involves, among other things, the question of the justification for asserting that in (21), for example, it is *Naomi* which bears the 1-relation, *that book,* the 2-relation, etc. Our ultimate claim is that the justification for such assignments (at the level of the c_1 coordinate) is universally determined by principles referring to the semantic role of the nominal. Thus, as traditionally recognized, agent nominals are initially 1s (although, of course, not all 1s represent agents), patients 2s, etc. Without over-looking the enormous difficulties in the way of making such an account precise, there is no doubt that even the rudimentary ideas lend significant language-independent empirical content to the claim that such and such nominal is an initial 1, 2, etc. Our claim in this study that a universal characterization of passivization is (only) possible in relational terms is to be relativized to a view of relations as given cross-linguistic substance (in part) by universal connections between the relational signs 1, 2, etc., and some representation of semantic relations.

It can be seen that the clause in (21) involves four distinct arcs, all of which share the same second node. In our representations, we have only written this node once, as a notational convenience. The alternative would be to represent the clause in (21) as follows:

(23)

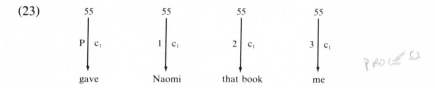

PROCESS

Moreover, since the particular identity of nonterminal nodes is never relevant, that is, structures which are the same except for distinct nonterminals are mere alphabetic variants, it is pointless to have a notation in which nonterminals are made explicit, since the presence of such a node is indicated by the intersection of arc lines. We will thus systematically suppress nonterminal nodes in our representations of clauses.

It can be seen that all of the arcs in (22) share a coordinate (c_1). This is not a necessary feature of arcs with the same second node. It defines, we claim, a crucial property of arcs, namely, the property of belonging to the same *stratum*. A stratum is simply the maximal set of arcs with the same second node sharing some coordinate. Thus any set of arcs like those in (22) will define from 1 to n strata. The notion 'stratum' can be used to reconstruct formally the notion of linguistic level.

In the example of an RN given above, each dependent node bears only one relation to its governing node; that is, each dependent node is the first node of only one arc. But this is by no means a necessary condition on RNs. Switching to artificial examples, for the moment, the following is a perfectly possible RN, where GR_x, GR_y, GR_z, GR_w, and GR_u are arbitrary relational signs:

relations between rels?

(24)

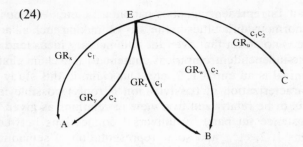

Here two of the dependent nodes, A and B, are first nodes of two different arcs. The RN in (24) has two distinct strata, one containing the arcs in (25a), the other those in (25b):

(25) a.

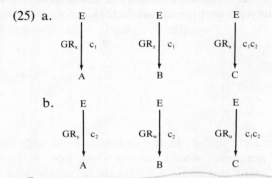

b.

Such an RN thus indicates that the same element, e.g., A, bears one relation (named GR_x) at the c_1 level, and another (named GR_y) at the c_2 level.

Now, it is convenient for presentational purposes to modify our notation for representing sets of stratified arcs (RNs). We can do this by eliminating the coordinates in favor of a more geometric representation of strata and by replacing sets of arcs which have both nodes in common by a single arc in which the relational signs are vertically ordered. If we do this, a structure like (24) is converted to the equivalent but presentationally more efficient structure:

(26)

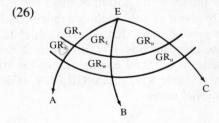

Here each stratum (set of arcs) defined by a single coordinate is represented as a single horizontal row, each set of arcs with the same nodes by a single graphic 'arc'. In what follows, we utilize exclusively notational forms like (26) as a way of representing the RNs relevant for clauses.

One of the consequences of representing clause structures by means of RNs can be seen by comparing the representation of (21) in (22) with that of the Japanese sentence:

(27) Naomi-tyan wa watasi ni   sono hon o   kureta.
      Naomi   I   DAT that book ACC gave
      'Naomi gave that book to me.'

A simplified RN for (27), again ignoring linear precedence among the various elements in (27), verb tense, and questions of how the grammatical particles *wa, ni,* and *o* and the 'Topic' relation are to be represented, is:

(28)

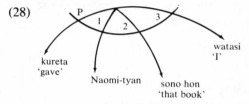

It is indicated in (28) that the verb *kureta* bears the predicate relation in the clause, *Naomi-tyan* the 1-relation, *sono hon* the 2-relation, and *watasi* the 3-relation. The basic clausal relations of the English and Japanese sentences represented here are the same, although the morphemes and linear order of elements in the two languages are different.

For an example that includes an oblique grammatical relation, consider the Malagasy sentence:

(29) Nividy ny vary ho an'ny ankizy   ny vehivavy.
      bought the rice for the   children the woman
      'The woman bought the rice for the children.'

A simplified RN for (29), ignoring verb tense, the preposition *ho,* and linear precedence relations among elements, is:

(30)

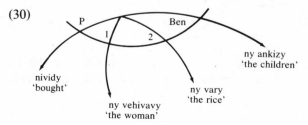

Example (30) represents the fact that in (29) *nividy* bears the predicate relation, *ny vehivavy* the 1-relation, *ny vary* the 2-relation, and *ny ankizy* the benefactive relation.

A primary goal of linguistic theory is to characterize the ways that human languages differ from each other and the ways that they are alike—that is, to distinguish what in language is universal from what is language-particular. The representation of sentence structure in terms of RNs is a significant step toward accomplishing this goal because it makes it possible to characterize what is universal in the clause structure of different languages despite such differences among languages as those involving linear order of elements.[11]

5   A Universal Characterization of Passivization

In §5 we argue that the representation of clause structures in terms of RNs makes possible a universal characterization of passivization. Once clause structure is conceived of in relational terms, it is possible to state the rule Passive in the same way (ignoring note 1) for every language manifesting passivization.

5.1   The Representation of Passive Clauses in RNs

Consider the English active-passive pair:

(31) a.   Louise reviewed that book.
     b.   That book was reviewed by Louise.

The simplified RN for (31a) is:

(32)
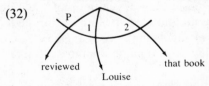

We propose that an *in*complete RN for (31b) is:

(33)
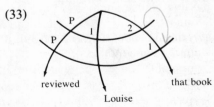

In addition to tense and linear order of elements, we also ignore here the question of how the auxiliary verb *was,* the participial form *re-*

viewed, and the preposition _by_ are to be represented. The key element of our proposal is this:

(34) a. The RN of a passive clause such as (31b) consists of (at least) two strata.

b. In the RN of a passive clause, a nominal (in this case, _that book_) that bears the 2-relation in one stratum bears the 1-relation in the immediately following stratum.

We postpone until §6 the question of what relation _Louise_ bears in the second stratum of (33). The important point is that _that book_ bears the 2-relation in the first stratum and the 1-relation in the second.

Our claim is that the RN of every passive clause in any human language has a nominal bearing the 2-relation and the 1-relation in successive strata. This holds regardless of the linear order of elements or the morphological concomitants of passivization. To cite just one example, an oversimplified RN for the Malagasy passive sentence:

(35) Novidin'   ny vehivavy ho an'ny ankizy   ny vary.
      was-bought the woman   for the   children the rice
      'The rice was bought for the children by the woman.'

is:

(36)

```
        P                    Ben
  P           1      2    Ben
                        1           ny ankizy
                                    'the children'
  novidin'              ny vary
  'was bought'          'the rice'
         ny vehivavy
         'the woman'
```

For an active clause such as (31a), one can ask which nominal is the 1 and which is the 2, and answer that _Louise_ is the 1 and _that book_ the 2. But with respect to a passive clause such as (31b) represented in (33), the answer to a parallel question is not so simple. Both _that book_ and _Louise_ are 1s in (33). While _that book_ is the 2 in (33), it is also a 1. However, it bears the 1- and 2-relations _in distinct strata._ Similarly, _Louise_ is a 1 in the initial stratum of (33), but it bears a different relation (specified in §6) in the second stratum. For passive clauses, one cannot simply say which nominal bears any given grammatical relation without specifying the relevant strata. This accounts for the sterility of much traditional argument about the 'real' subject of constructions like passives.

5.2   A Language-Independent Characterization of Passivization

We have taken sentences to be formally reconstructed by RNs, that is, by sets of arcs in the sense of §4. The crucial problem for a grammar (G) of a language is to divide the set of all arbitrary RNs into two sets, well-formed and ill-formed. We cannot here consider this problem seriously. But, informally, the basic relational grammar approach to characterizing well-formedness is as follows. We will specify a definition of RN well-formedness with respect to a fixed grammar G, this definition providing necessary and sufficient conditions for an arbitrary RN to be well-formed with respect to G. The underlying idea is that the rules of grammar are of two types, those which *positively sanction* the presence of arcs in RNs (say that such presence is 'legal') and those which *negatively sanction* the occurrence of arcs (say that the presence of such and such arcs is incompatible with well-formedness). The definition of well-formedness is then, very roughly, that an arbitrary RN is well-formed with respect to G if every arc in it is positively sanctioned by any rule in G. Intuitively, all of the rules are thus thought of as well-formedness conditions on RNs formed arbitrarily and 'presented' to the rules for evaluation.

In these terms, we can initially characterize Passive by saying that it is this rule that sanctions the existence of the 1-arc for, e.g., the nominal *that book* in (33). More generally, we suggest an informal characterization of Passive as follows:

(37)   Passive is the rule (more accurately, given note 1, any of the set of rules) that sanctions the existence of a 1-arc for a nominal N_a in stratum c_{k+1} of a clause node C, where N_a heads a 2-arc in stratum c_k of C, and where there is some nominal, N_b, which heads a 1-arc in stratum c_k.

Thus Passive is a rule which sanctions 1-hood in an immediately successive stratum for a nominal which is a 2 of a clause at a stratum in which some nominal is a 1. The reasons for the latter condition, restricting Passive to cases where the 'promoted' 2 cooccurs with some 1, can only be clarified in a more detailed study. For the present, however, it should be stressed that this clause does *not* imply that the other nominal bearing the 1-relation must show up on the surface. In many cases, this nominal is 'Unspecified' and silent, as in examples like *Mary was criticized*. In other terms, (37) informally characterizes Passive as a rule which sanctions the 1-relation for the nominal bearing the 2-relation in RN parts of the form:

(38)

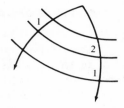

This account simultaneously states what Passive is and provides the following characterization of passive clauses in all languages:

(39)   If (i) the RN for a clause Q has a nominal N_a that bears the 2-relation in a stratum in which some nominal N_b bears the 1-relation, and (ii) if N_a bears the 1-relation in the following stratum, then Q is a passive clause. Thus, any clause in any language whose relational network contains a subpart of the form (38) is a passive clause.

6   Linguistic Universals That Interact with Passive

In proposing (17–18) as universals of passivization in §3, we noted that from the universality of (17–18) it does not follow that (17–18) are necessarily part of passivization itself. They could be due, at least in part, to other universals of language that interact with passivization. The universal characterization of passivization proposed in §5 makes more precise what we meant by (17). But it does not have (18) or (19) as consequences. We now turn to two hypothesized universals of language that interact with the universal characterization of passivization in §5 to give rise to the universals of passivization noted in (18) and (19).

6.1   The Stratal Uniqueness Law

Under our analysis of (1b), the nominal *that book* bears two distinct grammatical relations in the clause in two different strata. The question arises as to how many different nominals can bear a given grammatical relation in a single stratum. Consider the class of *term grammatical relations* (1, 2, 3). We claim that only one nominal can bear a given term relation *in a given stratum*. We propose this as the following universal law of grammar:[12]

(40)   The Stratal Uniqueness Law
       Let n be a variable ranging over the set of relational signs for term relations, let c_k be a single arbitrary coordinate, let c_x, c_y, etc., be variables over sequences of coordinates (which may be null) and let a, b, d be variables over nodes. Then, if, following

the notation in (20a), $[n(a,b)\langle c_x c_k c_y\rangle]$ and $[n(d,b)\langle c_w c_k c_z\rangle]$ are both arcs in some RN, a = d.

The Stratal Uniqueness Law thus says that only one dependent of a clause can bear a given term relation in a given stratum.

6.2   The Chômeur Condition

We now turn to the question of what relation *Louise* bears in the second stratum of (33). Since *that book* bears the 1-relation in this stratum, it follows from the Stratal Uniqueness Law that *Louise* can *not* bear the 1-relation in the second stratum. The relation borne by *Louise* in the second stratum of (33) is, we claim, an additional primitive relation we refer to as the chômeur relation. Nominals that bear this relation do so by virtue of a hypothesized universal condition of which the following is a highly oversimplified approximation:

(41) The Chômeur Condition
      Assume the same notational conventions as for (40). Then, if an RN, Q, contains the distinct arcs $[n(a,b)\langle c_x c_i c_y\rangle]$ $[n(d,b)\langle c_{i+1} c_v\rangle]$, where $d \neq a$, then Q contains the arc $[\text{Cho}\,(a,b)\langle c_{i+1} c_z\rangle]$.

The Chômeur Condition says that if some nominal, N_a, bears a given term relation in a given stratum, S_i, and some other nominal, N_b, bears the same term relation in the following stratum, S_{i+1}, then N_a bears the chômeur relation in S_{i+1}. Thus, since *Louise* in (33) bears the 1-relation in the first stratum and *that book* bears the 1-relation in the second, the Chômeur Condition stipulates that *Louise* bears the chômeur relation in the second stratum.

A nominal that bears the 1-relation in the last stratum before it bears the chômeur relation can be called a '1-chômeur', one that bears the 2-relation in the last stratum before it assumes the chômeur relation can be called a '2-chômeur', and likewise for 3-chômeurs. This terminology is convenient but cumbersome to write. Following a suggestion by Eugene Loos, we will write '1-chômeur' as '$\hat{1}$', '2-chômeur' as '$\hat{2}$', and '3-chômeur' as '$\hat{3}$'. For presentational purposes it does not matter whether one enters the value 'chômeur' or one of the values '$\hat{1}$', '$\hat{2}$', or '$\hat{3}$', since all are predictable from the information in RNs, given the Chômeur Condition. Thus, we can now give the simplified representation for (1b):

(42)

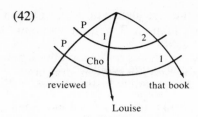

Similarly, the simplified RN for Malagasy (35) is:

(43)

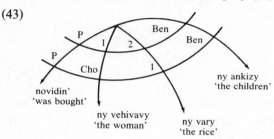

It should be stressed that the chômeur relation is in no way confined to passive clauses. Any rule that sanctions a term relation for some nominal bearing a distinct relation or no relation at all in an earlier stratum may produce an RN meeting the 'two arc' conditions referred to in (41). As a result, the earlier term must head a chômeur arc with the relevant coordinate. In future publications, we will introduce a typology of grammatical rules, including 'revaluation rules' (which include as a subclass the class of 'advancement rules'), 'ascension rules', and 'dummy rules'. This determines another classification of chômeurs, as 'revaluation chômeurs' (and, in some cases, as 'advancement chômeurs' as well), as 'ascension chômeurs', or as 'dummy chômeurs', depending on the type of rule determining that a given nominal bears the chômeur relation. Since Passive is both a revaluation rule and an advancement rule, *Louise* in (1b) and (42) and *ny vehivavy* in (35) and (43) are 'revaluation chômeurs' or 'advancement chômeurs', or more narrowly 'Passive chômeurs'.

The term 'chômeur' is a French word meaning 'unemployed' or 'idle'. A nominal that bears the chômeur relation in a given stratum is said to be 'en chômage' in that stratum. The choice of terminology is meant to reflect the idea that a nominal that is en chômage in a given stratum does not bear the term relation in that stratum that it bears in a higher stratum.[13]

Given the Chômeur Condition and the universal characterization of passivization in §5, the universals of passivization in (17–18) follow automatically. Example (17) is a consequence of the rule Passive itself, and (18), a consequence of the Chômeur Condition, can now be stated more precisely:

(44)   The subject of a monostratal active sentence is a chômeur in the second stratum of the corresponding bistratal passive.[14]

Some of the consequences of (44) are universal and some are language-particular. A universal consequence of (44), taken together with (17), is the intransitivity of passive clauses in the absence of another rule sanctioning the 2-relation for some other nominal. In individual languages, (44) will have various indirect consequences. Thus, one of the ways that passives obviously differ from language to language is in the marking of the Passive chômeur. Thus, one finds it marked with prepositions (*by* in English, *oleh* in Indonesian, *lé* in Achenese, *bèi* in Mandarin, *ʔoxwit* in Nitinaht, *ā* in Latin), sometimes with postpositions (*tarafindan* in Turkish, the instrumental postposition in Eskimo), sometimes with case (instrumental in Russian, ergative in Basque) and sometimes not at all (Malagasy).

Basque is particularly interesting in this respect. Superficially, actives and passives in Basque differ very little, since the nominal that is 1 of an active is in the ergative case in both the active and the 'corresponding' passive, and the nominal that is 2 of the active is in the absolutive case in both the active and the 'corresponding' passive. We have already seen that the 2 of the active is absolutive in the two sentences for different reasons. It is absolutive in the active because it is the 2 of a transitive clause, while it is absolutive in the passive because it is the 1 of an intransitive. We are now in a position to see that the 1 of the active is in the ergative case in the two sentences also for different reasons. It is ergative in the active because it is the 1 of a transitive clause, while it is ergative in the 'corresponding' passive because the ergative is the case used to mark passive chômeurs in Basque.[15] The claim that the relational status of the nominal is different in actives and passives receives support from the fact that in Basque, a language in which the (final) 1 triggers agreement on the verb, the ergative-marked nominal triggers agreement in the active but not in the passive (see note 7).

6.3   The Motivated Chômage Law

The Chômeur Condition stipulates the conditions under which a nominal bears the chômeur relation. We now make explicit an additional claim:

(45) The Motivated Chômage Law
      Only the Chômeur Condition can sanction the chômeur relation.

The empirical import of (45) is an exclusion from the class of possible grammatical rules and conditions any statment which sanctions the chômeur relation under conditions *distinct from* those specified in the Chômeur Condition. This law is stated quite informally here. Its content can ultimately be built into linguistic theory in a quite formal way which makes it redundant to have a separate statement like (45). This can be done simply by strengthening the Chômeur Condition to a biconditional (if and only if) statement.[16]

7   A Concluding Note

We have argued that passivization cannot be given a universal characterization in terms of word order, case, or verbal morphology. We have proposed a universal characterization of passivization that makes it necessary to conceive of clause structure in terms of grammatical relations (formally, in terms of arcs), and we have proposed that clause structure be represented in those terms. We have stated the Stratal Uniqueness Law and the Chômeur Condition and shown that, together with the universal relational characterization of passivization proposed, they account for the range of data concerning passives in various languages considered here.

But it should go without saying that at best this paper offers only the barest beginning of an account of passivization. There are many additional problems that must be faced and additional types of data that must be accounted for. We cite only a few examples:

(46) a.   The four-way contrast between passive types alluded to in note 1 must be elucidated. In particular, impersonal passives (particularly, those without surface dummy superficial subjects) have been cited by Keenan (1975), Comrie (1977), and Jain (1977) in support of the claim that there is 'spontaneous demotion' in natural languages, where this refers, in our terms, to nominals bearing the chômeur relation *without* the preconditions of the Chômeur Condition being met. Thus impersonal passives are an apparent counterexample both to the universal characterization of passivization offered here and to what we have called the Motivated Chômage Law.

     b.   Passive clauses in which a 3 (or some nominal bearing an oblique relation like benefactive, locative, instrumental, etc.) is superficial 1, such as English *Sue was given a watch.*

    c.   So-called pseudo-passives such as *That bed has been slept in* in English and *Le capitaine a été obéi,* 'the captain has been obeyed' in French. In these, apparently intransitive clauses (*obéir* does not permit a direct object in French active clauses) have passive correspondents in apparent conflict with our characterization.

Limitations of space preclude discussion of these and other such theoretically important phenomena here.

We began this paper by considering the possibility of a universal characterization of passivization in terms of such notions as word order, preposing, and postposing. We conclude by pointing out that not only do such notions fail to provide a universal characterization of passivization, they are inadequate even for the grossest statement of passivization internal to the grammars of particular languages. A theory that formulates passivization in terms of preposing and postposing, on the one hand, would be hard pressed to state passivization in any language where actives and passives have the same characteristic word order. Such a theory, if it makes any serious claims at all, predicts that such languages fall outside the class of possible human languages. A theory that states passivization in terms of grammatical relations, on the other hand, predicts that there can be languages in which the order of nominal elements in an active sentence and the 'corresponding passive' are the same.

Bell (1976) shows that Cebuano is such a language. In Cebuano, the predicate is normally clause-initial. It is followed by an advancement 1-chômeur (if there is one), the 1, a 2 (if present), and other nominals (if present), in that order. These facts can be given in tabular form as follows:

(47)   P (Adv-Î) 1 (2) . . .

Since the 2 of an active is final 1 of the 'corresponding' passive, and the 1 of an active is final Î of the 'corresponding' passive, the linear order of elements is the same in actives and passives, although the superficial grammatical relations are different.

(48) a.   Magluto' ang babaye ug bugas.
         cook-ACT NOM woman   rice
         'The woman will cook rice.'
     b.   Luto'on   sa   babaye ang bugas.
         cook-PASS GEN woman NOM rice
         'The rice will be cooked by the woman.'

The nominals *babaye* and *bugas* are in the same relative order in (48a–b), although their grammatical relations differ in the two sentences. The difference in superficial grammatical relations is manifested in several ways. First, the final 1 (*babaye* in (48a) and *bugas* in (48b)) has the nominative marker *ang*. Second, as Bell (1976) shows, in Cebuano only final 1s can be relativized. As a result, *babaye* can be relativized in (48a) but not in (48b), while *bugas* can be relativized in (48b) but not in (48a). Third, Bell shows that only final 1s can launch floating quantifiers in Cebuano. A plural nominal in place of *babaye* could launch floating quantifiers in (48a) but not (48b) while a plural substituted for *bugas* could launch floating quantifiers in (48b) but not in (48a).

Tzotzil is another language where element order is the same in 'corresponding' active and passive clauses. Like Cebuano, Tzotzil has verb-initial order. In Tzotzil, however, a final 2 precedes the final 1, which in turn precedes a passive chômeur. Since the 2 of an active is final 1 of the 'corresponding' passive and the 1 of an active is chômeur of the 'corresponding' passive, the relative order of elements is the same in 'corresponding' actives and passives as seen in the following examples from Cowan 1969 (p. 9):

(49) a. Lá snákan ti   vīnike ti   xpétule.
         seated   the man   the Peter
         'Peter seated the man.'

   b. Inákanat ti   vīnike yú?un ti   xpétule.
         seat-PASS the man   by   the Peter
         'The man was seated by Peter.'

The existence of languages whose active clause element order is the same as that of the 'corresponding' passive shows that notions of word order, preposing, etc., are not only inadequate as the basis for a universal characterization of passivization, but that they are hopeless for stating passivization internal to the grammars of particular languages such as Cebuano and Tzotzil. A conception of grammatical structure based on RNs, however, provides a means of stating passivization in the same way for all languages, regardless of such inessential and variable features as word order.

Notes

1. One of the major oversimplifications of this work is our failure to distinguish what are in fact four distinct though related types of passivization, for which we will use the terms in (i). These four types can be illustrated by the

corresponding sentences in (ii) from German, which is unusual in that it has all four:

(i) a. Plain Personal Passives
   b. Reflexive Personal Passives
   c. Plain Impersonal Passives
   d. Reflexive Impersonal Passives
(ii) a. Solche Sachen werden nicht oft gesagt
        'Such things aren't often said'
   b. Solche Sachen sagen sich nicht oft
        'Such things aren't often said'
   c. Es wird hier getanzt
        'Dancing takes place here'
   d. Es tanzt sich gut hier
        'One dances well here'

We claim that the characterization of passivization offered in this study holds for all four types (though this is far from obvious in the case of the impersonals). Thus what is most lacking is a universal specification of the differences between the four types, a specification which would involve stating just what it means to be a personal, impersonal, plain, or reflexive passive. We will show in future publications that such characterizations are also well within the bounds of a relational account of passivization.

2. This characterizes passivization even in those transformational treatments (such as that in Chomsky 1970) which claim that one or both of the operations (preposing and postposing) is accomplished by a rule also responsible for phenomena other than passivization.

3. *Hasan tarafından* is parenthesized because most Turkish speakers prefer so-called agentless passives in which the agent is 'Unspecified' and does not appear in the surface string. For those speakers who allow agents other than 'Unspecified' in passive sentences, (4a) has the corresponding passive (4b) with *Hasan tarafından*.

4. To state the facts of passivization in Turkish by means of a transformation it is necessary to posit some fixed word order so that the structural description of a Passive transformation can pick out the NPs that are to undergo Passive. It is unclear to what extent this imposes otherwise unmotivated complications on the grammar of Turkish.

5. To handle Passive in English and Turkish by means of the same transformation, one could, of course, propose a level of structure at which the two languages have the same relative order of constituents. But to do this would impose otherwise unmotivated complications on the grammar of at least one of the two languages.

6. There is also a problem of properly constraining the variable in (6), since Passive cannot apply to any two NPs in the string.

7. It is the auxiliary in such cases which expresses the agreement and (13b) has the intransitive auxiliary *da* which can manifest only a single agreement, that with an absolutive-marked nominal. In (13b), this is the superficial subject, *etchea*. The transitive auxiliary *du* in the active (13a), in contrast, manifests two agreements, with the ergative-marked subject and absolutive-marked direct object.

8. This is only an interim statement of the universal in question. It is given a more accurate formulation in §6.2.

9. This follows as a consequence of (17) and (18) only if we make the additional assumption that, at a given 'level' of structure (a notion to be made more precise in what follows), a clause can have only one direct object. We assume this and state it as a law of grammar in §6.1.

10. We have, of course, not characterized notions like 'nominal node' or 'clause node'. The obvious way to do this in terms of RNs is simply to recognize various terminal nodes Nom, C, etc., and to allow these to bear a fixed relation, that called 'Labels', to those terminal nodes to be characterized. Thus to say that some node, 55, is a nominal would be to specify:

The more interesting question is to determine what general conditions govern the distribution of such arcs. It may be, for instance, that they are predictable from the arcs having nodes like 55 as first node (so, for instance, all nodes which bear the subject, direct object, and indirect object relations are surely Nom, etc.).

11. 'Standard' transformational grammar assumes that there is such a thing as 'underlying' linear order distinct from that in actual strings of words. It is thus led to posit 'movement transformations' and suggests the possibility, discussed earlier, of a postposing or preposing theory of passivization, which faces the difficulties already considered. However, Sanders (1967, 1972, 1974, 1975a, 1975b) has developed a conception of transformational grammar which rejects in principle any linear order distinct from that actually observed in word sequences. If we understand his proposals properly, this leads to a conception of passivization in which differences in bracketing play a role analogous to differences of linear order in 'standard' transformational treatments. While such an account is not subject to exactly the criticisms we have leveled at linear order approaches, it is nonetheless vulnerable on many counts. In particular, it offers no account of passivization in those many cases (like those where active and passive word orders are identical [see the discussion of Cebuano and Tzotzil in §7]) where any constituency difference between active and passive would be perfectly arbitrary. We thus see no hope of a reconstruction of the essence of passivization in terms of bracketing. However, we strongly agree with Sanders's criticisms of 'standard' transformational grammar with respect to the role of linear order. That is, we agree with him that 'underlying order' is by and large an artifact. We disagree, however, with his view that the role of 'underlying order' is properly assigned simply to bracketing.

12. A similar principle, the Functional Uniqueness Principle, has been proposed independently by Harada (1975). Harada's principle is not stated with respect to strata, though presumably it would be if incorporated in a framework like ours. A number of researchers, including Comrie (1976), Gary and Keenan (1977), Kuno (1973), and Steele (1977), have claimed that a given sentence can have 'two subjects,' 'two direct objects,' etc. But most such claims have not been formulated precisely enough to determine whether they would be incompatible with the Stratal Uniqueness Law. For example, we ourselves claim that

all passive sentences have (at least) two subjects. But (in conformity with the Stratal Uniqueness Law) they can have at most one subject *in any given stratum*.

13. In earlier versions of relational grammar, such as that in Perlmutter and Postal 1974, we referred to the Chômeur Condition as the 'Relational Annihilation Law'. This name is used in some of the literature on relational grammar that is embedded in that earlier theoretical framework (e.g., chap. 6). Some of this literature refers to chômeurs as nominals that do not bear any grammatical relation whatsoever. This phrase is misleading in two respects: first, chômeurs *do* bear a grammatical relation, namely, the chômeur relation; second, the statement does not specify the stratum in which the chômeur nominal does not bear any other grammatical relation. All chômeurs bear some term relation in an earlier stratum.

14. We limit (44) to monostratal actives and bistratal passives to avoid discussing additional possibilities that arise in RNs having additional strata.

15. There are (at least) two possible analyses of this phenomenon within the framework we are proposing. Under one, Basque would simply have a rule marking passive chômeurs with the ergative case. Under the other, Basque grammar would contain a rule marking an initial ergative (1 of a transitive clause) that is a final nonterm with the ergative case. Harris (1976, 1977) argues for a rule of the latter kind for Georgian. The choice between these two alternatives for Basque would have to be made on the basis of additional data that we are not considering here. The question of which alternative is adopted does not affect the point at issue here.

16. The Motivated Chômage Law has, in effect, been challenged by various linguists including Keenan (1975), Comrie (1977), and Jain (1977). We intend to deal with this issue in a future publication.

References

Bell, Sarah. 1976. "Cebuano Subjects in Two Frameworks." Ph.D. diss., MIT.

Chomsky, Noam. 1957. *Syntactic Structures*. The Hague: Mouton & Co.

———. 1970. "Remarks on Nominalization." In R. Jacobs and P. Rosenbaum, eds., *Readings in English Transformational Grammar*. Waltham, Mass.: Blaisdell Publishing Co.

Chung, Sandra. 1976. "An Object-Creating Rule in Bahasa Indonesia." *Linguistic Inquiry* 7:41–87.

Cole, Peter, and Sadock, Jerrold, eds. 1977. *Syntax and Semantics 8: Grammatical Relations*. New York: Academic Press.

Comrie, Bernard. 1976. "The Syntax of Causative Constructions: Cross-Language Similarities and Divergences." In M. Shibatani, ed., *Syntax and Semantics 6: The Grammar of Causative Constructions*. New York: Academic Press.

———. 1977. "In Defense of Spontaneous Demotion: The Impersonal Passive." In Cole and Sadock, 1977.

Cowan, Marion M. 1969. *Tzotzil Grammar*. Summer Institute of Linguistics, University of Oklahoma, Norman.

Cummins, Sarah. 1976. "Relation-Changing Rules in Mandarin." University of Toronto.

Gary, Judith, and Keenan, Edward. 1977. "On Collapsing Grammatical Relations in Universal Grammar." In Cole and Sadock, 1977.

Harada, S. I. 1975. "The Functional Uniqueness Principle." *Attempts in Linguistics and Literature* 2:17–24. Society of Linguistics and Literature, International Christian University, Tokyo.

Harris, Alice. 1976. "Grammatical Relations in Modern Georgian." Ph.D. diss., Harvard University.

————. 1977. "Marking Former Terms: Georgian Evidence." In *Proceedings of the Seventh Annual Meeting of the North Eastern Linguistics Society.* Dept. of Linguistics, MIT.

Jain, Jagdish. 1977. "The Hindi Passive in Universal Grammar." San Francisco State University.

Keenan, Edward. 1972. "Relative Clause Formation in Malagasy." In P. Peranteau et al., eds., *The Chicago Which Hunt: Papers from the Relative Clause Festival.* Chicago: University of Chicago.

————. 1975. "Some Universals of Passive in Relational Grammar." In *Papers from the Eleventh Regional Meeting of the Chicago Linguistic Society.*

Klokeid, Terry. 1975. "On Grammatical Relations in Nitinaht." University of Calgary.

Kuno, Susumu. 1973. *The Structure of the Japanese Language.* Cambridge, Mass.: MIT Press.

Lafitte, Pierre. 1962. *Grammaire basque.* Bayonne: Editions des Amis du Musée Basque et 'Ikas'.

Lawler, John. 1977. "A Agrees with B in Achenese: A Problem for Relational Grammar." In Cole and Sadock, 1977.

Perlmutter, David, and Postal, Paul. 1974. Lectures on Relational Grammar at Summer Linguistic Institute of the Linguistic Society of America, Amherst, Mass.

Postal, Paul. 1977. "Antipassive in French." In *Papers from the Seventh Annual Meeting North Eastern Linguistic Society.* Cambridge, Mass.: MIT.

Rischel, Jørgen. 1975. "Some Characteristics of Noun Phrases in West Greenlandic." *Acta Linguistica Hafniensia* 13:214–45.

Sanders, Gerald. 1967. "Some General Grammatical Processes in English." Ph.D. diss., Indiana University.

————. 1972. *Equational Grammar.* The Hague: Mouton & Co.

————. 1974. "Precedence Relations in Language." *Foundations of Language* 2:361–400.

————. 1975a. *Invariant Ordering.* The Hague: Mouton & Co.

————. 1975b. "On the Exclusion of Extrinsic Ordering Constraints." In A. Koutsoudas, *The Ordering and Application of Grammatical Rules.* The Hague: Mouton & Co.

Steele, Susan. 1977. "On Being Possessed." In *Proceedings of the Third Annual Meeting of the Berkeley Linguistics Society.* Berkeley: University of California.

(J)

2 · The Relational Succession Law
David M. Perlmutter and Paul M. Postal

p-37

Editor's Foreword

The paper published here is a somewhat abridged version of a manuscript left unfinished in December 1972.[1] The basic framework and orientation of the paper are transformational throughout. As it was nearing completion, however, the authors' theoretical orientation began to change—most significantly in regarding grammatical relations as primitives of grammatical theory rather than as concepts defined in terms of other notions and in conceiving of the structures on which cyclical rules operate as representing grammatical relations but not the linear order of elements. The discrepancy between this view of linguistic structure and the transformational framework in which the paper was written led the authors to decide not to publish it at that time.

The paper consists of one basic idea—the Relational Succession Law—and a partial working out of its consequences. This idea, when pushed to the limit, had many more consequences than the authors saw at the time. In a sense, much of the subsequent development of relational grammar consisted of a further working out of the consequences of ideas that appear for the first time in this paper. Thus, although the paper is written in a transformational framework and although the authors saw themselves as advocating a more significant role for grammatical relations within transformational grammar rather than a new theory, in retrospect this was the first paper in relational grammar.

The editor is indebted to Judith Aissen, Sandra Chung, and Carlota Smith for discussion of the original manuscript and to Judith Aissen, Terry Klokeid, Stephen Marlett, Paul Postal, Geoffrey Pullum, Eduardo Raposo, and Carol Rosen for comments on the first draft of the Editor's Foreword and Afterword. Work on the Foreword and the Afterword was supported in part by the National Science Foundation through Grant No. BNS 78-17498 to the University of California, San Diego.

There are two reasons for including the paper in this volume. First, it gives a view of the earliest stage in the development of relational grammar. It argues that the *effect* of certain transformations is determined by grammatical relations. The subsequent attempt to make some of the ideas in this paper precise led us to abandon the transformational framework in which it is embedded. Second, this paper makes some theoretical claims that have played an important role in relational grammar but have not previously appeared in print.

The paper shares most of the basic assumptions of transformational grammar. The conception of sentence structure is that of a derivation (a sequence of structures), with transformations mapping one structure in the derivation onto the next. The structures themselves are constituent structure trees, with VSO constituent order assumed for English under the influence of the arguments in McCawley 1970a and Postal 1974. (The paper was written before Berman's [1974] now classic critique of the VSO hypothesis.) Consistent with its assumption of derivations and sequential rule application, the paper assumes a cyclical theory of grammar and a division of syntactic rules into (at least) two groups—cyclical and postcyclical.

The conception of ascensions in the paper is that of rules that move constituents, and there is considerable discussion of the derived constituent structure produced by such rules. This discussion is in tune with the transformational approach to grammatical relations which, following Chomsky 1965, conceived of grammatical relations as derivative concepts defined in terms of the positions of NPs in trees. The paper follows that tradition in speaking of raising "into subject position" and "into object position," "subject" and "object" being conceived of as terms referring to NPs occupying particular *positions* in trees.

The paper is also transformational in addressing itself to a number of issues that arise internal to a transformational framework, e.g., whether various sentential complements are dominated by NP-nodes, what is the relative order of application of Passive and Extraposition. Like most other transformational works at that time, it deals primarily with data from English. Examples from French and Portuguese are cited to show that the generalizations established for English are not confined to that language, and a construction in Malagasy is used to illustrate the generalizations' validity for a non-Indo-European language. The Afterword reexamines the paper from the perspective of current relational grammar.

The Relational Succession Law

1   Some Concepts Defined

Languages (may) contain, we claim, a subset of cyclic rules which we will refer to as 'Ascension Rules'. An ascension rule is a cyclic rule which takes some NP constituent, NP_a, from a position within some immediate constituent, A,[2] of an S, S_1, in an input tree, T_j, and, operating on the S_1 cycle, makes the correspondent of NP_a an immediate constituent of the correspondent of S_1 in the output tree, T_{j+1}.[3] Schematically:

(1)

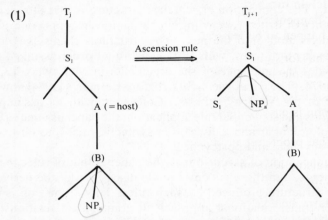

The NP (NP_a) that is moved by an ascension rule we will refer to as the 'ascendee'. The constituent A in (1) out of which the ascendee ascends we will call the 'host' constituent. Finally, we assume a linguistic theory in which grammatical relations such as 'subject of', 'direct object of', and 'indirect object of' are defined.[4] We will use the term 'object' as a cover term for both direct and indirect objects.

The schematization of ascension rules in (1) contains several so far unjustified assumptions—in particular, the asymmetry that the ascendee ends up *to the left* of its host. We return to this point below, suggesting, first, that this asymmetry is a characteristic of all ascension rule derivations and, second, that it is a consequence of the principle governing ascension rules that this paper proposes.

It should also be stressed that we are assuming that rules like Topicalization and WH-Movement are not cyclical and hence not even possible candidates for inclusion in the set of ascension rules.[5]

Most of the substantive points in this paper were presented by Perlmutter in talks at the University of London and Cambridge University in November 1972, by Postal at the Université de Paris VIII (Faculté de Vincennes) in February 1973, and by Perlmutter at the University of Tokyo in June 1973.

2   A Generalization Governing Well-Known Ascension Rules in English

In English, the best-known ascension rules are unquestionably the rules which have been called variously 'IT-Replacement', 'Pronoun Replacement', or '(Subject)-Raising',[6] on the one hand, and 'Tough Movement' or 'Object Shift',[7] on the other. We refer to these respectively as 'Subject Raising' and 'Object Raising'. The former has for some time been taken to be involved in the derivations of the b-examples of:

(2) a.   It turns out that Melvin is incoherent.
    b.   Melvin turns out to be incoherent.
(3) a.   It happens that I am leaving.
    b.   I happen to be leaving.

The latter has for some time been taken to be involved in the derivations of the b-examples in:

(4) a.   It is easy to please John.
    b.   John is easy to please.
(5) a.   It will be a cinch to solve that problem.
    b.   That problem will be a cinch to solve.

Subject Raising also operates, we claim, in the derivations of the b-examples in:

(6) a.   Harry believes (that) Joan is pregnant.
    b.   Harry believes Joan to be pregnant.
(7) a.   Harry expects (that) Joan will return.
    b.   Harry expects Joan to return.

This latter claim is challenged by Chomsky (1971, 1973) but defended at great length by Postal (1974). We are assuming here that the rule operative in (6b) and (7b) is the same as that operative in (2b) and (3b), an assumption now traditional (since Rosenbaum 1967), outlined by McCawley (1970a) and discussed by Postal (1974). There is nothing in the present discussion, however, that hinges on this assumption. Our remarks here would remain unaffected if it were assumed that there are two distinct rules, Subject Raising$_1$, operative in (2) and (3), and Subject Raising$_2$, operative in (6) and (7).

If one takes these assumptions as given, there is a regularity in the derivations sanctioned by the English rules Subject Raising and Object Raising which we believe has not previously been made explicit, a regularity governing the relations between the position which an ascendee assumes in the S$_1$ of T$_{j+1}$ of (1) and the position of the constituent A of T$_j$ from which the ascendee is removed. It is our purpose here to uncover this regularity and to suggest the hypothesis that it is the direct consequence of an invariant principle of Universal Grammar, which we will take steps toward formulating precisely.

Let us begin with the sentences in (2a) and (3a). We assume, as has been traditional in generative work and unchallenged until recently,[8] that sentences like (2a) and (3a) are derived by application of Extraposition,[9] and hence that *underlying these constructions are sentential subject NPs*. From this, together with the assumption that structures essentially like those underlying (2a), (3a), etc., also underlie respectively (2b), (3b), etc.,[10] it follows that in these cases an ascendee moves out of a sentential subject NP into subject position, or, put differently, that Subject Raising in these cases has the effect of mapping a tree with a main verb *turn out, happen,* etc., and a sentential subject into a derived tree in which these main verbs have ascendees as subjects. The operation performed by Subject Raising in these examples, then, is:[11]

(8)

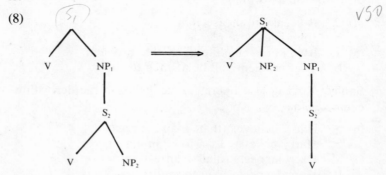

Turning next to (4) and (5), we also assume (as has been standard) that the a-examples involve application of Extraposition, and hence that these examples have underlying sentential subjects. It follows that, just as in the Subject Raising cases in (2) and (3), Object Raising has the effect of moving the ascendee out of a sentential subject into subject position. Thus, the operation performed by Object Raising is:

(9)

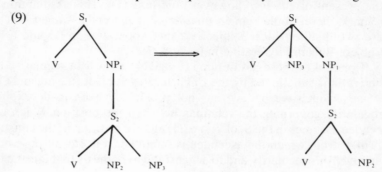

Finally, consider (6) and (7). Here the a-examples have 'sentential objects' and Subject Raising makes the ascendee a derived object, performing the operation:[12]

(10)

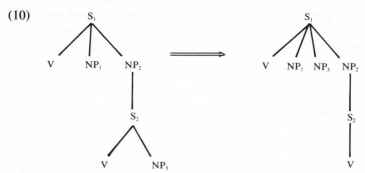

The table in (11) summarizes those aspects of Subject Raising into subject position, Object Raising, and Subject Raising into object position with which we are concerned here.

(11)

	GR of ascendee before ascension	GR of ascendee after ascension	GR of host NP before ascension
Subject Raising into subject position	Subject	Subject	Subject
Object Raising	Nonsubject	Subject	Subject
Subject Raising into object position	Subject	Direct Object	Direct Object

The table in (11) shows that there is no correlation between the grammatical relation of the ascendee after ascension and its grammatical relation before ascension. Strikingly, however, the grammatical relation of the ascendee after ascension is always the same as that of its host NP prior to ascension. If an NP ascends out of a (sentential) NP that is in subject position, it becomes a subject, and if it ascends out of a (sentential) NP that is in object position, it becomes an object.

Assuming that the constituent A in (1) is in all cases an NP, we can state the generalization:

(12)   The Relational Succession Law
       An ascendee assumes within the clause (S_1 in (1)) into which it ascends the grammatical relation of its host NP (the NP (A in (1)) out of which it ascends).

Under the assumptions we have made, the Relational Succession Law is true of all derivations involving Subject Raising and Object Raising in English.[13]

We now go one step further. We propose that the Relational Succession Law is not just a generalization about certain derivations in English, but rather a constraint on possible rules in human languages. That is, the Relational Succession Law is a principle of Universal Grammar to which all ascension rules in human languages conform. In §3, we examine some consequences of the incorporation of this principle into linguistic theory.

3   Some Consequences of the Relational Succession Law
3.1   Some Impossible Rules

An immediate consequence of the Relational Succession Law is that it rules out in principle certain rules that would otherwise be potential rules of human languages.

Consider first Subject Raising into subject position in English, as illustrated in (8). It is possible a priori that there could be a language just like English except that it has a Subject Raising rule which, instead of placing the raised NP to the left of the clause out of which it is promoted, as in (8), places it to the right of it, as in:

(13)

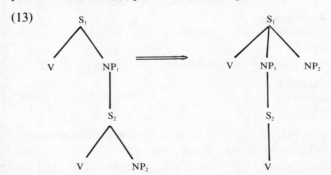

Call this rule 'Subject Raising 1A'. Subject Raising 1A would derive (14b) and (15b) from the structures that underlie (14a) and (15a), respectively.

(14) a.   It turns out that Melvin is incoherent.
b. *To be incoherent turns out Melvin.
(15) a.   It happens that I am leaving.
b. *To be leaving happens me.

Subject Raising 1A is easily formulable as a transformation, and no constraints on transformations have yet been established that would rule it out in principle.[14] Yet we claim that no language can have Subject

Raising 1A in its grammar. The Relational Succession Law predicts just this.

Turning now to Object Raising, it is possible a priori that natural languages could have rules which promote the object of the complement in (9) by placing it under S_1 immediately to the *right* of the host NP, NP_1. Call such a rule 'Object Raising A'. It would perform the operation:

(16)

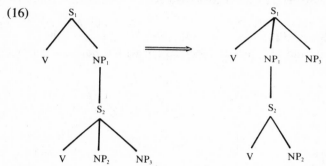

Thus, Object Raising A would derive (17b) and (18b) from the structures underlying (17a) and (18a), respectively.

(17) a.   It is easy to please John.
      b.   *To please is easy John.
(18) a.   It will be a cinch to solve that problem.
      b.   *To solve will be a cinch that problem.

Object Raising A is easily formulable as a transformation, but we claim that no such rule will be found in any natural language because any such rule would violate the Relational Succession Law.

Finally, consider Subject Raising into object position. Instead of putting the ascendee, NP_3 in (10), immediately to the left of the host NP, it is a priori possible that Subject Raising could place the ascendee to the right of the host NP, performing the operation:

(19)

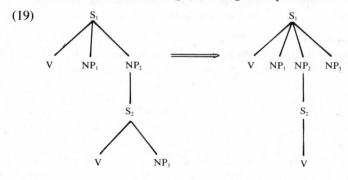

Call this rule 'Subject Raising 2A'. It would convert the structures underlying (20a) and (21a) into (20b) and (21b), respectively.

(20) a. Harry believes (that) Joan is pregnant.
     b. *Harry believes to be pregnant Joan.
(21) a. Harry expects (that) Joan will return.
     b. *Harry expects to return Joan.

There is also another possibility—a rule of Subject Raising that places the subject of the object complement in subject position in the matrix. Call this rule 'Subject Raising 2B'. It would perform the operation:

(22)

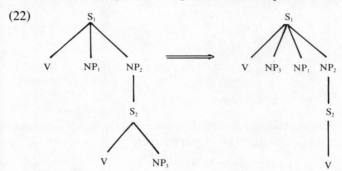

Subject Raising 2B would thus derive (23b) and (24b) from the structures underlying (23a) and (24a), respectively.

(23) a. Harry believes (that) Joan is pregnant.
     b. Joan believes Harry to be pregnant.
(24) a. Harry expects (that) Joan will return.
     b. Joan expects Harry to return.

Note that Subject Raising 2B would also generate (25b) from the structure underlying (25a).

(25) a. Jim expects (that) I will contradict myself.
     b. *I expect Jim to contradict myself.

Although Subject Raising 2A and Subject Raising 2B are formulable as transformations, both of these hypothetical rules violate the Relational Succession Law. They would therefore be impossible in any grammar constructed in accordance with a theory of Universal Grammar that incorporates the Relational Succession Law. Since such rules cannot, we claim, exist in any natural language, we propose that some appropriately precise formulation of the Relational Succession Law is a part of the theory of Universal Grammar.

In brief, the incorporation of the Relational Succession Law into Universal Grammar rules out in principle such hypothetical rules as

Subject Raising 1A, Object Raising A, Subject Raising 2A, and Subject Raising 2B, while allowing the rules of Subject Raising 1, Object Raising, and Subject Raising 2.

3.2   The Formulation of Ascension Rules

Once the Relational Succession Law is incorporated into linguistic theory as a universal, much that has previously been stated as part of particular ascension rules in particular languages is predictable, and hence need not be stated in these rules themselves. Thus, rules such as Subject Raising and Object Raising can be stated along the following lines:

(26)   Ascend the NP in the context U $[_{NP}$ X ___Y $_{NP}]$ W for appropriate specifications of U, X, Y, and W.

The fact that the ascendee ends up to the left of the host NP need not be stated as such; the position of the ascendee in the derived structure is predicted by the Relational Succession Law.

3.3   The Universal Component in Syntactic Rules

Formulation of syntactic rules along the lines proposed in §3.2 immediately calls into question the entire theory of the formulation of syntactic rules. The contrast between (26) and the formulations of Subject Raising and Object Raising that have been given in the past[15] shows how different a rule can look once its universal aspects have been factored out and stated in Universal Grammar. The formulations of rules in the past involve, we believe, ad hoc specifications of a variety of factors that are really universally governed, hence predictable, and which therefore need not be stated at all in particular rules or even in particular grammars.

3.4   The Role of Grammatical Relations in Grammar

The Relational Succession Law is formulated in terms of grammatical relations. It states that an ascendee takes over the grammatical relation of its host NP. The grammatical relation in question is thus "preserved" by being passed from the host NP to the ascendee.[16] Given this principle, formulated in terms of grammatical relations, it is apparent that grammatical relations play a key role in grammar. The fact that the Relational Succession Law makes it unnecessary to state some things that have previously been thought to be properties of particular rules, as pointed out in §3.2, means that certain aspects of transformations, previously stated in terms of (Boolean conditions on) analyzability in accordance with the theory of transformations proposed in Chomsky 1965, are actually to be stated in terms of the very different notion of grammatical relations. The extent to which the role of grammatical relations in grammar has been camouflaged by means of ad hoc statements in terms of (Boolean conditions on) analyzability as a part of particular transformations can only be determined by future research.

One conclusion can be drawn already, however. Since grammatical relations are the key notion in the operation of ascension rules such as Subject Raising and Object Raising, grammatical relations must be defined on transformationally derived structures. It is therefore necessary to abandon the theory proposed in Chomsky 1965, according to which grammatical relations are defined only at the level of 'deep structure' (because of their relevance to 'semantic interpretation of deep structures') and do not play a role in syntax. A syntax that cannot refer to grammatical relations cannot incorporate the Relational Succession Law. It is therefore forced to state in ad hoc ways as properties of particular transformations what has been shown to be predictable, thus failing to predict what is predictable and, by allowing such hypothetical rules as Subject Raising 1A, Object Raising A, Subject Raising 2A, and Subject Raising 2B, failing to place adequate constraints on the notion 'rule of grammar'.

We return to grammatical relations in §6.

3.5   The NP-hood of Sentential Complements

Acceptance of the Relational Succession Law entails rejection of all analyses that are inconsistent with it. One such analysis, proposed by Emonds (1970) and adopted by Chomsky (1973), by Bresnan (1972) in somewhat different form, and by others, is the non-NP analysis of *that*-clauses and infinitives. As was shown in the discussion of Subject Raising and Object Raising, such clauses serve as the host NPs from which NPs ascend. They must themselves be NPs in order to bear grammatical relations, which is necessary if they are to pass these grammatical relations on to the NPs that ascend out of them.[17] The Relational Succession Law thus provides an unexpected general class of arguments for determining NP-hood.

3.6   The Interaction of Subject Raising and Extraposition

In the absence of a theoretical framework that constrains possible grammars, Subject Raising could be thought to apply either to complements in subject position, or to sentential complements that have already undergone Extraposition. The latter analysis was adopted in Rosenbaum 1967. Once the Relational Succession Law is incorporated into linguistic theory, however, Rosenbaum's analysis is ruled out in principle, for the ascendee must ascend out of a subject NP in order to itself become a subject in derived constituent structure. Significantly, the only analysis permitted by the Relational Succession Law is supported by a variety of empirical facts of English that are independent of the Relational Succession Law.[18]

4   A Way of Strengthening the Relational Succession Law and Its Consequences

As formulated in (12), the Relational Succession Law states only that an ascendee assumes (within the clause into which it ascends) the grammatical relation of its host. Nothing is said about situations in which the host NP bears no grammatical relation. It is therefore possible to strengthen the Relational Succession Law as follows:

(27)   The Relational Succession Law
The only rules of the form:

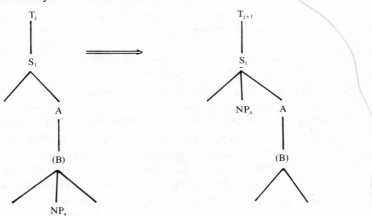

that exist in natural languages are rules whose application causes the moved NP, NP_a, to bear a grammatical relation to the verb whose sister[19] it becomes by virtue of being moved. The grammatical relation that the moved NP bears to its new verb-sister is the grammatical relation that its host constituent (A above) bore to that verb in the structure that served as input to the transformation.

This strengthened formulation of the Relational Succession Law has two additional consequences. First, it follows that the constituent A in (1) and in (27) will always be an NP, because only NPs bear grammatical relations. The second consequence of this formulation of the Relational Succession Law depends on the assumption, which we now make explicit, that there is only a small number of grammatical relations that an NP can bear to a verb (we would claim three—subject, direct object, and indirect object). Assuming a specification of the relational or nonrelational status of various NPs, the Relational Succession Law (27) predicts that no rule can ascend NPs out of constituents that are not subjects, direct objects, or (less likely) indirect objects.[20] Thus, under the assumption that a theory of grammatical relations does not recognize any relation of the relevant sort between the main verb and the underlined NPs in the constructions in (28), the Relational Succession Law (27) predicts that there can be no ascension rules operating on NPs like those italicized in (28).

(28) a.   Jim met Mary in *Teddy's barn.*
     b.   Ed married her because of *her money.*
     c.   Louise called the police on *three separate occasions at which I was present.*
     d.   Tom picked up the egg with *the blade of the shovel.*

As far as we know, this conclusion is correct; every ascension rule that has been proposed operates on NPs that are subjects or direct objects.[21]

5   Some Ascension Rules in Other Languages
5.1   Analogues of the English Rules Discussed

If the Relational Succession Law is a part of Universal Grammar, then we expect to find in other languages rules like Subject Raising 1, Object Raising, and so on, but never rules like Subject Raising 1A, Subject Raising 2A, Subject Raising 2B, or Object Raising A. While we have made no large-scale investigation of this matter, our general experience with languages supports it. For instance, the Romance languages have analogues of both the English rules Subject Raising and Object Raising. This can be seen for French, for example, from such pairs as[22]

(29) a.   Il semble que la porte de la cathédrale est fermée.
          'It seems that the door of the cathedral is closed.'
     b.   La porte de la cathédrale semble être fermée.
          'The door of the cathedral seems to be closed.'
(30) a.   Il est difficile de lire ces livres.
          'It is difficult to read these books.'
     b.   Ces livres sont difficiles à lire.
          'These books are difficult to read.'

In Portuguese, we also find analogues of Subject Raising and Object Raising, which relate such pairs as[23]

(31) a.   Parece que os brasileiros têm ganho o jogo.
          'It seems that the Brazilians have won the game.'
     b.   Os brasileiros parecem ter ganho o jogo.
          'The Brazilians seem to have won the game.'

(32) a.   Ele considera que essas pessoas são importantes.[24]
        'He considers that those people are important.'
   b.   Ele considera essas pessoas importantes.
        'He considers those people important.'
(33) a.   É impossível ler estes livros.
        'It is impossible to read these books.'
   b.   Estes livros são impossíveis de ler.
        'These books are impossible to read.'

The Relational Succession Law provides an essential link in explaining why French and Portuguese can have the rules needed to generate (29b), (30b), (31b), (32b), and (33b), but not those to generate the c-sentences below from the corresponding a-sentences.

(29) c.   *Etre fermé semble la porte de la cathédrale.
        'To be closed seems the door of the cathedral.'
(30) c.   *A lire est difficile ces livres.
        'To read is difficult these books.'
(31) c.   *Ter ganho o jogo parece os brasileiros.
        'To have won the game seems the Brazilians.'
(32) c.   *Essas pessoas consideram ele importantes.
        'Those people consider him important.'[25]
(33) c.   *De ler é impossível estes livros.
        'To read is impossible these books.'

We suggest, then, that many languages will contain analogues of Subject Raising and/or Object Raising, since the Relational Succession Law permits these and in each case makes it possible to state the rule with a minimum of language-particular apparatus. Rules which ascend an NP from a sentential subject into superordinate object position or from a sentential object into superordinate subject position, however, will never be found.

5.2   Possessor Ascension in Malagasy

If the Relational Succession Law is a part of Universal Grammar, as we suggest, then it should be possible for languages to have ascension rules that conform to it that are quite unlike any established rules of English. An interesting example of this kind has been discovered by Keenan (1971, 1972) in the course of his research on constraints on movement transformations in Malagasy and other languages.

Malagasy has an ascension rule that promotes Possessors out of NPs under conditions that are relevant here.[26]

Support from

(34)   Niantso ny anaran'   ny olona Rakoto
      called   the names-of the people Rakoto
      'Rakoto called the names of the people.'

In this sentence *ny anaran' ny olona* 'the names of the people' is the
direct object of *niantso* 'called.' Sentence (34) can be transformed into
a sentence with a different verbal voice in which *ny anaran' ny olona*
is the subject:

(35)   Nantsoin-dRakoto ny anaran'   ny olona.
      called   Rakoto the names-of the people
      'The names of the people were called by Rakoto.'

The parallel with Passive in English is obvious.[27]
    The Malagasy rule of Possessor Ascension operates on the structure
in (35) to produce the sentence

(36)   Nantsoin-dRakoto anarana ny olona.
      called   Rakoto name   the people
      'The people were name-called by Rakoto,' i.e., 'called by name.'

In (36), *ny olona* has been moved out of the NP *ny anaran' ny olona*
(compare (35)) and has become the subject of the sentence. Keenan's
evidence for this is solid. In Malagasy, only subjects can be relativized,
and *ny olona* in (36) is relativizable:

(37)   ny olona izay nantsoin-dRakoto anarana
      the people that called   Rakoto name
      'the people who were name-called by Rakoto,' i.e., 'whose names
         were called by Rakoto.'

In (35), by contrast, where *ny olona* is not the subject but is instead
inside the NP *ny anaran' ny olona,* it cannot be relativized:

(38)   *ny olona izay nantsoin-dRakoto ny anaran'ny
      (the people that called   Rakoto the names of)

In Malagasy, as in English, the Relational Succession Law automatically predicts the word order of the output of the ascension rule,
even though the actual word order resulting from ascension rules in
the two languages is different. In English, an NP that ascends out of
a subject NP goes to the left of the host NP, because subjects in English
are to the left, while in Malagasy an NP that ascends out of a subject
NP goes to the right of the host NP, since in Malagasy the subject is
to the right.[28]
    Of even greater interest is the fact that while Possessor Ascension
operates on (35), in which the host NP *ny anaran' ny olona* is the

subject, it cannot apply to (34), in which the host NP is the direct object. The ungrammatical sentence

(39) *Niantso anarana Rakoto ny olona.
    (called   name   Rakoto the people)

would result if *ny olona* ascended to subject position out of a direct object. The fact that the possessor NP can ascend to superordinate subject status only if the host NP is itself the subject is in accord with the Relational Succession Law.

Another fact, however, must also be accounted for. We have been assuming that the statement of Possessor Ascension in Malagasy will merely specify ascension of the possessor NP, letting the derived constituent structure follow automatically from the Relational Succession Law. Under these conditions, the grammar still needs to prevent Possessor Ascension from applying to the structure underlying (34), producing the derived structure

(40) *Niantso anarana ny olona Rakoto.
    (called   name   the people Rakoto)

in which *ny olona* is the direct object, having been promoted out of the direct object *ny anaran' ny olona* in (34). To prevent such derivations, the grammar must state that in Malagasy, *the host of Possessor Ascension must be a subject*. Thus, Possessor Ascension in Malagasy contrasts with Subject Raising in English, which is possible out of subjects and direct objects both. In these cases, the Relational Succession Law predicts the derived constituent structure produced by ascension.

6   On the Role of Grammatical Relations in Grammar

6.1   The Traditional Generative View of the Insensitivity of Transformations to Grammatical Relations

In the theory of syntax in Chomsky 1965, the grammatical relations *subject of* and *direct object of* were defined in terms of structural configurations at the level of deep structure.[29] In this theory, grammatical relations played a role in the semantic interpretation of deep structures but had no relevance for the syntactic component itself. A position on the role of grammatical relations in syntax that has been traditional in generative grammar is summarized succinctly in the following:

(41)   The basic property of transformations is that they map phrase-markers into phrase-markers. Each transformation applies to

a phrase-marker on the basis of the formal configurations expressed in it, and quite independently of the meanings or grammatical relations expressed by these formal configurations. Thus such sentences as *John received the book, John read the book, John expected the book to be good, John gave Bill the book,* and so on, undergo the passive transformation in exactly the same way. The transformation applies blindly to any phrase-marker of the proper form, caring nothing about meanings or grammatical relations. This situation is typical; I know of no exceptions, and no counterarguments that amount to more than terminological revision, although some intriguing proposals have been put forward and should obviously be explored. [Chomsky 1972, p. 118]

In another discussion of Passive, Chomsky (1971, pp. 29–31) makes much the same point, including some examples of what he means by 'grammatical relations':

(42)   We might propose, as a first approximation, that the passive is formed by the structure-dependent operation that locates the main verb and the noun phrase that follows it, inverting the two, and adding various modifications that need not concern us. . . .

   An interesting property of the formal operations of language is that though they are structure-dependent, they are, in an important sense, independent of meaning. Compare the sentences "I believed your testimony," "I believed your testimony to be false," and "I believed your testimony to have been given under duress." The corresponding passives are "Your testimony was believed," "Your testimony was believed to be false," and "Your testimony was believed to have been given under duress." In all cases, the passive is formed by the rule informally described a moment ago. *The rule pays no attention to the grammatical and semantic relations of the main verb to the noun phrase that follows it.* [Emphasis ours—DMP, PMP] Thus in "I believed your testimony," the noun phrase is the grammatical object of "believe." In "I believed your testimony to be false," it bears no relation to "believe," and is the subject of "be false." In "I believed your testimony to have been given under duress," it bears no relation to "believe" and is the grammatical object of the embedded verb "give." *Yet in all cases, the rule applies blindly, caring nothing for these differences.* [Emphasis ours—DMP, PMP] Thus in an important sense, the rules are structure-dependent and only structure-dependent. Technically, they are rules that apply to abstract labeled bracketing of sentences (abstract, in that it is not physically indicated), not to systems of grammatical or semantic relations.[30]

The view that grammatical relations play little or no role in syntax is not Chomsky's alone. For example, McCawley, who takes positions different from Chomsky's on many issues, is apparently in basic agreement with Chomsky's view of the insignificance of grammatical relations in syntax, as the following passage indicates:

(43)   I do not mean to imply by my choice of words that I regard the notion 'grammatical relation' as coherent, viable, or even useful. I am amazed at the extent to which the amount of space devoted by some transformational grammarians to defining that notion exceeds the amount of space that they devoted to using it, the difference often being by a factor of infinity. [McCawley 1970b, p. 444]

The examples Chomsky cites in denying any significant role for grammatical relations in syntax indicate a confusion of *grammatical relations* with *semantic relations,* which is perhaps linked to Chomsky's (1965) definition of grammatical relations solely at the level of deep structure. Consider the examples cited in (42), which we reproduce below:

(44)   I believed your testimony.
(45)   I believed your testimony to be false.
(46)   I believed your testimony to have been given under duress.

In (42) it was pointed out that all three sentences undergo Passive. It was also correctly pointed out that the NP *your testimony* in (44–46) bears different grammatical relations in 'underlying structure'. But there is nothing to support the claim that *your testimony* bears different grammatical relations to *believe* at *the stage of derivations at which Passive applies*. Such a claim is nothing more than an artifact of a theory that chooses to define grammatical relations on underlying structures but not on transformationally derived structures. Once grammatical relations are defined on derived structures as well, *your testimony* is the direct object of *believe* in all three sentences (44–46). Extensive evidence in support of this claim with respect to (45) and (46) is given in Postal 1974.[31] The examples cited in (41) and (42) in support of the claim that Passive applies to any NP immediately following the verb, without regard to its grammatical relation to the verb, are seen to be examples of the application of Passive to the 'direct object' of the verb, once the notion 'direct object of' is defined on transformationally derived structures.

6.2   Grammatical Relations in Derived Structure

In §3.4 it was pointed out that in order for the Relational Succession Law to be statable in linguistic theory, grammatical relations must be defined on structures that are transformationally derived. A theory that does not incorporate the Relational Succession Law not only fails to predict what is predictable, but, by allowing hypothetical rules such as those discussed which seem not to exist in any language, also fails to constrain adequately the notion 'rule of grammar'. In §6.1 we pointed out that grammatical relations must be defined on derived structures in order to account for certain sentences derived by Passive.

Another example where derived grammatical relations play a role comes from work on restrictive relative clause formation by Keenan and Comrie (1977). In a study of more than forty languages, they found that "the relativizability of certain NP positions is not independent of others, and further that the *dependencies* are the same in all languages studied despite considerable differences in the absolute relativizability of certain positions (e.g. in some languages direct objects can be relativized and in other languages they can't) and despite considerable differences in the syntactic properties of relative clause formation strategies in different languages". Of relevance here is the fact that the notions of 'subject', 'direct object', and 'indirect object' that play a role in the Accessibility Hierarchy are subject, direct object, and indirect object *in derived structure*. In all cases, derived subjects produced by movement rules like Passive in English[32] behave like subjects with respect to the Accessibility Hierarchy, objects produced by such movement rules act like objects with respect to the Accessibility Hierarchy, and so on. Thus, in Malagasy oblique case constituents must be made into subjects before they can undergo relativization, in Luganda they must at least be made into objects before they can be relativized, and so on. Similarly, possessor NPs in Malagasy must undergo Possessor Ascension before they can be relativized. The Accessibility Hierarchy discovered by Keenan and Comrie thus refers to *grammatical relations in derived structure*. A theory of language that does not define such grammatical relations is unable to incorporate the Accessibility Hierarchy.

6.3   Conclusions

In §§6.1–6.2 we have argued that:

(i)   Linguistic theory must define grammatical relations on transformationally derived structures.

(ii)   Once grammatical relations are defined on derived structures, the claim that Passive applies to verb-NP pairs in which the NP bears no grammatical relation to the verb dissolves; in each such case, the NP in question is an object of the verb.

(iii) The claim that Passive "applies blindly to any phrase-marker of the proper form, caring nothing about meanings or grammatical relations'' is based on a conception of grammatical relations as existing only at the level of deep structure. Once grammatical relations are defined on derived structures as well, the support for this claim vanishes.

We are *not* suggesting that *all* transformations are sensitive to grammatical relations. We suspect that grammatical relations play a key role in the operation of 'cyclical rules'. To discuss these matters here, however, would take us even further from the Relational Succession Law than we have strayed already.

7 The Syntax of the Host NP after Ascension

The Relational Succession Law states that each ascension rule has the effect of substituting for the term T of some grammatical relation of a verb an NP which was formerly a constituent of T. The question then naturally arises as to the status of the correspondent of the former term in the resulting structure. In other words, when part of a subject becomes the new subject, what is the relational status of (the remnant of) the old subject, and similarly for objects? This question takes on special importance in the context of attempts to define grammatical relations configurationally. For instance, if it is claimed that the direct object relation involves configurations like:

(47)

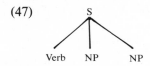

then application of an ascension rule to the sentential subject of an intransitive verb might turn the resulting verb into a transitive. Thus, given an underlying structure like:

(48)

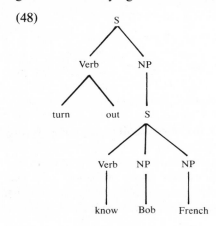

application of Subject Raising would generate:

(49)

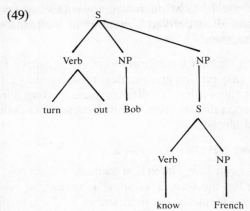

which has the form of (47), suggesting that the sentential remnant is now the direct object of *turn out*.

Such a result not only seems intuitively incorrect, there are certain grammatical facts which suggest that it is simply wrong. For instance, there is nothing to predict that Passive cannot apply to structures of the type (49). But it never can:

(50) a. *To know French was turned out by Bob.
     b. *To lie and cheat is tended by our president.
     c. *To be dead was happened by Napoleon.

Appeals to the stativity of the main verbs in such cases will not suffice, since many stative verbs permit passivization:

(51) a.   That was understood by the researchers.
     b.   That was believed by the troops.
     c.   Tea parties are adored by little children.

We conjecture that the failure of passivization in such cases is a function of two principles: (i) Passive is inherently defined as applying to the direct object of a verb; (ii) the host NP ceases to be the term of any grammatical relation. If (ii) is the case, and if (i) is not only true but a consequence of general principles defining cyclic rules, then we not only predict the facts in *(50) with no special statements, but we arrive at the stronger prediction that parallel sentences in any other language will be ill-formed.

Let us make a further conjecture. Suppose not only that (ii) is valid, but that it is itself a consequence of an even deeper principle which says that if any rule on a cycle S_j 'replaces' the term of one of the NP-verb relations, the NP bearing that relation then not only ceases to bear this relation, but cannot assume any new relation either. One consequence of this would be that in a case-marking language, where nominative is the case of the subject, accusative that of the direct object, operation of a rule like Passive could never turn the former subject into a direct object. This would mean that the analogue of Passive never functions in such a way that the former subject ends up marked accusative. Thus we do not expect to find paired sentences in any language of the form:

(52) a.   wrote Bill/NOM the letter/ACC
      b.   written the letter/NOM Bill/ACC

Rather, we expect the former subject to be either marked with some oblique case (as in Russian) or else fitted with a special prepositional or postpositional marker, as in English, French, or German. From this relational point of view, Passive is seen as a rule which creates new derived subjects and one which is prevented by a universal principle from creating new direct objects.

This means that Passive is properly looked upon as a rule whose nature is to create new subjects (out of direct objects), rather than to create new objects. This contrasts with the apparently symmetrical situation possible for a statement of this rule in a nonrelational theory of grammar, in which, for instance, given a structure of either the forms:

(53) a.   V   NP   NP
      b.   NP   NP   V

it seems quite arbitrary whether one says that the subject moves to the right or the object to the left. Our account leads us to a nonsymmetric statement of the form:

(54)   The direct object becomes the subject.

Given the Relational Succession Law governing ascension rules, a priori there are many possibilities as to the syntax of the host NP after ascension:

(55) a.   When the ascendee becomes superordinate subject, there will be two superordinate subjects; when it becomes superordinate object, there will be two superordinate objects.
      b.   After ascension, the host NP assumes a different grammatical relation.
      c.   After ascension, the host NP cannot bear any grammatical relation at all.
      d.   After ascension, the ascendee assumes a different grammatical relation if there is an independently motivated rule in the

grammar to achieve this effect, e.g., a rule that changes a direct object into an indirect object if there is more than one direct object. Otherwise, ascension entails no additional changes in grammatical relations, both the host and the ascendee bearing the same relation after ascension.

e. After ascension, the host NP assumes a different grammatical relation if there is an independently motivated rule in the grammar to achieve this effect, e.g., a rule that changes a direct object into an indirect object if there is more than one direct object. Otherwise, the ascendee and the host NP both bear the grammatical relation to the verb borne by the host NP prior to ascension.

These are only some of the possibilities. We have conjectured that (55c) is the case on the basis of rather slim evidence because (55c) makes the strongest possible claim that is consistent with the data we are familiar with. We hope that this claim will stimulate research into the question, so that data from a variety of languages can be brought to bear on the issue.

8   Conclusions

We have proposed that the Relational Succession Law is a part of Universal Grammar and have traced its consequences in a number of different areas. We have shown that it is a strong restrictive principle, constraining grammars by excluding certain rules that would otherwise be formulable as transformations. One important consequence of the Relational Succession Law is the necessity of defining grammatical relations on transformationally derived structures. This opens up the possibility of transformations being sensitive to grammatical relations. Another important consequence of the Relational Succession Law for the formulation of transformations can be seen in the formulation of ascension rules. Once the effect of the Relational Succession Law is factored out of the statement of the individual ascension rules, little need be stated in the rules themselves; the Relational Succession Law specifies the derived constituent structure automatically. We believe universal principles of this kind underlie most of what at first seem to be individual rules in particular languages. Such principles, when brought to light, will not only limit the power of individual grammars, but will completely change our notion of what particular rules consist of. The search for substantive universals of language like the Relational Succession Law should, we submit, have top priority in linguistic research.

Editor's Afterword

A1   The Basic Idea

The most basic idea in the accompanying paper (henceforth 'RSL') was the Relational Succession Law itself. It was given in two versions, in (12) and in (27). Version (12) simply states that an ascendee assumes the grammatical relation of the host out of which it ascends. The formulation in (27) attempts to incorporate (12) into a broader generalization that would limit the hosts of ascensions to subjects, direct objects, and indirect objects, that is, to what later came to be called *terms*. This further limitation was later separated from the Relational Succession Law, and in Perlmutter and Postal 1974 it was stated as a separate law, the Host Limitation Law. The 1974 formulations of the two laws are given below:

(A1)   Relational Succession Law
   An NP promoted by an ascension rule assumes the grammatical relation borne by the host out of which it ascends.
(A2)   Host Limitation Law
   Only a term of a grammatical relation can be the host of an ascension.

These two laws make distinct empirical claims, which can be illustrated with hypothetical examples. If a case were found where a nominal ascends out of a nonterm, say an instrument, to assume the instrument relation, that would be a counterexample to the Host Limitation Law but not to the Relational Succession Law. If an example were found where a nominal ascends out of a direct object, assuming a grammatical relation other than the direct object relation, that would be a counterexample to the Relational Succession Law but not to the Host Limitation Law. In RSL, however, these two laws are not clearly separated.

A2   An Immediate Consequence: The Role of Grammatical Relations in Grammar

An obvious and immediate consequence of the Relational Succession Law was that grammatical relations play a more significant role in grammar than they had been accorded in earlier generative work. This paper stressed the necessity of recognizing grammatical relations in derived structures, but this was but one aspect of the more general question of the linguistic level or levels at which grammatical relations are to be recognized in grammatical theory. In §A2.3 I briefly review the status of this issue at that time, §A2.1 comments on the class of grammatical relations posited in this paper, and §A2.2 comments on the paper's assumptions concerning the nature of grammatical relations.

A2.1   The Class of Grammatical Relations

This paper recognizes three grammatical relations: 'subject of', 'direct object of', and 'indirect object of'. On the one hand, this contrasts with Chomsky 1965, which defined only two grammatical relations—the subject and direct object relations. On the other hand, the recognition of only three grammatical relations in this paper contrasts with the much richer class of grammatical relations posited in later relational work (see Perlmutter and Postal (this volume, (13)).

A2.2   The Nature of Grammatical Relations

The accompanying paper shares with earlier generative work the assumption that grammatical relations are to be defined in terms of other concepts. This assumption appears in note 4, which states explicitly that the notion of grammatical relations in this paper "differs considerably from that in most past generative work, specifically in that we claim that derived structures play a basic role in characterizing such relations." This assumption can also be seen in note 20, which assumes "suitable definitions" of the subject and direct object relations. This paper thus shares with both Chomsky 1965 and Fillmore 1968 the assumption that the subject and direct object relations are to be characterized in terms of structural configurations in phrase markers. It also differs from later work in relational grammar in viewing nominals as bearing grammatical relations to the verb rather than to the clause.

A2.3   Grammatical Relations at All Stages of Derivations

RSL departs from earlier generative work in proposing the explicit recognition of grammatical relations at all stages of derivations. This proposal was a direct consequence of the Relational Succession Law, which crucially refers to grammatical relations in both the input and output structures of ascension rules. This position contrasts with that of Chomsky 1965, which recognizes grammatical relations in 'deep structure' but not in derived structures, as well as with that of Fillmore 1968, which recognizes the subject relation in surface structure, but not in earlier stages of derivations.

Comparison of the proposals in this paper with earlier work is complicated by the fact that there was a considerable disparity between generative grammarians' *theoretical* conceptions of grammatical relations and the notions they assumed *in practice*. I will therefore first compare the proposals in the present paper with generativists' theoretical conceptions of grammatical relations, and then briefly point out some examples of the discrepancy between those notions and their linguistic practice.

Chomsky (1965) took a configurational approach to grammatical relations, proposing that 'subject of' and 'direct object of' are *derivative* notions that can be read off structural configurations in phrase markers *at the level of deep structure*. Thus, he proposed that the subject is the NP immediately dominated by S, and the direct object is the NP immediately dominated by VP. Aside from the issue of grammatical relations in derived structures, these definitions are inadequate in several respects. First, they fail with respect to VSO languages, where the linear order of constituents makes it impossible to posit a VP constituent including the verb and direct object while excluding the subject. As a result, there is no single NP immediately dominated by S (which would be the subject in an SVO language) and no single NP immediately dominated by VP (which would be the direct object in an SVO language). Second, Chomsky's proposal in *Aspects* fails to provide a notion of 'indirect object.' Third, Chomsky's definition of 'direct object' relies on the fact that in English, indirect objects are marked with a preposition (usually *to*), while direct objects are not. Thus, in English the direct object would be the only NP immediately dominated by VP, the indirect object and other NPs in the VP being dominated by PP in an *Aspects*-type grammar.

For English it would therefore be possible to characterize the direct object as 'the NP immediately dominated by VP'. But in languages where neither direct nor indirect objects would be dominated by PP (e.g., Russian, Latin) and in languages where both direct and indirect objects would be dominated by PP (e.g., Nitinaht), Chomsky's definitions would fail to distinguish direct and indirect objects.[33]

However, we will not be concerned here with the inadequacies of Chomsky's definitions of grammatical relations. The crucial point for present concerns is that the definitions of grammatical relations that Chomsky proposed for deep structures do not provide the relevant notions for derived structures, even for English. Chomsky (1965, p. 220, footnote 30) states explicitly that his definitions of grammatical relations apply only to deep structures: "Observe that the definitions of grammatical relation or grammatical function that have been suggested here refer only to the base of the syntax and not to surface structures of actual sentences in other than the simplest cases. The significant grammatical relations of an actual sentence . . . are those which are defined in the basis (deep structure) of this sentence." The question then arises whether grammatical relations also exist in structures derived by transformations. Chomsky (1965, pp. 220–21, footnote 35) discusses the possibility of defining the grammatical relations on one class of derived structures—surface structures:

> Extension to surface structures of such functional notions as Subject-of is not an entirely straightforward matter. Thus in base structures, there is apparently never more than a single occurrence of a category such as NP in any structure immediately dominated by a single category . . . , and our definitions of these notions relied on this fact. But this is not true of surface structures. In the sentence "this book I really enjoyed," both "this book" and "I" are NP's immediately dominated by S. Apparently, then, order is significant in determining the grammatical relations defined by surface structures (not surprisingly), though it seems to play no role in the determination of grammatical relations in deep structures. Consequently, somewhat different definitions are needed for the surface notions.
>
> It might be suggested that Topic-Comment is the basic grammatical relation of surface structure corresponding (roughly) to the fundamental Subject-Predicate relation of deep structure. Thus we might define the Topic-of the Sentence as the leftmost NP immediately dominated by S in the surface structure, and the Comment-of the Sentence as the rest of the string. Often, of course, Topic and Subject will coincide, but not in the examples discussed.

The definitions of 'subject' and 'direct object' that Chomsky gave for deep structures do not work for surface structures. He therefore considers two alternatives, having different definitions for surface structures and dispensing entirely with the notions 'subject' and 'object' in surface structures. The matter is left unresolved. The status of grammatical relations at stages of derivations between deep structure and surface structure is not mentioned.

A different theoretical approach to grammatical relations within the framework of generative grammar is found in Fillmore 1968. Fillmore accepts Chomsky's configurational approach to grammatical relations and contrasts grammatical relations such as 'subject of', which can be defined in terms of position in phrase structure configurations, with what he calls 'labeled relations', such as 'recipient', 'actor', 'goal', 'experiencer', 'agent', 'instrument', 'locative', and so on. Fillmore (1968, p. 17) states his conclusion as follows:

> In my earlier paper (Fillmore, 1966) I pointed out that no semantically constant value is associated with the notion 'subject

of' (unless it is possible to make sense of the expression 'the thing being talked about,' and, if that can be done, to determine whether such a concept has any connection with the relation 'subject') and that no semantically relevant relations reside in the surface subject relation which are not somewhere also expressible by 'labeled' relations. The conclusion I have drawn from this is that all semantically relevant syntactic relations between NP's and the structures which contain them must be of the 'labeled' type. The consequences of this decision include (a) the elimination of the category VP, and (b) the addition to some grammars of a rule, or system of rules, for creating 'subjects.' The relation 'subject,' in other words, is now seen as exclusively a surface structure phenomenon.

Transformational grammar's basic insight in distinguishing between different levels of representation led to theoretical approaches to grammatical relations that differed with respect to the level or levels of representation at which these relations are recognized. Chomsky's characterization of these relational notions in terms of structural configurations in phrase markers resulted in a notion of 'grammatical relations' in deep structure that could not be extended to derived levels of representation. Fillmore's recognition that there is no semantically constant value associated with the notion 'subject of' led him to conclude that it is exclusively a surface structure phenomenon.

In their linguistic practice, however, generative grammarians often assumed notions of 'subject', 'direct object', etc., distinct from those characterized in theoretical discussions like those from Chomsky and Fillmore quoted above. But the notions of grammatical relations that such work appealed to were not made explicit.

I will illustrate with one example. Chomsky (1973) proposed what he calls the 'Specified Subject Condition' to account (inter alia) for the fact that a reflexive pronoun cannot be used to refer to *Tom* in *(A3b):

(A3) a. Tom_i expected Marie to give him_i the money.
     b.   *Tom_i expected Marie to give $himself_i$ the money.

Chomsky's account of this is that *Marie* is the subject of the complement in (A3) and that his Specified Subject Condition blocks the rule that would otherwise associate *himself* in *(A3b) with *Tom*. However, we find exactly the same phenomenon if the complement is passive:

(A4) a. Tom_i expected the money to be given him_i by Marie.
     b.   *Tom_i expected the money to be given $himself_i$ by Marie.

The reflexive facts are the same if the pronoun appears with the preposition *to* in surface structure:

(A5) a.   Tom₍ᵢ₎ expected the money to be given to him₍ᵢ₎ by Marie.
   b.   *Tom₍ᵢ₎ expected the money to be given to himself₍ᵢ₎ by Marie.

If the ungrammaticality of *(A4b) and *(A5b) is to be accounted for by the Specified Subject Condition, *the money* in these examples must be a subject. This means that subjects derived through the application of transformations (in this case, Passive) must count as subjects as far as the Specified Subject Condition is concerned. The notion of 'subject' on which Chomsky's Specified Subject Condition depends thus includes derived as well as deep structure subjects. It is thus a notion distinct from that defined in Chomsky 1965. Consequently, the conception of grammatical relations on which Chomsky's Specified Subject Condition depends is distinct from that in the quotations (41–42) in §6 of RSL. In those quotations his conclusion that Passive applies to noun phrases that bear different grammatical relations to the verb rests on the assumption that grammatical relations are defined only at the level of deep structure.

In the same vein, the quotation (43) from McCawley in §6 indicates that he disassociates himself from notions of grammatical relations on a theoretical plane. Yet, he makes use of them in concrete instances of linguistic analysis, as the following quotation (McCawley 1971) shows:

> I should also note that prelexical transformations include not only transformations which combine semantic material into possible lexical items, but also perfectly ordinary transformations such as Equi-NP-Deletion and *there*-insertion. One piece of evidence that Equi-NP-Deletion applies prelexically is that *apologize* has Equi-NP-Deletion under identity with its subject rather than indirect object in
>
> (7) a.   Tom apologized to Sue for kissing Lucy.,
>
> the deleted subject of *kiss* is *Tom,* not *Sue*. If *apologize* has the semantic structure proposed by Fillmore (1971), namely
>
> (7) b.   *x* apologizes to *y* for S = REQUEST(*x,y,*FORGIVE(*y,x,*S)),
>
> then the subject of the lowest sentence would be deleted under identity with the indirect object of FORGIVE. But since the indirect object of FORGIVE is identical to the subject of REQUEST and thus to the subject of *apologize,* there appears to be Equi-NP-Deletion under identity with the subject of *apologize:*

(7) c.

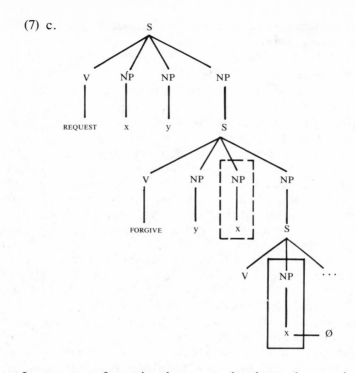

In sum, transformational grammar has been characterized by a curious and largely unnoticed discrepancy between the limited status accorded to grammatical relations on a theoretical plane and a widespread use of inexplicit or undefined relational notions by transformational grammarians in practice. In a sense, this is the very opposite of the situation described by McCawley in the quotation in (43). RSL departed from earlier generative work in proposing the recognition of grammatical relations at all stages of derivations, but it did not propose explicit definitions of grammatical relations in derived structures. As the quotations from Chomsky indicate, it is not clear whether or not the type of configurational definitions of grammatical relations in Chomsky 1965 can be extended to derived structures, even for English. One of the consequences of the Relational Succession Law—the recognition of the necessity of grammatical relations at all levels—was an important factor that led to making grammatical relations independent of positions in phrase structure configurations. The result was to abandon attempts to define grammatical relations in terms of other notions and to take them to be primitives of grammatical theory. This marked the beginning of relational grammar.

A3   **Some Further Consequences: Ideas That Appear Here
in Embryonic Form**

A3.1   The Separation of the Universal and Language-Particular
Components of Syntactic Rules

An important aspect of this paper was the explicit attempt to formulate
syntactic rules in a language-independent way—that is, to factor out
language-particular idiosyncrasies of a rule in individual languages from
a more general, language-independent statement of the rule that is
viewed as belonging to universal grammar. Most work in generative
grammar has assumed first, that grammatical rules vary from language
to language, within the very broad limits allowed by the general theory
of transformations, and second, that universal grammar is concerned
primarily with that general theory and, more particularly, with the
discovery of universal constraints on language-particular rules. Even
within generative grammar, however, certain works noted the similarity
of particular rules in different languages and attempted to capture this
in one way or another. The relevant literature here includes Bach 1965,
1971, Ross 1967, 1970, Fillmore 1968, Postal 1970, Hankamer 1971,
and Perlmutter and Orešnik 1973. In attempting to state what is common
to ascensions in all languages that have them, RSL can be viewed as
following this line of earlier work.

The particular attempt made here fails in a number of ways, but the
basic idea was that it is possible to characterize rules in the grammars
of different languages as instances of the 'same' syntactic rule. Subject-
to-Object Raising, for example, was conceived of as the 'same' rule,
though it can appear in the grammars of different languages with different word order patterns. The same is true of Passive, and ultimately
of a significant class of syntactic rules. The transformational conception
of such rules as movements of constituents to the left or right made
it difficult to extract what is common to these rules in different languages; in some languages a given rule might involve movement of an
NP to the left, in another to the right, in another it might involve
movement of several constituents. Further, the formulation of the rule
in terms of analyzability of phrase markers would make it necessary
in certain cases for the statement of the rule to mention language-
particular details simply because they are present in the class of structures to which the rule applies in one language or another.[34] Once a
significant class of syntactic rules was conceived of as operating not
on phrase markers representing linear order and dominance but rather
on grammatical relations, the identification of two rules in distinct
languages as instances of the 'same' rule became possible, and that
aspect of the rule that is the same in all languages could be factored
out and stated separately from the various language-particular details

of each language. This was the approach in Perlmutter and Postal 1974, where rules were conceived of as consisting of a universal 'core' and various language-particular 'side-effects'. One achievement of relational grammar has been to provide a conception of linguistic structure that makes it possible to capture what is common to the basic syntactic constructions in different languages in ways that were not possible in the transformational framework.

A3.2   The Universal Characterization of Passivization

In (54), RSL gives a characterization of passivization in terms of a direct object assuming subjecthood. This idea formed the basis of a talk by Postal at the 1973 meeting of the Chicago Linguistic Society. In Perlmutter and Postal 1974, in which rules were viewed as having a universal 'core' and language-particular 'side-effects', Passive was formulated in language-independent terms as follows:

(A6)   Passive

$$2 \longrightarrow 1$$

i.e., as advancement of a 2 (direct object) to 1 (subject). The morphological concomitants of passivization in particular languages, such as passive verb morphology and marking of the chômeur with a particular preposition, postposition, or case, were viewed as language-particular 'side effects' of passivization. This led to the universal characterization of Passive in Perlmutter and Postal 1977, where the relevant notions are made precise in terms of relational networks. The crucial step in this development was the factoring out from the statement of passivization in particular grammars what is common to passivization in all languages that have it, given in 1974 terms in (A6). Conceiving of the 'core' of the rule in relational terms made this possible.

A3.3   The Notion of 'Chômeur'

In §7, RSL considers the syntax of the host NP after ascension and conjectures that "the host NP ceases to be the term of any grammatical relation." This was the beginning of the notion of 'chômeur.'

The notion of 'chômeur' has itself undergone a certain evolution. The earliest work was embedded in a derivational framework and assumed the class of grammatical relations to consist of only the subject, direct object, and indirect object relations. A chômeur was a nominal that bore a grammatical relation at an earlier stage of the derivation but not at the stage under consideration. Terminology reflecting this set of assumptions is found in some early papers, e.g., Chung 1976. Later, as the class of nominal-clausal grammatical relations was enriched, a 'chômeur *relation*' was posited. With the introduction of relational networks in Perlmutter and Postal 1977, the notion of 'chômeur in a stratum c_i' was reconstructed as 'a nominal heading a Cho arc with coordinate c_i.'

RSL conjectures that the fact that the host NP ceases to be the term of any grammatical relation "is itself a consequence of an even deeper principle which says that if any rule on a cycle S_j 'replaces' the term of one of the NP-verb relations, the NP bearing that relation then not only ceases to bear this relation, but cannot assume any new relation either." This is the first statement of what in Perlmutter and Postal 1974 was called the 'Relational Annihilation Law', then stated as follows:

(A7)   Relational Annihilation Law
        When an NP, NP_i, assumes the grammatical relation borne by another NP, NP_j ($i \neq j$), then NP_j ceases to bear any grammatical relation whatsoever. Such NP_j are called 'chômeurs'.

This principle was called the 'Chômeur Condition' or 'Chômeur Law' in Perlmutter and Postal 1977. It predicts that the remainder of the host NP after ascension will be a chômeur and hence a nonterm. As shown in §A4.1.2 below, this is crucial for predicting word order in raising constructions in English.

The scope of the Chômeur Law is not limited to ascensions, for it also predicts chômage under parallel conditions in other types of constructions: revaluations (advancements and demotions) and constructions involving dummies. As such, it makes a wide range of empirical predictions. Perlmutter and Postal (chap. 3, §8) give grounds for the abandonment of the Chômeur Law as a linguistic universal, but a weaker version of this law can probably be maintained. In particular, it seems to be valid for ascensions, since no counterexamples in this domain are known at present.

A4   **Word Order in Ascension Constructions**
A4.1   Word Order in Ascension Constructions in Relational Grammar
A4.1.1 *The Necessary Concepts*

Relational grammar provides the following concepts to predict word order in the ascension constructions discussed here:

(A8) a.   the Relational Succession Law
     b.   the notion of chômeur
     c.   language-particular generalizations governing word order

The notion of chômeur is crucial. If it were necessary to state separately, for each ascension construction in each language, whether or not the host of the ascension heads a Cho arc, one could speak of giving an account of word order in ascension constructions in different languages, but not of predicting it. However, under a weakened version of the Chômeur Law applicable to ascensions, the chômage of the host is predictable. I also assume the Chômeur Advancement Ban, which guarantees that if a nominal heads a Cho arc in the c_k stratum of a clause b, it will head a Cho arc in the final stratum of b. Thus, ascension hosts head final-stratum Cho arcs in their clauses, a fact that is crucial for predicting word order in ascension constructions.

A4.1.2   *Word Order in Raising Constructions in English*

The word order in English basic clauses that do not involve WH-words, Topicalization, etc., can be given roughly in terms of *final-stratum* grammatical relations as follows:

(A9)   1 – P – 2 – 3 – Nonterm

That is, the final 1 precedes the predicate, the final 2 (if any) immediately follows the predicate, the final 3 (if any) comes next, and nonterms (if any) come last.

In conjunction with the universal characterization of Passive clauses in chapter 1, (A9) accounts for the word order in English passives:

(A10) a.   The press criticized that policy.
       b.   That policy was criticized by the press.

Sentence (A10a) involves only one stratum, in which *the press* heads a 1-arc, *criticized* a P-arc, and *that policy* a 2-arc; (A10b) is associated with the RN abbreviable as the following stratal diagram:[35]

(A11)

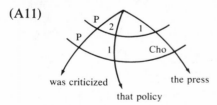

Thus, *that policy* is the final 1, *was criticized* the predicate,[36] and *the press* is a final chômeur. The word order in both (A10a) and (A10b) thus conforms to (A9).

Now consider:

(A12) a.   Tom gave the book to Louise.
       b.   Tom gave Louise the book.

Sentence (A12a) involves only one stratum, in which *Tom* heads a 1-arc, *the book* a 2-arc, and *Louise* a 3-arc. The word order in (A12a) thus conforms to (A9), but (A12b) involves 3-2 Advancement,[37] so its RN is abbreviable as follows:

(A13)

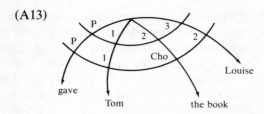

Louise thus heads a final-stratum 2-arc, and *the book* a final Cho arc. The word order in (A12b) consequently also conforms to (A9).

Although (A10b) and (A12b) are examples of different grammatical constructions, they illustrate the fact that in English, final-stratum chômeurs follow both the predicate and final terms. This generalization is not limited to these two constructions, but extends to ascensions as well.

Consider first so-called Subject-to-Subject Raising in English, illustrated by (2b) of RSL, repeated here for convenience:

(A14)   Melvin turns out to be incoherent.

Under the assumption that the complement clause is an initial 1 of the matrix clause,[38] the structure of (A14) is given in the simplified RN (with irrelevant details omitted) in (A15a), abbreviated as a stratal diagram in (A15b):

(A15) a.

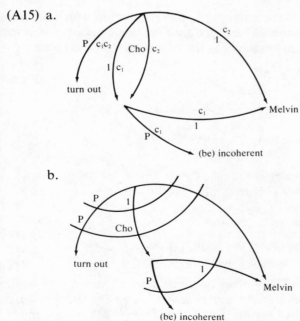

b.

By the Relational Succession Law, the ascendee (*Melvin*) assumes the 1-relation in the matrix clause, since that is the relation borne by the host (the complement) out of which it ascends under the assumptions made here. Since it heads a 1-arc in the final stratum of the matrix clause, it is the final 1 of the clause. Thus, by independent rules of English (whose effect is summarized in (A9)), it precedes the predicate of the main clause in normal word order.

Significantly, the linear position of *to be incoherent* is also predictable. Since the host nominal (the complement clause) heads a chômeur arc in the c_2 stratum of the matrix clause, it is a final chômeur, and hence, under the generalization in (A9), follows the predicate. The position of *to be incoherent* in (A14) follows from the same generalization that also governs the position of *the press* in (A10b) and that of *the book* in (A12b).

One further assumption must be made explicit. If a nominal *a* is an ascendee, so that it heads two arcs with distinct tails, it is the arc that is "higher" in the RN that determines the linear position of *a*. The question of how this principle is to be made precise, like the question of the range of phenomena for which it holds, is beyond the scope of this Afterword. What is relevant here is the fact that the linear position of *Melvin* in (A14) is determined by the fact that it heads a final 1-arc in the matrix clause, not by the 1-arc it heads in the complement. The principle that determines this is also crucial to the relational account of word order offered here for other raising constructions in English, as well as for the Possessor Ascension construction in Malagasy.

Now consider Object Raising in English, as exemplified by (4b) of RSL, repeated here for convenience:

(A16)   John is easy to please.

Again assuming ascension out of a 1, *John* ascends to assume the 1-relation in the matrix clause and therefore precedes the predicate in (A16). The host heads a c_2-stratum Cho arc in the main clause, so its remainder *to please* follows the predicate in (A16). Again, the linear position of both *John* and *to please* is predictable.

In the case of Subject-to-Object Raising, e.g.,

(A17)   Harry believes Joan to be pregnant.

the ascendee (*Joan*) ascends out of a 2, and so by the Relational Succession Law assumes the 2-relation in the matrix clause. The host heads a Cho arc in the final stratum of the matrix clause, so its remainder *to be pregnant,* a final chômeur, follows the final 2 *Joan* in (A17), according to the generalization in (A9).

Thus, there is a single generalization underlying the position of *the press* in (A10b), *the book* in (A12b), *to be incoherent* in (A14), *to please* in (A 16), and *to be pregnant* in (A17). Without the notion of chômeur, this generalization could not be captured.

In brief, the concepts in (A8), including the generalization in (A9) for English, predict word order in ascension constructions in English. They thus capture generalizations uniting word order in ascension constructions with that in other sentence types in English such as (A10) and (A12). At the same time, they provide an explanation of why some of the hypothetical possibilities discussed in §2.1 are not found.

A4.1.3   *Word Order in the Possessor Ascension Construction*
in Malagasy

Now consider Possessor Ascension in Malagasy. The following sentences ((35) and (36) of RSL) are relevant:

(A18)   Nantsoin-dRakoto ny anaran'   ny olona.
        called   Rakoto the names-of the people
        'The names of the people were called by Rakoto.'

(A19)   Nantsoin-dRakoto anarana ny olona.
        called   Rakoto names   the people
        'The people were called by name by Rakoto.'

Sentence (A18) does not involve Possessor Ascension, and is associated with the RN abbreviable as the following stratal diagram:[39]

(A20)
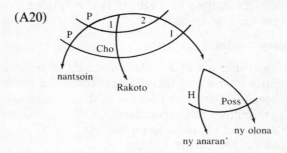

This is a Passive clause, whose final 1 is the possessive phrase *ny anaran' ny olona* 'the names of the people' in (A18). Sentence (A19), however, involves Possessor Ascension. It is associated with the RN abbreviable as the following stratal diagram:

(A21)

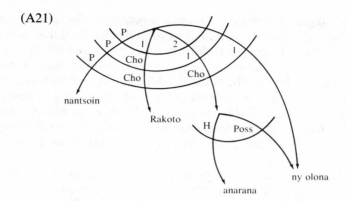

This, too, is a Passive clause, in which the host nominal heads a second-stratum 1-arc. The ascendee *ny olona* 'the people' thus ascends out of a 1 and therefore heads a 1-arc in the final stratum. Since nominals heading a final-stratum 1-arc occupy rightmost position in the clause in normal word order in Malagasy, *ny olona* does so in (A19).

An important difference between the transformational and relational treatments of ascensions lies in the fact that transformational grammar conceives of them as movement rules, and so must specify the direction of movement (rightward or leftward). The relational approach to ascensions, in contrast, conceives of them in terms of grammatical relations, with the ascendee assuming the grammatical relation of the host. The ascension itself has nothing to do with linear position. Independent rules of particular languages specify the linear position of nominals in the clause as a function of grammatical relations. In this way, the relational approach can make the differing linear positions of ascendees in different languages follow from language-particular differences in the rules that determine constituent order, capturing in terms of grammatical relations what is common to ascensions in different languages.

A4.2   Word Order in Ascension Constructions in RSL

At several points, RSL claims that the order of constituents resulting from ascensions is predicted by the Relational Succession Law. Thus, §3.2 states: "the fact that the ascendee ends up to the left of the host NP need not be stated as such; the position of the ascendee in derived structure is predicted by the Relational Succession Law." The entire discussion in §3.1 rests on similar assumptions; in order to rule out the a priori possible rules that §3.1 claims are excluded in principle, the Relational Succession Law must predict the order of constituents resulting from ascension. Further, §5.2 states: "the Relational Succession

Law automatically predicts the word order of the output of the ascension rule, even though the actual word order resulting from ascension rules in the two languages is different. In English, an NP that ascends out of a subject NP goes to the left of the host NP, because subjects in English are to the left, while in Malagasy an NP that ascends out of a subject NP goes to the right of the host NP, since in Malagasy the subject is to the right.'' The treatment of Malagasy is thus inconsistent with the characterization of ascensions in (1) and (27), which incorrectly assumes that in all ascensions the ascendee ends up to the *left* of the host.

Despite RSL's claim that the word order in ascension constructions in predictable, it fails to specify the mechanisms whereby adoption of the Relational Succession Law in a transformational framework would result in the automatic assignment of the correct word order in ascension constructions in different languages. RSL argues that the *effect* of certain transformations is determined by grammatical relations, but it fails to develop a coherent theory of the relation between grammatical relations and linear position. Subsequent work in relational grammar has developed the essential elements of such a theory, whose application to ascension constructions has been sketched in this Afterword. A significant step was the recognition that grammatical relations cannot be defined in terms of phrase structure configurations, but must be taken as theoretical primitives. It then becomes possible to state language-particular generalizations governing word order in terms of grammatical relations. As we have seen, the notion of chômeur has also been crucial. Although RSL failed to make linear position follow from grammatical relations, much subsequent work has attempted to achieve the goals set here.

Thus, the ideas in RSL in effect set two requirements for an adequate linguistic theory. First, such a theory must be able to state the cross-linguistic generalizations embodied in the Relational Succession Law and the Host Limitation Law. Second, where possible, it must make word order in ascension constructions follow from broader language-particular generalizations governing word order.

A5.   **The Current Status of the Claims in RSL**
A5.1   Different Analyses of Particular Phenomena
A5.1.1   *Raising and the Unaccusative Hypothesis*

RSL treats the raising constructions it exemplifies in (2–5) as instances of raising out of a subject. Under this assumption, the ascendee assumes the subject relation in the matrix clause, by the Relational Succession Law. This analysis is illustrated in (A15). More recently, however, it has been proposed (see Perlmutter and Postal, to appear a, Perlmutter 1978) that many intransitive clauses have an initial direct object but no initial subject. Such clauses are called 'initially unaccusative clauses', and the hypothesis that such clauses exist is called the 'Unaccusative Hypothesis'. Under this hypothesis, the relational network associated with (2b) would be given in simplified form as (A22a), or, abbreviated as a stratal diagram, as (A22b):

(A22) a.

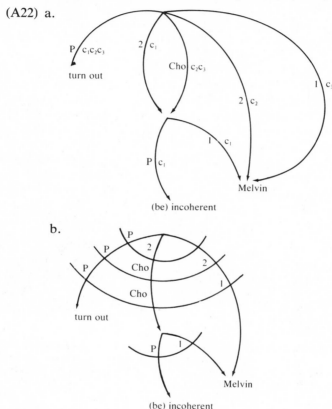

(Melvin should probably be analyzed as an initial 2 rather than initial 1, and *be* and *incoherent* as predicates of distinct clauses, but these matters are ignored here.) Under this analysis, the ascendee assumes the 2-relation in the matrix clause and advances to 1 in the Unaccusative Advancement construction (see Perlmutter and Postal, to appear a, and Perlmutter 1978 for discussion).

Some predicates that govern Raising also govern Inversion, under which a nominal heading a 1-arc in one stratum heads a 3-arc in a later stratum (see Harris 1981, to appear a, b and Perlmutter 1979, for evidence for Inversion in various languages and discussion). In the Inversion construction there is an unaccusative stratum (one containing a 2-arc but no 1-arc). However, this does not affect the analysis of Subject Raising, as can be seen in (A24), the stratal diagram for (A23).

(A23)   Marcia seems to me to be joking.

(A24)

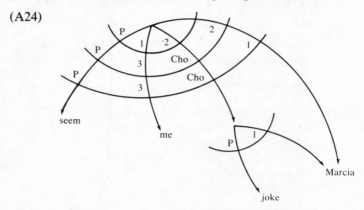

Under the Unaccusative Hypothesis, what has traditionally been called 'Subject-to-Subject Raising' is analyzed as raising to *direct object*. This differs from what has traditionally been called 'Subject-to-Object Raising' in that the latter construction involves raising to 2 in a *transitive* stratum (containing both a 1-arc and a 2-arc), while the former cases involve raising to 2 in an *unaccusative* stratum. However, justification of this analysis of raising constructions lies beyond the scope of this discussion.

A5.1.2   *The Relation between Grammatical Relations and Case*

RSL §7 assumes a very direct relation between grammatical relations and case. In particular, from the claim that "a rule like Passive could never function in such a way as to turn the former subject into a direct object," it concludes that "the analogue of Passive never functions in such a way that the former subject ends up marked accusative," citing (52) as an example that will not be found in any language. The unstated assumption is that the *only* way a nominal can be marked accusative is by being a direct object. However, this assumption is false. For example, under the analysis of Maasai proposed in Perlmutter and Postal (to ·appear b), certain nominals that are initial 2s and final chômeurs have accusative forms by virtue of rules that ensure accusative marking for "acting 2s."[40] Further, nothing rules out a language-particular rule marking chômeurs in the Passive construction with accusative case. The result would be examples like (52) of RSL. In fact, such cases exist. Thus, in Lardil, an Australian language discussed by Klokeid (1976), passive chômeurs occur in the genitive and accusative cases, the distribution of the two being predictable along aspectual lines:

(A25) a. Ngithun ngawa pethur   yadamankur.
           my   dog   bite-FUT horse-FUT
           'My dog will bite the horse.'
      b. Yadaman peyithur   ngithun-ngan ngawu-kan.
           horse   bite-PASS-FUT my-GEN   dog-GEN
           'The horse will be bitten by my dog.'

(A26) a. Ngithun ngawa petha-kun yadaman-in.
           my   dog   bite-ASP horse-ACC
           'My dog bit the horse.'
      b. Yadaman peyi-kun   ngithun-in ngawu-n.
           horse   bit-PASS-ASP   my-ACC   dog-ACC
           'The horse was bitten by my dog.'

As Klokeid's analysis makes clear, *ngithun-ngan ngawu-kan* in (A25b) and *ngithun-in ngawu-n* in (A26b) are final chômeurs rather than final 2s. That is, these examples have the structure in (A27) rather than that in (A28):

(A27)

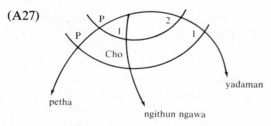

(A28)

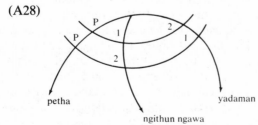

Two things are needed to guarantee that no language can have a passive clause in which the 1 is final 2: the characterization of passive clauses in which the 1 heads a Cho arc in the stratum in which the 2

heads a 1-arc and the Chômeur Advancement Ban (chap. 3), which rules out advancement of the chômeur to 2. Thus, RSL's claim that "a rule like Passive could never function in such a way as to turn the former subject into a direct object" may well be correct. The error lay in assuming that it therefore could not appear in the accusative case. As (A26b) in Lardil shows, the latter claim is false.

A5.2   On the Validity of the Relational Succession Law
and the Host Limitation Law

In the period since these laws were first formulated, two types of cases have been interpreted as challenges to their universality. The first concerns cases of Possessor Ascension in various languages. These are discussed in Perlmutter (to appear a) and will not be mentioned further here.

The second challenge to the validity of these laws is posed by Ruwet (1976), based on Subject Raising in French. Most of Ruwet's paper is devoted to the syntax of clauses with *sembler* 'seem' and similar verbs in French. In particular, Ruwet shows various ways in which the complement of *sembler* behaves like a direct object rather than a subject. He proposes (note 16) "an analysis which treats the sentential complement of *sembler* not as a direct object *stricto sensu* but rather as a predicate nominal." Since Ruwet assumes a rule of Subject Raising that raises the subject of the complement of *sembler* directly to so-called subject position, and since he gives various arguments that the complement of *sembler* is not its subject, he concludes that the French data he cites invalidates the Relational Succession Law.

Ruwet's argument against the Relational Succession Law is based entirely on the incompatibility between the nonsubject character of complements of *sembler* and the assumption that ascendees ascending from such complements ascend directly to subject. In a version of relational grammar (such as the current one) which incorporates the Unaccusative Hypothesis, however, the complement of *sembler* is an initial 2 of the matrix clause, and the ascendee ascends to 2, not to 1. The nominal ascending to 2 advances to 1 in the Unaccusative Advancement construction.[41] The structures that would be posited for *sembler*-clauses with raising in French are like those illustrated for English in (A22) and (A24) above, mutatis mutandis. Since such structures are compatible both with the objectlike behavior of *sembler*-complements pointed out by Ruwet (since the complement is the initial 2 of the *sembler*-clause) and with the Relational Succession Law, Ruwet's arguments have no bearing on the validity of that law.

A6   Conclusions

The main purpose of this Afterword has been to discuss RSL in the light of the status accorded grammatical relations in transformational grammar at the time it was written, and in the light of the subsequent development of relational grammar. It has been shown that the ideas in this paper led to the formulation of two distinct laws in Perlmutter and Postal 1974—the Relational Succession Law and the Host Limitation Law. Second, this Afterword has brought out some consequences of the paper and some ideas that appear here in embryonic form. The paper's claims about predicting word order in ascension constructions do not go through in the framework in which it is embedded, but it has been shown here how word order in these constructions *can* be predicted as a function of universals of grammar and language-particular generalizations. Finally, the current status of the paper's chief claims has been evaluated in the light of subsequent challenges and theoretical developments.

Notes

1. The terminology of the paper has been changed to conform to more recent usage.

2. A stronger definition would result if constraints were provided on the categories to which A could belong. We return to this below, arguing that A can be NP and nothing else.

3. This account is vague in not specifying whether an ascension rule is a pure movement rule or a doubling rule (leaving a pronominal 'copy' in the original position). We suggest that ascension rules can be of either type, and further that the contrast between the two may be at least partly predictable from the structure of the constituent A (e.g., where A is an island in the sense of Ross 1967, any ascension from A must be a doubling rule).

4. Grammatical relations are fundamental to our account. We claim that they play a key defining role for *cyclic* rules. However, our conception of grammatical relations differs considerably from that in most past generative work, specifically in that we claim that derived structures play a basic role in characterizing such relations.

5. It is worth noting that our view that such rules are not cyclic follows not only from particular empirical considerations (see Postal 1972) but from a general theory of the cyclic-postcyclic contrast according to which it is impossible for unbounded rules of this sort to be cyclic. [Editor's note: The allusion here is to the 'Cyclicity Law', which was stated in Perlmutter and Postal 1974 as follows: "If a rule creates or destroys termhood, it is a cyclical rule." In later versions of relational grammar, in which the notion of rules converting one structure into another was abandoned, the cycle, and hence the Cyclicity Law, ceased to have any meaning.]

6. See the discussion in Rosenbaum 1967, Ross 1967, Postal 1971, Perlmutter 1971, Kiparsky and Kiparsky 1970.

7. See the discussion in Postal 1971 and Bresnan 1971.

8. Emonds (1970, 1972) argues that the complements in such cases are generated directly at the right end of verb phrases, so that such sentences never involve sentential subjects. The development of the present argument provides one objection to this analysis. See also Higgins 1973 and Postal 1974. [Editor's note: Generating such complements at the right end of verb phrases was also proposed by Kajita (1966) and Bresnan (1972), and by Gross (1968) and Ruwet (1972) for French. This analysis was subsequently adopted in a number of other studies.]

9. For extensive discussion of this rule and its role in such derivations see Rosenbaum 1967 and Ross 1967.

10. This assumption is challenged by Bresnan (1971), who argues in an analysis partially similar to but distinct from that of Emonds (1970, 1972) that sentences like (2b) and (3b) are generated by a rule operating not on a sentential subject but rather on a complement generated directly at the extreme end of verb phrases. Again, the argument presented in the present paper provides an objection to that analysis.

11. We adopt here underlying structures in which English has verb-initial structure, as proposed by McCawley (1970a) and further supported by Bach (1971), Ross (1970), and Postal (1974). The argument of the present paper would be unaffected, however, if the underlying order of major constituents in English should turn out not to be VSO. In the absence of any evidence for a VP constituent, we assume that no such constituent exists. Subjects, direct objects, and indirect objects of a verb are thus its sisters.

12. In (10), as in (8), the embedded sentence contains an intransitive verb. Nothing of relevance to the argument is changed if the embedded verb is transitive.

13. If it were possible for Object Raising to raise NPs in embedded objects in subject clauses, deriving (i-b) from the structure underlying (i-a):

(i) a.   It will be a cinch to say you solved that problem.
    b.   That problem will be a cinch to say you solved.

that problem would still be moving out of a sentential subject: *to say you solved that problem*. As ascension rules are sketched in (1), the ascendee becomes the sister of the host constituent A. Since we find sentences like (i-b) of doubtful well-formedness, the point may be academic.

14. Emonds (1970, 1972) makes a proposal to this effect. Emonds' proposal, however, works only within his system, which requires that *that*-clauses and infinitives *not* be dominated by NP. However, Higgins 1973, Postal 1974, and the present paper present evidence that this aspect of Emonds's system is incorrect. His proposal to rule out transformations like 13 falls with it.

15. See the references in notes 6, 7, and 11.

16. What is 'preserved', then, is the grammatical relation, not the 'structure' in the sense of Emonds 1970.

17. For other evidence of the NP-hood of *that*-clauses and infinitives, see Higgins 1973 and Postal 1974.

18. See Postal 1974.

19. Under the assumption that no VP constituent exists, the subject of a verb (as well as its objects) is its sister.

20. We know of no cases where an ascension rule operates on indirect objects and thus consider it possible that a theory of ascension rules can be restricted

to A-constituents (hosts) which are either subjects or direct objects, given suitable definitions of these concepts.

21. Except for analyses which deny subject or object status (or even NP status) to such constituents (see the references in notes 8 and 10 and the discussion in §3.6).

The Relational Succession Law allows a grammar of English that derives (i-b) and (ii-b) from the structures underlying (i-a) and (ii-a), respectively.

(i) a.   The price of meat went up.
   b.   Meat went up in price.
(ii) a.   The protein content of tofu is high.
   b.   Tofu is high in protein content.

The rule in question would ascend an NP out of the subject of *went up* and *is high,* making the ascendee the new subject of these predicates. This rule would also be an ascension rule conforming to the Relational Succession Law, and hence formulable with minimal language-particular apparatus. The law would also explain the absence in English of related pairs like

(iii) a.   The price of meat went up.
    b. *The price went up meat.
(iv) a.   The protein content of tofu is high.
    b. *The protein content is high tofu.

Other examples of potential ascension rules similar to these could be cited.

22. For arguments supporting the analogue of Subject Raising 1 in French, see Ruwet 1970, 1972. For discussion of the analogue of Object Raising, see Kayne 1975, esp. pp. 16–17, and Gaatone 1970. For some further discussion of both rules in French, see Fauconnier 1971.

23. For evidence in support of the analogue of Subject Raising 1 in Portuguese, see Quícoli 1972, chap. 2.

24. Speakers of Portuguese differ on whether *considerar* takes *que*-complements in surface structure, as in (32a).

25. The English gloss is grammatical with a different meaning, derived from 'those people consider that he is important' rather than 'he considers that those people are important.' This confusion does not arise in Portuguese because of the plural ending on *importantes.*

26. Some of the Malagasy examples cited here are taken from Keenan 1972; the rest were kindly supplied by Keenan and Rodin Ramanantsoa. We are also indebted to Keenan for discussion of the issues involved.

27. The analogy with Passive in English is an oversimplification, since Malagasy has several such verbal voices. See Keenan 1971, 1972 for discussion

28. We have not investigated the question of whether the subject appears to the right of the object in underlying structure, as it generally does in surface structure, or whether this word order is the result of a rule that postposes the subject. If the latter is the case, the difference from English would be less striking, but in either case it is clear that the ascendee ascends into superordinate subject position.

29. Chomsky (1965) did not define the relation *indirect object of.* We claim that this relation must be included among the grammatical relations in an adequate syntactic theory.

30. While these quotations from Chomsky offer a particularly clear statement

of the view that has been traditional in generative grammar, we are somewhat reluctant to attribute them to Chomsky because in footnote 26 to the passage quoted above he states: "It should be noted that lexical properties of particular items determine the permissibility of transformations and that rules of semantic interpretation may be inapplicable in certain cases if transformations have applied. This 'filtering effect' of transformations in effect makes them inapplicable in certain cases." If "rules of semantic interpretation" have the power to filter out certain sentences, i.e., to characterize them as ungrammatical, on the basis of whether or not some transformation or transformations applied, there is then no clear content to the statement that "the rule pays no attention to the grammatical and semantic relations of the main verb to the noun phrase that follows it" or that "in all cases, the rule applies blindly, caring nothing for these differences." To say that "rules of semantic interpretation" have the power to characterize certain sentences as ungrammatical just in case a certain transformation has applied is equivalent to saying that the rule cannot apply under certain semantic conditions.

31. [Editor's note: At this point, the original manuscript contained a discussion of the examples offered in (41) in support of the claim that Passive is insensitive to grammatical relations, pointing out that although the *semantic* relation between *received* and *the book* in *John received the book* is not the same as that between *read* and *the book* in *John read the book,* in both cases *the book* is the direct object of the verb. It was then stated that this is also the case in *derived structure* in *John expected the book to be good.* There followed a discussion of *John gave Bill the book* and of the question of whether Passive applies to both direct and indirect objects. That discussion antedated the idea of 3–2 Advancement, under which an indirect object advances to direct object. Such an advancee to direct object can further advance to subject in many languages, including English, yielding sentences like *Bill was given the book by John.* The subsequent development of 3–2 Advancement thus made it possible to include such sentences as examples of a direct object advancing to subject. In the original text, they were treated as exceptional.]

32. We would claim that the relevant class of rules here is the class of *cyclical* rules. [Editor's note: See note 5.]

33. For Nitinaht, any attempt to make Chomsky's definitions of grammatical relations work would also face the difficulties posed by the fact that Nitinaht is a VSO language and the fact that subjects can also be marked with prepositions. See Klokeid (to appear) for arguments that configurational definitions of grammatical relations are inadequate for Nitinaht, and Johnson 1979 and Perlmutter (to appear) for arguments against configurational definitions of grammatical relations in general.

34. Certain aspects of these general points are argued in greater detail for Passive in Perlmutter and Postal 1977.

35. Explanations of the notation of relational networks (RNs) and stratal diagrams, of the notions 'arc', 'stratum', 'final stratum', etc., can be found in chaps. 1 and 3.

36. Treating *was criticized* as a single predicate is an oversimplification, since the structure may be biclausal, perhaps involving Clause Union of the type discussed by Aissen and Perlmutter (1976) for Spanish under the name 'Clause Reduction'. For a discussion of the periphrastic passives of German and Welsh in these terms, see Perlmutter and Postal (to appear b). The simplification is made throughout this Afterword.

37. The 3–2 Advancement construction in English is discussed briefly in chap. 3. Evidence for 3–2 Advancement in various languages can be found in Chung 1976, Allen and Frantz 1978, Crain 1979, Aissen, this volume, and Seiler and Frantz, to appear.

38. I thus ignore here the possibility that the complement is an initial 2, in accordance with the Unaccusative Hypothesis (see Perlmutter and Postal, to appear a, and Perlmutter 1978). If the complement is an initial 2, as proposed in Perlmutter and Postal (to appear b), the RN associated with (A14) would be abbreviable as the following stratal diagram:

(i)

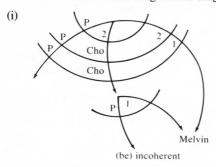

(be) incoherent

The question of whether (A14) has the structure in (i) or that in (A15) makes no difference, as far as word order is concerned, since in either case the correct word order is determined by the generalization in (A9). Thus, the Unaccusative Hypothesis is ignored throughout §A4. It is discussed briefly in §A5 in connection with a critique of the Relational Succession Law by Ruwet (1976).

39. 'H' and 'Poss' abbreviate 'Head' and 'Possessor', respectively.

40. On the notion 'acting Term$_x$', see Perlmutter and Postal (to appear b).

41. On the Unaccusative Hypothesis and Unaccusative Advancement, see Perlmutter and Postal, to appear a, and Perlmutter 1978.

References

Aissen, Judith (this volume). "Indirect Object Advancement in Tzotzil."

Aissen, Judith, and Perlmutter, David M. 1976. "Clause Reduction in Spanish." In *Proceedings of the Second Annual Meeting of the Berkeley Linguistics Society*. University of California, Berkeley. Reprinted in this volume.

Allen, Barbara J., and Frantz, Donald G. 1978. "Verb Agreement in Southern Tiwa." In *Proceedings of the Fourth Annual Meeting of the Berkeley Linguistics Society*. University of California, Berkeley. Revised version in this volume.

Anderson, Stephen R., and Kiparsky, Paul, eds. 1973. *A Festschrift for Morris Halle*. New York: Holt, Rinehart, & Winston.

Bach, Emmon. 1965. "On Some Recurrent Types of Transformations." In *Sixteenth Annual Round Table Meeting on Linguistics and Language Studies*. Georgetown University Monograph Series on Languages and Linguistics, no. 18, Washington, D.C.: Georgetown University Press.

———. 1971. "Questions." *Linguistic Inquiry* 2:153–66.

Berman, Arlene. 1974. "On the VSO Hypothesis." *Linguistic Inquiry* 5:1–37.

Bresnan, Joan W. 1971. "Sentence Stress and Syntactic Transformations." *Language* 47:257–81.

———. 1972. "Theory of Complementation in English Syntax." Ph.D. diss., MIT.

Chomsky, Noam. 1965. *Aspects of the Theory of Syntax*. Cambridge: MIT Press.

———. 1971. *Problems of Knowledge and Freedom*. New York: Pantheon.

———. 1972. "Some Empirical Issues in the Theory of Transformational Grammar." In Peters, 1972.

———. 1973. "Conditions on Transformations." In Anderson and Kiparsky, 1973.

Chung, Sandra. 1976. "An Object-Creating Rule in Bahasa Indonesia." *Linguistic Inquiry* 7:41–87. Reprinted in this volume.

Crain, Catherine. 1979. "Advancement and Ascension to Direct Object in Chamorro." *Linguistic Notes from La Jolla*, 6. San Diego: University of California.

Emonds, Joseph. 1970. "Root and Structure-Preserving Transformations." Ph.D. diss., MIT.

Emonds, Joseph. 1972. "A Reformulation of Certain Syntactic Transformations." In Peters, 1972.

Fauconnier, Gilles. 1971. "Theoretical Implications of Some Global Phenomena in Syntax." Ph.D. diss., University of California at San Diego.

Fillmore, Charles J. 1966. "A Proposal concerning English Prepositions." In *Seventeenth Annual Round Table Meeting on Linguistics and Language Studies*. Georgetown University Monograph Series on Linguistics and Language Studies, no. 19. Washington, D.C.: Georgetown University Press.

———. 1968. "The Case for Case." In Emmon Bach and Robert Harms, eds., *Universals in Linguistic Theory*. New York: Holt, Rinehart & Winston.

Gaatone, David. 1970. "La Transformation impersonnelle en français." *Le Français moderne* 38:389–411.

Gross, Maurice. 1968. *Grammaire transformationnelle du français: Syntaxe du verbe*. Paris: Larousse.

Hankamer, Jorge. 1971. "Constraints on Deletion in Syntax." Ph.D. diss., Yale University.

Harris, Alice. 1981. *Georgian Syntax*. Cambridge and New York: Cambridge University Press.

Harris, Alice C. (to appear a). "Case Marking, Verb Agreement, and Inversion in Udi," in Perlmutter and Rosen (to appear).

———. (to appear b). "Inversion as a Rule of Grammar: Georgian Evidence," in Perlmutter and Rosen (to appear).

Higgins, Roger. 1973. "On J. Emonds' Analysis of Extraposition." In John Kimball, ed., *Syntax and Semantics*, vol. 2. New York: Academic Press.

Johnson, David E. 1979. *Toward a Theory of Relationally-Based Grammar*. New York: Garland Publishing Co.

Kajita, Masaru. 1966. *A Generative-Transformational Study of Semi-Auxiliaries in Present-Day American English*. Toyko: Sanseido.

Kayne, Richard. 1975. *French Syntax: The Transformational Cycle*. Cambridge: MIT Press.

Keenan, Edward L. 1971. "Movement Transformations in a Family of Western Malayo-Polynesian Languages."

———. 1972. "Relative Clause Formation in Malagasy." In P. Peranteau et al., eds., *The Chicago Which Hunt: Papers from the Relative Clause Festival.* Chicago Linguistic Society, University of Chicago.

Keenan, Edward L., and Comrie, Bernard. 1977. "Noun Phrase Accessibility and Universal Grammar." *Linguistic Inquiry* 8:63–99.

Kiparsky, Paul, and Kiparsky, Carol. 1970. "Fact." In Manfred Bierwisch and Karl E. Heidolph, eds., *Progress in Linguistics.* The Hague: Mouton & Co.

Klokeid, Terry J. 1976. "Topics in Lardil Grammar." Ph.D. diss., MIT.

———. To appear. "Defining Grammatical Relations in Wakashan Languages."

McCawley, James D. 1970a. "English as a VSO Language." *Language* 46:286–99.

———. 1970b. Review of Jespersen, *Analytic Syntax. Language* 46:442–49.

———. 1971. "Prelexical Syntax." In *Twenty-Second Annual Round Table Meeting on Linguistics and Language Studies.* Georgetown University Monograph Series on Linguistics and Language Studies, no. 24. Washington, D.C.: Georgetown University Press.

Otsuka, Tatsuo. 1980. "Passivization in Japanese." In *Descriptive and Applied Linguistics,* vol. 13. Tokyo: International Christian University.

Perlmutter, David M. 1971. *Deep and Surface Structure Constraints in Syntax.* New York: Holt, Rinehart & Winston.

———. 1978. "Impersonal Passives and the Unaccusative Hypothesis." In *Proceedings of the Fourth Annual Meeting of the Berkeley Linguistics Society.* Berkeley: University of California.

———. 1979. "Working 1s and Inversion in Italian, Japanese, and Quechua." In *Proceedings of the Fifth Annual Meeting of the Berkeley Linguistics Society.* University of California, Berkeley.

———. 1980. "Relational Grammar." In Edith Moravcsik and Jessica Wirth, eds., *Syntax and Semantics,* vol. 13: *Current Approaches to Syntax.* New York: Academic Press.

———. (to appear a). "Possessor Ascension and Some Relational Laws."

———. (to appear b.) "Evidence for Inversion in Russian and Kannada."

———. (to appear c). "Grammatical Relations as Primitives of Linguistic Theory."

Perlmutter, David M., and Orešnik, Janez. 1973. "Language-Particular Rules and Explanation in Syntax." In Anderson and Kiparsky 1973.

Perlmutter, David M., and Postal, Paul M. 1974. Lectures on Relational Grammar, Summer Linguistic Institute of the Linguistic Society of America, University of Massachusetts, Amherst.

———. 1977. "Toward a Universal Characterization of Passivization." In *Proceedings of the Third Annual Meeting of the Berkeley Linguistics Society.* University of California, Berkeley. Reprinted in this volume.

———. (this volume). "Some Proposed Laws of Basic Clause Structure."

———. (to appear a). "The 1-Advancement Exclusiveness Law," in Perlmutter and Rosen (to appear).

———. (to appear b). "Impersonal Passives and Some Relational Laws," in Perlmutter and Rosen (to appear).

Perlmutter, David M. and Rosen, Carol, eds. (to appear). *Studies in Relational Grammar 2,* Chicago: University of Chicago Press.

Peters, Stanley, ed. 1972. *Goals of Linguistic Theory.* Englewood Cliffs, N.J.: Prentice-Hall.

Postal, Paul M. 1970. "The Method of Universal Grammar." In Paul Garvin, ed., *Method and Theory in Linguistics.* The Hague: Mouton & Co.

————. 1971. *Crossover Phenomena*. New York: Holt, Rinehart, & Winston.

————. 1972. "On Some Rules That Are *Not* Successive Cyclic." *Linguistic Inquiry* 3:211–22.

————. 1974. *On Raising*. Cambridge: MIT Press.

Quícoli, António Carlos. 1972. "Aspects of Portuguese Complementation." Ph.D. diss., State University of New York at Buffalo.

Rosenbaum, Peter. 1967. *The Grammar of English Predicate Complement Constructions*. Cambridge: MIT Press.

Ross, John R. 1967. "Constraints on Variables in Syntax." Ph.D. diss., MIT.

————. 1970. "Gapping and the Order of Constituents." In Manfred Bierwisch and Karl Erich Heidolph, eds., *Progress in Linguistics*. The Hague: Mouton & Co.

Ruwet, Nicolas. 1970. "Note sur la syntaxe du pronom *en* et d'autres sujets apparentés." *Langue française,* 6. Revised version in Ruwet, 1972.

————. 1972. *Théorie syntaxique et syntaxe du français*. Paris: Editions du Seuil.

————. 1976. "Subject-Raising and Extraposition." In Marta Luján and Fritz Hensey, eds., *Current Studies in Romance Linguistics*. Washington, D.C.: Georgetown University Press.

Seiler, Wolf, and Frantz, Donald G. (to appear). "The Instrumental Case in Iñupiat."

3 Some Proposed Laws of (κ) Basic Clause Structure

David M. Perlmutter and Paul M. Postal

P. 37

I Introduction

The goal of this paper is to present and give some limited support for several proposed laws of grammar that have played a basic role in relational grammar during the last several years. Some of these laws date to the beginnings of this work in 1972. Others developed later. All have undergone modifications as our conceptions of the underlying nature of grammatical structure have evolved.

In presenting these laws here, we occasionally give two distinct formulations. One represents for the most part the early or traditional formulation within relational grammar work, normally a formulation which presupposes a derivational conception of grammar. The other formulation is embedded within the so-called uninetwork relational grammar framework, represented by Postal 1977 and chapter 1, as well as some other papers included in this volume, and considerable unpublished work. In these terms, we represent the structure of sentences in terms of objects called relational networks (RNs). We adopt essentially the conventions of chapter 1 for representing these.

The laws to be considered here are concerned with a particular, limited subdomain of grammatical structure we shall refer to as 'basic clauses'. We will not attempt a precise definition of this notion here.[1] Suffice it to say informally that a basic clause involves at a minimum a nonnull set of 'nominals' and a nonnull, almost always unary, set of 'predicates' plus the relations these bear to an element we can call a

Perlmutter's work has been supported in part by the National Science Foundation through Grant No. BNS 76-00764 to the Massachusetts Institute of Technology and a fellowship from the John Simon Guggenheim Memorial Foundation. The authors are grateful to Judith Aissen, Sandra Chung, Matthew Dryer, Alice Harris, David Johnson, Terry Klokeid, Andrew Radford, Carol Rosen, Alan Timberlake, and Annie Zaenen for critical comments on the first draft of this paper.

'clause node'. We will not be concerned at all here with the internal structure of either nominals or predicates. In addition, we are not concerned here with the structure of flagging devices (prepositions, cases, etc.), the representation of linear precedence, or auxiliaries. We will, *artificially,* either ignore auxiliaries or treat them as parts of main predicates in all representations of examples containing auxiliaries.

The examples in (1a–g) illustrate basic clauses in English:

(1) a. Melvin sings.
    b. The rock sank.
    c. Ted tickled the alligator.
    d. Melvin handed a portion of snake liver to Gladys.
    e. The mush was eaten by the premier.
    f. It frightens me that his skin is turning green.
    g. Mercury seemed to us to be slippery.

Some examples of 'nonbasic clauses' are provided by:

(2) a. Joe sings and Mary dances.
    b. You can say that but I don't believe it.
    c. I bought for Louise and gave to Janet an enormous green tuffet.

Basic clauses are the kinds of things traditionally described as having subjects, predicates, etc. But this kind of description makes no sense for nonbasic clauses, which involve quite different relations. The overall clause in (2b), for example, has nothing that can be called a subject, nothing that can be called a predicate (although its component first and second clauses separated by *but* do have these). However, the two component clauses bear a definite relation to the overall nonbasic clause, one that can be called 'conjunct of'.

There is an obvious sense in which nonbasic clauses are composed of combinations of basic clauses. Thus it is natural to assume that any account of clause structure as a whole must be based on an account of basic clauses. These are truly basic in the sense that the existence of any kind of clause, basic or not, entails the existence of at least one basic clause. If, as seems plausible, sentences cannot exist without clauses, then every sentence must contain at least one basic clause.

Underlying the RG conception of grammatical structure and, in particular, its conception of basic clause structure is the view that sentence structure involves the following kinds of objects:

(3) a. Primitive linguistic elements
    b. Primitive grammatical relations
    c. Linguistic levels

Primitive grammatical relations hold between primitive linguistic elements. Although we cannot go into this here,[2] it seems that there are at least four distinct types of primitive linguistic elements, a purely formal type of element representing abstract constituent nodes, a type representing logical or semantic primitives, a type representing phonological primitives (features), and a type representing grammatical categories.

In a more formal treatment of these ideas only hinted at here, the fact that a certain primitive linguistic element bears a certain primitive grammatical relation to some other element can be given by formal structures notationally representable as follows:

(4)

The object in (4) is called an 'incomplete arc'.[3] Notation (4) is interpreted to mean that the primitive linguistic element b bears the relation whose name is GR_x to the primitive linguistic element a. If, for example, GR_x is '1', the name of the subject relation, then (4) indicates that b bears the subject relation to a, i.e., that b is a subject of a. If GR_x is '2', the name of the direct object relation, then (4) indicates that b is a direct object of a. However, this representational format is insufficient, for it ignores the question of linguistic levels. A basis for these can be provided by associating sequences of numbers called 'coordinates' with incomplete arcs like (4) to yield objects called 'arcs', notationally representable in either of two equivalent notations, given in (5a, b):

(5) a.   a

   $1 \mid c_1 c_2$

   b

   b. $[1 \ (b,a) <c_1 c_2>]$

The arc in (5) indicates that b bears the subject relation to a at both the first and second levels of a. Each node (like a) is associated with a finite, nonnull set of such levels.

It is then, in general, vague and necessarily inaccurate to say things like 'b is *the* subject of a', etc., without specifying levels. For b might be the subject of a at, e.g., the c_1 level, while a distinct element c might be the subject of a at the c_2 level. That is, a situation like the following often obtains:

(6)

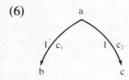

Structure (6) is typical of, e.g., passive clauses, where one nominal is the subject at c_1, a distinct nominal the subject at a later level.

Evidently, an account of basic clause structure in the terms just considered will have to specify the class of possible linguistic elements (what subtypes there are, etc.), the class of primitive grammatical relations, the possible linguistic levels, and the constraints that limit the combinations of all of these objects with each other.

Relational grammar differs from other approaches to grammatical description and theory in numerous ways, but especially notably in recognizing a much richer class of primitive grammatical relations. For example, it seems correct to interpret both structural and transformational views as recognizing at most three *primitive* grammatical relations, constituency, linear precedence, and labeling. While relational grammar also takes linear precedence and labeling as primitive relations, it does not adopt constituency as a primitive. Instead, it has a large class of distinct 'structural' grammatical relations. To illustrate, in structural or TG terms, French clauses of the form:

(7)   J'ai envoyé la machine à Marie.
       'I sent the machine to Marie.'
(8)   J'ai envoyé la machine à Paris.
       'I sent the machine to Paris.'

would both be analyzed as having prepositional phrase constituents of either the clause as a whole or of some VP or VP-like subconstituent. But in RG terms, the situation is quite different. *Marie* in (7) bears one primitive grammatical relation to the clause, which we refer to as the 'indirect object relation' (whose name is '3'), while *Paris* in (8) bears a distinct relation, which we can call 'directional' (whose name is 'Dir'). Hence, assuming that *je* bears the subject relation in both (7) and (8), and that 'P' is the name of the predicate relation, initial *partial* representations for the basic clauses in (7) and (8) would have the respective forms:

(9)

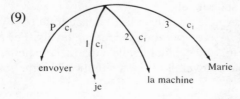

(10)

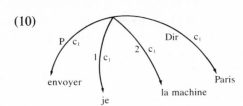

As is evident from structures like (9) and (10), constituency in these terms is, in a sense, derivative, since the structures give more information than sheer constituency. Roughly, a is a constituent of b if a is the head (at the arrowhead) of an arc whose tail is b, regardless of the grammatical relation name (henceforth, relational sign or R-sign) on the arc. Thus one comes closer to structural or transformational representations if all the arcs are stripped of their R-signs. One can then informally distinguish 'naked arc' approaches like these from approaches like RG, in which *every arc is labeled with the name of one and only one primitive grammatical relation*.

Given labeled arcs, certain problems which appear puzzling in naked arc frameworks become trivial. For instance, in French, when examples like (7) and (8) are changed by replacing the nominals *Marie* and *Paris* with pronouns, clitics appear on the verb. However, these contrast. That is, phrases of the 3-type yield the clitic *lui* (for third person singular), while those of the Dir-type yield the clitic *y*. The information required to state this distinction is provided by representations like (9) and (10), but not by those with naked arcs. Moreover, this distinction is *not* predictable from the choice of verb, since many verbs, including *envoyer,* accept both *y* and *lui:*

(11) a. J'ai envoyé la machine à cette ville-là.
        'I sent the machine to that city.'

  b. $\dfrac{\text{J'y ai}}{\text{*Je lui ai}}$ envoyé la machine (à cette ville-là).
        'I sent the machine there (to that city).'

(12) a. J'ai envoyé la machine à ce type-là.
        'I sent the machine to that guy.'

  b. $\dfrac{\text{Je lui ai}}{\text{*J'y ai}}$ envoyé la machine (à ce type-là).
        'I sent the machine to him (to that guy).'

Now consider basic clause structures. Constraints on these will be determined, inter alia, by different types of arcs, where types are defined by R-signs. Moreover, these types fall into a system of subtypes, yielding a hierarchy of classes of arcs defined by their R-signs. These classes correspond to classes of primitive grammatical relations under the interpretation of the formalism of arcs. We present what seems to us a reasonable initial classification of these R-signs (hence, ultimately, arcs and grammatical relations) relevant for describing the connections between nominals and basic clause nodes; we ignore here the R-signs relevant for describing the connections between other types of nodes.

(13)

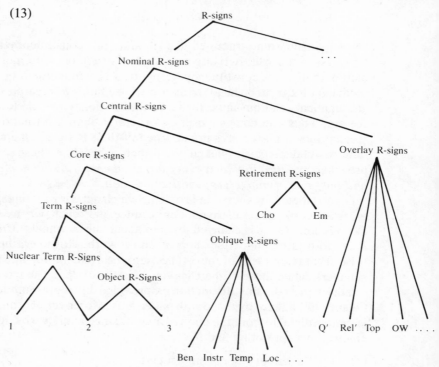

Let us briefly explicate this classification; '1', '2', and '3' are the names of relations corresponding to the traditional subject, direct object, and indirect object, respectively. These are categorized into two partially overlapping subsets, one defining ultimately the class of nuclear term relations, the other the class of object relations, the direct object relation being a member of both sets. The incompletely specified set 'Ben', 'Instr', 'Temp', 'Loc', involves the names of the set of oblique grammatical relations, relations like benefactive, instrumental, temporal, locative, etc. The limits of this class remain obscure. Note, however, that the chômeur and emeritus relations are *not* in this class.

'Cho' is the name of the chômeur relation, which figures centrally in the relational grammar of clause structure and is discussed in some detail below. 'Em' is the name of the emeritus relation, which appears to play a role primarily in clause union constructions. The present 'Em' corresponds to the R-sign 'Dead' of Johnson and Postal (1980).

The overlay R-signs 'Q'', 'Rel'', 'Top', and 'OW' (standing for 'overweight') are the names of the 'last' relations borne respectively by the italicized nominals in the following cases:

(14) a. *Who* do you think Ted met?
     b. the table *which* he is sending
     c. *That* I would never have believed he would do.
     d. I offered to Frederica at that time *the most beautiful pearl of the most expensive collection.*

Each R-sign defines a class of arcs, namely, the class of all arcs associated with that R-sign. It is convenient to refer to arcs by their R-signs. We will thus speak of 1-arcs, 2-arcs, Ben arcs, Cho arcs, Top arcs, etc. It is also convenient to refer to arcs by the names of the various classes of R-signs to which their R-signs belong. We will thus speak of overlay arcs (= arcs whose R-signs are members of the class of overlay R-signs), term arcs, nuclear term arcs, etc.

In what follows we will be concerned principally with term arcs and Cho arcs. It will be seen that term arcs in particular are fundamental to basic clause structure in a way in which other arcs are not.

Before turning to the laws to be considered, it is important to make one further observation about how the coordinates on arcs permit a characterization of level for a fixed element (node). This is done by defining the notion 'c_k stratum (b)', where b is a node and c_k an arbitrary coordinate. The c_k stratum of a node b is the set of all arcs with tail b which have the coordinate c_k. Hence in the 'flat' or unilevel structures in (9) and (10) all of the arcs are in a single stratum. The more interesting cases, those on which most work in RG has concentrated, involve basic clause structures in which there is more than one stratum. Consider, for example, the RN (16) associated with:

(15)   That book was reviewed by Louise.

(16)

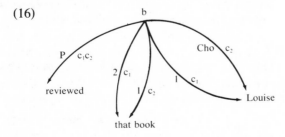

The first stratum of (16) is the set of all arcs with tail b which have the coordinate c_1, namely:

(17)

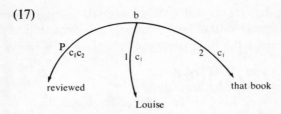

The second stratum of (16) is the set of all arcs with tail b which have the coordinate c_2, namely:

(18)

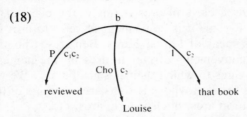

Sometimes we represent an RN such as (16) in terms of a 'stratal diagram' such as (19).

(19)

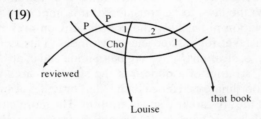

In (19), the R-signs of all the arcs in the first stratum are given in the first horizontal row and the R-signs of all the arcs in the second stratum in the second horizontal row. Stratal diagrams such as (19) are often more convenient for expository purposes, since they make the strata stand out more clearly. Pairs like (16) and (19) are, however, entirely equivalent notations for the same linguistic object (RN).

2   The Oblique Law

There is a basic asymmetry between the class of 'term relations' and that of 'oblique relations' (which together constitute the class of 'core grammatical relations'):

(20)   A nominal that bears a term relation in a given clause may or may not bear that relation in the initial stratum in that clause. A nominal that bears an oblique relation in a clause, in contrast, bears that relation in the initial stratum.

For example, in the English clause (21a) *Marvin* bears the 1-relation, but not in the initial stratum:

(21) a.   Marvin was criticized by Leslie.

b.

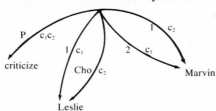

Similarly, in the Cebuano sentence[4]

(22)   Gipalitan ni   Rosa ug bugas ang   tindahan.
        buy-LOC GEN Rosa   rice NOM   store
        'The store will be bought rice at by Rosa.'

the final 1 (*tindahan*) is not the initial 1:

(23)

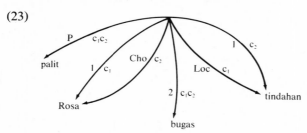

In the Indonesian sentence:

(24)   Ali membawakan adik   saya buku itu.
        Ali bring   sister I   book the
        'Ali brought my sister the book.'

adik saya bears the 2-relation, but not in the initial stratum:

(25)

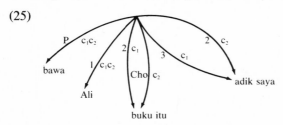

We claim, however, that in no language is there a well-formed RN having a nominal bearing an oblique relation in a noninitial stratum in some clause in which it does not also bear that relation in the initial stratum. Thus, sentences associated with RNs such as the following will not be well-formed in any language:

(26)

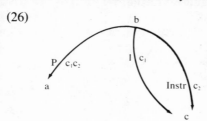

(27)

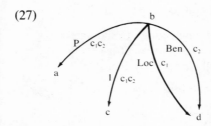

(28)

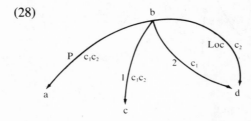

In (26), a nominal bears the instrumental relation in the second stratum but not in the first (where it bears the 1-relation); in (27) a nominal bears the benefactive relation in the second stratum but not in the first, and (28) has a locative in the second stratum that is not an initial locative.

A law excluding structures such as these from the class of well-formed RNs can be stated as follows:

(29)   Oblique Law
       We say that B is a c_i arc, if B is an arc one of whose coordinates is c_i.
       Then: If A is an oblique arc, A is a c_1 arc.

This principle thus requires that the first coordinate of every oblique arc be c_1. Therefore, any nominal that bears an oblique relation to a clause must bear it in the initial stratum (regardless of the other strata in which it is borne). Thus there can be no advancements or demotions *to* oblique grammatical relations.

Some additional possibilities ruled out by this law are also precluded independently by more specific conditions on RNs. Since dummy nominals never bear grammatical relations in initial strata, the Oblique Law renders ill-formed any RN in which a dummy heads an oblique arc. But this is also a consequence of the Nuclear Dummy Law (see §7). Since a nominal whose first grammatical relation in a clause is a consequence of Clause Union bears no relation in that clause in the initial stratum, the Oblique Law rules out RNs in which such a nominal heads an oblique arc in that clause. But this is independently a consequence of the nature of Clause Union constructions.

Since there is no counterpart to the Oblique Law for the term relations, the class of possible RNs includes those in which a nominal is the head of a 1-arc, a 2-arc, or a 3-arc in a noninitial stratum but not in the initial stratum. Such RNs correspond to well-formed sentences in particular languages where the language in question permits such term arcs.

The following tables summarize schematically the types of relational subnetworks that the Oblique Law allows and disallows with respect to arcs involving central R-signs (with the exception of Em, which is ignored here):

(30)   Allowed by the Oblique Law:

Oblique Oblique Oblique 3 3 3 2 2
   1   2   3   1 2 Cho 1 3

  2   1 1   1   Oblique Cho Cho Cho
Cho 2 3 Cho   Cho   1   2   3

(31)   Disallowed by the Oblique Law:

   1   2   3   Cho   Oblique$_x$
Oblique Oblique Oblique Oblique Oblique$_y$ where (x ≠ y)

These pairs of R-signs are to be interpreted as follows. 'Oblique/1' refers to a situation in which a nominal is the head of an oblique arc in one stratum and the head of a 1-arc in the next. Thus, the inclusion of 'Oblique/1' in (30) means that the Oblique Law is consistent with relational subnetworks having these properties. The inclusion of '1/ Oblique' in (31) means that the Oblique Law characterizes as ill-formed any RN in which a nominal heads a 1-arc in one stratum and an oblique arc in the next. The inclusion of 'Oblique$_x$/Oblique$_y$' in (31) means that the Oblique Law characterizes as ungrammatical any RN in which a nominal is the head of an arc with one oblique R-sign in one stratum and an arc with a *distinct* oblique R-sign in the next. It should be stressed that the presence of a pair of arc types in (30) does not mean that such situations are well-formed in some language. For although not excluded by the Oblique Law, they may be by others. In fact, all of the pairs of the form, 'Cho/Term' are universally characterized as ill-formed as a consequence of a principle called the Chômeur Advancement Ban (see §8 below). Similarly, the pair 'Oblique/Cho' is universally characterized as ill-formed by the Motivated Chômage Law (§5 below) and the Oblique Law.

We ignore Em arcs in this discussion since, to our knowledge, these are restricted primarily to Clause Union constructions and most of the logical possibilities for combining these with other parallel arcs are controlled by the principles relevant for those constructions.

In sum, the effect of the Oblique Law is to rule out the class of RNs with the subnetworks abbreviated in (31), embodying the claim that clauses associated with such RNs cannot be well-formed in any natural language.

3   The Stratal Uniqueness Law

Recall that a 'stratum' is a maximal, nonnull set of arcs with the same tail *sharing a single coordinate*. Hence, if b is a node and c_k is an arbitrary coordinate, 'the c_k stratum (b)' refers to the set of all arcs with tail b having the coordinate c_k.

A constraint characteristic of RG work since its inception is referred to as the Stratal Uniqueness Law. This principle limits the number of distinct *term arcs* (1-arcs, 2-arcs, 3-arcs) in a single stratum. It claims that no *stratum* can contain more than one 1-arc, one 2-arc, or one 3-arc. This is entirely distinct from what we take to be an obvious falsehood, namely, the claim that no *clause* can contain more than one 1-arc, one 2-arc, etc. The latter claim would, of course, entail the Stratal Uniqueness Law, though not conversely.

We can formulate the law as follows:[5]

(32)   Stratal Uniqueness Law
Let 'term$_x$' be a variable over the class of term R-signs, that is, '1', '2', or '3'.
Then: If arcs A and B are both members of the c_k stratum (b) and A and B are both term$_x$ arcs, then A = B.

One consequence of the Stratal Uniqueness Law can be illustrated for English sentences involving 3-2 Advancement:

(33)   a.   John sent the letter to Mary.
        b.   John sent Mary the letter.

The Stratal Uniqueness Law precludes (33b) having the structure in (34).

(34)

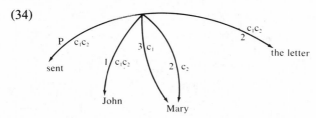

The structure in (34) is impossible, given (32), because it contains two 2-arcs in the c_2 stratum.

Rather, we claim that the RNs associated with (33a–b) are, respectively, (35) and (36):

(35)

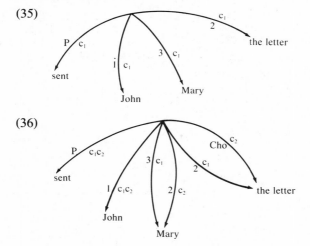

(36)

In (36), while *Mary* is the head of a 2-arc in the c_2 stratum, *the letter* is the head of a Cho arc (not a 2-arc) in that stratum. As a result, there is only one 2-arc in the c_2 stratum, and the Stratal Uniqueness Law is not violated. This law is, we believe, a primary reason for the existence of the chômeur relation. This relation permits structures such as (36), which are *similar* to (34), to exist without violating the Stratal Uniqueness Law.

Sentences (33a–b) have corresponding passives:

(37) a. The letter was sent to Mary by John.
     b. Mary was sent the letter by John.

The RNs associated with (37a–b) are (38) and (39), respectively (each given in the two equivalent notations).

(38) a.

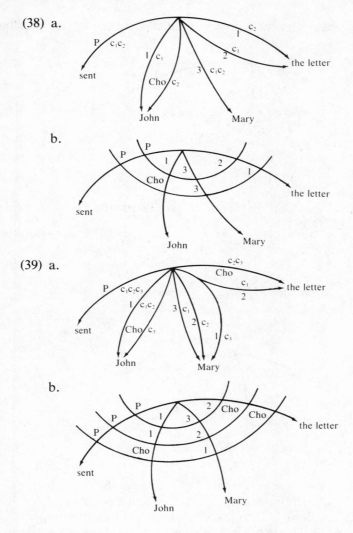

b.

(39) a.

b.

In (38), *the letter* is head of a 2-arc in the first stratum and head of a 1-arc in the second stratum. As a result, *John* is head of a Cho arc in the second stratum (see the discussion of the Chômeur Law in §§4 and 8). In (39), *Mary* heads a 3-arc, a 2-arc, and a 1-arc in successive strata, and *the letter* and *John* are heads of Cho arcs. All of these structures conform to the Stratal Uniqueness Law.

While we have imposed stratal uniqueness on term arcs, we have not done so for other arc types, in particular, not for Cho arcs or oblique arcs. This is likely an inadequacy in the case of oblique arcs, for we suspect that they are subject to an analogous principle. For Cho arcs, however, the absence of this restriction seems correct. Note that (39) has two distinct Cho arcs in the third stratum, headed by *John* and *the letter*.

As a consequence of the Stratal Uniqueness Law, statements referring to 1-arcs, 2-arcs, etc., pick out unique arcs *when they are specified for strata*. Thus, well-known rules whereby verbs agree with the heads of 1-arcs yield, for each relevant verb, a well-defined agreement with a single nominal if (as is common but not universal) the 1-arcs in question are specified to be 'final-stratum' 1-arcs. For the Stratal Uniqueness Law guarantees that each basic clause can have *no more* than a single 1-arc in its final stratum.[6]

Like any restrictive principle limiting the class of structures which can qualify as well-formed sentences in any language, the Stratal Uniqueness Law makes an empirical claim. Several attempts have been made to show that this claim is not correct. Most such attempts have been based on data concerning advancements to 2 in Bantu languages. These include Gary and Keenan 1977 and Duranti and Byarushengo 1977. Also potentially relevant are Gary 1977, Kimenyi 1976, and Kisseberth and Abasheikh 1977. For detailed discussion of data from one Bantu language that bears on this issue, see §8.

Some work that in effect purports to bear on the validity of the Stratal Uniqueness Law concludes, merely from the presence of two accusative-case nominals, that the clause in question has two direct objects, ignoring the question of whether or not there are two 2s *at a given linguistic level* (in our terms, in the same stratum). Thus, many of the examples with two accusative-case nominals that Comrie (1976) cites as examples of two direct objects in causative constructions should, we suggest, be analyzed as examples of 3-2 Advancement. Thus, each of the two accusative nominals would be the head of a 2-arc in our terms, as is the case in (36). But there would be *no stratum* containing two distinct 2-arcs.

4   The Chômeur Law

Relational grammar has introduced the concept of the chômeur relation and the derivative idea of a chômeur, that is, a nominal bearing the chômeur relation to some clause. These ideas have no real antecedents in traditional grammar or analogues in other approaches. In terms of these notions, it was assumed that there is a basic law determining the existence of the chômeur relation for a nominal under certain conditions. This law, originally called the Relational Annihilation Law, more recently the Chômeur Law, has been one of the cornerstones of the relational approach to clause structure. However, recent information made available, particularly about various Bantu languages, combines with other recent research (see Johnson and Postal 1980, chap. 8), to suggest rather strongly that certain predictions of this law are incorrect. This matter is taken up in greater detail in §8. In this section, we will present the relevant law and some of its motivations in a way which largely ignores the difficulties just mentioned.

The basic idea of the Chômeur Law, expressed differently at different times, is that under conditions that would otherwise lead to violations of the Stratal Uniqueness Law, nominals necessarily bear the chômeur relation. More precisely, if some nominal, N_a, bears a given term relation in a stratum, c_i, and some other nominal, N_b, bears the same (term) relation in the following stratum (c_{i+1}), then N_a bears the chômeur relation in c_{i+1}. The Chômeur Law can be formulated in the current framework along the following lines:

(40)   Chômeur Law
       If an RN contains arcs of the form $[\mathrm{Term}_x(a,b)\langle c_u c_k c_y\rangle]$ and $[\mathrm{Term}_x(c,b)\langle c_{k+1}c_z\rangle]$, then it contains an arc of the form $[\mathrm{Cho}(a,b)\langle c_{k+1}c_w\rangle]$.

Consider, for example, the partial structure of the Indonesian clause in (41a), given in (41b).

(41) a.   Yanti membawakan adik   saya buku itu.
          Yanti bring   sister I   book the
          'Yanti brought my sister the book.'

   b.

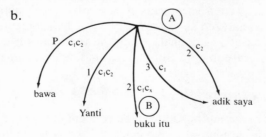

Here *adik saya* heads a 2-arc in the c_2 stratum. If *buku itu,* which heads a 2-arc in the c_1 stratum, also headed a 2-arc in the c_2 stratum, the Stratal Uniqueness Law would be violated. Given the Chômeur Law, however, this is avoided, since the proper structure for (41a) and analogous cases is then predicted to be of the form:

(42)

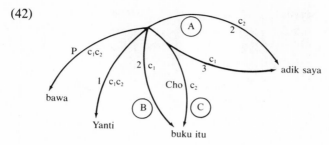

Here *buku itu* is, in the c_2 stratum, the head of a Cho arc, whose existence permits stratal uniqueness to be maintained.[7] In other words, conditions like those in (41b) determine the existence of the Cho arc in (42). Thus a language which permits pairs of arcs like A and B in (41b) determines 'automatically' the existence of an arc like C in (42). There is a function yielding the latter arc from the former two, this function being named the Chômeur Law.

The grammatical relation that a nominal bears in the last stratum before it bears the chômeur relation yields a typology of chômeurs in terms of the derivative categories '1-chômeur', '2-chômeur', and '3-chômeur'. Following a suggestion of Eugene Loos, we sometimes refer to these as '$\hat{1}$', '$\hat{2}$', and '$\hat{3}$', respectively, especially in stratal diagrams. There is another crosscutting typology of chômeurs based on the three types of 'new' term arcs which can bring about chômeur status for an earlier term. This yields the three types of 'revaluation chômeurs' (those due to advancements or demotion), 'ascension chômeurs' (those due to ascensions) and 'dummy chômeurs' (those put en chômage by dummy nominals). A priori, then, it would be possible for there to be at least nine distinct categories of chômeur. However, at least some of these are claimed not to exist as a function of other laws. For instance, as a function of the Nuclear Dummy Law (see §7), there are claimed to be no dummy 3s, and hence no possibility of dummy $\hat{3}$s.

The Chômeur Law predicts superficial *intransitivity* of certain clauses that might otherwise be thought to be transitive. Consider, for example, the passive of (41a/42) in Indonesian:

(43)   Adik saya dibawakan buku itu oleh Yanti.
        sister I   PASS-bring book the by   Yanti
        'My sister was brought the book by Yanti.'

The partial structure of (43) is given in (44).

(44) a.

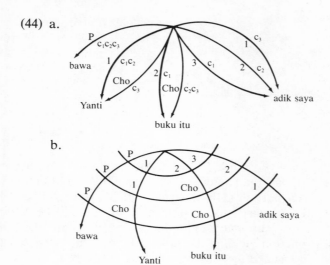

b.

As a consequence of the Chômeur Law, *buku itu* heads a Cho arc in the c_2 and c_3 strata. As a result, (43–44) is intransitive in the final stratum. As Chung (1976) shows, this has a number of empirical consequences, correctly predicting that *buku itu* does *not* behave as a 2 with respect to various syntactic phenomena in Indonesian. The Chômeur Law of course predicts intransitivity in analogous cases in other languages as well.

In assigning the chômeur relation to nominals under the conditions specified in (40), the Chômeur Law naturally makes varying predictions for different languages, depending on the phenomena in each language with which it interacts.

In a theory recognizing the chômeur relation, classes of nominals having nothing else in common are grouped together as chômeurs. One syntactic consequence of this is attested by Chung (1976). She shows that chômeurs of different types (passive chômeurs and 3-2 chômeurs) behave alike, and differently from both terms and other nonterms, with respect to a certain phenomenon (Quantifier Shift) in Indonesian. In a theory recognizing both an emeritus relation and a class of relations including just this and the chômeur relation, namely, retirement relations, a further, *otherwise* nonexistent, grouping of nominals is predicted.[8] It is an empirical question whether nominals having nothing else in common but being arguments of retirement relations ever behave alike in nonrandom ways in natural languages. Harris (1976, 1981) shows that in Georgian the two types of retirement nominals behave alike with respect to case marking, behaving differently in these respects from both terms and other nonterms. Indonesian and Georgian thus provide examples of syntactic generalizations that involve specific reference to the chômeur relation and to the class of retirement relations, offering a particular kind of support for the recognition of these concepts.

5   The Motivated Chômage Law

The Chômeur Law, discussed in §4, claims that under certain conditions, a Cho arc must exist and thus requires the chômeur relation to hold under the conditions defined by its antecedent. However, this law alone has nothing to say about the possibility of the chômeur relation in contexts distinct from those defined by its antecedent conditions. That is, the Chômeur Law does not preclude chômeurs existing under conditions distinct from those where the Chômeur Law requires chômeurs to exist. For example, the Chômeur Law does not block representations like (45a) which would yield sentences like (45b):

(45) a.

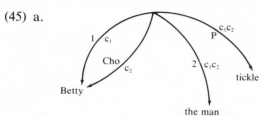

b. *(Was) tickled the man by Betty.

The relevant property of structures like (45a) is that a Cho arc exists even though the parallel term arc is not 'supplanted' by any later term arc. Hence cases like (45a) are those of 'unmotivated' or 'spontaneous' Cho arcs in the sense that the existence of the Cho arc plays absolutely no role in preserving stratal uniqueness.

Our claim is that spontaneous chômage is a logical possibility which is not an empirical possibility. This claim is embodied in the Motivated Chômage Law, which claims, in effect, that chômeurs exist only under the conditions described in the Chômeur Law, that is, only when the antecedent of this law is met. This further law would then claim that structures like (45a) cannot exist. We can formulate the Motivated Chômage Law as follows:

(46) Motivated Chômage Law
      An RN containing an arc of the form $[Cho(a,b)\langle c_i c_w \rangle]$ also contains distinct arcs of the form $[Term_x(a,b)\langle c_u c_{i-1} \rangle]$ and $[Term_x(c,b) \langle c_i c_z \rangle]$.

The Motivated Chômage Law embodies the claim that the conditions under which nominals bear the chômeur relation are limited by universal principles. One consequence of (46) is that Cho arcs can never occur in *initial* strata.

The Motivated Chômage Law has in effect been challenged by Keenan (1975), Comrie (1977), Jain (1977), and others, who cite impersonal passive clauses as an example of the need for spontaneous chômage[9] in violation of the Motivated Chômage Law. We discuss this matter in Perlmutter and Postal (in press a, b) and Perlmutter 1978.

6   The Final 1 Law

A basic RG claim is that every basic clause contains a final-stratum 1-arc, and thus that every basic clause involves some nominal as final 1. This is, of course, entirely distinct from the obvious falsehood that every basic clause contains a *surface* 1. The latter claim is hopeless in the face of any of the range of examples like (47):

(47) a.   Try and *tickle yourself.*
b.   *Kiss one salamander* and people say you are a pervert.
c.   Joe went home and then *called Betty.*
d.   Which of those nurses do you think *likes Ted the most?*

Each of the italicized clauses lacks a surface subject nominal, and in (47a–b) the relevant nominal is not even a surface nominal of the sentence as a whole. Such examples have no bearing on the law of interest here, which claims that basic clause final strata must contain 1-arcs, not that these must have surface realizations.

The Final 1 Law can be formulated as follows:

(48)   Final 1 Law
If there is a c_k stratum of b and no c_{k+1} stratum of $b,$ we say that the c_k stratum is the 'final' stratum of $b.$
Then: If b is a basic clause node, the final stratum of b contains a 1-arc.

There are, obviously, numerous examples of basic clauses in attested languages which *appear* not to have a final 1. This is the case, for example, in the Russian examples in (49) and the French examples in (50).

(49) a.   Morozit.
'It's freezing.'
b.   Menja   tošnit.
me-ACC nauseates
'I feel nauseous.'

(50) a.   Voilà Pierre.
          'There's Pierre.'
     b.   Le voici.
          'Here he is.'

Various contemporary scholars, e.g., Chvany (1975) for (49) and Martinet (1968) for (50), have cited such sentences as examples of subjectless sentences. There is, in fact, a copious literature going back centuries on so-called impersonal sentences, a category generally taken to include examples such as (49–50), as well as many other clause types. We claim that (49) and (50), as well as sentences of other types (such as 'impersonal sentences') that have been claimed to have 'no grammatical subject', do not violate the Final 1 Law because they have a dummy nominal as final 1. In some cases, such dummy nominals appear in the surface sentence. In many other cases, as in (49–50), they do not. The Final 1 Law predicts for such examples that, in cases of interaction with other syntactic phenomena in the languages in question, these clauses will behave as though they have dummies as final 1s, rather than behaving as though they have no final 1s. In some languages, there are numerous interactions where the presence or absence of a dummy as final 1 will make a difference; in other languages there may be no such cases.

7   The Nuclear Dummy Law

'Dummy nominals' have figured prominently in many discussions in the linguistic literature, where the term 'dummy' is used to refer to nominals such as those italicized in the examples below:

(51) English
     a.   *It* is clear that he is guilty.
     b.   *It's* amazing the things he's getting away with.
     c.   *It* didn't rain.
     d.   *There* is a daffodil under the pillow.
     e.   Terry made *it* clear that he would resign.

(52) French
     a.   *Il* est évident qu'il est coupable.
          'It is obvious that he is guilty.'
     b.   *Il* est arrivé trois inspecteurs.
          'Three inspectors arrived.'
     c.   *Il* pleut depuis cinq heures.
          'It has been raining for five hours.'
     d.   *C'*est étonnant le nombre de gens qui croient tout cela.
          'It's amazing the number of people who believe all that.'

(53) German
   a. *Es* ist nicht sicher, dass er schuldig ist.
      'It is not certain that he is guilty.'
   b. *Es* kamen zwei junge Männer an.
      'Two young men approached.'
   c. *Es* wurde den ganzen Abend getanzt.
      'Dancing went on all evening.' (Lit., 'It was danced all evening.')

(54) Welsh
   Yr oedd *hi* yn bwrw glaw ddoe.
   was   she   throw rain yesterday
   'It was raining yesterday.'

(55) Dutch[10]
   a. *Het* is niet zeker, dat hij te   laat kwam.
      it   is not certain that he too late came
      'It is not certain that he came late.'
   b. *Het* regent de hele   dag.
      it   rains the whole day
      'It has been raining all day.'
   c. *Er*   is geen onderscheid tussen   deze dingen.
      there is no   difference   between these things.
      'There is no difference between these things.'
   d. *Er* werd door de kinderen gespeeld en   gelachen.
      it was by   the children played and laughed.
      'The children played and laughed.'

   Given the existence of dummy nominals in natural languages, it is necessary to ask about the class of well-formed RNs with dummy nominals—in particular, about the class of possible arcs whose heads are dummy nominals. A priori one might think that there is no difference between dummy nominals and other nominals in this regard and that therefore in the RNs associated with well-formed clauses in natural languages there appear arcs such as the following (where 'D' stands for a dummy nominal node, '*b*' for a clause node):

(56) a.   b.   c.   d.

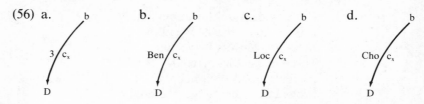

However, we claim that none of the arcs in (56) will be found in well-formed RNs. Their absence is accounted for by the Nuclear Dummy Law:

(57)   Nuclear Dummy Law
If A is an arc whose head is a dummy nominal, A is a nuclear term arc.

Before continuing, observe that we have not defined the notion 'dummy nominal' and thus technically there is no way this expression in (57) can pick out any particular arcs. This problem, though serious theoretically, does not preclude a practical testing of (57) as long as we can identify dummies extensionally in particular languages (i.e., as long as we accept that nominals like those in (51–55) are indeed dummies). The theoretical problem of defining dummy nominal is dealt with in detail in the APG framework in Johnson and Postal 1980, chap. 10.

The Nuclear Dummy Law characterizes as ill-formed any RN in which a dummy nominal is the head of an arc whose R-sign is other than '1' or '2'. This law has a number of immediate empirical consequences. The first four are implications of its prediction that dummies cannot head 3-arcs.

First, there will be no well-formed clauses where a dummy bears the 3-relation in the first stratum in which it bears a relation. Consider:

(58)   I sent gifts to six senators.

Here *I* bears the 1-relation, *gifts* the 2-relation, and *six senators* the 3-relation. A priori, one can conceive of a language with sentences just like (58) except that the associated RN contains a second stratum in which a dummy bears the 3-relation, and the initial 3 (as a consequence of the Chômeur Law) the chômeur relation:

(59)

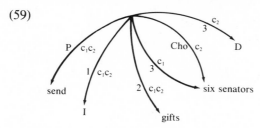

If the language in question were otherwise like English, and if the dummy in question were *there,* the resulting sentence would be one of the versions of (60), depending on whether or not the chômeur were marked with a preposition:

(60)   *I sent gifts to there (prep) six senators.

The Nuclear Dummy Law embodies the claim that RNs like (59) and hence sentences like *(60) will not be found in any natural language.

A second prediction of this law is that in Inversion clauses, where an earlier 1 is a later 3, a dummy will never be found as an Inversion 3. In Russian, for example, in Inversion clauses like (61), the initial 1 is the final 3.[11]

(61) a.   Takaja rubaška   nužna Borisu
            such   shirt-NOM needs Boris-DAT
            'Boris needs that kind of shirt.'

   b.

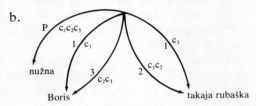

The Nuclear Dummy Law predicts that RNs like the following will not be well-formed in any language:

(62) a.

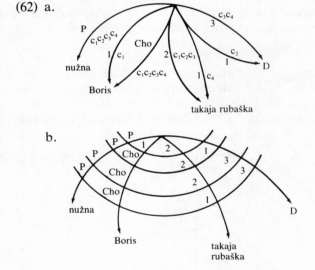

In (62), a dummy heads a 1-arc in the c_2 stratum, putting the initial 1 (*Boris*) en chômage. The dummy is also head of a 3-arc in the c_3 stratum, this being an Inversion construction. The initial 2 (*takaja rubaška*) is final 1 of the clause. Thus (62) parallels (61), which is grammatical in Russian, except that in (62) the dummy, rather than *Boris*, is the Inversion nominal. But this is excluded by the Nuclear Dummy Law, since it involves a dummy as head of a 3-arc. The sentence corresponding to (62) in Russian (assuming Russian to use the morpheme *to* as a dummy and to mark the î with the instrumental case) would be:

(63) *Takaja rubaška nužna tomu   Borisom
     such   shirt   needs D-DAT Boris-INSTR

The Nuclear Dummy Law predicts that sentences like *(63), corresponding to RNs like (62), will not be grammatical *in any language.*

Third, the Nuclear Dummy Law predicts that in cases where a language permits 2-3 Retreat, RNs in which a dummy nominal bearing the 2-relation also bears the 3-relation will not be well-formed. Thus, while clauses in which other 2s are final 3s will be well-formed, clauses in which dummy 2s are final 3s will not be.

A fourth class of cases for which the Nuclear Dummy Law makes predictions concerns Clause Union constructions in which the final 1 of a transitive complement heads a 3-arc in the matrix clause. Consider, for example, the Dutch sentence

(64)   Twee mensen hebben de nieuwe foto's gezien.
     'Two people have seen the new photos.'

If a clause like (64) (ignoring matters of verb tense and the auxiliary *hebben*) is embedded beneath the causative Clause Union trigger *laten*,[12] the result is:

(65)   Ik liet de nieuwe foto's aan twee mensen zien.
     'I let/had two people see the new photos.'
     'I showed the new photos to two people.'

The RN (66) is associated with (65); 'U' is the R-sign of the Union relation, which the complement predicate bears to the matrix clause in Clause Union constructions.

(66)

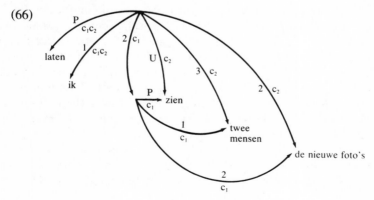

The complement 1 (*twee mensen*) is the 3 of the matrix clause in the Clause Union construction and is marked in (65) with the preposition *aan*. This is the preposition used in Dutch to mark final 3s.

Alongside (64), Dutch has grammatical sentences of the form

(67)   Er hebben twee mensen de nieuwe foto's gezien.
       'Two people have seen the new photos.'

in which the dummy *er* is arguably the final 1. Like other final 1s, it can, for example, be found in 'inverted word order' in questions.[13]

(68)   Hebben er twee mensen de nieuwe foto's gezien?
       'Have two people seen the new photos?'

Just as (64) can be embedded beneath *laten* in Clause Union constructions, (67) would a priori be embeddable in this construction as well. Such a complex sentence would have the RN:

(69)

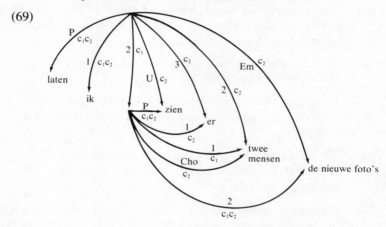

Structure (69) represents the fact that in the complement, the dummy *er* heads a 1-arc in the second stratum, and the initial 1 of the complement (*twee mensen*) heads a Cho arc in the second stratum. Since this is a clause union construction, the final 1 of the transitive complement lawfully heads a 3-arc in the matrix clause. But the Nuclear Dummy Law predicts that (69) is ill-formed, because a dummy (*er*) is head of a 3-arc. And, in fact, there are no grammatical sentences in Dutch corresponding to (69). In the realization of (69), the dummy *er* should be marked with the preposition *aan*, yielding the form *daaraan*. But such expressions are ill-formed:

(70) a. *Ik liet de nieuwe foto's daaraan twee mensen zien.
      b. *Ik liet de nieuwe foto's twee mensen daaraan zien.

There is no way to obtain a grammatical sentence from *(70) by varying the word order. The Nuclear Dummy Law predicts that a dummy that is the final 1 of a transitive complement can never be head of a 3-arc in the matrix clause in a Clause Union construction.

A fifth consequence of the Nuclear Dummy Law is that a dummy cannot head an oblique arc. Thus, there are predicted (correctly as far as we know) to be no cases in natural languages where dummies bear relations such as temporal, locative, instrumental, benefactive, etc.

Sixth, the Nuclear Dummy Law predicts that dummies cannot head Cho arcs. This predicts the ungrammaticality of *(71b) and *(71d), passive counterparts of (71a) and (71c).

(71) a. It bothers me that he is getting away with so much.
    b. *I am bothered by it that he is getting away with so much.
    c. It bothers me the things he's getting away with.
    d. *I am bothered by it the things he's getting away with.

In the RNs associated with *(71b) and *(71d), the dummy *it* heads Cho arcs in violation of the Nuclear Dummy Law. Hence *(71b) would have the RN:

(72)

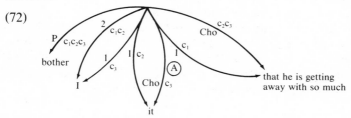

Here arc A conflicts with the Nuclear Dummy Law.

Seventh, the Nuclear Dummy Law predicts that there can be no Em arcs headed by dummies. But since clearly attested Em arcs have heads which are also heads of 3-arcs, oblique arcs or Cho arcs, there is presently no obvious way to test this claim independently of previous implications of the Nuclear Dummy Law.

Eighth, the Nuclear Dummy Law prevents dummy nominals from heading arcs with overlay R-signs. Thus, dummies are predicted not to be possible heads of Top arcs. As a result, examples like *(73b) and *(74b) are necessarily ill-formed in English:

(73) a. I hate it very much for you to scream like that.
    b. *It I hate very much for you to scream like that.
(74) a. Sue believes there to be life on Mars.
    b. *There Sue believes to be life on Mars.
    c. Sue believes Joe lives there.
    d. There Sue believes Joe lives.

Example *(74b) contrasts with (74d), where *there* is not a dummy.

However, it is not clear whether, or to what extent, the claim that dummies cannot head overlay arcs is independently testable. It may be that each such arc is independently limited by one or another semantic constraint of a sort which would preclude overlay arcs headed by dummies even without a principle like the Nuclear Dummy Law.

In testing the empirical consequences of the Nuclear Dummy Law, it is essential not to confuse 'dummies' with 'pronominal copies' (of other nominals). Copies are illustrated by the italicized pronouns in the following English examples:

(75) a.   Your father, everybody thinks *he* is a great guy.
     b.   Everybody I know told *him* to go to hell, your father.
     c.   Those kids, everybody is always giving things to *them*.
     d.   Your Aunt Harriet, we did it all just for *her*.

A pronominal copy normally agrees with the nominal of which it is a copy. This can be seen in the examples in (75), where in each case, the pronominal copy agrees in gender and number with its antecedent. Unlike dummies, pronominal copies can be heads of 3-arcs, oblique arcs, Cho arcs, etc., as (75c–d) illustrate.

We use the term 'Extraposition' exclusively to refer to constructions in which a nominal, clausal or otherwise, is put en chômage by a dummy. There are sentences for which it is not obvious whether a pronominal form is a dummy or a copy, i.e., whether the sentences are instances of Extraposition or, e.g., Dislocation:

(76)   German
       Ich wusste es nicht, dass er hungrig war.
       I   knew it not   that he hungry was
       'I didn't know that he was hungry.'
(77)   Hungarian
       János azt   mondta, hogy visszajön.
       János it-ACC said   that he-return
       'János said that he would return.'

There are in our terms two (or more) possible analyses of these examples. Under the first analysis, they involve Extraposition. In this case, the pronominal form (*es, azt*) is a dummy and the complement, which is an initial 2, is a final chômeur. Under the second analysis, these sentences involve so-called 'Right Dislocation'. In this case, the complement, which is an initial 2, is head of an overlay arc (with R-sign 'Disloc'), and the pronominal form is a copy of the dislocatee. We have not investigated these alternatives for these examples.

There are certain cases, including the following examples, however, where the Nuclear Dummy Law *excludes the dummy analysis:*

(78)   German
Die Kinder freuten sich darüber, dass die Mutter
the children rejoiced REFL about-it that the mother
zurückkam.
returned
'The children were glad that their mother had returned.'

(79)   Dutch
De kinderen verheugen er zich over, dat hun moeder
the children rejoice   it REFL about that their mother
terug kwam.
back came
'The children are glad that their mother returned.'

Examples analogous to (78) and (79) can be constructed for Hungarian. Examples (78) and (79) have pronominal elements (realized as *da-* in (78) and as *er* in (79)) that are heads of oblique arcs in the associated RNs. Since the Nuclear Dummy Law specifically prevents dummies from being heads of arcs with R-signs other than '1' or '2', the only analysis of (78) and (79) compatible with this law must involve Dislocation rather than Extraposition, with the pronominal elements as pronominal copies rather than dummies. For cases such as these, the Nuclear Dummy Law predicts that, where there are clear differences between Extraposition and Dislocation (or other phenomena involving pronominal copies), sentences like (78) and (79) will behave like the latter.

8   **Kinyarwanda versus the Stratal Uniqueness Law and the Chômeur Law**

In earlier sections, we stated the Stratal Uniqueness and Chômeur Laws, which have played a fundamental role in the development of the relational grammar view of clause structure. These laws have recently come under criticism. We suggest in this section that the criticisms of the former can be met. Thus we continue to claim that stratal uniqueness is a genuine property of human clause structures. However, to maintain this view, it becomes necessary to abandon the Chômeur Law. This is consistent with other recent work also leading to the conclusion that this constraint is overly restrictive.

Perhaps the best-known critique of stratal uniqueness so far is that of Gary and Keenan (1977) based on facts from the Bantu language Kinyarwanda. We will indicate why we believe the Kinyarwanda data does not violate the Stratal Uniqueness Law. This does not mean, however, that all the problems raised by Kinyarwanda with respect to this domain are resolved. They are not. In particular, the conditions permitting pronominal cliticization are unresolved. However, the data on this matter is inadequate and we do not think any serious claims can be based on this area as yet. (We will discuss clitic pronouns briefly at the end of this section.)

Gary and Keenan's objection is based essentially on the properties of examples like:

(80) a.   Gary and Keenan's (13)

                                ⎧ ibaruwa   Maria ⎫
      Yohani y-oher-er-eje   ⎪ letter   Mary   ⎪
      John   he-send-?-ASP   ⎨ Maria   ibaruwa ⎬
                                  ⎩ Mary   letter ⎭
      'John sent a letter to Mary.'

    b.   Gary and Keenan's (20b)
      Ibaruwa y-ø-oher-er-ej-w-e   Maria na Yohani.
      letter   it-PAST-send-?-ASP-PASS-ASP Maria by John
      'The letter was sent to Mary by John.'

    c.   Gary and Keenan's (20c)
      Maria y-ø-oher-er-ej-w-e   ibaruwa na Yohani.
      Mary she-PAST-send-?-ASP-PASS-ASP letter   by John
      'Mary was sent the letter by John.'

Translating to our terms, Gary and Keenan argue in effect that the structure of examples like (80a) has only one stratum, in which there are two 2-arcs, one headed by *ibaruwa,* the other by *Maria.* Restated in our framework, then, Gary and Keenan attribute the following structure to (80a):

(81)

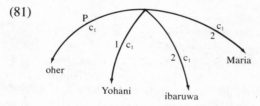

Their argument takes the following general form. There are a number of properties arguably typical of 2s in Kinyarwanda which can be established independently of constructions like (80a). Such properties relate to passivization, reflexivization, relativization, etc. With respect to these properties, both *ibaruwa* and *Maria* in (80a) behave like 2s.

This is illustrated for passivization in (80b, c), in which either *ibaruwa* or *Maria* can be the subject of a passive clause, indicating apparently that both are 2s.

Let us focus on the possibility of relativizing. In fact, either *Maria* or *ibaruwa* can relativize in sentences like (80a). Gary and Keenan take this as strong evidence for a violation of stratal uniqueness, i.e., as evidence that sentences like (80a) are incompatible with the Stratal Uniqueness Law, for the following reasons. Significantly, they show that most nominals, oblique nominals in particular, are not directly subject to the relativization 'strategy' in question. More significantly, final chômeurs are arguably not subject to this. Hence the 1-chômeur in a passive and the 2-chômeur 'created' when a *locative* advances to 2-hood are *not* relativizable. Gary and Keenan (1977, p. 90) assume that the relevant constraint on this relativization in Kinyarwanda is:

(82)   Only (final) 1s and 2s relativize.

From this, they conclude that the Kinyarwanda example (80a) cannot have a structure like (36) above. That analysis would make *ibaruwa* a chômeur, and thus, by (82), not subject to relativization, when in fact it is subject to relativization.

Particularly relevant is the contrast between:

(83)   Gary and Keenan's (21)
       Nabonye ibaruwa Yohani yoher-er-eje Maria.
       I saw   letter   John   sent-ASP   Mary
       'I saw the letter John sent Mary.'

where what we would regard as the initial 2 *ibaruwa* is relativizable in a construction with what we (but not Gary and Keenan) would regard as an initial 3 (*Maria*) and the following:

(84)   Gary and Keenan's (57a)
       *Nabonye impiyisi Yohani y-ø-iish-e-mo   ishyamba.
       I saw   hyena   John   he-PAST-kill-ASP-LOC forest
       'I saw the hyena that John killed in the forest.'

That is, when a locative advances to 2, the initial 2 is not relativizable, indicating, given (82), that it is a chômeur. Gary and Keenan conclude, in effect, that since the initial 2 in examples like (83) cannot be a chômeur, it must be a final 2. And since what corresponds to a 3 in other languages also behaves like a 2, the clauses in question must have two 2s. In other words, in our terms, Gary and Keenan's conclusions would mean that (80a) would have the structure in (81) and (80b) would have that in:

(85)

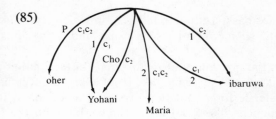

Both of these structures counterexemplify the Stratal Uniqueness Law, since they contain two 2-arcs in the c_1 stratum.

However, Gary and Keenan's conclusion is unwarranted by this array of facts. There are analyses of such data distinct from that of the form (81/85) that are compatible both with the generalizations they cite for Kinyarwanda and with the Stratal Uniqueness Law. We first consider one analysis, which renders Kinyarwanda quite like English (with respect to the domain in question) except for certain morphological features. We then consider one type of fact not fully compatible with this treatment, but which is compatible with either a slight extension or revision of it.

Kinyarwanda clauses such as (80a) correspond to distinct *pairs* of English examples like:

(86) a.   John sent the letter to Mary.
      b.   John sent Mary the letter.

Under the analyses we proposed for these English clauses in (35/36), either *the letter* or *Mary* is passivizable, *even under the assumption that (English) passive constructions are those in which a nominal that heads a 2-arc in one stratum heads a 1-arc in the next.* The passives corresponding to (86a, b) and their respective structures are given in (37) and (38).

Gary and Keenan's initial generalizations about Kinyarwanda are captured in a grammar that does not violate the Stratal Uniqueness Law *if* Kinyarwanda clauses like (80a) are *structurally ambiguous* over the two analyses manifested by the pair of English clauses in (86). That is, (80a) could represent two structures which, except for lexical differences, are identical to those of (33), represented in (35) and (36). Hence, on the analysis corresponding to (35), the initial (and final) 2 can passivize, yielding (80b), which is parallel to (37a). On the analysis of (80a) corresponding to (36), the initial 3, which is a 2 in the second stratum, can passivize, yielding (80c), which is parallel to (37b). Example (83) is accounted for by relativization of the initial (and final) 2 in the structure corresponding to (35). This analysis is consistent with both (82) and the Stratal Uniqueness Law. No generalizations in Kinyarwanda are violated and almost all of the properties attested are accounted for without ad hoc statements. On this treatment, the Stratal Uniqueness Law is no more disconfirmed by the relevant facts in Kinyarwanda than it is by those like (37) from English.

In the terms just suggested, the Kinyarwanda treatment of 3s differs from that in English chiefly in not involving flagging with a preposition or any other device. This has the effect of making it not immediately clear from the superficial forms of clauses whether one is dealing with (inter alia) a final 3 or a final 2.

There is, however, a problem with the treatment of Kinyarwanda 3s just sketched, one raised by a further example cited by Gary and Keenan. This is the form in (87a), *whose subordinate clause* would have to be represented as in (87b):

(87) a.   Gary and Keenan's (59)
      ibaruwa Maria y-ø-ohér-er-ej-w-e
      letter   Mary she-PAST-send-BEN-ASP-PASS-ASP
      'the letter that Mary was sent.'

    b.

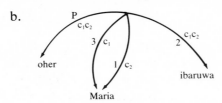

That is, we take (87a) to show that some morphologically 'passive' clauses in Kinyarwanda must be analyzed as having direct advancement of 3s to 1, with no intermediate 2-stage. This treatment is forced because the initial 2 in (87a) is relativizable and thus, if (82) is to be maintained, must not be a final chômeur. But, given the Chômeur Law and the Stratal Uniqueness Law, it would be a final chômeur if the 3 advanced to 2 before advancing to 1.

We see no objection to an analysis like (87b). Such structures are independently attested in other languages, particularly Western Austronesian (see Keenan 1972, 1976 and Bell 1976 and chap. 5) and hence cannot be precluded on universal grounds. It would thus follow that Kinyarwanda allows both 2s and 3s to advance directly to 1.[14] This raises the following question. Given the possibility of direct advancement of 3 to 1, is it ever necessary to recognize, in our terms, that Kinyarwanda allows advancement of 3 to 2? We are confident that the answer to this question is positive. But a defense of it would require analysis of much other data from Kinyarwanda (Kimenyi 1976), particularly data involving Possessor Ascension constructions. And this is beyond the scope of this discussion. Moreover, it does not really matter for present purposes. Our goal here is limited to arguing that the data cited by Gary and Keenan does not require abandonment of the Stratal Uniqueness Law. And for this, it suffices to note that a treatment recognizing advancement of 3s directly to 1 accounts for the data either alone or in combination with advancement of 3s to 2.

Observe that taking some Kinyarwanda passive clauses to involve advancement of 3 to 1 with no intermediate stratum where the 3 is a 2 causes no problems for determining the choice of chômeur marking or verb marking in such cases.[15] The choice of the passive chômeur marker *na* would be determined by the advancement of either a 2 or a 3 to 1-hood, that is, by the advancement of an *object*. Just so, the passive verbal morphology would be predicted by the advancement of an *object*. These statements would be no less general than those of a language like Indonesian or English, where the analogous properties would be limited to the more restricted situations in which only 2s advance directly to 1-hood.[16] In these terms, Kinyarwanda contrasts with many Western Austronesian languages in *not* having distinctive verbal morphologies for the distinct cases where 3s advance to 1 and where 2s advance to 1.

Under Gary and Keenan's analysis of Kinyarwanda, there is some latitude as to how the condition on relativizability could be formulated. The constraint in (82) can be restated in our terms as:

(88)   Only final nuclear terms relativize.

But there is also another possibility:

(89)   Only final terms relativize.

Under Gary and Keenan's analysis, (88) and (89) are extensionally equivalent internal to Kinyarwanda because they posit no 3s in this language. Under our analysis, (88) and (89) both account for the relativizability of all three nominals in (80a) because (80a) is relationally ambiguous. If (88) were adopted, on the one hand, *Maria* in (80a) would *not* be relativizable in the structure in which it is a final 3, but it would be in the structure in which it is a final 2. If (89) is adopted, on the other hand, *Maria* in (80a) would be relativizable in either structure. In our discussion of Instrumental–2 Advancement in Kinyarwanda below, we show that there are grounds for rejecting (88) in favor of (89).

We conclude that nothing about indirect object constructions in Kinyarwanda adduced by Gary and Keenan suggests any genuine difficulty for the Stratal Uniqueness Law. Their conclusion that this domain is inconsistent with this law and, in particular, their view that clauses like (80a) involve a single stratum with two 2-arcs, appears to be based on a failure to consider certain analyses of the data consistent with this law. Notably, they fail to consider the possibility that clauses like (80a) might be relationally ambiguous or the possibility that 3s in Kinyarwanda might advance directly to 1. But since no principles of grammar with any known support preclude either of these possibilities, and since neither of them leads to any clear loss of generalization internal to the language, these hypotheses about the Kinyarwanda data adduced by Gary and Keenan are initially superior to their hypothesis, which involves an otherwise unmotivated widening of the class of possible linguistic structures which grammatical theory must recognize.

Even if one grants that the proposals just put forward 'save' the Stratal Uniqueness Law from facts involving the domain of 2s and 3s in Kinyarwanda, it would be inaccurate and misleading to let stand any implication that all the data recently brought forward from Kinyarwanda is consistent overall with the 'traditional' relational grammar framework, much of which is stated in this paper. For we believe that when the data in Kimenyi 1976 is analyzed in greater detail, it will provide important materials supporting *an abandonment of the Chômeur Law*. Hence we take it that Kinyarwanda's real negative relevance to past relational grammar claims at this stage is that it provides solid grounds for the conclusion considered rather abstractly in Johnson and Postal (1980, chap. 8, §7) that the Chômeur Law is mistaken. Since we have stated this traditional relational principle in this paper, it is important to consider the Kinyarwanda facts which suggest its inadequacy.

The grounds for regarding Kinyarwanda as incompatible with the Chômeur Law are related to the considerations discussed by Gary and Keenan, that is, they are related to the restriction of a number of syntactic phenomena in the language to terms or objects. However, the real problem for the Chômeur Law is brought out not by constructions involving initial 3s discussed by Gary and Keenan but by, e.g., the contrast between those involving advancement of locatives to 2 and those involving advancement of (inter alia) instrumentals to 2.

As already noted in the text, when locatives advance to 2, the original 2 can *not* participate in constructions limited to terms, i.e., relativization. This is predicted by the Chômeur Law and thus in itself, far from causing difficulties, supports the principle in question. The problem arises from, e.g., instrumental advancement. For, when instruments advance to 2, the initial 2 does *not* (in a large class of cases)[17] lose the potentiality for participating in grammatical phenomena otherwise apparently restricted to terms.

We will illustrate with examples from chapter 4 of Kimenyi 1976. The superficial consequences of what we assume (with Kimenyi) to be advancement of instrumentals to 2 are illustrated by contrasts like:

(90) a.   Kimenyi's (4.1.6a)
      Umugabo a-ra-andik-a   íbarúwa n'   ííkarámu.
      man   he-PRES-write-ASP letter   with pen
      'The man is writing a letter with the pen.'
   b.   Kimenyi's (4.2.6b)
      Umugabo a-ra-andik-iish-a   íbarúwa íkarámu.
      man   he-PRES-write-INSTR-ASP letter   pen
      'The man is writing a letter with the pen.'

Advancement of the instrumental to 2 leads to an *absence* of the instrumental preposition *na* (or *n'*) and to the presence of the instrumental marker *-iish-* on the verb of the clause.

There are strong grounds for the assumption that *ííkarámu* is a 2 in (90b) though not in (90a). Namely, the phenomena restricted to terms in Kinyarwanda are possible with this nominal in cases like (90b) but not in (90a). Thus the nominal can relativize, etc., only in the former cases. This is extensively documented by Kimenyi and we will not say more about it here.

So far, then, instrumental advancement is not distinguished from, e.g., locative advancement, and indeed from typical advancements to 2 in other languages, including other Bantu languages, English, Indonesian, etc. However, the relatively special properties of Kinyarwanda instrumental advancement are brought out by the fact that when instrumentals advance, the initial 2, if any, does not normally (in contrast to, e.g., the original 2 in a locative advancement construction) lose its ability to participate in phenomena of the sort restricted to objects or terms. That is, the initial 2 does not behave like a final chômeur. This is illustrated by such forms as (91) which show that the initial 2 can relativize:

(91)   Kimenyi's (4.1.18)
      Ng'iíyi   íbarúwa umugabo y-aándik-iish-a   íkarámu.
      that this letter   man   he-REL-write-INSTR-ASP pen
      'Here is the letter that the man is writing with a pen.'

If, as Kimenyi and Gary and Keenan have argued, e.g., relativization is restricted to final terms (e.g., (89) is valid), then there is only one way to maintain the Chômeur Law and the Stratal Uniqueness Law simultaneously in the face of examples like (91). This would be to say that the initial 2 in the relative clause retreats to chômeur and then only subsequently advances to 3. However, this analysis, while perhaps not definitively excluded by the data, forces rejection of an otherwise plausible principle, namely, the Chômeur Advancement Ban:

(92)   Chômeur Advancement Ban
        Chômeurs cannot advance. That is, if an RN contains an arc of the form $[Cho(a,b)\langle c_x c_i \rangle]$, then it contains no arc of the form $[Term_y(a,b)\langle c_{i+1} c_w \rangle]$.

This principle,[18] though not traditional in relational grammar in the way that the Chômeur Law is, is at least as plausible as the latter. There is no obvious gain in saving one law only at the cost of another. Moreover, allowing chômeurs to advance would vastly diminish the empirical content of the 'saved' Chômeur Law. While it would remain in principle possible to falsify this law, we know of no type of evidence that would in fact be relevant to this, without (92). Consequently, even if the Chômeur Law were 'saved' by abandoning (92) and adopting particular analyses in which chômeurs advance, the principle would have thereby lost most of its significance.

On the face of it, examples like (91) might seem to suggest, more strongly than those cited by Gary and Keenan, that the Stratal Uniqueness Law is falsified by Kinyarwanda. It might seem that in the second stratum of the subordinate clause in an example like (91) there must be two 2-arcs if principle (88/89) is to be maintained. If this analysis were adopted, then the subordinate clause in (91) would have the representation:

(93)

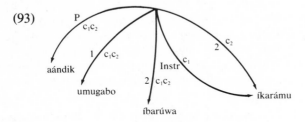

This analysis would force the abandonment of *both* the Stratal Uniqueness Law and the Chômeur Law, although it would not require giving up the Chômeur Advancement Ban. However, we reject (93). Taking advantage of our earlier proposal that final 3s in Kinyarwanda have the unusual (for Bantu languages) property of not being morphologically distinct from final 2s, we propose that the initial 2 in such cases is a final 3. Thus we suggest that the proper structure for a simple instrumental advancement clause like that in (91) is rather:

(94) a.

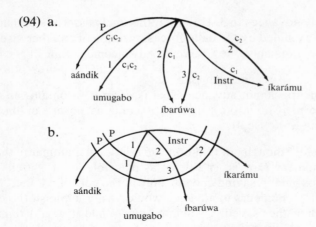

b.

This structure claims that the initial 2, *íbarúwa,* is a final 3 in the subordinate clause of (91). Hence it is subject to processes restricted to final terms not because it is a final 2 but because it is a final 3. Note that (94) involves the kind of 'simultaneous' revaluation typical of chômeur situations forced by the Chômeur Law. But instead of the original term being revalued to chômeur, it is demoted to 3.

Since (94) meets the antecedent conditions of the Chômeur Law, but not the consequent, we cannot maintain a structure like (94) without abandoning the Chômeur Law. However, (94), if sustainable, does permit maintenance of the Stratal Uniqueness Law and causes no problem for the Chômeur Advancement Ban. Nor does it seem to be in any way inferior to (93) with respect to Kinyarwanda-internal generalizations. If (89) is adopted in preference to (88), the grammaticality of (91) is accounted for. We conclude tentatively that the best analysis of examples like (91) involves structures of the form (94).

While we cannot attempt to justify (94) in detail further, there are several reasons why it is plausible to think both that: (i) it is proper to abandon the Chômeur Law rather than other universal principles, and (ii) structures like (94) are possible in human languages. As to the former, several grounds having nothing to do with Kinyarwanda are brought forward in Johnson and Postal (1980, chap. 8, §7) which suggest the inadequacy of the Chômeur Law. See also the appendix to Perlmutter and Postal (in press a).

Judith Aissen and Paul Schachter have independently pointed out to us that there is a possible description of these Kinyarwanda facts consistent both with the known generalizations about Kinyarwanda and with the Chômeur Law. According to this account, in the instrumental cases the instrument advances to 3, rather than to 2. Thus the fact that the earlier 2 in these constructions behaves like a final term (object) is predicted, since this nominal would be a 2 in all strata. In particular, the Motivated Chômage Law would not permit it to demote to chômeur. In these terms, instrumental advancement in Kinyarwanda would contrast with locative advancement, which would be to 2, thus determining (by the Chômeur Law) chômeur status for the earlier 2.

The analysis under which an instrumental advances to 3 certainly deserves further study. We know of no Kinyarwanda-internal arguments against it and in favor of the advancement-to-2 description proposed here, or conversely. Its main virtue is that it would preserve the Chômeur Law against the Kinyarwanda data. However, this result is of limited relevance if, as we believe, there is other data that is also incompatible with that law. Moreover, the proposal that instrumentals advance directly to 3 in Kinyarwanda may itself conflict with another otherwise valid law. There are a number of documented cases, in languages other than Kinyarwanda, where instrumentals advance to 2, but we know of no case where they clearly advance to 3. This raises the question of whether instrumental advancement to 3 is possible in natural languages. There may be an as yet unformulated law precluding such advancement. That is, one should resist adopting an instrumental-to-3 analysis for data that can be analyzed differently, unless clear cases can be shown that require universal grammar to permit direct advancement of an instrument to 3. As indicated in the discussion of Pocomam and Dyirbal immediately below, the analysis we propose, in which instruments advance to 2 with the original 2 demoting to 3, seems attestable independent of Kinyarwanda.

Structures like (94) are plausible (see (ii) above) because we have found in several other language families indications that when instrumentals advance to 2, the original 2 is revalued not to chômeur but to 3. For instance, Smith-Stark (1976, p. 23) provides some brief information on this for the Mayan language Pocomam, specifying that:

> Curiously, instruments behave something like agents in that they are not questioned directly. Instead, there is a special verb form, which I call *instrumental voice*. Formally, this is a derived transitive verb which takes an instrument 'patient'. What would otherwise be a patient appears as an indirect object (actually, things are a good bit more complex). The instrumental voice is used among other places, when an instrumental phrase is questioned. Compare, for example,

i) pila? šake?ex
what you-ground-it
'What did you grind?'

ii) pila? šakiew'ieh   reh
what you-ground-with-it to-it
'What did you grind it with?'

We interpret this as saying that when the instrumental advances to 2 ('patient' in Smith-Stark's terms), the initial 2 is demoted to 3, hence appearing in a dative form, indicated by *reh*. Similarly, as kindly pointed out to us by David Johnson, treatment of the initial 2 as subsequent 3 when instrumentals advance to 2 is the standard situation in the Australian language Dyirbal, discussed in detail by Dixon (1972).

There are two types of instrumental constructions in Dyirbal, one without advancement illustrated by:

(95) Dixon's (242)
balan   ḍugumbil   baŋgul   yaṛangu
THERE-NOM-II woman-NOM THERE-ERG-I man-ERG
baŋgu   yuguŋgu   balgan
THERE-INSTR-IV stick-INSTR hit-PRES/PAST
'Man is hitting woman with stick.'

Here the initial 2, referring to 'woman', is as expected for Dyirbal in the absolutive case (i.e., Dixon's nominative), the initial 1 referring to 'man' as expected in the ergative case, and the instrumental is in the instrumental case. The verb has no special marking. The other type of instrumental construction is illustrated by:

(96) Dixon's (253)
bala   yugu   baŋgul   yaṛaŋgu
THERE-NOM-I stick-NOM THERE-ERG-I man-ERG
balgalman   bagun   ḍugumbilgu
hit-INSTR-PRES/PAST THERE-DAT-II woman-DAT
'Man is hitting woman with stick.'

Example (96) differs from (95) inter alia in that the initial instrumental is in the absolutive case, the verb bears a suffix absent in (95), and the initial 2 is in the dative case. We take this to indicate that (96) has the structure:

(97)

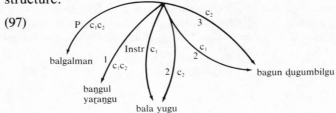

That is, the initial instrumental is a final 2, while the initial 2 is a final 3. Hence, if we are correct, Smith-Stark's (ii) and (96) are instances of the same stratal subpattern in (98) which we have taken to be the proper structure for the Kinyarwanda examples like (91):

(98)

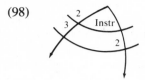

Thus, our tentative conclusion is that the relevant facts in Kinyarwanda, like those in Pocomam and Dyirbal, are in no way inconsistent with the Stratal Uniqueness Law. However, the best analysis of them, that represented by the structure in (94) rather than that in:

(99)

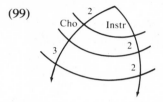

is clearly inconsistent with the Chômeur Law.

For these reasons, our current view is that the Chômeur Law is not a valid principle of human linguistic structure. This does *not* constitute an abandonment of the chômeur relation. On the contrary, as pointed out in §4, the chômeur relation accounts for a wide array of linguistic data (and is one of the features distinguishing relational grammar from other conceptions of linguistic structure, both contemporary and traditional). What the foregoing discussion suggests is that the Chômeur Law is overly restrictive in *requiring* the chômeur relation to exist under the conditions defined by its antecedent. The data from Kinyarwanda, Pocomam, and Dyirbal suggest that the range of possible linguistic variation is greater than that allowed by the Chômeur Law, since in these languages the nominal that the Chômeur Law requires to bear the chômeur relation in the first stratum in which an instrumental bears the 2-relation seems to bear the 3-relation instead. Additional empirical investigation needs to be undertaken to determine more precisely the range of cases in natural languages where nominals required by the Chômeur Law to bear the chômeur relation in a particular stratum bear some other relation instead.

In the light of the data known to us at present, it seems that many of the empirical claims of the Chômeur Law are correct. The antecedent conditions of this law are satisfiable in three known ways, namely, when terms arise in strata via revaluations (advancements and demotions), ascensions, or the existence of dummy nominals. All cases known to us where 'new' terms do *not* result in earlier terms of the same type bearing the chômeur relation involve *advancements*. Further, in all of these cases, the nominal for which the Chômeur Law predicts the chômeur relation seems to bear the 3-relation instead. Conceivably then, a weaker version of the Chômeur Law can be retained. We leave this as a possibility for further investigation. For the present, we propose the Motivated Chômage Law and the Chômeur Advancement Ban as universal constraints on the chômeur relation.

To conclude this discussion of the Stratal Uniqueness Law and the Chômeur Law as they relate to Kinyarwanda, we want to say something about the principles governing the possibility of pronominal object clitics in this language. Both Kimenyi (1976) and Gary and Keenan assume that object clitics, like passivization, relativization, and reflexivization, are properties determined by 2s. More precisely, they seem to assume that such verbal clitics are determined by *final* 2s. Since there exist Kinyarwanda verbs with two or three such clitics cooccurring, the only analyses of Kinyarwanda consistent with this assumption would falsify the Stratal Uniqueness Law. In continuing to support this law, we must reject the assumption that object clitics are in all cases determined by final 2s.

Moreover, given the existence of cases of three cooccurring object clitics, even the recognition of final 3s in Kinyarwanda does not permit a natural extension of the assumption that clitics are determined by final 2s. One cannot account for the full range of pronominal clitics in terms of a principle limiting such to final objects (2s and 3s), for this would falsely yield a maximum of two clitics, when the real maximum is at least three, as shown by such examples as:

(100)   Kimenyi's (7.2.15)
        Abáana   ba-zaa-ha-*ki-mu-b*-eerek-er-a.
        Children they-FUT-there-it-him-them-show-BEN-ASP
        'The children will show it to him for them there.'

Here the italicized forms are three cooccurring object clitics. Since at most two of these could represent *final* objects, an analysis of Kinyarwanda clitics consistent with the Stratal Uniqueness Law cannot limit them to final objects.

However, there is a generalization about clitics consistent with Kimenyi's basic generalization and compatible with the Stratal Uniqueness Law:

(101)   So-called object clitics are determined by objects that are not final 1s.

The crucial feature of (101) is that though the nominals referenced must be objects (2s or 3s), they need not be *final* objects. They can be final chômeurs as long as they are 2s or 3s in some stratum.

To illustrate, suppose that the appropriate RN for (100) were roughly:

(102)

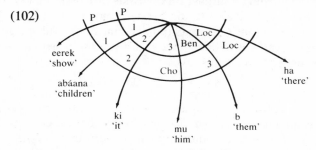

Then, the initial 2, 3, and benefactive would all meet the condition in (101) and could consequently determine clitic pronouns. Note, however, that the benefactive would not meet (101) if it had not advanced. Hence, just as in Kimenyi's account, advancement is crucial here. But the initial 3 determines a clitic although it is not a final object, since *final* objecthood is irrelevant to (101).

As it stands, (101) is somewhat too general. For example, there are at least some 2-chômeurs that cannot determine clitics, e.g., at least some of those put en chômage by the advancement of a locative to 2 (Kimenyi 1976, p. 97).[19] Other constraints may also be required. Unfortunately, the available data on clitics is too skimpy to study the matter in detail from the literature. Moreover, the accounts in the literature cannot fail to raise skepticism since they are partly incompatible. For example, Kimenyi (1976, p. 199) makes the following claim: "If the verb has four incorporated pronouns, which is usually the maximum number the verb can take, these pronouns must be locative, patient, recipient, and benefactive." Yet, Gary and Keenan (1977, p. 117) cite the following sentence:

(103)   Gary and Keenan's (68)
        Y-a-yi-ki-bi-ba-andik-iish-ir-ije-ho.
        he-PAST-it-it-it-them-write-INSTR-BEN-ASP-LOC
        'He wrote it on it with it for them.'

Example (103) is inconsistent with Kimenyi's claim cited above, since one of the clitics is instrumental. We are hard pressed to understand this discrepancy. It cannot be due to dialectal or idiolectal differences, since Kimenyi was Gary and Keenan's only consultant.

In view of the limited data available and the discrepancies in the literature, we see no point in attempting to improve on (101) at this point. We see no basic objection to (101), which provides a strong generalization covering the overwhelming majority of cases. In any event, anyone wishing to argue, on the basis of Kinyarwanda, that the facts of cliticization invalidate the Stratal Uniqueness Law will have to provide a much more far-reaching account of the full range of cliticization facts and show that there is a description better than (101) that is incompatible with this law.

Postscript

After completing this paper, we became acquainted with Dryer's work on Kinyarwanda (chap. 4), which gives independent arguments for the existence of 3s in Kinyarwanda and the failure of the Kinyarwanda data cited by Gary and Keenan to invalidate the Stratal Uniqueness Law.

Notes

1. This concept is precisely defined in terms of the 'arc pair grammar' (APG) framework in Johnson and Postal 1980.

2. This question is discussed in Johnson and Postal 1980, chap. 2.

3. For formal definitions of 'incomplete arc', 'arc', 'coordinate sequence', and related notions, see Johnson and Postal 1980, chap. 2.

4. Cebuano and Indonesian examples cited in this paper and their analyses are taken respectively from the work of Bell (chap. 5, below) and Chung (chap. 6, below).

5. This formulation, which rules out cases where a nominal is the head of more than one arc with the same R-sign in the same stratum, is stronger than that in chap. 1, which was stated in terms of identity of *nodes*. The stronger formulation based on arc identity is due to David Johnson.

The Functional Uniqueness Principle, which is similar to the Stratal Uniqueness Law, has been proposed independently by Harada (1975). Harada's principle is, however, not stated in terms of strata.

6. The Final 1 Law in §6 guarantees that there can be *no less* than one.

7. The existence of such an arc, though a sufficient condition for maintaining stratal uniqueness in such cases, is not necessary (see Johnson and Postal 1980, chap. 8, and §8 of this paper).

8. For a discussion of the emeritus relation, see Bell and Perlmutter, in preparation.

9. Comrie (1977) uses the term 'spontaneous demotion' to designate essentially what we call 'spontaneous chômage'. We use the latter term to distinguish this phenomenon from other cases of demotion such as Inversion, 2-3 Retreat, and Antipassive (under the analysis proposed in Postal 1977).

10. We are indebted to Annie Zaenen both for checking the Dutch examples in this paper and for stimulating discussion of the issues involved.

11. For evidence for Inversion in Russian, see Perlmutter (to appear).

12. On Clause Union in Dutch, see Zaenen 1976.

13. Maling and Zaenen (1978) discuss two dialects of Dutch. In one, the dummy appears in 'inverted' word order in interrogatives such as (68). In the other, no surface dummy appears in this construction.

14. The reader might assume at this point that in postulating that both 3s and 2s can advance directly to 1, we are forced to posit an 'extra rule' as against a treatment which recognizes only that 2s can advance to 1. However, no such argument against the present proposal can be maintained. A single rule of the form 'objects advance to 1' would suffice.

15. The fact that in Kinyarwanda, clauses in which 3s advance directly to 1 have the same morphological trappings as clauses in which 2s advance to 1 shows that passive clauses need not always be morphologically unique. Passive clauses (as characterized in Perlmutter and Postal (1977, in press a) should actually be seen as a special case of a whole set of structures in which a nominal of type x cooccurring with a 1 at a stratum advances to 1. Hence the type of clauses defined by direct advancement of 2s to 1 is only a special subtype of advancement to 1. It is an empirical question whether in a particular case where a nominal of type x, $x \neq 2$, advances to 1, it does so directly or, e.g., by way of 2. See note 16.

16. George Lakoff (1977 and unpublished work) has suggested, in effect, that all advancements to termhood are direct, that is, that no nominal can bear more than two relations to a fixed node. Hence he would analyze in these terms, e.g., (37b), as involving no 2-arc headed by *Mary*. Although we do not accept this position, it is less easy to argue against in particular cases than one might assume.

A key issue here is the status of the initial 2 when a 3 with which it occurs advances to 1. If the advancement is direct, there is no reason why the initial 2 should not stay a 2. If, however, the 3 advances by an intermediary 2-stage, the initial 2 should be a later chômeur. Our account allows both possibilities, and we claim that both are instantiated. Thus, in Kinyarwanda, as seen from the discussion of (91), one finds a 3 advancing to 1 with the 2 continuing to behave like a term. In contrast, as discussed extensively by Chung (1976), in Indonesian, when the 3 of a ditransitive clause advances to 1, the original 2 behaves like a chômeur. We take this as a classic case of advancement to 1 with an intermediate 2-stage. Hence key evidence for the possibility of the intermediate stage involves contrasts between the behavior of initial 2s in such cases.

17. When both a locative and an instrumental advance to 2 in the same clause, only the initial locative behaves like a final term for the phenomena of relevance. The initial 2 and initial instrumental behave like chômeurs. Thus, in contrast to structures like (94), proposed for simple instrumental advancement structures, we would propose the RN in (i-b) as the appropriate structure for a multiadvancement case like (i-a):

(i) a.   Kimenyi's (4.6.1.4d)
         Umwáalímu y-a-andik-iish-ijé-ho   ikibaho imibáre íngwa.
         teacher   he-PAST-write-INSTR-ASP-on board   math   chalk
         'The teacher wrote math on the blackboard with chalk.'

b.

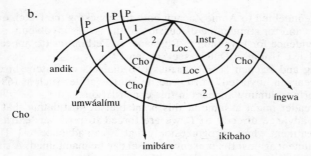

Of the demotion options allowed by linguistic theory when an instrument advances to 2 in a structure containing an earlier 2—demotion of the 2 to chômeur or to 3—the grammar of Kinyarwanda must specify that only the former is allowed in clauses involving both instrumental advancement and locative advancement. Further, the grammar must characterize as ill-formed any structure of the form:

(ii)

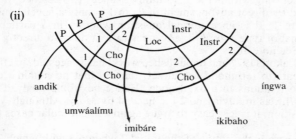

If (ii) were allowed, Kinyarwanda would have grammatical clauses with both instrumental and locative advancement to 2 in which the initial instrument behaves like a final 2 and the initial locative like a final chômeur.

18. A version of this constraint is formalized in APG terms in Johnson and Postal 1980 as "PN Law 63," the "Cho Arc No Local Successor Law."

19. Further, in cases we would analyze as Possessor Ascension, with a possessor ascending to 2, the initial 2 cannot determine an object clitic, nor can it passivize, cleft, or relativize. All of this is evidence that it is a final chômeur and suggests further that 2-chômeurs in general cannot determine object clitics.

References

Bell, Sarah J. 1976. "Cebuano Subjects in Two Frameworks." Ph.D. diss., MIT; Indiana University Linguistics Club.

Bell, Sarah J. (this volume). "Advancements and Ascensions in Cebuano."

Bell, Sarah J., and Perlmutter, David M. In preparation. "Clause Union and Advancements in Three Philippine Languages."

Chung, Sandra. 1976. "An Object-Creating Rule in Bahasa Indonesia." *Linguistic Inquiry* 7:41–87. Reprinted in this volume.

Chvany, Catherine. 1975. *On the Syntax of BE-Sentences in Russian.* Cambridge, Mass.: Slavica Publishers.

Cole, Peter, and Sadock, Jerrold, eds. 1977. *Syntax and Semantics 8: Grammatical Relations.* New York: Academic Press.

Comrie, Bernard. 1976. "The Syntax of Causative Constructions: Cross-Language Similarities and Divergences." In M. Shibatani, ed., *Syntax and Semantics 6: The Grammar of Causative Constructions.* New York: Academic Press.

———. 1977. "In Defense of Spontaneous Demotion: The Impersonal Passive." In Cole and Sadock 1977.

Dixon, R. M. W. 1972. *The Dyirbal Language of North Queensland.* Cambridge University Press, Cambridge.

Dryer, Matthew. (this volume). "Indirect Objects in Kinyarwanda Revisited".

Duranti, Alessandro, and Byarushengo, Ernest R. 1977. "On the Notion of 'Direct Object.'" In E. Byarushengo, A. Duranti, and L. Hyman, eds., *Haya Grammatical Structure.* Southern California Occasional Papers in Linguistics, no. 6, University of Southern California.

Gary, Judith O. 1977. "Object Formation Rules in Several Bantu Languages: Questions and Implications for Universal Grammar." *Papers from the Thirteenth Regional Meeting of the Chicago Linguistic Society.* Chicago: University of Chicago.

Gary, Judith O., and Keenan, Edward L. 1977. "On Collapsing Grammatical Relations in Universal Grammar." In Cole and Sadock 1977.

Harada, S.-I. 1975. "The Functional Uniqueness Principle." *Attempts in Linguistics and Literature* 2:17–24. Society of Linguistics and Literature, International Christian University, Tokyo.

Harris, Alice C. 1976. "Grammatical Relations in Modern Georgian." Ph.D. diss., Harvard University.

———. 1981. *Georgian Syntax: A Study in Relational Grammar.* Cambridge: Cambridge University Press.

Jain, Jagdish. 1977. "The Hindi Passive in Universal Grammar." San Francisco State University.

Johnson, David E., and Postal, Paul M. 1980. *Arc Pair Grammar.* Princeton: Princeton University Press.

Keenan, Edward L. 1972. "Relative Clause Formation in Malagasy." In *The Chicago Which Hunt.* Chicago Linguistic Society, University of Chicago.

———. 1975. "Some Universals of Passive in Relational Grammar." *Papers from the Eleventh Regional Meeting of the Chicago Linguistic Society.* Department of Linguistics, University of Chicago.

———. 1976. "Remarkable Subjects in Malagasy." In Li 1976.

Kimenyi, Alexandre. 1976. "A Relational Grammar of Kinyarwanda." Ph.D. diss., UCLA.

Kisseberth, Charles, and Abasheikh, Mohammad. 1977. "The Object Relation in Chi-Mwi:ni, a Bantu Language." In Cole and Sadock 1977.

Lakoff, George. 1977. "Linguistic Gestalts." *Papers from the Thirteenth Regional Meeting of the Chicago Linguistic Society.* Department of Linguistics, University of Chicago.

Li, Charles, N. 1976. *Subject and Topic.* New York: Academic Press.

Maling, Joan, and Zaenen, Annie. 1978. "The Nonuniversality of a Surface Filter." *Linguistic Inquiry* 9:475–97.

Martinet, André. 1968. "Réflexions sur les universaux du langage." *Folia Linguistica* 1:125–34.

Perlmutter, David M. 1978. "Impersonal Passives and the Unaccusative Hypothesis." In *Proceedings of the Fourth Annual Meeting of the Berkeley Linguistics Society*. University of California, Berkeley.

————. (to appear). "Evidence for Inversion in Russian and Kannada."

Perlmutter, David M., and Postal, Paul M. 1977. "Toward a Universal Characterization of Passivization," *Proceedings of the Third Annual Meeting of the Berkeley Linguistics Society*. Reprinted in this volume.

————. (in press a). "The 1-Advancement Exclusiveness Law," in Perlmutter and Rosen (in press).

————. (in press b). "Impersonal Passives and Some Relational Laws," in Perlmutter and Rosen (in press).

Perlmutter, David M., and Rosen, Carol G. (eds.) (in press) *Studies in Relational Grammar* 2.

Postal, Paul M. 1977. "Antipassive in French." *Linguisticae Investigationes* 1:333–74.

Smith-Stark, Thom. 1976. "Ergativity, Grammatical Relations, Accessibility Hierarchies, Pocomam, and Cosmic Consciousness." Holyoke, Mass.

Zaenen, Annie. 1976. "Dutch Causatives and Relational Grammar." Harvard and MIT.

4 Indirect Objects in Kinyarwanda Revisited

Matthew S. Dryer

In a recent paper, Gary and Keenan (1977) argue that Kinyarwanda, a Bantu language spoken in Rwanda and Burundi, lacks a distinction between direct objects and indirect objects. They argue that in Kinyarwanda the grammatical relations of direct object (DO) and indirect object (IO) are collapsed into the single grammatical relation of DO and that more than one NP in a clause can bear the DO relation to the verb. In this paper, I argue that, contrary to the claims of Gary and Keenan, DO and IO *are* distinct grammatical relations in Kinyarwanda.

1 Summary of Gary and Keenan's Arguments

Let me first summarize briefly Gary and Keenan's arguments. Gary and Keenan claim that in (1), both *Maríya* 'Mary' and *íbárúwa* 'letter' are DOs.

(1) Yohaâni y-oher-er-eje   Maríya íbárúwa.
     John   he-send-BEN-ASP Mary   letter
     'John sent a letter to Mary.'

The structure of their argument is as follows. There exists a large set of properties possessed by DOs and IOs in Kinyarwanda that are not possessed by oblique NPs.[1] These include the ability to relativize, reflexivize, passivize, and, when pronominal, to be incorporated into the verb. Example (2a) illustrates reflexivization of a DO, (2b) reflexivization of an IO, (3a) passivization of a DO, (3b) passivization of an IO, (4a) incorporation of a DO pronoun, and (4b) incorporation of an IO pronoun.

Most of the data in this paper are from Kimenyi 1976. The remaining data were obtained directly from Alexandre Kimenyi in personal communication. I am greatly indebted to him for his assistance and comments. I also thank John Lawler, David Perlmutter, Rich Rhodes, and Russ Tomlin for their comments.

129

(2) a. Umukoôbwa a-r-íi-reeb-a.
        girl   she-PRES-REFL-watch-ASP
        'The girl is watching herself.'
    b. Yohaâni y-a-yi-oher-er-eje   íbárúwa.
        John   he-PAST-REFL-send-BEN-ASP letter
        'John sent himself a letter.'

(3) a. Íbárúwa y-oher-er-ej-w-e   Maríya na Yohaâni.
        letter   it-send-BEN-ASP-PASS-ASP Mary   by John
        'The letter was sent to Mary by John.'
    b. Maríya y-oher-er-ej-w-e   íbárúwa na Yohaâni.
        Mary   she-send-BEN-ASP-PASS-ASP letter   by John
        'Mary was sent a letter by John.'

(4) a. Yohaâni y-a-y-oher-er-eje   Maríya.
        John   he-PAST-it-send-BEN-ASP Mary
        'John sent it to Mary.'
    b. Yohaâni y-a-mw-oher-er-eje   íbárúwa.
        John   he-PAST-her-send-BEN-ASP letter
        'John sent a letter to her.'

Gary and Keenan show that oblique NPs cannot be relativized, reflexivized, passivized, incorporated, and so on, unless they are advanced to DO. The reader is referred to their paper for details. (A more
detailed account is given in Kimenyi 1976.)

Gary and Keenan refer to their analysis as the 'Two Objects Analysis'
(TOA). In defending the TOA, most of their discussion is directed
against what they call the 'Promotion Analysis' (PA). According to the
PA, Kinyarwanda has an obligatory dative rule which promotes IOs
to DO. One argument they give against the PA is that it would predict
that the underlying DO would be a chômeur in clauses containing an
IO, and therefore lack the various object properties. As Gary and
Keenan show, in sentences containing both a DO and an IO, both NPs
possess the various object properties. For example, (3a) and (4a) above
illustrate, respectively, the passivization and pronoun incorporation of
a DO in a clause containing an IO. Example (5) below illustrates simultaneous incorporation of DO and IO pronouns.

(5) Yohaâni y-a-yi-mw-oher-er-eje.
     John   he-PAST-it-her-send-BEN-ASP
     'John sent it to her.'

2   An Alternative Analysis

In the conclusion to their paper, Gary and Keenan mention briefly a
third hypothesis suggested to them by Peter Cole. According to this

hypothesis, DOs and IOs are distinct in Kinyarwanda; however, IOs happen to be very similar to DOs in their syntactic properties. It is this hypothesis that I will defend here. I will refer to it as the 'Indirect Object Analysis' (IOA). According to the IOA, DOs and IOs are distinct grammatical relations in Kinyarwanda. The TOA, in contrast, claims that what the IOA claims to be DOs and IOs are actually subcategories of the category DO, in Kinyarwanda.

The set of properties that distinguish DOs from IOs is rather limited. Gary and Keenan claim, without further argument, that the differences between DOs and IOs in Kinyarwanda are insufficient to justify making a distinction in grammatical category and are more naturally attributed to subcategory differences between NPs bearing the same grammatical relation to the verb. Unfortunately, this is the only argument that they give against the IOA. In the remainder of this paper, I will argue that the IOA is correct.

3   Distinguishing IOs from Benefactives

Now it is first necessary to note that there are two types of NPs in Kinyarwanda that might be considered IOs. The first type is illustrated in (6), the second type in (7).

(6) a.   Yohaâni   y-oher-er-eje   Maríya íbárúwa.
           John   he-send-BEN-ASP Mary   letter
           'John sent a letter to Mary.'
    b.   Umukoôbwa a-ra-som-er-a   umuhuûngu igitabo.
           girl   she-PRES-read-BEN-ASP boy   book
           'The girl is reading the book for the boy.'
    c.   Umugóre a-ra-kor-er-a   umugabo.
           woman   she-PRES-work-BEN-ASP man
           'The woman is working for the man.'

(7) a.   Umugabo y-a-haa-ye   umugóre igitabo.
           man   he-PAST-give-ASP woman   book
           'The man gave the book to the woman.'
    b.   Umugóre y-iim-ye   abáana ibiryo.
           woman   she-refuse-ASP children food
           'The woman refused food to the children.'
    c.   Umugabo y-eerets-e   abáana igitabo.
           man   he-show-ASP children book
           'The man showed the book to the children.'

There are two differences between the sentences in (6) and those in (7). First, in each of the sentences in (6), the verb bears a suffix -er 'benefactive'. This suffix does not occur in the sentences in (7). Second, the NPs which immediately follow the verb in (6) bear what can be described as a benefactive relationship to the verb, while the NPs which follow the verb in (7) are 'prototypical' IOs. For this reason, Kimenyi (1976) calls NPs like those in (6) 'benefactives' (Bens), and NPs like those in (7) 'indirect objects' (IOs). I will use Kimenyi's terminology for the remainder of this paper. The NPs which Gary and Keenan call IOs, and which I called IOs in §§1 and 2, are actually Bens according to this terminology.

Using Kimenyi's terminology, what Gary and Keenan claim to have shown is that Bens are a subcategory of DO. Kimenyi (1976) supports Gary and Keenan's conclusion and further argues that IOs are also a subcategory of DO. He shows that the arguments for considering Ben a subcategory of DO also apply to IOs. Thus, on Kimenyi's analysis, each of the sentences in (7) above contains two DOs.

The structure of the remainder of this paper is as follows. In §4, I outline differences between DOs and IOs that are consistent with either the TOA or the IOA. In §§5 and 6, I give two arguments that show that DOs and IOs are distinct grammatical relations in Kinyarwanda. In §7, I turn my attention to Bens and argue that Bens are also distinct from DOs.

4   Basic Differences between DOs and IOs

Let me now examine the properties that distinguish DOs from IOs in Kinyarwanda. The first is the order of DO and IO NPs. Both tend to follow the verb immediately. In sentences with both a DO and an IO, the IO normally precedes the DO, as in (7a).

The second property that distinguishes DOs from IOs is the order of pronouns incorporated into the verb. When DO and IO pronouns are simultaneously incorporated into the verb, the order is fixed: DO precedes IO, as in (8).

(8)   Umugabo y-a-ki-ba-haa-ye.
       man   he-PAST-it-them-give-ASP
       'The man gave it to them.'

It is necessary to distinguish DOs from IOs to state the order of DO and IO NPs, and the order of DO and IO pronouns incorporated into the verb. Such facts, however, are equally consistent with either the TOA or the IOA. On the IOA, they are facts about the order of DO and IO. On the TOA, they are facts about the order of the two types of DOs.

5   First Argument for the IOA, Based on Causatives

The facts from the last section are relevant to my first argument that the IOA is correct and the TOA incorrect. This argument is based on morphological causatives in Kinyarwanda. Examples (9) and (10) illustrate causative sentences.

(9) a.   Abáana ba-ra-som-a   ibitabo.
         children they-PRES-read-ASP books
         'The children are reading books.'

    b.   Umugabo a-ra-som-eesh-a   abáana ibitabo.
         man   he-PRES-read-CAUS-ASP children books
         'The man is making the children read the books.'

(10) a.   Abaantu ba-r-úubak-a   inzu.
          people   they-PRES-build-ASP house
          'The people are building the house.'

    b.   Umugabo a-r-úubak-iish-a   abaantu inzu
          man   he-PRES-build-CAUS-ASP people   house
          'The man is making the people build the house.'

Kimenyi argues that causative sentences are another case of object "doubling" in Kinyarwanda. In other words, he claims that both *abáana* 'children' and *ibitabo* 'books' are DOs in (9b). Now according to Perlmutter and Postal 1974 (and others), the normal result of causative clause union in universal grammar will be as follows: the subject (SU) of an embedded transitive clause will become the IO of the resultant clause, and the DO of the embedded clause will become the DO of the resultant clause. Thus it should not be surprising that causative sentences in Kinyarwanda should be candidates for object doubling.

Now the TOA makes no prediction about the order of the two object NPs in causative sentences, nor about the order of pronouns incorporated into the verb. The IOA, however, predicts that the SU of the embedded clause should have the properties of an IO in the resultant clause, and the DO in the embedded clause should have the properties of a DO in the resultant clause. In other words, the IOA predicts that the SU of the embedded clause should precede the DO of the embedded clause in the resultant clause. This prediction is confirmed by (9b) and (10b). In (9b), *abáana* 'children' is the SU of the embedded clause and hence the IO in the resultant clause, and should therefore precede *ibitabo* 'books'.

The IOA also predicts, correctly, the order of pronouns incorporated into the verb.

(11) Umugabo a-ra-yí-b-uubak-iish-a.
      man   he-PRES-it-them-build-CAUS-ASP
      'The man is making them build it.'

In (11), -yi- 'it' is the DO of the embedded clause and hence DO of the resultant clause. The element -b- 'them' is the SU of the embedded clause and hence IO of the resultant clause. The fact that -yi- precedes -b- is explained by the IOA: incorporated DO pronouns precede incorporated IO pronouns.

Thus the IOA correctly predicts these facts about Kinyarwanda causatives, whereas the TOA makes no prediction at all.

6   Second Argument for the IOA, Based on Locative Advancement

The second argument for the IOA over the TOA is stronger than the first argument. In this second case, not only does the IOA make the correct prediction, but furthermore, the TOA makes the wrong prediction.

Kinyarwanda has a rule, mentioned by Gary and Keenan, but discussed at much greater length by Kimenyi (1976), which advances locatives to DO. This rule relates (12a) to (12b) and (13a) to (13b).

(12) a.   Umwáana y-a-taa-ye   igitabo mu máazi.
          child   he-PAST-throw-ASP book   in water
          'The child has thrown the book into the water.'
     b.   Umwáana y-a-taa-yé-mo   amáazi igitabo.
          child   he-PAST-throw-ASP-in water   book
          'The child has thrown the book into the water.'

(13) a.   Umwáalímu y-oohere-je igitabo kw-iishuûri.
          teacher   he-send-ASP book   to-school
          'The teacher sent the book to the school.'
     b.   Umwáalímu y-oohere-jé-ho ishuûri igitabo.
          teacher   he-send-ASP-to school book
          'The teacher sent the book to the school.'

When a locative NP is advanced to DO, the underlying DO loses its object properties, as predicted by the Relational Annihilation Law of Perlmutter and Postal 1974 (and the Chômeur Condition of Perlmutter and Postal 1977). Thus of the two postverbal NPs in (13b), only the underlying locative NP *ishuûri* 'school' possesses the various object properties. This is demonstrated by the examples in (14) through (16). Example (14) demonstrates it with passivization, (15) with pronoun incorporation, and (16) with relativization. The grammaticality of the a-examples in (14) through (16) demonstrates that the underlying locative NP *ishuûri* 'school' has acquired the various object properties. The ungrammaticality of the b-examples demonstrates that the underlying DO *igitabo* 'book' has lost the various object properties.

(14) a. Ishuûri ry-oohere-j-w-é-ho   igitabo n-úmwáalímu.
         school it-send-ASP-PASS-ASP-to book by-teacher
         'The school was sent the book to by the teacher.'
     b. *Igitabo cy-oohere-j-w-é-ho   ishuûri n-úmwáalímu.
         book   it-send-ASP-PASS-ASP-to school by-teacher
         (The book was sent to the school by the teacher.)

(15) a. Umwáalímu y-a-ry-oohere-jé-ho   igitabo.
         teacher   he-PAST-it-send-ASP-to book
         'The teacher sent the book to it.'
     b. *Umwáalímu y-a-cy-oohere-jé-ho   ishuûri.
         teacher   he-PAST-it-send-ASP-to school
         (The teacher sent it to the school.)

(16) a. Umugabo y-a-tw-eerets-e   ishuûri umwáalímu
         man   he-PAST-us-show-ASP school teacher
         y-oóhere-jé-ho   igitabo.
         he-send(REL)-ASP-to book
         'The man showed us the school to which the teacher sent the book.'
     b. *Y-a-tw-eerets-e   igitabo umwáalímu
         he-PAST-us-show-ASP book   teacher
         y-oóhere-jé-ho   ishuûri.
         he-send(REL)-ASP-to school
         (He showed us the book that the teacher sent to the school.)

These facts are consistent with both the TOA and the IOA.

The TOA and the IOA make different predictions, however, about what will happen in clauses with an IO in which a locative NP gets advanced to DO. This possibility is illustrated in (17).

(17) a. Umugabo y-eerets-e   umukoóbwa ibíryo mw-iíshuûri.
         man   he-show-ASP girl   food   in-school
         'The man showed food to the girl in the school.'
     b. Umugabo y-eerets-é-mo   ishuûri umukoôbwa ibíryo.
         man   he-show-ASP-in school girl   food
         'The man showed food to the girl in the school.'

Both the IOA and the TOA predict that in (17b), the underlying DO *ibíryo* 'food' will be a chômeur and lack object properties. However, the IOA predicts that *umukoôbwa* 'girl' in (17b) will still possess the object properties because it is an IO, not a DO. Since the locative is being advanced to DO, not to IO, only the DO should become a chômeur. The TOA, however, predicts that *umukoôbwa* 'girl' should also be a chômeur in (17b), since according to the TOA, both *ibíryo* 'food' and *umukoôbwa* 'girl' are DOs in (17a). The examples in (18) through (20) show that it is the IOA that makes the correct predictions. Example (18) shows that the underlying DO *ibíryo* 'food' has lost its ability to be advanced to SU by Passive, but that the IO *umukoôbwa* 'girl' and the locative advanced to DO *ishuûri* 'school' can both be advanced to SU by passive. Examples (19) and (20) show analogous facts for pronoun incorporation and relativization, respectively.

(18) a. Ishuûri ry-eerets-w-é-mo   umukoôbwa ibíryo n-úmugabo.
     school it-show-PASS-ASP-in girl   food by-man
     Lit.: 'The school was showed-in food to the girl by the man.'

   b. Umukoôbwa y-eerets-w-é-mo   ishuûri ibíryo
       girl   she-show-PASS-ASP-in school food
       n-úmugabo.
       by-man
       'The girl was shown food in the school by the man.'

   c. *Ibíryo by-eerets-w-é-mo   ishuûri umukoôbwa n-úmugabo.
       food   it-show-PASS-ASP-in school girl   by-man
       (The food was shown to the girl in the school by the man.)

(19) a. Umugabo y-a-ry-eerets-é-mo   umukoôbwa ibíryo.
     man   he-PAST-it-show-ASP-in girl   food
     'The man showed food to the girl in it.'

   b. Umugabo y-a-mw-eerets-é-mo   ishuûri ibíryo.
       man   he-PAST-her-show-ASP-in school food
       'The man showed food to her in the school.'

   c. *Umugabo y-a-by-eerets-é-mo   ishuûri umukoôbwa.
       man   he-PAST-it-show-ASP-in school girl
       (The man showed it to the girl in the school.)

(20) a. N-a-boon-ye   ishuûri umugabo y-eérets-é-mo
     I-PAST-see-ASP school man   he-show(REL)-ASP-in
     umukoôbwa ibíryo.
     girl   food
     'I saw the school in which the man showed food to the girl.'

   b. N-a-boon-ye   umukoôbwa umugabo y-eérets-é-mo
       I-PAST-see-ASP girl   man   he-show(REL)-ASP-in
       ishuûri ibíryo.
       school food
       'I saw the girl to whom the man showed the food in the school.'

    c. *N-a-boon-ye   ibíryo umugabo y-eérets-é-mo
      I-PAST-see-ASP food   man   he-show(REL)-ASP-in
      ishuûri umukoôbwa.
      school girl
      (I saw the food which the man showed to the girl in the school.)

These facts are completely mysterious under the TOA but are explained naturally by the IOA, in conjunction with the Relational Annihilation Law: the advancement of a locative NP to DO should place an underlying DO en chômage but leave an IO unaffected. It is necessary to conclude that DOs and IOs are distinct grammatical relations in Kinyarwanda.[2]

7 Benefactives

Let us turn now to Kinyarwanda benefactives, which Gary and Keenan refer to as "putative IOs" and which they use as the basis of their argument that Kinyarwanda lacks a distinction between DOs and IOs. Since I have demonstrated that DOs and IOs are in fact distinct in Kinyarwanda, Gary and Keenan's claim must be modified to say that DOs and Bens are not distinct in Kinyarwanda. Thus on this modification of their analysis, in (21), both *umugabo* 'man' and *ibíryo* 'food' would be DOs and *ímbwa* 'dog' would be IO.

(21) Umugóre a-ra-hé-er-a   umugabo ímbwa ibíryo.
       woman she-PRES-give-BEN-ASP man   dog   food
       'The woman is giving food to the dog for the man.'

Kimenyi (1976) shows that all three of the postverbal NPs in (21), *umugabo* 'man', *ímbwa* 'dog', and *ibíryo* 'food', possess the various 'object' properties. For example, all three can be incorporated into the verb as pronouns, as in (22).

(22) Umugóre a-ra-bi-yí-mu-he-er-a.
       woman she-PRES-it(DO)-it(IO)-him(BEN)-give-BEN-ASP
       'The woman is giving it to it for him.'

   It is possible to show that Bens are distinct from DOs, just as IOs are distinct from DOs. As Kimenyi shows, locatives can be advanced to DO in clauses containing Bens but only if the clause lacks an underlying DO. Thus locative advancement relates (23a) to (23b).

(23) a. Umwáana y-iicar-i-ye   umugabo kuú ntebe.
         child   he-sit-BEN-ASP man   on   chair
        'The child is sitting on the chair for the man.'
    b. Umwáana y-iicar-i-yé-ho   íntebe umugabo.
        child   he-sit-BEN-ASP-on chair man
        'The child is sitting on the chair for the man.'

It is crucial that the advancement in (23) does not cause the Ben to lose its 'object' properties. Example (24) shows that Passive can apply to either of the postverbal NPs in (23b). Examples (25) and (26) show the same for pronoun incorporation and relativization, respectively.

(24) a. Íntebe y-iicar-i-w-é-ho   umugabo n-uúmwáana.
        chair   it-sit-BEN-PASS-ASP-on man   by-child
        'The chair is sat on for the man by the child.'

  b. Umugabo y-iicar-i-w-é-ho   íntebe n-uúmwáana.
        man   he-sit-BEN-PASS-ASP-on chair   by-child
        Lit.: 'The man is sat-on-the-chair-for by the child.'

(25) a. Umwáana a-mw-iicar-i-yé-ho   íntebe.
        child   he-him-sit-BEN-ASP-on chair
        'The child is sitting on the chair for him.'

  b. Umwáana a-y-iicar-i-yé-ho   umugabo.
        child   he-it-sit-BEN-ASP-on man
        'The child is sitting on it for the man.'

(26) a. N-a-boon-ye   íntebe umwáana y-iicar-i-yé-ho
        I-PAST-see-ASP chair   child   he-sit(REL)-BEN-ASP-on
        umugabo.
        man
        'I saw the chair that the child was sitting on for the man.'

  b. N-a-boon-ye   umugabo umwáana
        I-PAST-see-ASP man   child
        y-iicar-i-yé-ho   íntebe.
        he-sit(REL)-BEN-ASP-on chair
        'I saw the man that the child was sitting on the chair for.'

These examples show that locative advancement does not cause a Ben to lose its 'object' properties. This contrasts with the fact, demonstrated in §6, that locative advancement does cause a DO to lose its 'object' properties.[3] As in the case with IOs, these facts can be naturally explained if we interpret the benefactive NP in (22) as a Ben rather than as a second DO, as claimed by Gary and Keenan. The advancement of a locative NP to DO should place an underlying DO (if there is one) en chômage but leave a Ben unaffected. This is exactly what happens, as demonstrated above.

8 Conclusion

We must conclude then that, contrary to the claims of Gary and Keenan, both IO and Ben are distinct from DO in Kinyarwanda, and that Kinyarwanda does not provide evidence against the Stratal Uniqueness Law of Perlmutter and Postal (1977), which states, in effect, that no more than one NP in a clause can bear the same grammatical relation to the verb at a single point in the derivation. The host of properties shared by DOs, IOs, and Bens are not properties that characterize DOs alone, but rather properties that characterize a continuous segment of the relational hierarchy that includes DOs, IOs, and Bens. The properties shared by DOs, IOs, and Bens include the ability to passivize, reflexivize, relativize, and, when pronominal, to be incorporated into the verb.[4] The properties that distinguish DOs, IOs, and Bens include their word order, the order of pronouns incorporated into the verb, the effect of locative advancement, and, in the case of Bens, the presence of a benefactive suffix on the verb.

I hope that I have shown that the fact that DOs and IOs are very similar does not mean that they are the same. Although DOs and IOs may share a host of properties, a single argument, such as the one given in §6, is enough to show that the two are distinct.

I do not claim to have solved all the mysteries of grammatical relations in Kinyarwanda. Kimenyi (1976) discusses many other examples of phenomena in Kinyarwanda that appear to bring into question many of the claims of relational grammar. I only claim to have shown that one set of facts is consistent with the theory when examined with greater scrutiny.

Notes

1. I use the terms 'direct object' (DO) and 'indirect object' (IO) to refer to those NPs which are underlying DOs and IOs if I am correct that the two are distinct. Even in Gary and Keenan's analysis, there exist two subclasses of DO, which they refer to by the terms "patient" and "recipient." My use of the terms DO and IO is the same as that in Kimenyi 1976.

2. A possible rejoinder might be as follows: The TOA allows there to be two DOs in a clause; hence when a locative is advanced to DO, only one of the underlying DOs need be placed en chômage. One of the underlying DOs could remain a DO, since that would leave two DOs in the clause, which is consistent with the TOA.

The most obvious problem with this is that the TOA would still fail to predict which DO would become a chômeur. The IOA correctly predicts that the NP which the IOA claims is the DO, not the IO, will become a chômeur.

Worse still, the hypothesis that there can be two DOs in a clause completely fails to make the correct predictions elsewhere in the language. As Kimenyi shows, it is possible for there to be three NPs in a clause all possessing the various object properties. (Sentences (21) and (22) in this paper are examples of such.) Furthermore, the hypothesis would seem to predict that the application of locative advancement in a clause with only one DO would not cause that DO to become a chômeur. But this is false, as illustrated by the examples in (14) through (16) of this paper.

3. Note that I cannot illustrate this fact as neatly as I could illustrate the fact that locative advancement causes DOs to lose their 'object' properties but

does not cause IOs to lose their 'object' properties. It is possible to illustrate the latter fact by demonstrating the effect of locative advancement in a sentence containing both a DO and an IO, as I did in (18) through (20). This is not possible in the case of Bens, since locative advancement is not possible in a clause containing both a DO and a Ben. Instead, I have had to illustrate the effect of locative advancement on DOs in (14) through (16) and the effect of locative advancement on Bens separately in (24) through (26). The logic of the argument is just as strong with Bens as it is with IOs, although it may not be as pleasing aesthetically.

4. It follows that the rule I am calling Passive is actually a rule that advances any of DO, IO, or Ben to SU.

References

Gary, Judith, and Keenan, Edward. 1977. "On Collapsing Grammatical Relations in Universal Grammar." In Peter Cole and Jerrold Sadock, eds., *Syntax and Semantics 8: Grammatical Relations*. New York: Academic Press.

Kimenyi, Alexandre. 1976. "A Relational Grammar of Kinyarwanda." Ph.D. diss., UCLA. A revised version was published by the University of California Press in 1980.

Perlmutter, David, and Postal, Paul. 1974. Lectures on Relational Grammar at Summer Linguistics Institute of the Linguistic Society of America, Amherst, Mass.

————. 1977. "Toward a Universal Characterization of Passivization." In *Proceedings of the Third Annual Meeting of the Berkeley Linguistics Society*.

Part 2

5 Advancements and Ascensions in Cebuano

Sarah J. Bell

Advancements

1 **Subjects in Verb-Containing Sentences**

1.1 The Voice System in Cebuano

Like most other Philippine languages, Cebuano[1] is a verb-initial language with a rich voice system. A simple verb-containing sentence consists of a verb followed by a series of nominal phrases.

The verb consists of a stem plus affixes which show mode (real or unreal), aspect (durative, potential, or volitional), and voice (active, objective, locative, and instrumental). Details of verbal affixes are found in Appendix A.

The nominals are marked for nominative, genitive, or oblique case. Pronouns have different forms for the different cases. The case of other nominals is marked by a particle which precedes the rest of the nominal. Details about case marking are found in Appendix B.

The different voices are used to mark different relationships of the nominative nominal in the clause. To see how voice and case are coordinated, let us look at the different sentences that could be used to say that a definite woman will cook rice in the ricepot.

In a sentence with an active verb (marked by *mag-*), *babaye* 'the woman' is in the nominative case.

(1) *Mag*luto' *ang babaye ug bugas sa kulon.*
     ACT-cook NOM woman OBL rice OBL ricepot
     'The woman will cook rice in the ricepot.'

With many verbs, the nominative nominal in an active sentence designates the one performing the action. The nominative nominal in an active sentence is frequently referred to as the 'actor' in consequence. As shown in (2), the so-called actor need not be an agent.

143

(2) *Naka*dawat *si   Fred* ug libro gikan kang Tomas.
     ACT-receive NOM Fred OBL book from OBL Tomas
     'Fred received a book from Tomas.'

Moreover, it may even be an abstraction, as in (3):

(3) Wolff 1972
     *Mi*santup sa   iyang bu'ut *ang usa ka sayun nga pa'agi.*
     ACT-enter OBL his-LN mind NOM one LN easy   LN way
     'An easy way (of doing it) came to his mind.'

'Actor' is therefore a misleading name. I will later propose that the so-called actor is the initial subject. However, until the proposal is made and supported, I will retain the term 'actor', despite the inaccuracy of its semantic content, to designate the nominal which is nominative in an active sentence or the active correlate of a sentence.

In the situation with the woman cooking rice in the ricepot, if a definitely determined rice is involved, *bugas* 'rice' may be in the nominative case. The verb will then be in the objective voice, and the actor will be in the genitive case, the case always used with nonnominative actors.

(4) Luto'*on* sa   babaye *ang bugas* sa   kulon.
     cook-OBJ GEN woman NOM rice   OBL ricepot
     'The rice will be cooked in a ricepot by the woman.'

The ricepot may also be chosen as the nominative nominal. It will then follow the actor. The verb will be in the locative voice, as in (5).

(5) Luto'*an* sa   babaye *ang kulon*   ug bugas.
     cook-LOC GEN woman NOM ricepot OBL rice
     'The woman will cook rice in *the ricepot.*'

(In this sentence and others in which the nominative cannot be the subject of an English sentence, I will simply italicize the English translation of the Cebuano nominative, without changing the voice in English.)

The locative is also used when an initial indirect object is selected as the nominative nominal. In (6a), the verb is active, and the indirect object *Perla* is in the oblique case. When the initial indirect object is nominative, the verb is in the locative voice, as in (6b).

(6) a. Mosulat si   Inday ug sulat kang Perla.
         ACT-write NOM Inday OBL letter OBL Perla
         'Inday will write a letter to Perla.'

b. Sulatan   ni   Inday si   Perla ug   sulat.
    write-LOC GEN Inday NOM Perla OBL letter
    'Perla will be written a letter by Inday.'

With verbs which do not take an initial indirect object, the locative voice may be used if an initial benefactive is chosen as the nominative nominal. In (7a), an active sentence, the benefactive is in a prepositional phrase *para kang Pedro* 'for Pedro'. When the initial benefactive is in the nominative case, the verb may be in the locative voice, as in (7b).

(7) a. Moluto' si   Maria ug   kalamay   para kang
         ACT-cook NOM Maria OBL brown-sugar candy for   OBL
         Pedro.
         Pedro
         'Maria will cook some candy for Pedro.'
    b. Luto'an   ni   Maria si   Pedro ug   kalamay.
         cook-LOC GEN Maria NOM Pedro OBL candy
         'Pedro will be cooked candy by Maria.'

This use of the locative voice will be discussed later in §3.3.2.[2]

The remaining voice is the instrumental voice. It is a residual voice used when the nominative nominal is not the actor, an initial 2, an initial 3, or an initial locative.[3] For example, it is used when an initial instrument is in the nominative case. In (8a), the instrument is found in the phrase *gigamit ang lapis* 'a pencil being used'.[4] In (8b), the instrument is the nominative nominal for the whole sentence, and the verb is in the instrumental voice.

(8) a. Mosulat   si   Linda ug   sulat gigamit   ang lapis.
         ACT-write NOM Linda OBL write being used NOM pencil
         'Linda will write a letter with the pencil.'
    b. Isulat   ni   Linda ang lapis ug   sulat.
         INS-write GEN Linda NOM pencil OBL letter
         'Linda will write a letter with *the pencil*.'

The instrumental voice may also be used when an initial benefactive is in the nominative case, chiefly in requests, to which it imparts a high degree of politeness.

(9) a. Motawag ka   ug   taksi para sa   ako'.
         ACT-call you-NOM OBL taxi for   OBL I-GEN
         'Call a taxi for me.'
    b. Itawag ra   mo   ako   ug   taksi.
         INS-call only you-GEN I-NOM OBL taxi
         'Please call *me* a taxi.'

As a third example, the instrumental voice is used when the nominative nominal gives the suitable time for an action.

(10) a. Mogikan ang barko sa alas   sayis.
    ACT-from NOM ship   OBL o'clock 6
    'The ship will leave at 6 o'clock.'
  b. Igikan   sa barko ang alas   sayis.
    INS-from GEN ship   NOM o'clock 6
    'The ship leaves at 6 o'clock.'

This use is rare, except in relative clauses. According to Wolff (1966, 10A4, p. 385), only the unreal mode is found in such sentences.

In summary, the voice depends on the role of the nominative nominal in the sentence. If it is the actor, the verb is in the active voice. Objective voice is used when the initial direct object is in the nominative. If the nominative nominal is an initial indirect object or an initial locative, the verb is in the locative voice. Either locative or instrumental voice may be used when an initial benefactive is in the nominative case. Elsewhere, the instrumental voice is used.[5]

1.2   The Question of Subjects

Early American descriptions of Philippine languages assumed that the nominative nominal (or the nominative nominal in topicalized position) was the subject of the sentence (Blake 1904, Bloomfield 1917). For instance, in writing about Tagalog, Bloomfield calls *ang aklat* 'the book' the subject in (11).

(11) *Ibini*gay niya   sa akin *ang aklat.*
    INS-give he-GEN LOC I-obl NOM book
    'The book was given by him to me.'

Bloomfield (1917, p. 154) noted that while in English the active construction is generally preferred, in Tagalog "the active construction is avoided whenever any other than the actor is available as subject." He found a correlation between the nominative nominal and the bearer of old information. As he put it, "the definite known object [i.e., substantive, more or less] underlying the predication as starting-point of discourse is chosen as subject."

The predominance of the new/old information organization as a factor in selecting the nominal to be nominative eventually led to regarding the nominative as the 'topic' of the sentence rather than the subject. The change was introduced by McKaughan (1958) and paralleled an earlier shift from 'voice' to 'focus' as a name for the verbal category we have been discussing.[6] The topic is characterized as "the thing which the sentence is about'' by Bowen (1965, p. 182). It is said to be ''highlighted'' (Dean 1958, p. 59) or ''foremost in the speaker's mind'' (Bowen 1965, p. 182) or even ''the most important element in the sentence'' (Interchurch Language School 1962, p. 62, §1.312).

Kess (1975) has noted the distortions caused by the use of the terms 'topic' and 'focus'. He points out, for example, that some authors apparently confuse one or the other with emphasis. As Bloomfield's more sober statement implies, the nominative is ''foremost in the speaker's mind'' as being known or predictable or having background information, not as being the most important or emphatic element.

Besides leading some people astray, referring to the nominative nominal as the topic is inaccurate. Dahl (1976, p. 120) points out that the bearer of old information and the nominative nominal do not coincide in relative clauses.[7] Schachter (1976, pp. 496–97) gives additional constructions with nonnominative topics. Coincidence of nominative nominal and topic, then, is a tendency, not a rule. Recognition of this fact led McKaughan (1973) to abandon his innovative use of *topic* and analyze the nominative nominal as the subject, but so far, his innovation has attracted more followers than his retraction, and the nominative nominal is still analyzed as topic by many Philippinists.

Those who call the nominative nominal the topic have dealt in different ways with the question of what is the subject. Some, for example Wolfenden (1961), do not mention subjects at all, apparently taking the position that Philippine languages differ from other languages of the world in having topics rather than subjects. Others, for example Reid (1966), consider the actor the subject in active and nonactive sentences alike. Schachter (1976) argues that Philippine languages have no single nominal as subject, subject properties being shared by the nominative nominal and the actor.

In brief, then, the following views about the subject in Philippine languages are current: (1) the nominative nominal is the subject; (2) the actor is the subject in active and nonactive sentences; (3) the nominative nominal and actor together correspond to the subject in other languages; (4) Philippine languages do not have subjects.

1.3   Proposal for an Analysis

Does Cebuano have subjects? If so, is the subject of a verb-containing sentence the nominative nominal or the actor? These questions cannot be answered in a vacuum, but only in a theory in which the notion of 'subject' has some role to play. In what follows, I will show that the questions can be given a consistent answer in the theory of relational grammar. In that theory, the actor is the initial subject, the nominative nominal is the final subject, and active sentences are related to their nonactive counterparts by having identical initial strata in their networks, the networks differing in that those of the nonactive sentences involve advancements and hence at least one additional stratum. Before this proposal can be elaborated and illustrated, however, a few comments about the theoretical framework may be helpful.

1.3.1   *The Framework*

The proposal for the analysis of subjects in verb-containing sentences of Cebuano was stated above in the terminology of the uninetwork version of relational grammar sketched in Perlmutter and Postal (1977) (see chap. 1, above). With certain modifications, this is the version used in the rest of the paper.

In the uninetwork version, as in other versions, grammatical relations are of primary importance in the theory. Clausal grammatical relations are divided into two main sorts: central relations and overlay relations; see (13) in chap. 3, above. Overlay relations include relations such as 'topic', a relation that will be used later. A nominal may bear an overlay relation in a clause in which it does not bear a central relation.

Central relations are further subdivided into oblique and pure relations. The oblique relations include benefactive (Ben), locative (Loc), instrumental (Instr), and so on.

The pure relations are the term relations and the retirement relations, the latter class consisting of the chômeur relation and the emeritus relation.[8] The term relations are subject (1), direct object (2), and indirect object (3). Chômeurs in one stratum are dependents which are terms in an earlier stratum.

Chômeurs, emeriti, and nominals bearing oblique grammatical relations are referred to collectively as nonterms. The terms are distinguished from nonterms because there are certain syntactic processes in which only terms participate. The central relations are arranged in a hierarchy in which the terms outrank the nonterms:

(12)   Relational hierarchy: $1 > 2 > 3 >$ nonterms

Associated with each sentence is a network of arcs. Perlmutter and Postal (chap. 1) give a technical definition of an arc as consisting of a governing node, a dependent node, a relation sign (the name of the grammatical relation of the dependent to the governor), and coordinates specifying the strata in which the dependent bears the relation. They show how the information in technically defined arcs can be represented in stratal diagrams by showing the sequences of grammatical relations of each dependent to a given governor in successive strata. In stratal diagrams, the lines on which the successive relations of a dependent to a governor are written are also called arcs. I will use these arcs throughout in informal or semiformal statements of rules.

Rules are well-formedness conditions on networks. Two types of rules will be used in this paper: advancements and ascensions.

An advancement rule states that there may (or must) be a transition from one grammatical relation to a relation higher in the hierarchy on the arc of a dependent. For example, the rule of Passive permits a transition from 2 to 1. It can be stated semiformally as shown below:

(13) Passive:
       If a is a 2 of clause b in stratum c_i, it may be a 1 of clause b in stratum c_{i+1}.

Alternatively, the permitted transition may simply be displayed.

(14) Passive
       The following transition is permitted:

Paired with Passive will be a marking rule.

(15) Voice Marking Rule:
       If a is a predicate of clause b and the arc of some dependent of b shows a transition 2–1, then a is in the passive voice.

The Voice Marking Rule does not mark the verb, but specifies what the voice marking must be for the network to be well-formed. In the stratal diagram, the voice is shown as bearing the relation 'voice' (V) to the verb stem.

Passive and the Voice Marking Rule above are among the rules which accept the network represented in stratal diagram (16) as well-formed.

(16)

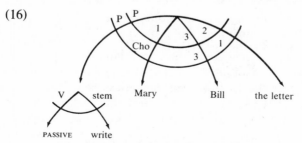

'The letter was written by Mary to Bill.'

Case marking rules, stated in terms of grammatical relations, are also conditions on well-formed networks. In the stratal diagrams, the case is shown as bearing the relation 'case' (C) to the noun that bears the head (H) relation to a nominal node.

The representations of case and voice in stratal diagrams are tentative. When not of direct interest, they will be omitted.

An ascension rule states that a dependent of a dependent of a clause may itself be a dependent of the clause in a later stratum. The dependent of a dependent which becomes the dependent of the clause is called the 'ascendee'. The dependent from which it ascends is called the 'host'. Subject Raising is an example of an ascension rule. It can be stated semiformally as:

(17)   Subject Raising
       If *a* is a 1 of clause *b* and *b* is a 1 of clause *c,* then *a* may be a
       1 of *c.*

The grammar will include information about which predicates govern Subject Raising. In English, for instance, 'likely' will be marked as governing the rule. Ignoring the question of the internal relations of 'is likely' and 'to win', Subject Raising will be among the rules which accept the network shown in (18) as well-formed.

(18)

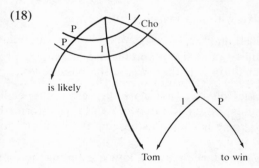

'Tom is likely to win.'

Any rule sanctioning transitions along an arc may have consequences for the status of transitions along other arcs, in accordance with the Chômeur Condition (chap. 1):

(19)   Chômeur Condition
       If a network contains a subnetwork of the form

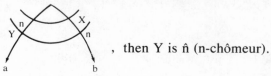   , then Y is ñ (n-chômeur).

To slip back into derivational terminology, when a term's grammatical relation is assumed by another dependent, it becomes a chômeur (goes en chômage). In the stratal diagram for 'The letter was written by Mary to Bill', shown in (16), there is one such subnetwork, given in (20) below.

(20)

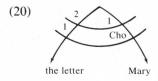

the letter   Mary

Certain rules are restricted to apply only to terms in a given stratum. Such rules, of course, do not apply to chômeurs in that stratum. Rules which apply generally to central dependents or to nonterms in particular may apply to chômeurs.

A marking rule may specify the marking used for the chômeurs created by a given rule. Otherwise, the chômeur's marking follows the Chômeur Marking Principle:

(21)   Chômeur Marking Principle
Unless otherwise specified, an n-chômeur is subject to the same marking rules as an n.

In addition to the conditions regarding chômeurs, advancement rules and ascensions are subject to certain laws. The 1-Advancement Exclusiveness Law (22a) and the Host Limitation and Relational Succession Laws (22b) will be of importance here:

(22) a.   The 1-Advancement Exclusiveness Law:
There can be at most one advancement to 1 per clause.[9]
  b.   The Host Limitation Law:
Only terms can serve as hosts;
  c.   Relational Succession Law:
An ascendee takes on the grammatical relation of its host. (See chap. 2, above).

Besides these general conditions on rules, there are conditions on particular rules. One of the common conditions is that a particular rule applies only to dependents above a certain rank in the heirarchy. Such a rule might apply to all dependents in one language, to terms in a second, to subjects and direct objects (nuclear terms) in a third, and only to subjects in a fourth. It would not apply to, say, just direct objects or just direct objects and indirect objects. Rules which are restricted in this manner are said to be subject to line-drawing (Perlmutter and Postal 1974).

1.3.2   *Preliminary Statement of the Proposal*

Now that the framework has been sketched, it is possible to state the proposal more fully, although detailed consideration of the exact form of the rules involved will be postponed to §3, which follows the arguments in favor of the analysis.

I am proposing that the so-called actor in the active sentence is the initial subject, that the nominative nominal is the final subject, and that the networks of nonactive sentences contain transitions to 1 sanctioned by advancement rules.

In an active sentence, the initial and final subject will be one and the same. The network for sentence (1) can accordingly be represented as shown in stratal diagram (23).

(23)

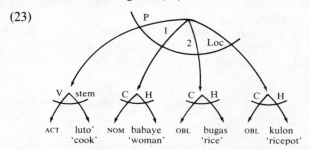

In a nonactive sentence, the arc of one of the dependents will show a transition from some other grammatical relation to 1. The diagram for (4), in which *bugas* 'rice' is the final subject, will be as shown in (24).

(24)

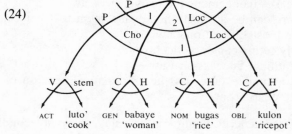

In accordance with the Chômeur Condition, the initial 1 is a final 1-chômeur in nonactive sentences. In sentence (5), *kulon* 'ricepot' is the final 1. Its arc will show a transition from locative to 1, as illustrated in (25).

(25)

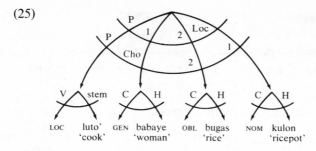

	LOC	GEN	OBL	NOM
	luto'	babaye	bugas	kulon
	'cook'	'woman'	'rice'	'ricepot'

As a final example, the stratal diagram for (10b), in which the temporal is the final 1, will be (26).

(26)

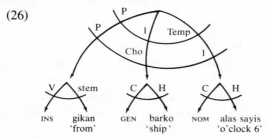

	INS	GEN	NOM
	gikan	barko	alas sayis
	'from'	'ship'	'o'clock 6'

In §2, I give arguments to support the proposal. Arguments based on Quantifier Float and accessibility of dependents to relativization are given to establish that the nominative nominal is the final subject. Next, it is shown that the actor behaves like a subject in Reflexivization and Equi, supporting my claim that it is the initial subject.[10] Finally, an argument is given that advancement rules sanction the transitions to 1 in the networks of nonactive sentences.

The form of the advancement rules and the case and voice marking rules are discussed in §3. Finally, I reply to Schachter's (1976) arguments against this analysis in §4. The analysis of ascension rules begins with §5.

2 Arguments for the Analysis
2.1 Arguments That the Nominative Nominal Is the Final 1
2.1.1 *The Argument from Quantifier Float*

It has been proposed that a rule of Quantifier Float relates the pairs in sentences (27–29):[11]

(27) a.   All the men are coming.
　　 b.   The men are all coming.
(28) a.   Each man was hurrying.
　　 b.   The men were each hurrying.

(29) a.   Both the boys will arrive tonight.
     b.   The boys will both arrive tonight.

Perlmutter and Postal (1974) proposed that Quantifier Float is subject to line-drawing. In English, for example, the line is drawn at 1. Quantifiers can float only from final subjects.

(30) *Tom was all reading the books.

Perlmutter and Postal observed that in Japanese the line is drawn at 2 and in French the line is drawn at 3.[12]

Assuming that Quantifier Float is governed by line-drawing, it follows that if quantifiers can float only from a single dependent, that dependent is the subject.

2.1.2   *Quantifier Float in Cebuano*

In Cebuano, the quantifier *tanan* 'all', and apparently only this quantifier, can float from its nominal phrase and follow the verb. In postverbal position, it is interpreted as having come from the nominative nominal. I conclude that the nominative nominal is a subject.

To establish this claim, it is necessary to show that the quantifier does float. This in turn requires us to look at adjectives in Cebuano.

In Cebuano, an adjective may precede or follow its head. It is linked to the head by the linker (LN) *nga* (*ng* after vowels, glottal stops, or nasals) in either position. If *nga* is absent, then the adjective and the noun are not part of a single nominal. In (31c), for example, *pula* 'red' is the predicate.

(31) a.   bulak nga pula
           flower LN red
           'red flower'
     b.   pulang bulak
           red-LN flower
           'red flower'
     c.   Pula ang bulak.
           red NOM flower
           'The flower is red.'

The quantifier *tanan* 'all' is usually found within its nominal. Like other adjectives, it may appear before or after the noun. When it precedes the noun, as in (32a), it follows the case marking particle. In either position, it is linked to the noun by *nga*. *Tanan* 'all', but no other quantifier, can also appear in postverbal position.

(32) a. Ningdagan ang tanan nga bata'.
ACT-run NOM all LN child
'All the children ran off.'

   b. Ningdagan ang batang tanan.
ACT-run NOM child-LN all
'All the children ran off.'

   c. Ningdagan *tanan* ang *bata'*.
ACT-run all NOM child
'The children all ran off.'

When it follows the verb, *tanan* is outside the nominal, for it precedes the case marking particle and is not attached to the noun by *nga*. The quantifier, that is to say, has floated from its nominal.

A quantifier found in postverbal position is construed with the nominative nominal and with it alone.[13]

(33) a. Nagbasa *tanan ang istudiente* sa mga libro ni Rizal.
ACT-read all NOM student OBL PL book GEN Rizal
'The students were all reading Rizal's books.'

   b. Gibasa *tanan* sa mga istudiente *ang mga libro*
OBJ-read all GEN PL student NOM PL book
ni Rizal.
GEN Rizal
'Rizal's books were all being read by the students.'

(34) a. Nagbutang *tanan ang mga babaye* sa mga pinggan
ACT-place all NOM PL woman OBL PL dish
sa mga lamisa.
OBL PL table
'The women were all putting the dishes on the tables.'

   b. Gibutangan *tanan* sa mga babaye *ang mga lamisa*
place-LOC all GEN PL woman NOM PL table
ug mga pinggan.
OBL PL dish
'The tables were all having dishes put on them by the women.'

(35) a. Nagluto' *tanan ang mga babaye* ug dulsi para
ACT-cook all NOM PL woman OBL candy for
sa mga bata'.
OBL PL child
'The women were all cooking candy for the children.'

b. Giluto'an *tanan* sa   mga babaye *ang mga bata'*
cook-LOC all   GEN PL   woman NOM PL   child
ug   dulsi.
OBL candy
'The children were all cooked candy by the women.'

Tanan may also precede the verb. In such a position, it is still construed with the nominative nominal.

(36) a. *Tanan* nagluto' *ang mga babaye* ug   dulsi   para sa
all   ACT-cook NOM PL   woman OBL candy for   OBL
mga bata'.
PL   child
'The women were all cooking candy for the children.'

b. *Tanan* giluto'an sa   mga babaye *ang mga bata'*
all   cook-LOC GEN PL   woman NOM PL   child
ug   dulsi.
OBL candy
'The children were all cooked candy by the women.'

Tanan floats, then, only from the nominative nominal. Since Quantifier Float is limited by line-drawing and only the nominative nominal launches quantifiers, the nominative nominal must be a subject in some stratum; presumably, it is the final subject.

2.1.3   Support from Relative Clause Formation

Keenan and Comrie (1977) examined relative clauses in a number of languages. Assuming a derivational model, they spoke of "relativizing into" the position which would be occupied by a nominal coreferential to the head of the relative clause. As a result of their examination, they concluded that the grammatical relation of a nominal had a bearing on its accessibility to relativization. In particular, nominals were found to be ranked according to the accessibility hierarchy:

(37)   Accessibility hierarchy
a.   Subj $\geq$ DO $\geq$ IO $\geq$ Obj of Prep $\geq$ Possessor $\geq$ Obj of Comparative
b.   If X $\geq$ Y and Y $\geq$ Z, then X $\geq$ Z, where '$\geq$' means 'greater than or equal to in accessibility.'

Languages draw the line at different points along the hierarchy. If a language permits relativization of a given nominal by its major relative clause formation strategy, then it also permits relativization of any nominal which is of greater or equal accessibility by the major strategy,[14] which applies to subjects. It follows that if relativization in a given language is restricted to a single nominal, that nominal must be the subject.

In Cebuano, a relative clause is linked to its head by the general linker *nga*. The relativized nominal does not appear in the relative clause.

(38) Nakakita' ako   sa   tawo   nga nagdagan diba'.
      ACT-see   I-NOM OBL person LN   ACT-run   there
      'I saw the man who was running there.'

The nominative nominal can be relativized. Thus, corresponding to (39a), we find the relative clause italicized in (39b). No other nominal in (39a) can be relativized. For example, there is no relative clause corresponding to (39a) with *karabao* as its head.

(39) a. Nagpalit ang magdadaro ug   karabao.
         ACT-buy NOM farmer   OBL waterbuffalo
         'The farmer bought a buffalo.'
     b. Nakakita' ko   sa   magdadaro *nga nagpalit ug   karabao*.
         ACT-see   I-NOM OBL farmer   LN   ACT-buy OBL buffalo
         'I saw the farmer who had bought a buffalo.'
     c. *Nakakita' ko   ug/sa karabao *nga nagpalit ang*
         ACT-see   I-NOM OBL buffalo LN   ACT-buy NOM
         magdadaro.
         farmer
         (I saw a/the buffalo which the farmer had bought.)

In order for *karabao* to be relativized, it must be nominative. Thus, corresponding to (40a), we can form the relative clause in (40b). No relative clause corresponding to (40a) can be formed with *magdadaro* as head.

(40) a. Gipalit   sa   magdadaro ang karabao.
         OBJ-buy GEN farmer   NOM buffalo
         'The buffalo was bought by the farmer.'
     b. Nakakita' ko   ug   karabao *nga gipalit   sa   magdadaro*.
         ACT-see   I-NOM OBL buffalo LN   OBJ-buy GEN farmer
         'I saw a buffalo which had been bought by the farmer.'
     c. *Nakakita' ko   sa   magdadaro *nga gipalit   ang karabao*.
         ACT-see   I-NOM OBL farmer   LN   OBJ-buy NOM buffalo
         (I saw the farmer by whom the buffalo had been bought.)

Similarly, in the sets of sentences below, the nominative nominal, and only the nominative nominal, can be relativized.

(41) a. Giluto'an niya   ang lata ug bugas.
        cook-LOC he-GEN NOM can OBL rice
        'He cooked rice in *the can.*'

    b. Hugaw ang lata nga giluto'an niya   ug bugas.
        dirty   NOM can LN cook-LOC he-GEN OBL rice
        'The can in which he cooked rice is dirty.'

    c. *Hugaw ang bugas nga giluto'an niya   ang lata.
        dirty   NOM rice   LN cook-LOC he-GEN NOM can
        (The rice which he cooked in *the can* was dirty.)

(42) a. Giluto'an ko   ang bata' ug kalamay.
        cook-LOC I-GEN NOM child OBL candy
        'The child was cooked candy by me.'

    b. Nagtawag siya   sa bata' nga giluto'an ko   ug
        ACT-call he-NOM OBL child LN cook-LOC I-GEN OBL
        kalamay.
        candy
        'He called the child for whom I had cooked candy.'

    c. *Lami' ang kalamay nga giluto'an nako ang bata'.
        tasty   NOM candy   LN cook-LOC I-GEN NOM child
        (The candy which I cooked for the child was delicious.)

(43) a. Ipalit   ko   kining   baynti ug saging.
        INS buy I-GEN this-NOM-LN 20   OBL banana
        'I'll buy some bananas with *this 20 centavo piece.*'

    b. Gihatag nako ni   Go. Abaya kining   baynti nga
        INS-give I-OBL GEN Mr. Abaya this-NOM-LN 20   LN
        ipalit   ko   ug saging.
        ins-buy I-GEN OBL banana
        'This 20 centavo piece with which I'll buy some bananas was
        given to me by Mr. Abaya.'

    c. *Dako' ang mga saging nga ipalit   ko
        big   NOM PL banana LN INS-buy I-GEN
        kining   baynti.
        this-NOM-LN 20
        (The bananas which I'll buy with *this 20 centavo piece* are
        large.)

Only the nominative nominal is accessible to relativization. If relative clause formation is indeed restricted according to the Accessibility Hierarchy, the nominative nominal must be a subject.

2.1.4 *Summary of the Arguments*

If either the proposal that Quantifier Float is subject to line-drawing or the claim that relative clause formation is restricted according to the

Accessibility Hierarchy is correct, then the nominative nominal is a subject in the stratum with respect to which these rules are stated, for only the nominative nominal can launch floating quantifiers or be relativized.

The nominative nominal's behavior in Quantifier Float and relative clause formation supports the proposal that it be analyzed as the final subject. It remains to be shown that it is not the subject in all strata in nonactive sentences.[15]

2.2   Arguments That the Actor Is the Initial 1
2.2.1   *The Argument from Reflexives*

Languages differ as to which dependents can be antecedents for reflexives. In Russian, for example, traditional grammars state that the reflexive pronoun "refers back to the subject of the sentence" (Stilman and Harkins 1964). In English, on the other hand, subjects, indirect objects, and perhaps certain other dependents can be antecedents of reflexives which are lower in the hierarchy.

(44) a.   John shaved himself.
     b.   *Himself shaved John.
(45) a.   Bob talked to Sue about himself/herself.
     b.   *Bob talked to herself about Sue.
     c.   *Bob talked about Sue to herself.
(46) a.   Bob received a letter from Sue about himself/herself.[16]
     b.   *Bob received a letter about Sue from herself.

In view of examples like these in diverse languages, Perlmutter and Postal (1974) proposed that the antecedent must be higher on the hierarchy than the reflexive in the stratum with respect to which reflexive anaphora is stated. This generalization is called the Reflexive Rank Law.

The Reflexive Rank Law has certain consequences. First, since subjects rank highest in the hierarchy, it follows that if a language has reflexives, the subject must be able to serve as the antecedent of a reflexive. Second, if a dependent can be the antecedent of a reflexive which is a direct object, it must be a subject, since only subjects outrank direct objects. Finally, in a simple clause if a dependent can be a reflexive, it cannot be the subject in the stratum with reference to which rules of reflexive anaphora are stated.

These consequences can be applied to Cebuano to form an argument for the analysis in which the actor is the initial 1 and the nominative nominal is the final 1.

So far, arguments have been given to show that the nominative nominal is a final 1. These arguments dispose of the possibility that Cebuano has no subject or that the actor is the subject in all strata. This leaves us with at least two alternatives: the proposal that the actor is the initial 1 and the nominative nominal is the final 1 and the proposal that the nominative nominal is the 1 in all strata, as suggested by McKaughan (1973) and Kess (1975).

Data from reflexives provide a basis for choosing between these two alternatives. We shall see that the nominative nominal can be a reflexive. This fact establishes that it is not a 1 in the stratum with respect to which reflexive anaphora is stated. It will further be shown that the actor can serve as the antecedent of a reflexive direct object. It follows that the actor is the subject in the stratum with respect to which reflexive anaphora is stated.

These conclusions are incompatible with an analysis in which the nominative nominal is the subject in all strata. They are compatible with an analysis in which the actor is the initial 1 and the nominative nominal is the final 1, requiring only that the rules of reflexive anaphora refer to initial termhood. In a theory which includes the Reflexive Rank Law, then, Cebuano reflexives support the analysis being proposed in this paper.

The reflexive nominal in Cebuano is formed of the preposed genitive form of the pronoun plus the noun *ka'ugalingon* 'self'.

When used as a dependent in a clause, the reflexive requires an antecedent.

(47) a. Nagsulat siya   sa iyang ka'ugalingon.
        ACT-write he-NOM OBL his-LN self
        'He was writing to himself.'
    b. *Nagsulat siya   sa imong ka'ugalingon.
        ACT-write he-NOM OBL your-LN self
        (He was writing to yourself.)

The antecedent must be a dependent of the same clause as the reflexive; that is, reflexive anaphora is clause-bound. For example, a reflexive in a *pag*-complement (§2.2.2) cannot have its antecedent in the main clause (48a). Similarly, a reflexive in a relative clause cannot refer to an antecedent in the main clause (48b).

(48) a. Naghuna'huna' ako   sa pagtan'aw ni Linda sa
        ACT-think about I-NOM OBL looking at GEN Linda OBL
        iyang/*akong ka'ugalingon sa   salamin.
        her-LN/my-LN self   OBL mirror
        'I was thinking about Linda's looking at herself/*myself in the mirror.'

b. Nakita' ko   ang tawo   nga nagtawag sa
    OBJ-see I-GEN NOM person LN ACT-call OBL
    iyang/*akong ka'ugalingon.
    his-LN/my-LN self
    'The man who called himself/*myself was seen by me.'

The actor can be the antecedent of a reflexive direct object in both active and nonactive sentences.

(49) a. Motan'aw ako   sa   akong ka'ugalingon sa   salamin.
         ACT-look at I-NOM OBL my-LN SELF   OBL mirror
         'I'll look at myself in the mirror.'
     b. Tan'awon nako' ang akong ka'ugalingon sa   salamin.
         look at-OBJ I-GEN NOM my-LN self   OBL mirror
         'I'll look at *myself* in the mirror.'

According to the Reflexive Rank Law, the antecedent must be higher on the hierarchy than the reflexive. Only the subject is higher than the direct object on the hierarchy. Since the actor can be the antecedent of a reflexive direct object, it must be a subject in the stratum with respect to which the rule of reflexive anaphora is stated.

If the actor is the subject in the stratum with respect to which rules of reflexive anaphora are stated, then it should not be possible for the actor itself to be a reflexive. This prediction is borne out. In neither active (50a) or nonactive (50b) sentences can the actor be a reflexive.[17]

(50) a. *Motan'aw   nako' ang akong ka'ugalingon sa   salamin.
         ACT-look at I-OBL NOM my-LN self   OBL mirror
         (Myself will look at me in the mirror.)
     b. *Tan'awon ako   sa   akong ka'ugalingon sa   salamin.
         look at-OBJ I-NOM GEN my-LN self   OBL mirror
         (I will be looked at by myself in the mirror.)

Sentences (49a) and (49b) show that the actor is a subject in the stratum to which the reflexive rules refer. Sentence (49b) also shows that the nominative nominal is not a subject in that stratum, for the subject cannot itself be a reflexive, as the nominative nominal is in (49b).

Yet another consequence may be drawn from the sentences in (49). Since the same dependents can serve as antecedents of reflexives in active and nonactive sentences alike, rules of reflexive anaphora must refer to initial termhood.[18] It follows that the actor is the subject in the initial stratum.

Assuming that the Reflexive Rank Law is correct,[19] then, Cebuano reflexives show that the nominative nominal is not the subject in all strata, that the actor is the initial subject, and that reflexive anaphora rules in Cebuano refer to initial termhood.

2.2.2   *The Argument from Equi*

In certain constructions the subject of a complement clause or nominal cannot be lexically present in the sentence. The missing subject is understood to be coreferential to the subject of the main clause with certain verbs and to the direct object of the main clause with other verbs. Because the absent subject is coreferential to a dependent of the main clause, I retain the name 'Equi' for this phenomenon without taking any position as to the form of the rule(s) responsible for it.

Since it is the subject which is obligatorily absent in an Equi construction, if a dependent is subject to Equi (i.e., is obligatorily absent), it must be the 1 of the complement in the stratum with respect to which Equi is stated. Since the missing subject is coreferential with the subject of the main clause with certain verbs, if a dependent of a main clause with one of those verbs as predicate is coreferential with an absent subject, it must be a subject of the main clause at the level with respect to which Equi is stated.

Data with Equi constructions in Cebuano provide additional support for the claim that the actor, not the nominative nominal, is the initial 1.

In Cebuano, the actor is obligatorily absent in the *pag*-complement of certain verbs. With verbs such as *sa'ad* 'promise' and *sábot* 'agree', the missing actor is taken to be coreferential with the actor of the main clause in active and nonactive sentences alike. With verbs such as *sugo'* 'order' and *pílit* 'insist on, force', the missing actor is taken to be coreferential with the initial direct object in active and nonactive sentences. These are Equi constructions. From this, certain consequences follow.

First, since it is the actor of the *pag*-complement that is obligatorily absent, the actor is the subject of the *pag*-complement. As it happens, this conclusion has no bearing on the question of whether the actor or the nominative nominal is the initial subject. As will be shown, *pag*-complements do not exhibit differences in voice. The initial and final subject will therefore coincide under either of the alternatives being considered.

Second, since the missing complement subject is coreferential with the actor with verbs such as 'promise' *sa'ad,* the actor is the subject in the stratum with respect to which Equi is stated.

Third, since the voice makes no difference in the coreference possibilities, Equi rules refer to initial relations in Cebuano.

Before we proceed to the argument, certain preliminaries are required.

In Cebuano, there is a deverbal form made by adding *pag-* to the verb stem (for example, *pagluto'*, 'cooking', from *luto'*, 'cook'; *pag-balik*, 'returning', from *balik*, 'return'; *pagulan*, 'raining', from *ulan*, 'rain'). The *pag*-form may be followed by dependent nominals. The actor is genitive, and the other dependents are oblique.

(51)   pagluto' ni   Rosa ug   bugas
    cooking GEN Rosa OBL rice
    'Rosa's cooking of rice'

Pag-forms appear to be nominals. They may be preceded by nominal markers. When used as time expressions, for example, they are in the oblique case.

(52)   sa   pag'abot ni   Jose sa   balay
    OBL arriving   GEN Jose OBL house
    'upon Jose's arriving at the house' 'when Jose got to the house'

Pag-constructions also serve as subjects in attributive sentences.

(53) a.   Lami' ka'ayo ang   bebingka.
      tasty very   NOM bebingka (a type of cake)
      'Bebingka is very tasty.'
    b.   Lisod ka'ayo ang   pag'adto   didto.
      hard very   NOM going-there there
      'Going there is very hard.'

Pag-constructions may also be dependents in verb-containing sentences.

(54)   Naghuna'huna' si   Rosa sa   pag'abot ni   Jose sa
    ACT-think about NOM Rosa OBL arriving   GEN Jose OBL
    siyudad.
    city
    'Rosa was thinking about Jose's arrival in the city.'

Finally, they can be preceded by adjectives and numerals.

(55)   usa ka malinaw nga paghukum sa   corte
    one LN clear   LN judging   GEN court
    'a clear decision of the court'

A *pag*-nominal has the same set of dependents as its stem verb. For example, the verb *dagan* 'run' does not take a direct object (56a, b), and *pagdagan* 'running' does not take a direct object (56c, d).

(56) a.   Midagan ang   bata'.
      ACT-run NOM child
      'The child ran.'

b. *Midagan ang bata' sa   kahoy.
   ACT-run NOM child OBL tree
   (The child ran the tree.)

c. sa   pagdagan sa   bata'
   OBL running GEN child
   'upon the child's running off'

d. *sa   pagdagan sa   bata' sa   kahoy
   OBL running GEN child OBL tree
   (upon the child's running the tree)

The appropriateness of particular lexical items is also the same for a *pag*-nominal and for its stem verb. For example, except in stories, both *tu'o* 'believe' and *pagtu'o* 'believing' require animate subjects.

(57) a. Nagtu'o   si   Juan/# ang kahoy sa   mangangahoy.
        ACT-believe NOM Juan   NOM tree   OBL woodcutter
        'Juan/#the tree believed the woodcutter.'

     b. pagtu'o ni   Juan/# sa   kahoy sa   mangangahoy.
        believing GEN Juan   GEN tree   OBL woodcutter
        'Juan's/#the tree's believing the woodcutter'

The fact that the stem verb and the *pag*-nominal take the same dependents is a consequence of the fact that with a very few exceptions (e.g., *pagka'on,* 'food' as well as 'eating'), the meaning of the *pag*-nominal is predictable from the meaning of the stem verb.

Pag-nominals are also morphologically regular and productively formed.

The relational analysis of nominals is as yet less fully developed than the relational analysis of clauses. Two possible analyses suggest themselves. First, *pag*-constructions are nominals whose head noun takes the same dependents as a verb. Second, the *pag*-prefix may be a complementizer used to embed clauses as nominals.

The second alternative has one advantage over the first: It allows a simpler statement of coreference possibilities of reflexives. In (48a), we saw that a nominal in the main clause cannot be the antecedent of a reflexive in a *pag*-construction. There are other nominals with dependents of which this is not true. In (58), a dependent in the main clause is the antecedent of a reflexive in the nominal *ug sulat bahin sa iyang ka'ugalingon* ('a letter about herself').

(58) Nakadawat si   Maria ug   sulat bahin sa   iyang
     ACT-receive NOM Maria OBL letter about GEN her-LN
     ka'ugalingon.
     self
     'Maria received a letter about herself.'

Under the second analysis, (58) presents no problem. *Pag*-constructions differ from other nominals by containing a clause, and the reflexive rule is stated on clause-mates. Under the first alternative, in contrast, some sort of distinction between *pag*-nominals and other nominals must be built into the statement of the reflexive rule.

One condition is required on *pag*-clauses. No advancements to 1 are permitted in *pag*-clauses, to assume for a moment that there are advancements to 1. Advancements to 1 have consequences for case marking and for voice marking. The 1 of a *pag*-construction is in the genitive case. If another nominal can advance to 1, it should be found in the genitive case. The verb is marked for various voices depending on the transition in question. If there is a transition from 2 to 1, the verb is in the objective voice. Thus, if a 2 in a *pag*-construction could be a 1 in another stratum, the *pag*-form should be in the objective voice, and the final 1 should be in the genitive case. The predicted construction would thus be (59).

(59) *pagtawgon ni   Rosa ni   Perla
      calling-OBJ GEN Rosa GEN Perla
      (Perla's being called by Rosa)

But (59) is not an acceptable nominal form. Advancements to 1 must therefore be forbidden in *pag*-constructions. This condition is also required in the complements of causative constructions, as discussed in Bell and Perlmutter, to appear, and in *inig*-clauses, which will be mentioned later.

In Cebuano, there are two types of clausal complements. One is the *pag*-construction just discussed (60a). The other is a clause which could appear independently, linked to the main clause by *nga* (60b). There is a slight difference in the meaning of the two complements. According to informants, the *pag*-construction is somehow more real, a difference I have tried to reflect in the glosses.

Both types of complements act like dependents in the main clause. For example, either can be the final subject. When a *pag*-complement is the final 1, it is overtly marked by *ang,* like any common noun (60c). When a full sentence is the final subject, it is still linked to the main clause by *nga* (60d). No overt nominative marker appears.[20]

(60) a. Naka'alinggat siya   sa   pagka'on sa   iho   sa
         ACT-notice   he-NOM OBL eating   GEN shark OBL
         karabao.
         buffalo
         'He noticed the shark's eating the buffalo.'

b. Naka'alinggat siya   nga nagka'on ang iho   sa
    ACT-notice   he-NOM LN ACT-eat   NOM shark OBL
    karabao.
    buffalo
    'He noticed that the shark was eating the buffalo.'
c. Na'alinggatan niya   ang pagka'on sa iho   sa
    notice-LOC   he-GEN NOM eating   GEN shark OBL
    karabao.
    buffalo
    'The shark's eating of the buffalo was noticed by him.'
d. Na'alinggatan niya   nga nagka'on ang iho   sa
    notice-LOC   he-GEN LN ACT-eat   NOM shark OBL
    karabao.
    buffalo
    'That the shark was eating the buffalo was noticed by him.'

Pronouns are omitted rather freely in Cebuano if the antecedent is clear, especially if the antecedent appear elsewhere in the sentence.

(61) Nagsugo' siya_i   kang Rodolfo_j nga mokuha' (siya_j)   sa
     ACT-order he-NOM OBL Rodolfo LN ACT take he-NOM OBL
     bag.
     bag
     'He ordered Rodolfo that he should take the bag.'

The omission of the pronoun is optional. The sentence is grammatical if the pronoun is present, even when the pronoun is not emphatic.
With certain verbs, the actor cannot appear in the *pag*-complement.

(62) a. Ningsugo' ako   kang Rosa sa   pagdagan ø/*niya.
         ACT-order I-NOM OBL Rosa OBL running   she-GEN
         'I ordered Rosa to run.'
     b. Ningsa'ad   ako   kang Lus sa   pagluto' ø/*nako' ug
         ACT-promise I-NOM OBL Lus OBL cooking   I-GEN OBL
         panihapon.
         dinner
         'I promised Lus to cook dinner.'

The fact that the actor must be omitted shows that these sentences are not cases of Pronoun Drop.
As shown earlier, in (48a), reflexives in a *pag*-complement cannot have an antecedent in the main clause. However, a reflexive may be found in a *pag*-complement in which the actor is obligatorily absent.

(63) Nagsulay ako   sa   pagbantay   sa   akong ka'ugalingon.
      ACT-try I-NOM OBL looking after OBL my-LN self
      'I try to look after myself.'

The generalization that a reflexive in a *pag*-nominal cannot have an antecedent in the main clause can be retained if the complement has an actor which serves as an antecedent for the reflexive. To account for the absence of this actor, a rule will be needed. As can be seen from (62), with verbs of one class (*sa'ad* 'promise'), the missing complement actor is coreferential with the matrix actor, while with verbs of the other class (*sugo'* 'order'), the missing actor is coreferential with the object. This difference in coreference relations is the same as that found with Equi constructions in other languages. If we take the absence of the complement actor to be due to Equi, no new sort of rule will be required. I propose, then, that the grammar of Cebuano contains Equi, which will account for the absence of the actor in *pag*-complements of verbs of the *sa'ad* and *sugo'* classes.

Since it is the complement subject which is obligatorily absent in Equi constructions, the actor must be the subject of *pag*-constructions. Since, however, no advancements can occur in *pag*-constructions, this fact has no bearing on the argument that the actor is the initial subject in nonactive as well as active sentences.

To make such an argument, it is necessary to look at nonactive sentences. The coreference relations are the same in nonactive sentences as in active sentences.

(64) a. Gisugo'   nako' si   Rosa sa   pagdagan.
         OBJ-order I-GEN NOM Rosa OBL running
         'Rosa was ordered by me to run.'
     b. Gisa'aran   nako' si   Lus sa   pagluto' ug panihapon.
         promise-LOC I-GEN NOM Lus OBL cooking OBL dinner
         'I promised *Lus* to cook dinner.'

This fact can be accounted for very simply if Equi rules are stated with respect to initial grammatical relations in Cebuano if the actor is the initial 1. We can simply say that with *sa'ad* 'promise', *sulay* 'try', *sabot* 'agree', and so on, the missing complement 1 is coreferential with the initial 1 of the matrix, while with verbs such as *sugo'* 'order', *pilit* 'force', and the like, the missing complement 1 is coreferential with the initial matrix 2.[21]

The alternative is more complicated. In (62a) and (64a) alike, *Rosa* is coreferential with the missing complement 1. In (64a), *Rosa* is the nominative nominal, and hence by our earlier arguments, a subject. Now, if the nominative nominal in both (62a) and (64a) is the initial 1,

Rosa will have different grammatical relations in all strata in the two sentences, and separate rules will be required to state the coreference relations for active and nonactive sentences. Similarly, if Equi is stated on final grammatical relations, then since *Rosa* will have different final grammatical relations in the two sentences, different rules will be needed for active and nonactive sentences. The only simple solution is to have *Rosa* as the initial 2 of both sentences and to state the rule referring to the initial stratum.

A similar complexity is introduced if the actor is not the initial 1. *Ako* 'I' would then have different initial grammatical relations in (62b) and (64b), resulting in the need for different rules for active and nonactive sentences. The actor, then, must be the initial 1 in active and nonactive sentences alike.

2.2.3   *Summary of the Arguments*

It was proposed that the actor is the initial 1 and the nominative nominal is the final 1 in verb-containing sentences in Cebuano. To support the proposal, arguments from Quantifier Float and relative clauses were advanced to show that the nominative nominal is the subject in some stratum. Next, arguments from reflexives and Equi were presented showing that the actor is the subject in the stratum with respect to which the rules governing these constructions are stated. Finally, an argument was presented to show that Equi rules are stated with respect to initial grammatical relations. It follows that the actor is a subject in the initial stratum. The nominative nominal must then be a subject in the final stratum.

Since the actor is the initial subject in nonactive sentences as well as active sentences and the nominative nominal is the final subject, there must be a rule or rules sanctioning transitions to 1 in the networks of nonactive sentences; that is to say, there must be advancement rules. Advancements to 1 are subject to the 1-Advancement Exclusiveness Law (see Perlmutter and Postal (to appear)). In the next subsection, it will be shown that the proposed advancements conform to this law, providing further support for the analysis.

2.3   Two Consequences of the 1-Advancement Rules

The arguments so far have supported the claim that the actor is the initial 1 and the nominative nominal is the final 1. It follows that in the network of a nonactive sentence the arc of some dependent shows a transition from non-1 to 1. There must, then, be a rule of Advancement to 1 in the grammar of Cebuano to sanction such transitions. The 1-Advancement rules have two consequences in addition to permitting a transition. One is a result of the 1-Advancement Exclusiveness Law;

the other of the Chômeur Condition. The data from Cebuano are in accord with both of these consequences, a fact which further supports an analysis with a 1-Advancement Rule.

First, according to the 1-Advancement Exclusiveness Law, there cannot be two advancements to 1 in the same clause. This prediction is borne out in Cebuano. To see this, let us examine a set of active and nonactive sentences. Sentence (65a) is an active sentence whose stratal diagram is found in (65b).

(65) a. Nagsulat si   Lito sa   balita kang Maria.
          ACT-write NOM Lito OBL news OBL Maria
          'Lito was writing the news to Maria.'

b.

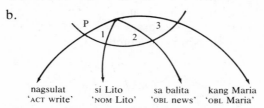

nagsulat   si Lito   sa balita   kang Maria
'ACT write'   'NOM Lito'   'OBL news'   'OBL Maria'

There are two nonactive sentences corresponding to (66a). Either *balita* 'news' or *Maria* may be the final 1. In the first instance, there is a transition from 2 to 1 along the arc of *balita,* as shown in (66b), the stratal diagram for (66a).

(66) a. Gisulat   ni   Lito ang balita kang Maria.
          OBJ-write GEN Lito NOM news OBL Maria
          'The news was written to Maria by Lito.'

b.

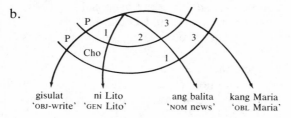

gisulat   ni Lito   ang balita   kang Maria
'OBJ-write'   'GEN Lito'   'NOM news'   'OBL Maria'

When there is a transition from 2 to 1, the verb is in the objective voice, and the 1-chômeur is in the genitive case.

When *Maria* is the final 1, the arc of *Maria* shows a transition from 3 to 1, as shown in the stratal diagram (67b), corresponding to (67a).

(67) a. Gisulatan ni   Lito si   Maria sa   balita.
          write-LOC GEN Lito NOM Maria OBL news
          'Maria was written the news by Lito.'

b.

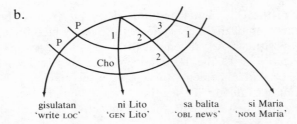

gisulatan	ni Lito	sa balita	si Maria
'write LOC'	'GEN Lito'	'OBL news'	'NOM Maria'

When there is a transition from 3 to 1, the verb is in the locative voice and the 1-chômeur is in the genitive case.

The 1-Advancement Exclusiveness Law predicts that it will be impossible for there to be transitions to 1 on the arcs of both *balita* 'news' and *Maria*. That is, it predicts that there is no grammatical sentence corresponding to the stratal diagram shown in (68), no matter how the voice and case markings may be combined.

(68)

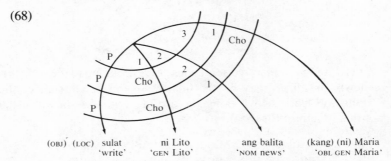

(OBJ) (LOC) sulat	ni Lito	ang balita	(kang) (ni) Maria
'write'	'GEN Lito'	'NOM news'	'OBL GEN Maria'

This prediction is borne out. No such sentence is found. The correctness of the prediction supports the proposal that there are 1-advancements in nonactive sentences in Cebuano.

The second consequence of advancement rules has been indicated in the diagrams already. If there is a transition to 1, the Chômeur Condition predicts that the initial 1 must be a 1-chômeur. The chômeur status of the actor in nonactive sentences is shown by the fact that it cannot be relativized, as illustrated in (40c), or launch floating quantifiers, as illustrated in (33), (34), and (35). That this prediction is also verified further supports the analysis.

2.4   Two Digressions

There are two additional characteristics of 1-chômeurs from advancement rules: they are in the genitive case, and they occur in postverbal position. At the risk of disrupting the argument, I would like to digress about genitive actors and about word orders, to provide some information which will be needed later.

2.4.1   *Genitive Actors*

In a nonactive sentence, the actor is a final 1-chômeur. As such, it will be in the genitive case. It is important to note that these 1-chômeurs are not the only actors in the genitive case. We saw earlier in §2.2.2 that the subject of a *pag*-construction is in the genitive case (51). There is another type of nonfinite construction in Cebuano formed by adding *inig*- to a verb stem. These clauses are used as temporal expressions, always expressing a future time. The subject of an *inig*-clause is in the genitive case.

(69)   Wolff 1966, 3.a.25
     Inig'abot ninyo   sa   Sanciangko, liko' sa   tu'o.
     arriving you-GEN OBL Sanciangko turn OBL right
     'When you get to Sanciangko, turn right.'

The final subject of a finite clause is nominative. The subject of a nonfinite clause is genitive. Some genitive actors are 1-chômeurs from advancements, while others are final 1's of nonfinite clauses.

2.4.2   *Word Orders*

A full network includes a statement of linear precedence relations obtaining among dependents of a single governor. To simplify diagrams, I prefer simply to state the word order in terms of final grammatical relations. In such terms the basic word order is shown in (70).

(70)   Verb (*tanan*) (Advancement 1-chômeur) 1 (2) (3) (Nonterms)

Of the 1-chômeurs, *tanan* 'all' precedes the 1-chômeur from advancement rules.
    The final subject can appear in preverbal position.

(71)   Ang bagong kalaha'   giluto'an sa   babaye sa isda'.
     NOM new-LN frying pan cook-LOC GEN woman OBL fish
     '*In the new frying pan,* the woman cooked the fish.'

This word order is felt as marked, but the nature of the marking is not clear. It is sometimes said to be 'emphatic', but it seems to be less a matter of emphasis than of giving the topic of the sentence, telling what the sentence is about. In relational grammar, Topic is an overlay relation. Sentence (71) can be accounted for by having a rule sanctioning the overlay topic relation and having a topicalized word order with the topic before the verb. Such an analysis will be in accord with the position taken by McKaughan (1973) that not all (final) subjects, but only preposed subjects, are topics.
    The topicalized word order is simply stated.

(72)   Topic   Verb (1-chômeurs) (1) (2) (3) (Nonterms)

Since 'Topic' is not in parentheses but 1 is, (72) indicates that a nominal
that is both Topic and final 1 precedes the verb.

Problems arise, however, in the statement of the Topic rule. A dependent of one clause may bear an overlay relation in another clause
in which it bears no central relation. In Cebuano, a nominal, nom_i,
which bears no central grammatical relation in a clause, C_i, can be the
topic of C_i just in case nom_i is the final 1 of some clause C_j, where C_j
is either (i) the final 1 of C_i or (ii) the final 1 of a clause contained in
C_i. Examples may make this clearer. Sentence (73a), whose stratal
diagram is shown in (73b), is grammatical.

(73) a.   Ang iho   na'alinggatan sa   mananagat nga mibalik.
          NOM shark notice-LOC   GEN fisherman LN ACT-return
          'That THE SHARK had returned was noticed by the fisherman.'

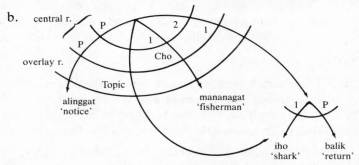

In (73), *iho* 'shark' is the final 1 of the dependent clause. The dependent
clause itself is the final 1 of the governing clause. The conditions are
met.

Sentence (74a), diagrammed in (74b), provides a more complex
example.

(74) a.   Ang iho   gi'ingon ni   Fred kang Perla nga misinggit
          NOM shark OBJ-tell GEN Fred OBL   Perla LN ACT-shout
          si   Lito nga na'alinggatan sa   mananagat nga mibalik.
          NOM Lito LN   notice-LOC   GEN fisherman LN ACT-return
          'It was told by Fred to Perla that Lito had shouted that it had
          been noticed by the fisherman that THE SHARK had returned.'

b.

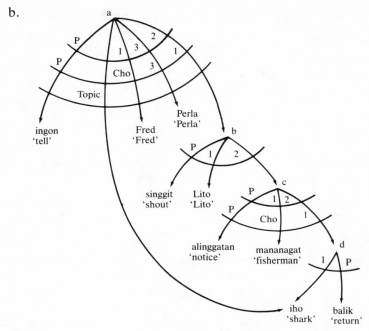

Network (74b) would be ill-formed if *iho* were not final 1 of *d,* or if *d* were not final 1 of *c,* or if *b* were not final 1 of *a.*

If the conditions are not met, there will be no grammatical sentence corresponding to the network. For example, in (75a), the clause containing *iho* is not the final 1 of the clause of which *iho* is a topic, and (75b) is ungrammatical. Similarly, in (75c), the clause of which *iho* is the final 1 is not itself a final 1, and (75d) is ungrammatical.

(75) a.

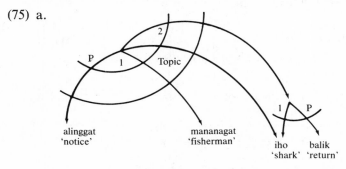

b. *Ang iho   naka'alinggat ang mananagat nga mibalik.
    NOM shark ACT-notice   NOM fisherman LN ACT-return
    (The shark, the fisherman noticed that it had returned.)

c.

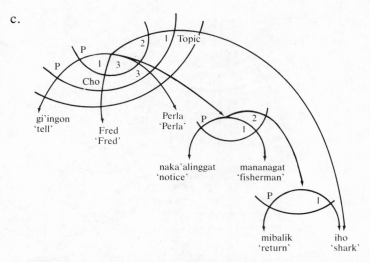

d. *Ang iho   gi'ingon ni   Fred kang Perla nga naka'alinggat
   NOM shark OBJ-tell GEN Fred OBL Perla LN ACT-notice
   ang   mananagat nga mibalik.
   NOM fisherman LN ACT-return
   (The shark, it was told by Fred to Perla that the fisherman had
   noticed that it had returned.)

Semiformally, the conditions illustrated above can be incorporated
into the Topic Rule as follows:

(76) Topic Rule:
      If *a* is a Topic of clause *b,* then either *a* is the final 1 of *b* or *a*
      is the final 1 of some clause *c* which is itself a final 1 and is
      (contained in) the final 1 of *b.*

Indirect objects and impure dependents may also precede the verb,
as shown in (77) and (78). Example (77a) shows the basic order. In
(77b), the temporal phrase precedes the verb.

(77) a. Mo'ani'   kami   ug humay sa bulan sa
        ACT-harvest we-NOM OBL rice   OBL month GEN
        Nobyember.
        November
        'We harvest rice in the month of November.'
    b. Sa bulan sa Nobyember mo'ani'   kami   ug
        OBL month GEN November ACT-harvest we-NOM OBL
        humay.
        rice
        'In November, we harvest rice.'

The final 3 can precede the verb, as shown in (78).

(78) a.   Nagsulat si   Lito sa   balita kang Maria.
          ACT-write NOM Lito OBL news OBL Maria
          'Lito was writing the news to Maria.'
      b. Kang Maria nagsulat   si   Lito sa   balita.
          OBL Maria ACT-write NOM Lito OBL news
          'To Maria, Lito wrote the news.'

The final 2 cannot precede the verb.

(79) a. *Ug humay mo'ani   kami   sa   bulan sa
          OBL rice   ACT-harvest we-NOM OBL month GEN
          Nobyember.
          November
          (Rice we harvest in November.)
      b. *Sa   balita nagsulat   si   Lito kang Maria.
          OBL news ACT-write NOM Lito OBL Maria
          (The news, Lito wrote to Maria.)

The 1-chômeur, too, is unable to precede the verb.[22]

(80) *Sa   babaye giluto'an ang bagong kalaha'   ug   isda'.
     GEN woman cook-LOC NOM new-LN frying pan OBL fish
     (By the woman, the new frying pan is being cooked fish in.)

The word order with nonnominative elements in front of the verb is not felt as marked, as is the topicalized word order. It seems to be stylistic, rather like the diverse positions of certain adverbs in English. Accordingly, I call it the adverbial word order. Since the 1 and 2 together are called 'nuclear terms', this word order can be stated as below, referring to final relations:

(81)   Adverbial Word Order
       Nonnuclear dependent   Verb (1-chômeur) 1 (2) (3) (Nonterms)

Like the basic word order, the adverbial word order is stated in terms of central grammatical relations, not in terms of overlay relations. Consequently, it would not permit a network in which the relation of linear precedence held between the nonnuclear dependents of one clause and the verb of another clause. In (82a), the temporal expression is in the dependent clause; (81) will permit it to appear before the verb which is predicate of that clause as in (82b), but not to appear before the verb which is predicate of the governing clause as in (82c).

(82) a. Gi'ingon ni   Maria kanako' nga mo'ani'   sila   ug
         OBJ-tell GEN Maria I-OBL   LN ACT-harvest they-NOM OBL
         humay sa   bulan sa   Nobyember.
         rice   OBL month GEN November
         'That they harvest rice in November was told me by Maria.'
     b. Gi'ingon ni   Maria kanako' nga sa   bulan sa
         OBJ-tell GEN Maria I-OBL   LN OBL month GEN
         Nobyember mo'ani'   sila   ug humay.
         November ACT-harvest they-NOM OBL rice
         'It was told me by Maria that in November they harvest rice.'
     c. *Sa bulan sa   Nobyember gi'ingon ni   Maria kanako'
         OBL month GEN November OBJ-tell GEN Maria I-OBL
         nga mo'ani'   sila   ug humay.
         LN ACT-harvest they-NOM OBL rice
         (In November, it was told me by Maria that they will harvest
         rice.)

(If the temporal expression is in the same clause as *ingon* 'tell', then
naturally sentence (82c) is grammatical.)

This ends the digression into word order. Let us proceed to the next
topic: the form of the advancement, case marking, and voice marking
rules.

3   The Rules
3.1   The Advancement Rule(s): One Rule or Many?

We have seen that a dependent with any initial central relation can be
the final 1 with some verb or other, although not every dependent can
be the final 1 with every verb. This raises a question: Should there be
a separate rule sanctioning the transition from each central relation to
1, or can all be combined?

If all are combined, the advancement rule can be stated as in (83)
below.

(83) Advancement rule:
      If a bears a central grammatical relation in clause b in stratum
      c_i, it may be a 1 of b in stratum c_{i+1}.

If the advancements are not combined, a multitude of rules will be
required, as shown in (84).

(84) AR1: If a is a 2 of b in stratum c_i, it may be a 1 of b in stratum
           c_{i+1}.
     AR2: If a is a 3 of b in stratum c_i, it may be a 1 of b in stratum
           c_{i+1}.

> AR3: If a is a locative of b in stratum c_i, it may be a 1 of b in stratum c_{i+1}.
>
> AR4: If a is a benefactive of b in stratum c_i, it may be a 1 of b in stratum c_{i+1}.
>
> AR5: If a is an instrument of b in stratum c_i, it may be a 1 of b in stratum c_{i+1}.
>
> AR6: If a is a temporal of b in stratum c_i, it may be a 1 of b in stratum c_{i+1}.

Economy favors (83). It is clearly simpler to have one rule than six or more.

3.2   The Case Marking Rules

The case marking rules are straightforward. The final subject is in the nominative case, a 1-chômeur from an advancement is in the genitive, and other dependents are in the oblique case, except that a final benefactive is marked by the preposition *alang* 'for' or the preposition *para* 'for' as well.[23] The case marking rules may be stated semiformally as in (85).

> (85) CMR1: If the predicate of clause c is a finite verb, the final 1 of c is in the nominative case.
>
> CMR2: A final 1-chômeur is in the genitive case.
>
> CMR3: A final benefactive is marked with *para* or *alang*.
>
> CMR4: Other central dependents in a clause are in the oblique case.[24]

As mentioned earlier, the case marking rules do not mark cases but rather accept as well-formed those networks with the correct case markings. Returning to the more detailed stratal diagrams showing case and voice marking, we can see that the rules above will accept (86a) as well-formed while rejecting (86b).

(86) a.

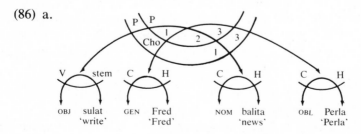

b.

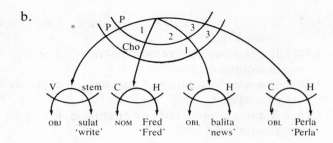

3.3 The Voice Marking Rules
3.3.1 *Preliminary Statement*

The voice marking rules will specify the voice marking which must be present when a given dependent has advanced to 1. When an initial 2, 3, locative, instrument, or temporal has advanced, only one voice marking is possible. However, as was shown in §1.1, the verb may be in either locative or instrumental voice when an initial benefactive is the final 1. The problem of stating correct voice marking in such cases is discussed in §3.3.2, where it is proposed that there is a rule of Benefactive-3 Advancement.

For the straightforward cases, the voice marking rules may be stated semiformally as in (87).

(87) VMR1: If verb *a* is the predicate of clause *b* and there is no transition from non-1 to 1 on the arc of any dependent of *b*, then *a* is in the active voice.

VMR2: If verb *a* is the predicate of clause *b* and the arc of some dependent of *b* shows a transition from 2 to 1, then *a* is in the objective voice.

VMR3: If verb *a* is the predicate of clause *b* and the arc of some dependent of *b* shows a transition from 3 to 1, then *a* is in the locative voice.

VMR4: If verb *a* is the predicate of clause *b* and the arc of some dependent of *b* shows a transition from locative to 1, then the verb is in the locative voice.

VMR5: If a verb *a* is the predicate of clause *b* and any dependent of *b* shows a transition from any other non-1 relation to 1, the verb is in the instrumental voice.

3.3.2 *Benefactive-3 Advancement*

As was mentioned in §1.1, either locative or instrumental voice may be used when an initial benefactive is a final 1. In the active sentence (88a), the benefactive is expressed in the prepositional phrase *para sa ako'* 'for me'. There are two sentences corresponding to (88a) with the initial benefactive as final 1: (88b) with the verb in the locative voice and the more polite (88c) with the verb in the instrumental voice.

(88) a. Magpalit ka   ug   kok   para sa   ako'.
        ACT-buy you-NOM OBL coke for   OBL me
        '(You) buy me a coke.'
    b. Paliti   mo   ako   ug   kok.
        buy-LOC you-GEN I-NOM OBL coke
        '(You) buy *me* a coke.'
    c. Ipalit   mo   ako   ug   kok.
        INS-buy you-GEN I-NOM OBL coke
        '(You) buy *me* a coke, please.'

There is a restriction on the use of locative voice when an initial benefactive is the final 1. Locative voice cannot be so used with a verb which can take an initial 3. In (89), for instance, the final 1, *Go. Santos* 'Mr. Santos', can only be an initial 3, not an initial benefactive.

(89) Gisulatan ni   Go. Abaya si   Go. Santos ug
      write-LOC GEN Mr. Abaya NOM Mr. Santos OBL
      rekomendasyon.
      recommendation
      'Mr. Abaya wrote a recommendation to *Mr. Santos*.'
      (*Not:* 'Mr. Abaya wrote a recommendation for *Mr. Santos*.')

The possibility of having either of two voices on all but a small class of verbs when an initial benefactive is a final 1 must be accounted for. In what follows, I will compare two solutions: using a voice marking rule and proposing an advancement from benefactive to 3.

If there is no rule sanctioning a transition from benefactive to 3, there will be no difference in the networks for (88b) and (88c), except in voice marking. Both will share the network of central relations shown in stratal diagram (90).

(90)

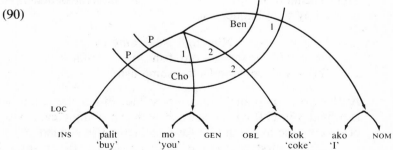

To account for the possibility of using either instrumental or locative voice, the following voice marking rule will be required:

(91) If verb *a* is the predicate of clause *b* and the arc of some depen-
      dent of *b* shows a transition from benefactive to 1, then the verb
      is in either the instrumental or the locative voice, but not both.

If there is a rule sanctioning a transition from benefactive to 3, no
special voice marking rule will be required. The networks for (88b) and
(88c) will differ. In the network for (88b), show in diagram (92), there
is a transition from benefactive to 3 and from 3 to 1. The regular voice
marking rule VMR3 in (87) will require that the verb be in the locative
voice.

(92)

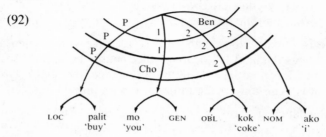

```
LOC    palit    mo    GEN   OBL   kok   NOM   ako
       'buy'   'you'             'coke'       'i'
```

In the network for (88c), there will be no transition from benefactive
to 3. Instead, there will be a transition from benefactive to 1, so that
the central clausal relations will again be as shown in (90). VMR5 in
(87) will then require the verb to be in the instrumental case.

There is evidence in favor of Benefactive-3 Advancement. As noted
earlier, the final benefactive is usually marked by *para* 'for' or *alang*
'for', as shown in (93).

(93) Nagluto' si   Nina ug isda' para kang Dolfin.
      ACT-cook NOM Nina OBL fish for   OBL Dolfin
      'Nina was cooking some fish for Dolfin.'

Some speakers also accept sentences in which the benefactive is simply
marked by the oblique case.

(94) Nagluto' si   Nina ug isda' kang Dolfin.
      ACT-cook NOM Nina OBL fish OBL Dolfin
      'Nina was cooking Dolfin some fish.'

At this point, two analyses are possible. Either the initial benefactive
is a final 3 in (94) and is marked with the oblique case like other 3s,
or a new case marking rule for benefactives is needed.

Under the first alternative, the rule of Benefactive-to-3 Advancement, among other rules, will accept the network diagrammed in (95)
as the network for (94).

(95)

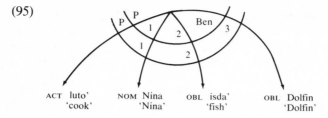

In (95), *Dolfin* is a final 3. Like other final 3s, it will be required to be in the oblique case by case marking rule 4. No additional complications will be required to account for (94).

If there is no rule of Benefactive-to-3 Advancement, the central clausal relations in the networks for (93) and (94) will be the same, as shown in (96).

(96)

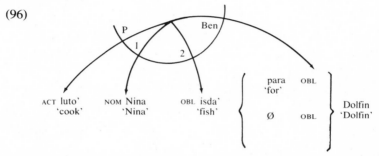

To account for the difference in marking of *Dolfin,* a more complex case marking rule, like that shown in (97), will be needed.

(97)   A final benefactive is marked with *para* or *alang* or else it is simply in the oblique case.

The analysis with Benefactive-3 Advancement is simpler. It requires no new rules and allows us to keep the simpler case marking rules. The irregular case marking analysis, in contrast, requires more complicated marking rules.

There is one more fact which favors the analysis with Benefactive-to-3 Advancement. The preposition may be absent only if the verb cannot take an indirect object. Sentence (98) is unambiguous. *Go. Santos* 'Mr. Santos' cannot be understood as a benefactive.

(98)   Nagsulat si   Go. Abaya ug   rekomendasyon kang
       ACT-write NOM Mr. Abaya OBL recommendation OBL
       Go. Santos.
       Mr. Santos
       'Mr. Abaya wrote a recommendation to Mr. Santos.'
       (*Not:* 'Mr. Abaya wrote a recommendation for Mr. Santos.')

The same class of verbs can appear only in the instrumental voice when an initial benefactive is a final 1. If there is a rule of Benefactive-3 Advancement, these verbs can be considered irregular in not permitting that one rule. If there is no rule of Benefactive-3 Advancement, these verbs will have to be treated as irregular in two unrelated rules.

By adding one rule to the grammar, two complications of the marking rules can be avoided and two irregularities of certain verbs can be connected. Let us, then, include the following rule of Benefactive-3 Advancement in the grammar of speakers who accept sentences like (94).

(99)   Benefactive-3 Advancement:
   If a is an initial benefactive of clause b in stratum c_i, it may be a 3 of b in stratum c_{i+1}.

One fact remains to be accounted for. Some speakers reject sentences like (94) in which an initial benefactive which is not a final 1 is not marked with *para* or *alang*, while accepting sentences with the verb in the locative voice when an initial benefactive is a final subject. Rule (99) does not describe the dialect of these speakers as it stands; yet, if these speakers have no rule permitting a transition from benefactive to 3, the complicated voice and case marking rules given above will be needed. It seems simpler to complicate (99) be adding another condition for the grammar of these speakers.

The Benefactive-3 Advancement rule can be amended in either of two ways. One could simply forbid the initial benefactive to be a final 3 by adding the condition in (100) to rule (99).

(100)   . . . but a may not be the final 3 of b.

Alternatively, one might state the rule permitting a transition from benefactive to 3 as a multistratum advancement, Benefactive-3-1 Advancement, as shown in (101):

(101)   If a is a benefactive of clause b in stratum c_i and a 1 of b in stratum c_{i+2}, it may be a 3 of b in stratum c_{i+1}.

There is some evidence from causative constructions that suggests that the first alternative is the right one. (See Bell and Perlmutter, to appear, for details.)

I propose that (99) be included in the grammar for speakers who do not require a preposition before an initial benefactive and that rule (99) with the condition in (100) be included in the grammar for speakers who do.

3.3.3   *Locative-3 Advancement?*

In §3.3.2, we dealt with an instance in which there were two possible voice markings when an initial benefactive is a final 1. In the remaining voice marking rules, there is a case of the opposite sort. The same voice (the locative) is used with a transition from 3 to 1 and with a transition from locative to 1. It might be proposed that VMR4 be eliminated by proposing an advancement from locative to 3. Under such a proposal, the arc of an initial locative which is a final 1 would show the transitions locative-3-1. VMR3 would then correctly require that the verb be in the locative voice.

Such a suggestion would ignore two large differences between Benefactive-3 Advancement and Locative-3 Advancement. First, Benefactive-3 Advancement is a rule in other languages. Using it does not require proposing an otherwise unknown rule. Locative-3 Advancement is, as far as I know, not found elsewhere.

Second, there is independent evidence that Benefactive-3 Advancement is a rule of Cebuano. Using the rule allows simplification of case marking rules as well as elimination of a particularly complicated voice marking rule. With a rule of Locative-3 Advancement, however, one straightforward rule would simply be replaced by another, with no net gain in simplicity.

On the basis of present evidence, then, Locative-3 Advancement should not be included in the grammar of Cebuano.

3.3.4   *A Note on Irregularity*

Normally, when an initial 2 is a final 1, the verb is in the objective voice as required by VMR2 in (87). With certain verbs, however, apparent irregularities are observed.

With verbs of transferral or conveyance, one would expect the thing transferred or conveyed to be an initial 2. By VMR4, it would follow that the verb should be in the objective voice when the thing transferred or conveyed is the final 1. Instead, the verb is in the instrumental voice.

(102) a.   Mosulod   ang lalaki sa   mga butang sa   sakyanan.
　　　　　ACT-inside NOM man   OBL PL   thing   OBL vehicle
　　　　　'The man will put the things into the vehicle.'
　　　b.   Isulod   sa   lalaki ang mga butang sa   sakyanan.
　　　　　INS-inside GEN man   NOM PL   thing   OBL vehicle
　　　　　'The things will be put into the vehicle by the man.'

With many verbs of perception and mental activity (*alinggat,* 'notice, perceive'; *hinumdum,* 'remember'; *kalimot,* 'forget', and others) and with certain other verbs (*kapot,* 'grab') the verb is in the locative voice when the dependent that would be expected to be an initial 2 is the final 1. For example, the thing grabbed would be expected to be an initial 2, but as shown below, the verb is in the locative voice rather than the objective voice when the thing grabbed is the final 1.

(103) a. Ningkapot ang kawatan sa   akong bag.
     ACT-grab NOM thief   OBL my-LN bag
     'The thief grabbed my bag.'

   b. Gikaptan sa   kawatan ang akong bag.
     grab-LOC GEN thief   NOM my-LN bag
     'My bag was grabbed by the thief.'

   c. *Gikapot sa   kawatan ang akong bag.
     OBJ-grab GEN thief   NOM my-LN bag
   (My bag was grabbed by the thief.)

These irregularities might be treated in at least four ways. First, it might be claimed that the final 1s in these sentences are not really initial 2s. Second, some other factor in addition to grammatical relation may be influencing choice of voice affix.[25] Third, the initial 2 may bear some other nonfinal grammatical relation. Fourth, the rules for verbal voice marking may be different with different classes of verbs; that is, the marking may be irregular.

I follow Wolff (1966), Kess (1967), Kerr (1965), and others in treating certain classes of verbs as irregular. With verbs of conveying, the instrumental voice marks, among other things, a transition from 2 to 1. Similarly, with another class of verbs including *kapot* 'grab' and the verbs of perception, a transition from 2 to 1 is marked by the locative voice.

3.4   Summary of the Rules Proposed

The analysis proposed has a single rule of advancement to 1:

(104)   If a is a central dependent of a clause b in stratum c_i, it may be a 1 of b in stratum c_{i+1}.

It has one of two rules of Benefactive-3 Advancement, depending on the dialect.

(105)   If a is a benefactive of clause b in stratum c_i, it may be a 3 of b in stratum c_{i+1}.

(106)   If a is a benefactive of clause b in stratum c_i, it may be a 3 of b in stratum c_{i+1}, but it may not be a final 3 of b.

The voice marking rules are as given earlier in (87).

VMR1:   If verb a is a predicate of clause b and no arc of a dependent of *b* shows a transition from non-1 to 1, then *a* is in the active voice.

VMR2:   If verb *a* is the predicate of clause *b* and the arc of some dependent of *b* shows a transition 2-1, then *a* is in the objective voice.

VMR3:   If verb *a* is the predicate of clause *b* and the arc of some dependent of *b* shows a transition 3-1, then *a* is in the locative voice.

VMR4:   If verb *a* is the predicate of clause *b* and the arc of some dependent of *b* shows a transition locative-1, then *a* is in the locative voice.

VMR5:   Elsewhere, if verb *a* is a predicate of clause *b, a* is in the instrumental voice.

Irregular voice marking will be stated in special voice marking rules restricted to certain verbs or verb classes.

The following rules will require the correct case markings for benefactives and for central dependents whose relations are not marked by prepositions. To these rules may be added a rule for the case of the final 1 in *pag-* and *inig*-clauses.

CMR1:   A final 1 in a finite clause is in the nominative case.

CMR2:   A final 1-chômeur from an advancement is in the genitive case.

CMR3:   A final benefactive is marked by *para* or *alang* 'for'.

CMR4:   Other central dependents are in the oblique case.

CMR5:   A final 1 in a *pag*-clause or *inig*-clause is in the genitive.

Prepositions will govern the case of the dependents they mark.

4   Schachter's Objections

I have proposed that the so-called actor is the initial 1, the nominative nominal is the final 1, and advancement rules sanction transitions to 1 in the networks of nonactive sentences, supported the proposal with arguments from Quantifier Float, relativization, reflexivization, and Equi, and discussed the form of the rules required. Schachter (1976, 1977) has objected to the analysis proposed. In his 1976 paper, using data from Tagalog, he presents three arguments against considering the actor as initial 1 and the 'topic' (i.e., the nominative nominal) as final 1 in Philippine languages.

4.1   Objection Based on Sentences without Actors

The 'actor' was defined earlier as the dependent which is in the nominative case when the verb is in the active voice. Schachter points out that Tagalog has several classes of sentences which have no actor. He argues that if the initial subject in all sentences were the actor, these sentences without actors would have no initial subject. Assuming that every logically complete declarative sentence must contain a subject and a predicate, he concludes that the initial subject cannot be the actor in all sentences, but only in those with certain verbs as predicates.

First, it should be noted that the proposal is to analyze the actor as the initial subject, not to claim that the initial subject is the actor in all sorts of sentences. Moreover, the analysis is proposed only for verb-containing sentences. The absence of actors in verbless sentences—equational, attributive, and existential sentences—is irrelevant. In equational and attributive sentences, exemplified below, the nominative nominal is the initial and final 1, the adjective or first nominal being the predicate.

(107)   Abagado ang lalaki.
        lawyer   NOM man
        'The man is a lawyer.'
(108)   Matalino ang lalaki.
        intelligent NOM man
        'The man is intelligent.'

Whether the nominal is a 1 in an existential sentence such as (109)

(109)   May akisidente kagabi.
        E   accident   last night
        'There was an accident last night.'

or whether the subject is a dummy cannot be decided without further study. In any case, the verbless sentences have no bearing on the claim that the actor is the initial 1 in verb-containing sentences.

Schachter's other class of sentences without actors contains verbs which cannot occur in the active voice. There is a large class of de-nominal verbs in Tagalog and in Cebuano which can occur in the loc-ative voice, but not in the active voice, and which do not have actors.

(110) a.   Papawisan ang lalaki
           sweat-LOC NOM man
           'The man will sweat.'
      b.   *Papawis ng/sa   lalaki.
           sweat   GEN/REF man
           (The man will sweat.)

Since these sentences have no actor, Schachter concludes that the actor is not what he calls 'the primary subject', that is, a dependent which is both initial and a final 1. Returning to the assumption that every logically complete predication has a subject and a predicate, he concludes further that the initial 1 in these sentences is not the actor.

Schachter's first conclusion, that the actor is not the primary subject in these sentences, is correct, but irrelevant. In the analysis proposed here, the sentences in question would have no initial subject. Perlmutter and Postal have proposed that a large number of verbs be analyzed as taking an initial 2 rather than an initial 1 (see Perlmutter 1978). If *pawis* 'sweat' belongs to this class, the network for (110a) can be diagrammed as in (111).

(111)

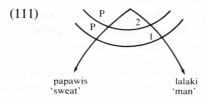

The use of locative voice with a transition from 2 to 1 can be accounted for as an irregularity or be correlated with the use of locative affixes on the verb to mark a transition from 2 to 1 with verbs denoting actions not under one's control, as mentioned in note 2. Schachter's requirement that every logically complete declarative sentence have a subject is met by this analysis, since *lalaki* 'man' is the final 1. The assumed need for a subject could present problems for this analysis only if it were further assumed that a subject must be present in the initial stratum.

Moreover, "the rather common assumption that logically complete declarative sentences must contain a subject and a predicate" (Schachter 1976, pp. 498–99) is itself open to question. In Cebuano, verbs describing meteorological conditions occur without any nominal dependents at all.

(112)   Nagulan.
        ACT-rain
        'It's raining.'

I see no reason to suppose that a sentence with one of these verbs has a subject in any stratum, yet the sentences are clearly "logically complete." Even in English, it is difficult to analyze the subject *it* in 'It's raining' as being *logically* necessary for the sentence to be complete.

Of the actorless sentences Schachter discusses, then, the verbless sentences are irrelevant. The verb-containing sentences do meet the assumed requirement that a logically complete declarative sentence have a subject. The requirement itself is debatable.

4.2   Objection Based on Restricted Occurrence of Active Forms of Certain Verbs

Schachter shows that in Tagalog the active form of certain verbs is more restricted in occurrence than the nonactive forms. For example, the active form of *takot* 'frighten' can occur only in relative clauses.

(113) a. *T*u*makot   ang lalaki ng bata.
          ACT-frighten NOM man   OBL child
          (The man frightened a child.)

      b. Nasa'an ang lalaki ng tumakot   ng bata?
          where   NOM man LN ACT frighten OBL child
          'Where's the man who frightened a child?'

To account for the ungrammaticality of (113a), Schachter presumes that "the verbs in question would have to be marked with a lexical feature that would have the effect of making the goal-subject rule apply obligatorily in just the right cases. . . . On the other hand, if goal-topic constructions are not transformationally derived, all that is needed to account for the distribution is a contextual feature on certain actor-topic verbs, constraining their insertion to the appropriate contexts" (Schachter 1976, pp. 511–12). The distribution, that is to say, can more easily be described if active and nonactive forms are inserted independently.

Continuing for the moment to follow Schachter and speak of transformations and derivations, one could reply that Schachter's objection holds only in a version of transformational grammar which does not permit surface filters.[26] In any other version, Schachter's presumption that the distribution would have to be stated using a lexically governed rule sensitive to the verb's position in a relative clause is incorrect. A surface filter would more appropriately be used.

In the uninetwork version of relational grammar, of course, no question of transformations arises. Rules are well-formedness conditions on networks. Active and nonactive sentences are related not because one is derived from the other, but because they have identical initial strata. The required condition can be stated much in line with Schachter's suggestion.

(114)   If a verb *a* is a member of the *takot* class and *a* is the predicate of clause *b,* then *b* must be a relative clause in some nominal *c* if *a* is in the active voice.

Schachter's objection, then, does not hold in the uninetwork version of relational grammar.

4.3   Objection to Busy Chômeurs

The Chômeur Condition requires that an initial 1 be a 1-chômeur in a network in which the arc of some dependent shows a transition from non-1 to 1. As a chômeur, it "will no longer have those properties that are associated uniquely with terms" (Schachter 1976, p. 512). Among those properties are "control over Reflexivization and control over Equi-Noun Phrase Deletion (coreferential complement deletion)." The chômeur, then, should not be able to control Reflexivization or Equi. But in fact, the actor controls Reflexivization and Equi in active and nonactive sentences alike. The actor, then, cannot be a chômeur even in nonactive sentences. Therefore, nonactive and active sentences cannot be related by advancement rules, if the Relational Annihilation Law (now the Chômeur Condition) is to be maintained.

Schachter's argument does not go through as it stands. Another premise is covertly assumed. The premise may be that a rule cannot refer to relations in particular strata, or it may be that all rules relating to coreference are stated with respect to final grammatical relations.

If neither of these premises is added, the coreference rules can refer to initial grammatical relations. For example, consider Equi. A lexically governed rule can require that with matrix verbs like *sa'ad* 'promise' the initial 1 of the matrix clause and the initial 1 of the complement be the same. Equi can then require that the initial 1 of a *pag*-clause with these verbs not be realized. Similarly, the reflexive rule can specify permissible anaphoric links between a reflexive and another dependent on the basis of initial grammatical relations. If these rules are stated with respect to initial 1s, the fact that an initial 1 is a final 1-chômeur in nonactive sentences will be irrelevant to the rules. The argument thus requires one of the premises above to rule out this possibility if the objection is to be valid.

There is, however, no reason to assume either of the premises. Neither is a principle of the uninetwork version of relational grammar. Rules may refer to initial and final grammatical relations, permitting the analysis outlined above. Moreover, there is evidence that coreference rules must be able to refer to nonfinal strata. In Russian, for example, a reflexive pronoun may have as its antecedent the initial 1 even in a passive sentence. (See Perlmutter, to appear, for examples and discussion.) To require that rules concerning coreference refer only to final strata would not permit an adequate description of Russian reflexives, quite apart from the problem of Philippine reflexives. Since reference to nonfinal strata must be permitted, the rules of Equi and Reflexive can refer to initial grammatical relations. The fact that an initial 1 may be a final 1-chômeur will be irrelevant.

Since there is no reason to make either of the assumptions required to complete the argument,[27] and since indeed there is reason *not* to make them, Schachter's objection does not hold.

4.4   Conclusion

Schachter discussed the arguments for and against the subjecthood of the 'topic' (nominative nominal), the 'actor', and the 'actor-topic' (a nominative actor). He concluded that "these three different constituent classes in fact share the properties commonly associated with subjects" (Schachter 1976, p. 493). From this, he went on to claim that "it cannot be the case that 'subject' represents a linguistic universal" (p. 515). He concluded that 'subject' cannot be taken as a primitive term in a theory of grammar.

In order for his first conclusion to hold, Schachter had to dispose of one possible analysis which would account for the apparent sharing of "properties commonly associated with subjects" by the nominative nominal and the actor, an analysis in which the actor is an initial subject and the nominative nominal is a final subject. This analysis is the one proposed here. As I hope I have shown, none of the objections Schachter advances holds. Schachter's first conclusion is thereby undermined. Without the first conclusion, the subsequent conclusions cannot be established. It follows that it has not been shown that the 'subject' cannot be taken as a linguistic universal or that theories of grammar taking 'subject' as a primitive can be ruled out. On the contrary, one such theory has been shown to permit a coherent analysis of verb-containing sentences in a Philippine language.

Ascensions

5   Introduction

In the section on advancements, it was proposed that the actor be analyzed as the initial 1 in verb-containing sentences, the nominative nominal be analyzed as the final 1, and an advancement rule sanction diverse transitions to 1 in the networks of nonactive sentences. Here the proposed analysis is extended in the examination of two more constructions. There are two reasons for extending the analysis. First, if it is shown that the nominative nominal acts like a 1 in other constructions, the analysis in which it is the final 1 is strengthened. Second, the various laws of relational grammar, being empirical hypotheses, are logically independent. Showing that these logically independent laws impose a coherent analysis on the data should increase our confidence in the laws.

Since the constructions will be analyzed as ascensions, it may be useful to repeat what was said in §1.3.1 about ascensions. In an ascension, a dependent of a dependent of a clause in one stratum is itself a dependent of a clause in another stratum. The dependent from which it ascends (the host) must be a term, by the Host Limitation Law. The ascendee assumes the grammatical relation of the host, by the Relational Succession Law. In accordance with the Chômeur Condition, the rest of the host is a chômeur.

It is the Host Limitation Law and the Relational Succession Law that will confirm that the nominative nominal is a 1, for we shall see that both ascensions are restricted to the nominative nominal.

6 Possessor Ascension

6.1 The Construction

Cebuano has a class of verb-containing sentences with two nominatives. Except for topic, (115a) is synonymous with (115b). In (115a), the possessor *sakup ni Iyo' Bruno* appears in front of the verb and is in the nominative case. In this construction, it is also possible for a possessive pronoun to appear in the normal position.

(115) Wolff 1967, p. 348

    a. Ang sakóp ni   Iyo' Bruno nagkadugo'   ang mga
        NOM group GEN Iyo' Bruno ACT-be bloody NOM PL
        ba'ba'.
        mouth
        'Iyo' Bruno's group, (their) mouths were bloody.'

    b. Nagkadugo'   ang mga ba'ba' sa   sakop ni
        ACT-be bloody NOM PL   mouth GEN group GEN
        Iyo' Bruno.
        Iyo' Bruno
        'The mouths of Iyo' Bruno's group were bloody.'

    c. Ang sakóp ni   Iyo' Bruno nagkadugo'   ang ilang
        NOM group GEN Iyo' Bruno ACT-be bloody NOM their-LN
        mga ba'ba'.
        PL   mouth
        'Iyo' Bruno's group, their mouths were bloody.

A preverbal possessor is unambiguously associated with the nominative nominal. In (116a), the possessor is not a dependent of the nominative nominal. If the possessor is in preverbal position, the sentence is ungrammatical (116b). In the corresponding passive sentence (116c), the possessor is in the nominative nominal. The nominative possessor can be found in preverbal position (116d).

(116) a. Miputol   na   siya   sa sungay sa baka.
       ACT-cut off already he-NOM OBL horn   GEN COW
       'He has already cut off the cow's horns.'

     b. *Ang/*Sa baka miputol   na   siya   sa mga
       NOM/GEN COW ACT-cut off already he-NOM OBL PL
       sungay.
       horn
       (The cow, he cut off (its) horns.)

     c. Giputlan   na   niya   ang sungay sa baka.
       cut off-LOC already he-GEN NOM horn   GEN COW
       'The cow's horns were already cut off by him.'

     d. Ang baka giputlan   na   niya   ang (iyang) sungay.
       NOM COW cut off-LOC already he-GEN NOM (its)   horn
       'The cow, (its) horns were already cut off by him.'

Moreover, when my informant was asked to correct (117a), he gave (117b). Asked to correct (117c), he responded with (117d).

(117) a. *Ang pangulo nagbisita ang mga sulugu'on sa   balay.
       NOM chief   ACT-visit NOM PL   servant   OBL house
       (The chief, (his) servants visited the house.)

     b. Nagbisita ang mga sulugu'on sa   pangulo sa   balay.
       ACT-visit NOM PL   servant   GEN chief   OBL house
       'The chief's servants visited the house.'

     c. *Ang pangulo gibisitahan sa   mga sulugu'on ang balay.
       NOM chief   visit-LOC   GEN PL   servant   NOM house
       (The chief, (his) house was visited by the servants.)

     d. Gibisitahan sa   mga sulugu'on ang balay sa   pangulo.
       visit-LOC   GEN PL   servant   NOM house GEN chief
       'The chief's house was visited by the servants.'

In both cases, the sentence was corrected by associating an improperly fronted possessor with the nominative nominal. The pattern of grammatical and ungrammatical sentences in (116) and (117) shows clearly that the preverbal possessor must modify the nominative nominal.

When a possessor is nominative, it must appear before the verb.

(118) Giputlan   niya   ang sungay ang baka.
     cut off-LOC he-GEN NOM horns   NOM COW
     (The cow, its horns were cut off by him.)

Preverbal position is the position of the topic. We can account for the preverbal position of the nominative possessor if we analyze it as a topic. As indicated in the discussion of topicalized word order in §2.4.2, the topic must be a final 1 of the clause of which it is a central dependent.

The preposed possessor, that is to say, is a dependent of a 1 (the nominative nominal) in one stratum and is also a final 1 of a clause. Clearly an ascension rule is needed.

6.2   The Analysis

A rule is needed to allow a possessor to be a final 1 provided that it is also a topic. Such a rule can be stated informally as follows:

(119)   Possessor Ascension

If *a* is a possessor in nominal *b* and *b* is a 1 of clause *c*, then *a* may be a 1 of *c* if it is also a topic. It may optionally leave a pronominal copy bearing the possessor relation in nominal *b*.

Two conditions must be satisfied for a possessor to ascend. Its host must be a 1, and it itself must be a topic. Since, as mentioned above, only a final 1 can be a topic, the requirement that the possessor be a topic if it ascends entails that the ascendee must be a final 1. The ascendee cannot be, for example, a 1-chômeur.

The rule of possessor ascension, among others, will sanction the networks in (120a) and (120b). The network in (120a) corresponds to that in (116d) without the pronoun copy and (120b) to (116d) with the pronoun copy. In (120b), AL stands for anaphoric link. Because the treatment of pronouns as resulting from multiple attachments has not been firmly established, (120b) should be regarded as tentative.

(120) a.

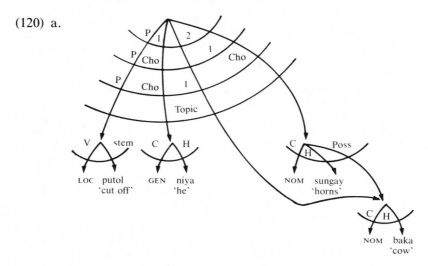

b.

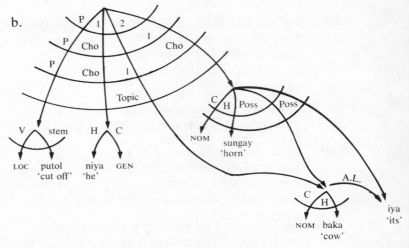

As the rule is stated, it does not require that the possessor be the topic of the same clause of which it is the final 1. As usual with topics, the possessor may be the final 1 in one clause and the topic in another, as shown in (121a) and (121b).

(121) a. Gi'ingon sa   babaye kang Fred nga giputlan   nako'
          OBJ-tell GEN woman OBL Fred LN cut off-LOC I-GEN
          ang sungay sa   baka.
          NOM horns   GEN cow
          'That the cow's horns were cut off by me was told by the woman to Fred.'

      b. Ang baka gi'ingon sa   babaye kang Fred nga giputlan
          NOM cow OBJ-tell GEN woman OBL Fred LN cut off-LOC
          nako' ang sungay.
          I-GEN NOM horn
          'The cow, that (its) horns were cut off by me was told to Fred by the woman.'

The ascendee must be a topic, but it need not be the topic of the clause into which it ascends. In such cases, topics from Possessor Ascension are subject to the usual restrictions on topics. If the possessor is a topic of a clause of which it is not the final 1, then it must be part of the clause which is the final 1 of that clause, as in (121b).

6.3   Consequences of the Analysis

The rule of Possessor Ascension permits the possessor to be a final 1. By the Chômeur Condition, the rest of the host must be a chômeur. Both of these consequences of the rule interact with the earlier analysis and with principles of the theory.

We saw earlier in §2.1.3 that only the final 1 is relativizable. If the rule of Possessor Ascension is correct, the ascended possessor should be relativizable and the chômeur should not be relativizable. This prediction is fulfilled.[28] In (122), the ascendee has been relativized.

(122) Nahadlok siya   sa   sakop ni   Iyo' Bruno nga
       ACT-fear he-NOM OBL group GEN Iyo' Bruno LN
       nagkadugo'   ang ba'ba'.
       ACT-be bloody NOM mouth
       'He was afraid of Iyo' Bruno's group, who (their) mouths were
       bloody.'

In contrast, the chômeur cannot be relativized.

(123) *Nakakita' siya   sa   mga ba'ba' nga ang sakop ni
       ACT-see   he-NOM OBL PL   mouth LN   NOM group GEN
       Iyo' Bruno nagkadugo'.
       Iyo' Bruno ACT-be bloody
       (He saw the mouths which, Iyo' Bruno's group, (theirs) were
       bloody.)

The relations sanctioned by Possessor Ascension and the Chômeur Condition are also borne out by the case marking. Since the possessor has ascended to be the final 1, it should be in the nominative case by CMR1, as indeed it is. By the Chômeur Marking Principle, unless there is a special case marking rule for the chômeur, an *n*-chômeur has the same case marking as a final *n*. If no special marking rule is set up, the host will be in the nominative case. The use of the nominative case for the ascension chômeur thus follows naturally from an ascension analysis.

The presence of two nominative nominals in a sentence, which is natural enough under the analysis proposed, presents difficulties for those who simply identify the topic with the nominative nominal, denying that the Philippine languages have subjects. In (116d), will they say that *ang baka* 'cow' or *ang sungay* 'horn' is the topic? For us, there is no question. *Ang baka* is the final subject and the topic; *ang sungay* is a 1-chômeur.

Case marking and accessibility to relativization, then, support the ascension analysis.[29]

7   Pag-Ascension
7.1   The Construction

In the discussion of *pag*-clauses in §2.2.2, it was noted that the 1 of a *pag*-construction is in the genitive case and that other dependents are in the oblique case. As shown in (124), none of the dependents can be in the nominative case.

(124) sa   pagkapot sa/*ang   kawatan sa/*ang   manok
       OBL grabbing GEN/NOM thief   GEN/NOM chicken
       'upon the thief's grabbing the chicken'

Pag-complements of certain verbs (e.g., *sugud* 'begin'; *huna'huna'* 'think about'; *hadlok* 'fear'; *hinumdum* 'remember'; *sulay* 'try') appear to contradict this generalization.

(125) Gihuna'huna'   ni   Lito sa   pagsulat ni   Maria ang
       OBJ-think about GEN Lito ?OBL writing GEN Maria NOM
       balita kang Jose.
       news OBL Jose
       'Maria's writing *the news* to Jose was being thought about by Lito.'

On the face of it, (125) is exceptional in another way as well. An independent clause with *huna'huna'* 'think about' as predicate must have a nominative dependent.

(126) a. Gihuna'huna'   ni   Lito ang iyang anak.
          OBJ-think about GEN Lito NOM his-LN child (offspring)
          'Lito was thinking about *his child*.'
      b. *Gihuna'huna'   ni   Lito sa   iyang anak.
          OBJ-think about GEN Lito OBL his-LN child
          (Was thought about his child by Lito.)

In (125), *huna'huna'* is the predicate of the main clause, but there appears to be no nominative nominal in that clause.

7.2   The Analysis

The two apparent anomalies in (125) vanish if the nominative nominal *ang balita* 'the news' has ascended to be a dependent of the same clause as *huna'huna'* 'think about' by an ascension rule. Under such an analysis, *balita* will be nominative because it is the final 1 of the main clause. The clause with *huna'huna'* as predicate will have the final 1 it requires. Before the ascension rule can be stated, it is necessary to consider further possible ascendees and possible hosts.

Turning first to possible ascendees, we saw in (125) that the initial 2 of the complement can ascend. In (127), *Jose* is in the nominative case, showing that an initial 3 of the complement can ascend.

(127) Gihuna'huna' ni Lito sa pagsulat ni Maria sa balita
       OBJ-think about GEN Lito ?OBL writing GEN Maria OBL news
       si   Jose.
       NOM Jose
       'Maria's writing the news to *Jose* was thought about by Lito.'

As shown in (128), the initial 1 of the complement cannot ascend; *Maria*
cannot be in the nominative case.

(128) *Gihuna'huna' ni Lito sa pagsulat si Maria sa
       OBJ-think about GEN Lito ?OBL writing NOM Maria OBL
       balita kang Jose.
       news OBL Jose
       (*Maria's* writing the news to Jose was thought about by Lito.)

The ascendee, that is to say, can be an initial 2 or 3 of the *pag*-clause.
    Now let us turn to possible hosts. The same voice found on the verb
when the complement is the final 1 is found with the ascension. Example
(129a) shows that the verb is in the locative voice when the complement
is the final 1. Example (129b) shows that this same voice is used when
kahoy 'tree' ascends. No other voice can be used when *kahoy* ascends.
The verb cannot be in the active voice, for example.

(129) a. Gisugdan ni   Juan ang pagpilay   sa kahoy.
          begin-LOC GEN Juan NOM cutting down OBL tree
          'Cutting down the tree was begun by Juan.'
      b. Gisugdan ni   Juan sa   pagpilay   ang kahoy.
          begin-LOC GEN Juan ?OBL cutting down NOM tree
          'Cutting down *the tree* was begun by Juan.'
      c. *Misugud si/ni   Juan sa   pagpilay   ang kahoy.
          ACT-begin NOM/GEN Juan ?OBL cutting down NOM tree
          (Juan began cutting down *the tree*.)

There are two ways of accounting for the sameness of voice marking:

(130) Ascension From 1
       The host of the ascension must be a 1. In order for ascension
       to be permitted, the *pag*-complement must be a 1. That is, its
       arc will show a transition to 1. Because of this transition, the
       usual voice marking found with an advancement of the com-
       plement to 1 will be required on the verb. Since the ascendee
       ascends from a 1, it must be a 1 by the Relational Succession
       Law. Under this hypothesis, the network for (125) will be as
       diagrammed in (131).

(131)

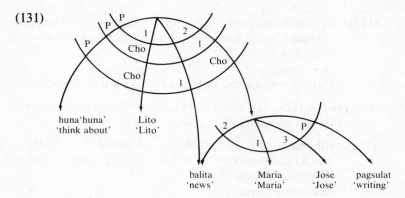

(132)   **Ascension from 2**
The host of the ascension is a 2. The ascendee ascends from a 2. By the Relational Succession Law, it is a 2 of the main clause. If it is a 1 in a later stratum, its arc in the main clause will show a transition from 2 to 1. The voice marking rule will accordingly require that the verb be in the case used with a transition 2-1 with the verb in question. Under this analysis, the network for (125) will be as diagrammed in (133).

(133)

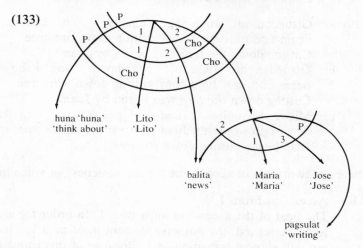

These two analyses make different predictions. First, under the Ascension-from-1 analysis, the *pag*-complement is a final 1-chômeur, while under the Ascension-from-2 analysis, it is a final 2-chômeur. Second, under the Ascension-from-2 analysis, but not under the Ascension-from-1 analysis, the following stratal diagram will be well-formed.

(134)

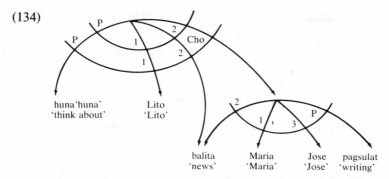

In (134), *balita* has ascended from the complement to be a 2 of the main clause, as permitted by the Ascension-from-2 analysis. Since advancement to 1 is optional, (134) should be well-formed. Under the Ascension-from-1 analysis, the *pag*-complement must be a 1 to serve as a host. Since the *pag*-complement in (134) is not a 1, *balita* cannot ascend, and (134) is not well-formed.

Unfortunately, neither of these differences in predictions leads to a clear argument favoring one analysis over the other. The first difference provides the basis for a weak argument in favor of the Ascension-from-2 analysis, while the second provides a weak argument in favor of the Ascension-from-1 analysis.

Under the Ascension-from-2 analysis, the *pag*-complement is a final 2-chômeur. As such, it will be marked like a 2 in accordance with the Chômeur Marking Principle, unless there is a special chômeur marking rule. Since a final 2 is in the oblique case, the marking of the *pag*-complement will follow without any special rule under the Ascension-from-2 analysis.

This argument has two weaknesses. First, a special rule of case marking is possible. Although, all other things being equal, an analysis without such a special rule is to be preferred, the fact that a special rule is needed does not show that the Ascension-from-1 analysis is impossible.

Second, the argument holds only if the *pag*-complement really is in the oblique case. As I have indicated by the question mark preceding the gloss 'OBL', the case marking is uncertain. The case marker is *sa*. *Sa* is used to mark either genitive or oblique case. Normally, one can determine which case is being marked by substituting a personal name or a personal pronoun for the nominal marked by *sa*. If the case is genitive, the personal name marker will be *ni* and the pronoun will be genitive. If the case is oblique, *kang* will mark a personal name and the oblique pronouns will be used. Since *pag*-constructions are obviously not personal names or animates and since *pag*-ascension occurs only out of *pag*-constructions, there is no way to determine whether *sa* is being used to mark genitive or oblique case with the chômeur. In a description, the choice is arbitrary. I have chosen to suppose that the *pag*-complement is in the oblique case, but no argument should be based on this assumption.

Returning to the other difference in the predictions of the two analyses, one can make a similarly inconclusive argument favoring the Ascension-from-1 analysis. If (134) is well-formed, there should be a good sentence corresponding to it. As can be seen by comparing (129a) and (129b), for example, in *pag*-ascension, the ascendee occupies the same position in the sentence which it would occupy if it had not ascended. The sentence corresponding to (134) would accordingly be (135).

(135) Naghuna'huna' si   Lito sa   pagsulat ni   Maria sa   balita
       ACT-think about NOM Lito OBL writing   GEN Maria OBL news
       kang Jose.
       OBL Jose
       'Lito thought about Maria's writing the news to Jose.'

Now, (135) is also the sentence which will be associated with a network in which ascension has not occurred. That is, (136) as well as (134) will be associated with (135).

(136)

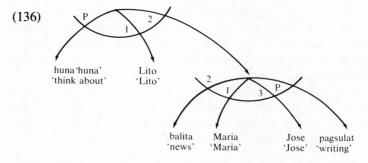

Under the Ascension-from-2 analysis, (135) is relationally ambiguous. This ambiguity is not reflected in meaning or in any marking or in word order. If the absence of any overt sign of ambiguity in (135) can be taken as an indication that the ambiguity predicted by the Ascension-from-2 analysis is spurious, then the Ascension-from-1 analysis, which does not accept (134) as well-formed, is to be preferred. Because it is unclear whether relational ambiguity must have some overt manifestation, this argument, too, is weak. However, because some question of the genuineness of the ambiguity remains, I prefer to adopt the

Ascension-from-1 analysis and not to risk introducing possibly spurious networks.

The host, then, will be a 1. Accordingly, the rule of *Pag*-Ascension will be roughly as follows:

(137) *Pag*-Ascension
   If the predicate of *a* is a *pag*-nominal and *a* is a 1 of clause *b*, then a 2 or 3 of *a* may be a 1 of *b*.

This rule will be governed by the verbs in the class indicated earlier.

Since the Ascension-from-1 analysis has been accepted, the *pag*-complement is a final 1-chômeur. Since it is not in the nominative case, a special case marking rule will be needed.

(138) A final 1-chômeur from *Pag*-Ascension is in the oblique (genitive?) case.

7.3 Consequences of the Analysis

The rule of *Pag*-Ascension permits a 2 or 3 of a *pag*-complement to be the 1 of the main clause. The ascendee should act like a 1 in relativization, Possessor Ascension, Quantifier Float, the Topic Rule, and the word orders. We shall see that it does act like a 1 in accessibility to relativization, the Topic Rule, Possessor Ascension, and possibly in Quantifier Float. It does not occur in the position of a 1 in the basic word order. Let us go through these one by one.

7.3.1 *Relativization of the Ascendee*

We have seen that only final 1s can be relativized. Thus, *kahoy* 'tree' cannot be relativized in (138a), as shown in (138b).

(138) a. Gisugdan ni   Juan ang pagpilay   sa   kahoy.
          begin-LOC GEN Juan NOM cutting down OBL tree
          'Cutting down the tree was begun by Juan.'
      b. *Ta'as ka'ayo ang   kahoy nga gisugdan   ni   Juan ang
          tall   very   NOM tree   LN begin-LOC GEN Juan NOM
          pagpilay.
          cutting down
          (The tree that Juan began cutting down was very tall.)

If *kahoy* ascends, as in (139a), it can be relativized, as in (139b).

(139) a. Gisugdan ni   Juan sa   pagpilay   ang kahoy.
          begin-LOC GEN Juan OBL cutting down NOM tree
          'Cutting down *the tree* was begun by Juan.'

b. Ta'as ka'ayo ang kahoy nga gisugdan ni   Juan sa
    tall   very   NOM tree   LN begin-LOC GEN Juan OBL
    pagpilay.
    cutting down
    'The tree the cutting down of which was begun by Juan was
    very tall.'

It follows that the ascendee is the final 1, as the analysis predicts.

7.3.2 *Ascendee as Topic*

The ascendee can appear before the verb in at least some instances[30]
in topicalized word order. *Kanang taytayana* 'that bridge' has ascended
in (140a) and can appear before the verb as in (140b).

(140) a. Gikahadlokan ko'   sa   pag'agi kanang
          fear-LOC   I-GEN OBL passing that-NOM-LN
          taytayana.
          bridge-SPECIFIC
          'I'm afraid to go over *that bridge*.'
      b. Kanang   taytayana gikahadlokan ko'   sa   pag'agi.
          that-NOM-LN bridge-SPEC fear-LOC   I-GEN OBL passing
          'That bridge I'm afraid to go over.'

Preverbal position alone does not establish that *kanang taytayana* is
the topic in (140b), since a dependent can precede the verb in either
topicalized word order or adverbial word order. Now, (140b) cannot
be an example of adverbial word order. In that word order, nonnuclear
dependents precede the verb which is predicate of the clause of which
they are dependents. If (140b) were an example of adverbial word order
kanang taytayana would have to be a nonnuclear dependent; it could
not have ascended. But if it had not ascended, it would still be a
dependent of the clause of which *pag'agi* 'passing' is the predicate.
The adverbial word order would not justify its appearance in front of
the predicate of the matrix clause. Therefore, (140b) cannot be taken
to be an example of adverbial word order, but must rather be an example
of topicalized word order. *Kanang taytayana* is therefore a topic. Since
only final 1s are topics, it follows that *kanang taytayana* is a final 1,
as permitted by the ascension rule.

7.3.3 *Possessor Ascension and Pag-Ascension*

In §6.1, we saw that possessors can ascend from 1s. The ascendee of
Pag-Ascension can host Possessor Ascension, as shown in (141b).

(141) a.   Gisugdan niya   sa   pagputol   ang sungay sa   baka.
        begin-LOC he-GEN OBL cutting off NOM horn   GEN COW
        'Cutting off *the cow's horns* was begun by him.'
    b.   Ang baka gisugdan   niya   sa   pagputol   ang sungay.
        NOM cow begin-LOC he-GEN OBL cutting off NOM horn
        'The cow, cutting off (its) horns was begun by him.'

In Possessor Ascension, too, the ascendee of *Pag*-Ascension acts like a 1.

7.3.4   *Quantifier Float and Pag-Ascension*

In §2.1.2, it was shown that only 1s can launch floating quantifiers. If being a 1 is a sufficient condition for launching floating quantifiers, then *Pag*-Ascension predicts that the ascendee should launch floating quantifiers.

Unfortunately, it is not clear whether this prediction is fulfilled or not. The responses of the two informants I questioned were inconsistent. Both sometimes accepted and sometimes rejected sentences like (142).

(142) ?Gisugdan *tanan* sa   mangangahoy sa   pagpilay
      begin-LOC all   GEN woodcutter   OBL cutting down
      ang   kahoy.
      NOM tree
      'The trees were all begun to be cut down by the woodcutter.'

In view of the inconsistent responses, Quantifier Float appears neither to support nor to disconfirm the proposed rule of *Pag*-Ascension.

7.3.5   *The Problem of Word Order*

In the basic word order, the final 1 follows the 1-chômeur. The ascendee of *Pag*-Ascension can sometimes appear in this position, as in (143), but sometimes it cannot, as in (144).

(143)   Gisugdan ni   Juan ang kahoy sa   pagpilay.
      begin-LOC GEN Juan NOM tree   OBL cutting down
      'The tree was begun to be cut down by Juan.'
(144) *Gihuna'huna'   ni   Lito ang balita sa   pagsulat ni   Maria
      OBJ-think about GEN Lito NOM news OBL writing GEN Maria
      kang Jose.
      OBL Jose
      (Lito was thinking of Maria's writing *the news* to Jose.)[31]

In any case, the most natural position for the ascendee in this construction is after the subject of the *pag*-construction. To state the word order heretofore we have had to refer only to final relations. Here, it will be necessary to refer to initial relations as well. For ease of statement, I shall write the predicate as a subscript, 'm' for the main verb and 'p' for the *pag*-clause, and put an 'i' before an initial grammatical relation. Thus 'i3p' will mean the initial 3 of the *pag*-construction, for example. The *Pag*-Ascension word order can then be stated as:

(145) *Pag*-Ascension Word Order
V_m (1_m) *pag*-form (1_p) 1_m ($i2_p$) ($i3_p$) ($nonterm_p$)

While *Pag*-Ascension leads us to this complicated statement for word order, it makes correct predictions with respect to relativization, topicalization, and Possessor Ascension.

8   Conclusion

Two ascensions have been proposed for Cebuano: Possessor Ascension and *Pag*-Ascension. In both, only a 1 can serve as the host. I have not found any ascensions from any term except 1. If there are none, it would seem that in restricting the grammatical relation of possible hosts in ascensions, as in relativization, Cebuano draws the line at 1.

If the earlier analysis of advancements is correct, both these ascensions are well-behaved, conforming to the Host Limitation Law and the Relational Succession Law. Their conformity supports the analysis of advancements. In Possessor Ascension, the Chômeur Marking Principle helped to account for the presence of two nominatives in a clause with a single verb, a matter difficult to explain for those who claim that the nominative nominal is the topic alone, not a 1 as well.

Two awkward points remain. First, in sentences with Possessor Ascension, being a subject is not a sufficient condition for being relativizable, although it seems to be a sufficient condition in other constructions. Second, the rule of *Pag*-Ascension required a special word order which required reference to initial relations, unlike the other word orders.

To sum it all up, one set of laws of relational grammar proposed by Perlmutter and Postal supports an analysis of simple verb-containing sentences of Cebuano in which the actor is the initial 1, the nominative nominal is the final 1, and an advancement rule sanctions transitions to 1 in the networks of nonactive sentences. When this analysis was extended to additional data, it was found to permit an analysis of the data which is in accordance with other laws and rules of relational grammar. That is to say, although there is no logical connection between the laws, they support a straightforward and consistent analysis of the data from Cebuano.

Appendix A: Verbal Affixes

The verbal affixes are summarized in the table below.

1. Active	Real Mode	Unreal Mode	
Durative	nag(a)-	mag(a)-	
Volitional	ni-/mi-/ning-/ ming-	mo-	
Potential	naka-	maka-	

2. Objective	Real Mode	Unreal Mode 1	Unreal Mode 2
Durative	gi(na)-	(pag(a)-) . . . -on	(pag(a)-) . . . -a
Volitional	gi-	-on	-a
Potential	na-	ma-	ma- . . . -a

3. Locative			
Durative	gi(na)- . . . -an	(pag(a)-) . . . -an	(pag(a)-) . . . -i
Volitional	gi- . . . -an	-an	-i
Potential	na- . . . -an	ma- . . . -an	ma- . . . -i

4. Instrumental	gi(pag(a))-	i(pag)-/i(ga)-	i(pag)-
Durative	gi(pag(a))-	i(pag)-/i(ga)-	i(pag)-
Volitional	gi-	i-	i-
Potential	gika-/na	ika-/ma-	ika-/ma-

(These tables are based on Wolff 1966 and Bunye and Yap 1971.) The parts of affixes in parentheses are rare except in formal writing.

In the table above, I have used Wolff's names for aspects and voices. Bunye and Yap (1971) use "neutral" for "volitional," "progressive" for "durative," and "aptative" for "potential." Writers on other languages use "nonvolitional" for "potential," and "referential" for "locative."

Unreal mode 1 is used for future and habitual actions; unreal mode 2 (Wolff's "subjunctive"), for imperatives and negated past action.

Appendix B: Case Markers and Pronouns

1. Case Marking Particles

		Nominative	Genitive	Oblique
Personal Name		si	ni	kang
	Specific	ang	sa	sa
Other				
	Nonspecific	y (?)/ ø	sa	ug

Note that the genitive *sa* differs from the oblique *sa* in that it occurs in the same environments as *ni* rather than those of *kang* and in that it is not marked for specificity.

There is some question about the proper analysis of *ug*. See note 23 for further information.

2. Personal Pronouns

Person	Nominative	Genitive		Oblique
		Postposed	Preposed	
Singular				
1	ako (ko)	nako' (ko')	ako'	kanako' (nako')
2	ikaw (ka)	nimo (mo)	imo	kanimo (nimo)
3	siya	niya	iya	kaniya (niya)
Plural				
1 (excl)	kami (mi)	namo' (mo')	amo'	kanamo' (namo')
1 (incl)	kita (ta)	nato' (to')	ato'	kanato' (nato')
2	kamo (mo)	ninyo	inyo	kaninyo (ninyo)
3	sila	nila	ila	kanila (nila)

The forms in parentheses are short forms. *Ka* is obligatorily used instead of *ikaw* except when *ikaw* is the predicate or is somehow separated from the verb. Use of the other short forms is optional. Short forms are placed after the verb or a preverbal deictic or negative. See Wolff 1966, 6D for details about order of pronouns.

Bunye and Yap (1971) do not separate the postposed genitive forms from the short forms of the oblique pronouns, which are homophonous with them. However, the forms do belong to different substitution classes. The postposed genitive forms can always be replaced by the preposed genitive forms, while the short forms of the oblique pronouns cannot. The short forms of the postposed genitive cannot be used in place of the short forms of the oblique pronouns.

3. Demonstratives

	Nominative	Genitive/Oblique
Near me, not near you	kiri (ri)	ni'iri
Near us	kini (ni)	ni'ini
Near you, not near me	kana' (na')	ni'ana'
Not near us	kadto (to)	ni'adto

A noun preceded by a demonstrative may be marked specific by the suffix -a.

These tables are all based on information from Wolff 1966.

Notes

1. Cebuano is a member of the Philippine branch of the Austronesian (Malayo-Polynesian) family. It is spoken by between 7 and 10 million people in the

Philippines, principally in the middle islands or Visayas, but also in parts of northern and central Mindanao. It is also known as Visayan or Bisayan or Bisaya' or Binisaya'. However, since Waray, Hiligaynon, and other languages are also spoken in the Visayas, I prefer the name Cebuano, even though the language is spoken in many places besides Cebu.

The chief works on Cebuano are John Wolff's thesis *Cebuano Visayan Syntax* (1965), his *Dictionary of Cebuano Visayan* (1972), and his excellent pedagogical grammar *Beginning Cebuano,* part 1 (1966), part 2 (1967). Bunye and Yap 1971 is more limited and less carefully done.

For the most part, I use regular Cebuano orthography. The spelling deviates from the phonemic structure in the following ways: (1) *i* and *e* are not phonemically distinct, contrasting only in some borrowed words. Neither are *o* and *u*. (2) The single phoneme /ŋ/ is represented by *ng*. (3) In the usual orthography, glottal stops are represented by a hyphen between a C and a V and omitted elsewhere. I use an apostrophe for a glottal stop, except word initially. All words written with an initial vowel really begin with a glottal stop. (4) Stress is phonemic and shifts when affixes are added. It is not represented in the usual orthography, and I, too, omit it.

My chief informant has been Mr. Angelo Larraga. Mr. Larraga was born in Leyte, and his first language was Waray. Since he was sent to school in Cebu from the time he was ten years old, he also has native competence in Cebuano. He was at one time a writer for the *Bisaya* magazine. He has a good imagination and can dream up contexts for otherwise improbable sentences. Because he has lived in the United States for more than eight years and lived in Manila for some time before that, his Cebuano may be influenced by English or Tagalog. Mrs. Divina Lynch, who was born in Cagayan de Oro and worked in Valencia, Bukidnon, in Mindanao, Mrs. Lolita de la Pena from Cebu, and Miss Lucy Castillo from Cebu also provided comments on some sentences.

The following abbreviations of verbal voice markings are used in this paper:

ACT   active
INS   instrumental
LOC   locative
OBJ   objective
REF   referential

The following are used as R-signs (names of grammatical relations):

AL   anaphoric link (see n. 19)
C   case
H   head
P   predicate
TOPIC   topic
V   voice

2. The locative voice has two additional uses which do not seem to be connected with the use just described. First, the locative voice may be used when the nominative nominal refers to something indirectly affected by the action of the verb, as shown in the following examples from Wolff 1966 (8A4).

(i)   Tinalig   *ma*gabhi'*an ta.*
       maybe-CONJ night-LOC   we-INCL-NOM
       'Perhaps we'll be benighted.'

(ii) *Gi*mahala*n si   Ju̜an* sa   pliti ngadto sa   Ormok.
     dear-LOC   NOM Juan OBL fare thither OBL Ormoc
     'Juan considered the fare to Ormoc expensive.'

The nominative nominals in these sentences seem rather like *on* phrases in sentences such as 'The dog ate the meat on me.' They may be analogous to 'datives of interest' or 'ethical datives'. They require separate treatment, and I will not deal with them.

The second use is the use of the locative voice when an action is accidental. The nominative in such a sentence may be an initial 2 or an initial locative. In (iii), the seeing may be by chance or on purpose; in (iv), it is by chance (Wolff 1967 (24A2)):

(iii) *Gi*kita' ko'   *siya*   sa   simbahan.
      OBJ-see I-GEN he-NOM OBL church
      'He was seen by me at church.'
(iv) Kit'*an* ko'   *siya*   sa   simbahan.
      see-LOC I-GEN he-NOM OBL church
      'He was seen by me at church (by chance).'

In these sentences, the locative voice is no longer determined purely by the relationship of the nominative in the clause. This use of the locative voice is also peculiar in that the verb is in the unreal mode, regardless of the circumstances of the action. This deviance from the normal pattern seems to indicate that the category of voice is taking on some other function in accidental locatives. I exclude them, too, from my discussion.

3. Directionals and sources are treated like locatives in case marking and voice marking. I therefore use the term 'locative' so as to include directionals and sources as well.

4. *Gigamit* is clearly the objective form of *gamit* 'use' and thus takes a nominative complement. That it is used as a preposition in sentences like (8) is suggested by the fact that it cannot take additional nominal complements in these constructions. It may, however, be being used in some sort of nominative absolute. The analysis of this form is an open question.

5. This summary is somewhat oversimplified. Irregular voice marking is discussed briefly in §3.3.4.

6. According to Elkins 1970, p. 2, note 3, the term 'focus' began to replace 'voice' among members of the Summer Institute of Linguistics in 1953.

7. Relative clauses are discussed in §2.1.3.

8. The emeritus relation is found in clauses with some type of clause union and is borne roughly be what were called 'dead terms'. See Bell and Perlmutter, to appear, for details.

9. For discussion of this law, see Perlmutter and Postal (to appear).

10. Actually, the first arguments show that the nominative nominal is a subject in some stratum or other. They do not establish that the nominative nominal is the final 1. The arguments given in §§2.2.1 and 2.2.2 show that the actor is the *initial* subject. It is from these arguments taken together with the arguments that the nominative nominal is a subject in some stratum that it follows that the nominative nominal is the final 1. Anticipating the later arguments, I will speak of an argument's showing that the nominative nominal is a final 1, rather than of its showing that the nominative nominal is a 1 in some stratum or other.

It is worth noting that the arguments showing that the actor is the initial subject support Perlmutter and Postal's hypothesis of universal assignment of initial termhood; that is, the hypothesis that, given verbs in different languages with the same meaning, the same participant in the action will be the initial 1 in all the languages, that the same participant will be the initial 2 in all the languages, and that the same participant will be the initial 3 in all the languages.

11. It should be noted that only quantifiers which are detached from their nominal phrases are considered to have floated off the nominal. In (i), the quantifier follows the noun, but it still seems to be a part of the nominal phrase since one cannot, for instance, insert an adverb or particle between the quantifier and the noun.

(i)   Bob gave the books all away to the Salvation Army.
(ii) *Bob gave the books recently all to the Salvation Army.
(iii) *Bob gave the books away all to the Salvation Army.

12. Some speakers of Japanese will allow quantifiers to float from 3s as well, but these sentences are less natural than those with quantifiers floating from 1s and 2s. See Shibatani 1978 for some unresolved problems with Japanese quantifier float.

In French, quantifier float from 2s and 3s is subject to additional conditions which do not apply to quantifier float from 1s. See Kayne 1975 and Perlmutter 1972 for details.

13. If construing *tanan* with the nominative nominal is semantically anomalous, for example, if the nominative nominal is a singular personal name, the quantifier is associated with the nearest nominal which might be considered plural, but the sentence is not fully acceptable.

One informant reports that the dialect of Cebuano spoken in Talisay has different conditions on which dependent is construed with *tanan*.

A quantifier in postverbal position may also be taken to modify the verb. *Tanan* in such a position may be taken to mean 'wholly' or 'totally'. When other quantifiers are found postverbally, they are always interpreted as modifying the verb.

14. Keenan and Comrie's Accessibility Hierarchy has been challenged by R. Cena (1977) and S. Kuno (1973).

Cena claims that in Tagalog the final 1, objects of certain prepositions, and possessors can be relativized by the primary relativization strategy, while the direct and indirect objects cannot be, casting doubt on the claim that any relative clause forming strategy must apply to a continuous segment of the Accessibility Hierarchy.

If Tagalog, like Cebuano, has a rule of Possessor Ascension (§6), then examples with relativization of the possessor, such as (i) below, present no problem.

(i) a.   Palaging umi'iyak ang anak ng   doktor.
          always   ACT-cry NOM child GEN doctor
          'The child of the doctor is always crying.'
     b.   Nadismaya ang doktor na palaging umi'iyak ang anak.
          disappoint NOM doctor LN always   ACT-cry NOM child
          'The doctor whose child is always crying was disappointed.'

The possessor can be taken to have ascended to 1 and to be eligible for relativization.

The examples with objects of prepositions remain troublesome. In (ii-a), *doktor* is the object of the preposition *kasama*, but it can be relativized as in (ii-b).

(ii) a. Kasama ng doktor ang anak.
     ka + with OBL doctor NOM child
     'The child is with the doctor.'
   b. Nadismaya ang doktor na kasama ang anak.
     disappointed NOM doctor LN *ka* + with NOM child
     'The doctor who is with his child was disappointed.'

All the examples are with *ka* + root. Cena glosses these forms as abstract nouns as well as *ka* + preposition. He glosses *kasama* both as '*ka* + with' and as 'companion'. If *kasama* can be glossed as 'companion' in (ii) and *ng* can be taken as genitive rather than oblique, then an alternative gloss for (ii-a) would be 'The child is the doctor's companion.' Example (ii-b) would then be another example of relativization of a possessor, with the gloss 'The doctor whose companion is the child is disappointed.'

Whether the analysis suggested here can be sustained can only be determined by further investigation of Tagalog. If it can, then Cena's examples do not weaken the hierarchy.

Kuno's objection is of another sort. He claims that relativization in Japanese is limited with respect to topic rather than grammatical relation. He shows that a nominal can be relativized only if the particle following it can be deleted before the topic marker *wa* when that nominal is the topic. For example, *ni* 'to' can be deleted before *wa*, as shown in (iii).

(iii) a. Oozei no hito   ga sono mura ni kita.
     many GEN people SUBJ the   village to came
     'Many people came to the village.'
   b. Sono mura (ni) wa oozei no hito   ga kita.
     the   village to TOP many GEN people SUBJ came
     'As for the village, many people came there.'

Kara 'from' cannot be deleted before *wa*.

(iv) a. Oozei no hito   ga sono mura kara kita.
     many GEN people SUBJ the   village from came
     'Many people came from the village.'
   b. Sono mura kara/*ø wa oozei no hito   ga kita.
     the   village from   TOP many GEN people SUBJ came
     'As for the village, many people came from there.'

A relative clause can be formed by relativizing the nominal with *ni*, but not the one with *kara*. Example (v) can mean only 'the village that many people came to', not 'the village that many people came from.'

(v) oozei no hito   ga kita mura
     many GEN people SUBJ came village
     'the village that many people came to'

If both *ni* and *kara* are postpositions, the difference in relativizability of their objects is not accounted for by the Accessibility Hierarchy. If Kuno is correct, his analysis casts doubt on the universality and, hence, on the meaningfulness, of Keenan and Comrie's Accessibility Hierarchy.

Kuno's alternative, that relativization is restricted to topics in Japanese, cannot be extended to account for generalizations about relativization in other languages. In Indonesian, for example, the primary relativization strategy is restricted to 1s and 2s, not to topics (Chung 1976). The Accessibility Hierarchy does seem to account for certain facts even if Kuno's analysis is correct. The status of the Accessibility Hierarchy thus remains uncertain.

In view of this uncertainty, I can only say that relative clauses support the claim that the nominative nominal is a 1 to the extent that accessibility to relativization is restricted in accordance with the Accessibility Hierarchy.

15. See Kess 1975 for a proposal that the nominative nominal be analyzed as the only subject.

16. The ungrammaticality of (45c) and (46b) shows that we are dealing with hierarchical relations, not just with word order.

17. In (50a) and (50b), the would-be antecedent of the reflexive is a pronoun. Since the short forms of the oblique pronouns follow the verb, the pronouns precede the reflexive. Accordingly, the ungrammaticality of (50) cannot be attributed to surface word order.

18. One way of dealing with anaphora that Perlmutter and Postal have considered is by using nodes which are multiply attached in the initial stratum. In a later stratum, the multiple attachment may be broken. A pronoun or reflexive may assume one of the relations borne by the dependent, in which case the network must show an anaphoric link between antecedent and pronoun or reflexive. Diagrams (i) and (ii) exemplify such networks.

(i)   John shaved himself.

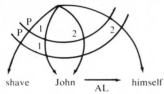

(ii)   John said he would go.

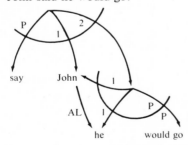

Another way of breaking a multiple attachment would be by not requiring any overt anaphoric phrase to bear one of the relations. I will indicate this by showing a transition to zero, showing that one relation is no longer borne, although this treatment is only tentative.

(iii)   John promised to go.

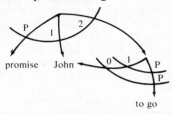

If anaphora is treated in this manner, the Reflexive Rule in Cebuano can be stated roughly as in (iv).

(iv)   Reflexive Rule
        If *a* bears initial relation *n* and initial relation *m* in clause *b,* then a reflexive must bear the lower of the two relations in *b* in the next stratum.

Given this rule, the diagram for (49b), for example, will be as in (v).

(v)

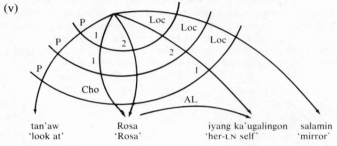

tan'aw   Rosa   iyang ka'ugalingon   salamin
'look at'   'Rosa'   'her-LN self'   'mirror'

19. The argument just given rests on the Reflexive Rank Law, which states that the antecedent must be higher in the hierarchy than the reflexive. Certain sentences in Cebuano present one problem for the law. In (i), *bata'* 'child' is a benefactive and *iyang ka'ugalingon* 'himself', 'herself' is a source. Both are nonterms. Since benefactive is no higher on the hierarchy, it should not be possible for *bata'* to be an antecedent for *ka'ugalingon.* Yet, as shown in (i), *bata'* can be the antecedent.

(i)   Nagdawat si   Maria ug sulat para sa bata' gikan
       ACT-receive NOM Maria OBL letter for   OBL child from
       sa   iyang   ka'ugalingon.
       OBL his/her-LN self
       'Maria received a letter for the child from himself/herself.'

Several alternatives are open in light of (i). One alternative that seems to me to merit further study is that some or all of the nonterms are also hierarchically ranked. Such a ranking might also help to explain the conditions on relativization in Japanese mentioned in note 14. However, no alternative can be chosen until rules governed by line-drawing have been investigated in more languages.
       20. The *nga*-clause in (60d) is a nominative nominal. It specifies the situation noticed, and when the verb is locative, the thing noticed is the nominative nominal, as in (i).

(i)   Na'alinggatan niya   ang iho.
      notice-LOC   he-GEN NOM shark
      'The shark was noticed by him.'

Moreover, if the *nga*-clause were not a nominative nominal, (60d) would be
an independent clause with the predicate *alinggat* but without any nominative
nominal. But there must be a nominative nominal in an independent clause
with *alinggat* as predicate, as shown in (ii).

(ii) *Na'alinggatan niya   sa   iho.
      notice-LOC   he-GEN OBL shark
      (Noticed the shark by him.)

What is crucial here, in terms of the analysis being discussed, is that a *nga*-
clause can be a final 1. *Ang* simply does not appear before *nga*.
     21. If we use the treatment of anaphora sketched in note 18, two rules of
Equi can be stated, the first for verbs of the *sa'ad* 'promise' class, the second
for verbs of the *sugo'* 'order' class.
     The first rule can be stated informally as in (i).

(i)   If nominal *a* is the initial 1 of clause *b,* and the 2 of *b* is a *pag*-complement
      c, and *a* is the initial 1 of *c,* then *a* is detached from *c* by Equi.

If the same highly tentative way of representing Equi that was used in note 18
is used here, the network for (64b) can be diagrammed as in (ii).

(ii)

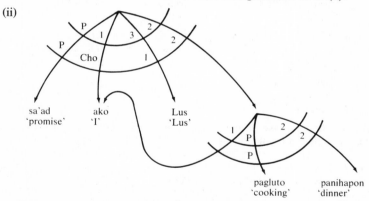

The second rule is somewhat more difficult to state. I am uncertain of the
relation of the *pag*-complement to the main clause. The use of objective voice
when the one ordered to act is the final 1 shows that, not the *pag*-complement,
but the one ordered to act, is the penultimate 2. In the rough statement of the
second rule, I will use *n* to designate the relation of the *pag*-complement in the
main clause, whatever it may be.

(iii) If nominal *a* is an initial 2 of clause *b,* and the *n* of clause *b* is a *pag*-
      complement *c,* and *a* is the initial 1 of *c,* then *a* is detached from *c* by
      Equi.

Under the same assumptions as before, the network for (64a) can be diagrammed as in (iv).

(iv)

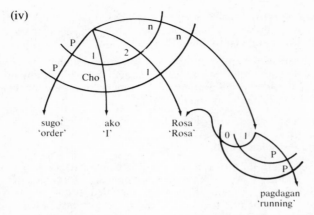

It is likely that these two rules of Equi should be collapsed into one rule in a more formal and thorough treatment.

22. Genitive pronouns come in three forms: long postposed pronouns, short postposed pronouns, and preposed pronouns. The postposed forms follow the verb or noun without any linker, as shown in (i-a–b).

(i) a. balay nako'   b. balay ko   c. akong balay
     house I-GEN   house I-GEN   my-LN house
     'my house'   'my house'   'my house'

The preposed genitive pronoun precedes the noun or verb and is linked to it by *nga,* as in (i-c). When a 1-chômeur is a pronoun, a preposed form may be used, as in (ii).

(ii) Akong giluto'   ang isda'.
     my-LN OBL-cook NOM fish
     'the fish was cooked by me.'

This is the only case in which a 1-chômeur may precede the verb. In view of the examples in (i), it seems to be a purely morphological matter.

23. In the case marking rules, I have followed Wolff 1966 in setting up three cases. It is not certain that this is correct. The case marker *ug* is included in this analysis in the oblique case markers. Yet it cannot be used with all dependents in the oblique case. All my informants permit its use with dependents which are initial and final 2s. Two permit its use with derived 2s as well; two do not. One permits its use with final instruments. None permit its use with locatives or 3s. It may be that the case marking system is changing to or from a system like Tagalog with nominative, genitive, referential, and oblique cases. In view of the confused situation, the analysis here should be taken as tentative.

24. An additional rule can be added for the 1 of *pag-* and *inig-*clauses.

(1) The final 1 in a nonfinite clause is in the genitive case.

25. As mentioned in note 2, the locative voice can be used to indicate that an event occurred by chance. This is an example in which something other than grammatical relations influences the voice.

26. Schachter's preferred alternative, "a contextual feature on certain actor-topic verbs, constraining their insertion to the appropriate contexts" could not,

I think, be stated in the *Aspects* model of transformational grammar. The active forms can appear only in relative clauses. Now, relative clauses would be described by using category symbols rather than features such as animacy. The statement of their occurrence would be a matter of strict subcategorization, not of selectional restrictions. But Chomsky places a condition on strict subcategorization: An item *a* can be strictly subcategorized with respect to category *b* only if the same phrase structure rule which introduces the node dominating *a* also introduces *b*. Since different rules introduce V and the relative clause structure, verbs cannot be strictly subcategorized to occur in relative clauses.

27. A very early version of relational grammar did hold that all relational rules applied before any coreference rules (Bell 1974a). It is likely that the earlier version led Schachter astray.

28. There are also sentences in which the ascendee cannot be relativized. For example, the ascendee cannot be relativized in (i).

(i) *Kusgan ang baka nga giputlan   niya   ang sungay.
    strong NOM COW LN cut off-LOC he-GEN NOM horns
    (The cow, which (its) horns were cut off by him, is strong.)

In the case of Possessor Ascension, at least, being a final 1 is not a sufficient condition for a nominal to be relativizable.

29. The rule of Possessor Ascension is quite limited, but I am uncertain of the exact restrictions on its use. It can apply only with certain verbs. For example, it cannot apply with *palit* 'buy'.

(i) *Kadtong   baka gipalit niya   ang sungay.
    that-NOM-LN COW OBJ-buy he-GEN NOM horn
    (That cow, (its) horns were bought by him.)

Moreover, as shown in (ii), increased complexity of material between two nominatives reduces acceptability.

(ii) a. Ang pangulo gibisitahan nila   ang balay.
        NOM chief   visit-LOC they-GEN NOM house
        'The chief, (his) house was visited by them.'
    b. *Ang pangulo gibisitahan sa   sulugu'on ang balay.
        NOM chief   visit-LOC GEN servant NOM house
        (The chief, (his) house was visited by the servants.)

Yet there is no absolute prohibition on having a nonpronominal form between the two nominatives, as shown in (iii).

(iii) Ang baka giputlan   sa magdadaro ang sungay.
     NOM COW cut off-LOC GEN farmer   NOM horn
     'The cow, (its) horns were cut off by the farmer.'

In trying to determine the conditions on Possessor Ascension, the following facts should be considered.

(A) Possessor Ascension is not limited to inalienable possession.

(iv) Ang sakop ni Iyo' Bruno nagkadugo'   ang mga bangkaw.
     NOM group GEN Iyo' Bruno ACT-be bloody NOM PL spear
     'Iyo' Bruno's group, (their) spears were bloody.'

(B) Possessor Ascension may be too narrow a name. Genitives which are not possessors may also ascend.

(v) a. Ma'ayo ang librario ni'ining lungsura.
      good   NOM library this-GEN city-SPECIFIC
      'This city's library is good.'
   b. Kining   lungsura   ma'ayo ang librario.
      this-NOM city-SPECIFIC good   NOM library
      'This city, (its) library is good.'

(C) As (v) shows, this construction can be used with inanimates.
(D) The construction occurs with abstracts.

(vi) a. Dili' malinaw ang pagsabot sa   hustisya.
      not   clear   NOM concept GEN justice
      'The concept of justice is not clear.'
   b. Ang hustisya dili' malinaw ang pagsabot.
      NOM justice not clear   NOM concept
      'Justice, (its) concept is not clear.'

30. There are sentences in which the final 1 from *Pag*-Ascension cannot precede the verb. For example, if the ascendee precedes the verb in (i), the sentence cannot be understood as one in which *Pag*-Ascension has occurred. The remnant of the *pag*-clause is treated instead as a complete temporal expression.

(i) Ang balita gihuna'huna'   ni   Lito sa   pagsulat ni
    NOM news OBJ-think about GEN Lito OBL writing   GEN
    Maria kang Jose.
    Maria OBL Jose
    'The news was thought about by Lito while Maria was writing to Jose.'
    (*Not:* The news, Lito thought about Maria's writing it to Jose.)

I suspect that the temporal reading takes precedence over the ascension reading and that the ascension reading comes through only when there is something missing from the *pag*-clause which prevents it from being interpreted as a temporal expression.

31. Here, too, a temporal reading is possible. Example (144) is grammatical with the reading 'Lito was thinking about *the news* while Maria was writing to Jose.'

References

Barnard, M., and Foster, J. 1954. "Introduction to Dibabawon Sentence Structures." *Journal of East Asiatic Studies* 3 (2): 227–31.

Bell, S. 1974a. "Some Notes on Cebuano and Relational Grammar." MIT.

———. 1974b. "Two Consequences of Advancement Rules in Cebuano." In E. Kaisse and J. Hankamer, eds., *North East Linguistics Society* 5:257–64. Cambridge, Mass.: Linguistics Dept., Harvard University.

Bell, S., and Perlmutter, D. To appear. "Causative Clause Union in Hiligaynon."

Blake, F. 1904. "Differences between Tagalog and Bisayan." *Journal of the American Oriental Society*, 25/1:162–69.

Bloomfield, L. 1917. *Tagalog Texts with Grammatical Analysis*. University of Illinois Studies in Language and Literature, 3 (3) Urbana, Ill.: University of Illinois.

Bowen, J. D. 1965. *Beginning Tagalog: A Course for Speakers of English*. Los Angeles: University of California Press.

Bunye, M., and Yap, E. 1971. *Cebuano Grammar Notes*. Honolulu: University of Hawaii Press.

Cena, R. 1977. "Relativization in Tagalog and the Accessibility Hierarchy." University of Alberta, Edmonton.

Chung, S. 1976. "An Object-Creating Rule in Bahasa Indonesia," *Linguistic Inquiry* 7, 41–87. Reprinted in this volume.

Dahl, D. 1976. *Proto-Austronesian*. London: Curzon Press.

Dean, J. 1958. "Some Principal Grammatical Relations in Bilaan." In *Studies in Philippine Linguistics*. Oceania Linguistic Monographs, no. 3, pp. 51–64. University of Sydney, Sydney, Australia.

Elkins, R. 1970. *Major Grammatical Patterns of Western Bukidnon Manobo*. Summer Institute of Linguistics Publications, no. 26. Norman, Okla.: Summer Institute of Linguistics, University of Oklahoma.

Fiengo, R., and Lasnik, H. 1976. "Some Issues in the Theory of Transformations." *Linguistic Inquiry* 7:182–92.

Interchurch Language School. 1962. *Cebuano for Missionaries*. Manila.

Kayne, R. 1975. *French Syntax: The Transformational Cycle*. Cambridge, Mass.: MIT Press.

Keenan, E. 1972. "Relative Clause Formation in Malagasy." In Peranteau et al. 1972.

———. 1976. "Towards a Universal Definition of 'Subject.' " In Li 1976.

Keenan, E., and Comrie, B. 1977. "Noun Phrase Accessibility and Universal Grammar." *Linguistic Inquiry* 8:63–100.

Kerr, H. 1965. "The Case-Marking and Classifying Function of Cotabato Manobo Voice Affixes." *Oceanic Linguistics* 4:15–48.

Kess, J. 1967. *Syntactic Features of Tagalog Verbs*. Ann Arbor, Mich.: University Microfilms.

———. 1975. "On the Semantics of Focus." *Anthropological Linguistics* 17:

Kuno, S. 1973. *Structure of the Japanese Language*. Cambridge, Mass.: MIT Press.

Li, C., ed. 1976. *Subject and Topic*. New York: Academic Press.

McKaughan, H. 1957. "Relation Markers in Maranao." In *Proceedings of the Ninth Pacific Science Congress of the Pacific Science Association* 3:81–83. Bangkok, Thailand: Secretariat, Ninth Pacific Science Congress, Department of Science, 1963.

———. 1958. *The Inflection and Syntax of Maranao Verbs*. Manila: Institute of National Language, Bureau of Printing.

———. 1962. "Overt Relation Markers in Maranao." *Language* 38:45–51.

———. 1973. "Subject Versus Topic." In *Parangal Kay Cecilio Lopez*, A. Gonzalez, ed., *Journal of Philippine Linguistics*, Special Monograph no. 4.

Peranteau, P.; Levi, J.; and Phares, G.; eds. 1972. *The Chicago Which Hunt: Papers from the Relative Clause Festival*. Chicago Linguistic Society, University of Chicago.

Perlmutter, D. 1972. "Evidence for Shadow Pronouns in French Relativization." In Peranteau et al. 1972.

———. 1978. "Impersonal Passives and the Unaccusative Hypothesis." In

Proceedings of the Fourth Annual Meeting of the Berkeley Linguistics Society. University of California, Berkeley.

Perlmutter, D. (to appear a) "Evidence for Inversion in Russian and Kannada."

Perlmutter, D. and Postal, P. 1974. Lectures at Linguistic Institute of the Linguistic Society of America, University of Massachusetts, Amherst.

————. 1977. "Toward a Universal Characterization of Passivization," in K. Whistler et al. (eds.) *Proceedings of the Third Annual Meeting of the Berkeley Linguistics Society.* University of California, Berkeley. Reprinted in this volume.

Perlmutter, D. and P. Postal (this volume a) "The Relational Succession Law."

Perlmutter D. and P. Postal (this volume b) "Some Proposed Laws of Basic Clause Structure."

Perlmutter, D. and P. Postal (to appear) "The 1-Advancement Exclusiveness Law," in Perlmutter and Rosen (to appear).

Perlmutter, D. and C. Rosen (eds.) (to appear) *Studies in Relational Grammar 2.*

Reid, L. 1966. *An Ivatan Syntax. Oceanic Linguistics,* Special Publication, no. 2.

Schachter, P. 1976. "The Subject in Philippine Languages: Topic, Actor, Actor-Topic, or None of the Above" in Li 1976, pp. 491–518.

————. 1977. "Reference-Related and Role-Related Properties of Subjects." *Syntax and Semantics* 8:279–306.

Schachter, P., and Otanes, F. 1972. *Tagalog Reference Grammar.* Los Angeles: University of California Press.

Shibatani, M. 1977. "Grammatical Relations and Surface Cases." *Language* 53(4): 789–809.

Stilman, G., and Harkins, W. 1964. *Introductory Russian Grammar.* Waltham, Mass.: Blaisdell Publishing Co.

Wolfenden, E. 1961. *A Re-statement of Tagalog Grammar.* Manila: Summer Institute of Linguistics and the Institute of National Language.

Wolff, J. 1965. *Cebuano Visayan Syntax.* Ph.D. thesis, Yale University. Ann Arbor, Mich.: University Microfilms.

————. 1966. *Beginning Cebuano,* Part I. New Haven, Conn.: Yale University Press.

————. 1967. *Beginning Cebuano,* Part II. New Haven, Conn.: Yale University Press.

————. 1972. *Dictionary of Cebuano Visayan.* Data Paper no. 87. Ithaca, N.Y.: South Asia Program, Dept. of Asian Studies, Cornell University.

Yap, E. and H. Bunye. 1971. *Cebuano-Visayan Dictionary.* Honolulu: University of Hawaii Press.

6 An Object-Creating Rule in Bahasa Indonesia

Sandra Chung

Introduction

A standard assumption of transformational grammar is that all syntactic operations can be expressed in terms of category labels (e.g. NP, V) and the relations of dominance and linear order. In this article, I present evidence against this assumption from Bahasa Indonesia, a Western Austronesian language. The evidence involves a productive rule of Dative, which relates the transitive sentences in (1) to those in (2):

(1) a. Saja mem-bawa   surat itu kepada Ali.
     I   TRANS-bring letter the to   Ali
     'I brought the letter to Ali.'
    b. Mereka men-dapat suatu pekerdjaan untuk anak-ku.
     they   TRANS-find a   job   for   child-my
     'They found a job for my daughter.'

(2) a. Saja mem-bawa-kan   Ali surat itu.
     I   TRANS-bring-BEN Ali letter the
     'I brought Ali the letter.'

Reprinted by permission from *Linguistic Inquiry* 7 (winter 1976): 41–87.

   The Bahasa Indonesia described here is the Indonesian spoken in Jakarta. I am grateful to Arief Budiman, Ibrahim Hasan, Iwan Hirsan, Johnny Basuki, Leila Budiman, Adela Hadiwono, and several others for providing native speakers' judgments on the Indonesian sentences. I also wish to thank David Perlmutter, Paul Postal, Susumu Kuno, Alan Stevens, and Jorge Hankamer for their valuable criticisms of earlier versions of this article. Earlier versions were presented at MIT, UCLA, and the 1974 Winter LSA Meeting, and I have profited from the comments and suggestions of people there. The usual disclaimers apply.

   This work was supported in part by the Department of Linguistics, Harvard University.

   In order to agree with the secondary sources, I have written the examples in the orthography used prior to the spelling reform of 1972. In this orthography, j = [y], tj = [č], dj = [j], nj = [ñ], sj = [š], and reduplication is indicated by the number 2 (e.g., *tahanan2* = *tahanan-tahanan* 'prisoners'). I differ from the standard orthography in writing unstressed prepositions as separate words rather than as clitics.

219

b. Mereka men-dapat-kan anak-ku suatu pekerdjaan.
they   TRANS-find-BEN child-my a   job
'They found my daughter a job.'

Roughly, Dative permutes a direct object with an indirect object or benefactive, and deprives the indirect object/benefactive of its preposition (either *kepada* 'to' or *untuk* 'for'). Some form of the benefactive suffix (here *-kan*) is typically added to the verb.

I will first examine the interaction of Dative with other syntactic rules and establish that Dative has two basic effects: first, it is an 'object-creating rule', in the sense that it turns the indirect object/benefactive into a direct object, and, second, it displaces the underlying direct object so that it is inaccessible to later syntactic rules. I will then argue that these effects of Dative cannot be accounted for if the rule is stated in terms of dominance and linear order; they can only be explained if the rule is stated in terms of grammatical relations. Dative therefore provides evidence in favor of a theory of grammar that allows rules to refer directly to grammatical relations. Such a theory has recently been proposed by Perlmutter and Postal (1974).

The article is organized as follows. In §1 I discuss some syntactic processes that can be used to identify direct objects in Bahasa Indonesia. In §2 I examine the interaction of these processes with Dative and conclude that Dative is an object-creating rule. In §3, several alternatives are presented for describing the behavior of Dative within the framework of transformational grammar. It is shown that none of these alternatives is adequate and that only a solution that makes reference to grammatical relations will account for all of the facts. Finally, §4 proposes a relational analysis for Dative and shows that this analysis is supported by an independent set of facts in Indonesian.

1   Identifying Direct Objects
1.1   General Properties

Bahasa Indonesia is an SVO language in which functional distinctions between NPs are indicated by prepositions. In this language, there are two surface characteristics of direct objects that distinguish them from other NPs. First, the direct object (like the subject) is prepositionless, whereas the indirect object and oblique NPs occur in a prepositional phrase. Second, although this position may be changed by scrambling, the direct object usually occurs to the immediate right of the verb:

(3) a. Monjet men-gigit   saja.
monkey TRANS-bite me
'A monkey bit me.'

    b.   Setiap anak mem-bawa buku ke (dalam) kelas-nja.
           each   child TRANS-bring book to inside class-his
           'Each child brought a book to his class.'

Direct objects can also be distinguished from other NPs by their ability to undergo certain syntactic operations; these processes are allowed for direct objects and, in some cases, for subjects as well, but never for indirect objects or oblique NPs. These syntactic processes provide a clear set of tests for determining whether or not a particular NP is a direct object.

We will appeal to five such processes to test for the direct objecthood of an NP.

1.2   Passive

Passive turns the direct object into a subject, removes the underlying subject to a prepositional phrase (with *oleh* 'by'), and adds a prefix *di-* to the verb.[1] The prefix replaces the active transitive prefix *meng-*, whose (optional) appearance on the verb is conditioned by semantic and stylistic parameters (Danoesoegondo 1971, p. 20; Dyen 1964, 7a.6):

(4) a.   Saja di-gigit   oleh monjet.
        I   PASS-bite by   monkey
        'I was bitten by the monkey.'
    b.   Pelarian itu di-tembaki oleh pendjaga pendjara.
        escapee the PASS-fire at by   guard   prison
        'The escapee was fired at repeatedly by the prison guards.'
        (Danoesoegondo 1971, p. 33)

Passive applies to direct objects, but it does not apply to indirect objects or oblique NPs, which are expressed by means of a prepositional phrase:

(5) a.   Seseorang men-djual mobil kepada paman saja.
        someone TRANS-sell car   to   uncle my
        'Someone sold a car to my uncle.'
    b.   Mereka ber-lajar ke Amerika.
        they   INTR-sail to America
        'They sailed to America.'

(6) a.   *Paman saja di-djual mobil (kepada) (oleh seseorang).
        uncle my PASS-sell car   by someone
        (My uncle was sold a car (to) (by someone).)
    b.   *Amerika di-(ber)-lajar (ke) oleh mereka.
        America PASS-INTR-sail to by   them
        (America was sailed (to) by them.)

Because the starred examples in (6) are prepositional phrases, it might be suggested that they are ungrammatical because Indonesian never allows stranding of prepositions. Under such a proposal, the right statement about Passive would be that it is limited to prepositionless postverbal NPs. Such a proposal is plausible because (i) indirect objects and oblique NPs are usually accompanied by prepositions, and (ii) it appears that prepositions can never be stranded in Indonesian.

In §2, however, I will show that no such proposal can be correct, because there are prepositionless postverbal NPs in Indonesian that cannot undergo Passive or any of the other processes discussed in this section. I will therefore ignore the possibility that the rules discussed here could be stated so that they refer to prepositionless NPs.

1.3 Reflexive

True reflexives are formed with *diri* 'self' plus an optional possessive pronoun. The presence or absence of the pronoun in this construction is determined by conditions that are poorly understood:

(7) a.   Saja me-lihat   diri saja dalam air.
         I   TRANS-see self my in   water
         'I saw myself in the water.'
     b.   Saja men-tjoba bunuh diri (*saja).
          I   TRANS-try kill   self   my
          'I tried to kill myself.'
     c.   Apakah dia mem-bunuh diri di kebun?
          Q   he TRANS-kill   self in garden
          'Did he kill himself in the garden?'

The presence or absence of the pronoun also intersects with the scrambling possibilities of the reflexive. Reflexives that include a possessive pronoun can scramble like ordinary objects:[2]

(8) Saja me-lihat   dalam air   diri saja.
      I   TRANS-see in   water self my
      'I saw myself in the water.'

But reflexives that do not include a pronoun must occur to the immediate right of the verb:

(9) *Apakah dia mem-bunuh di kebun diri?
      Q   he TRANS-kill in garden self
     (Did he kill himself in the garden?)

The contrast between (8) and (9) suggests that *diri* cliticizes to the verb when it is by itself, but that the combination of *diri* plus possessive pronoun behaves like a full NP. That the latter kind of reflexive is allowed to scramble at all will become important in the discussion in §2.

Reflexives consisting of *diri* plus a possessive pronoun can replace direct objects but no other NPs. The reflexive of an indirect object or oblique NP is usually expressed by means of a personal pronoun plus *sendiri* '(by) oneself', which is an emphatic rather than a true reflexive (Dyen 1964, 17a.11):[3]

(10) a.   Sjahrir men-tjerita-kan sesuatu tjerita kepada dia sendiri.
          Sjahrir TRANS-tell-BEN a   story   to   him EMP
          'Sjahrir told a story to himself.'
     b.   Kakak saja mem-beli   sepasang sepatu merah untuk
          sibling my TRANS-buy a pair   shoe   red   for
          dia sendiri.
          him EMP
          'My brother bought a pair of red shoes for himself.'

(11) a. *Sjahrir men-tjerita-kan sesuatu tjerita kepada diri-nja.
          Sjahrir TRANS-tell-BEN a   story   to   self-his
          (Sjahrir told a story to himself.)
     b. *Kakak saja mem-beli   sepasang sepatu merah untuk
          sibling my TRANS-buy a pair   shoe   red   for
          diri-nja.
          self-his
          (My brother bought a pair of red shoes for himself.)

That *sendiri* is an emphatic reflexive can be seen from (12a); (12b) shows that the true reflexive *diri* is ungrammatical in this sentence.

(12) a.   Saja mau lihat buku itu sendiri.
          I   want see book the EMP
          'I want to see that book myself.' (Dyen 1964, 17a.11)
     b. *Saja mau lihat buku itu diri saja.
          I   want see book the self my
          (I want to see that book myself.)

1.4   Object Preposing

An unusual process that is restricted to direct objects optionally moves the object to the beginning of its clause when the subject is a pronoun (Danoesoegondo 1971, p. 12).[4] The verb is not marked with the transitive prefix *meng-*, and the subject can be inverted with a following auxiliary:

(13) a.   Ikan merah itu dia sudah tangkap.
          fish red   the he PERF catch
          'The red fish he already caught.'

b. Itu dapat kita lihat pada mata-nja.
    that can we see in   eye-its
    'We can see this in its eyes.' (MacDonald and Dardjowidjojo
    1967, p. 238)

The true nature of this process, which I refer to as 'Object Preposing',
is rather obscure. Sentences like (13) are usually identified by native
speakers as versions of active sentences, and their surface form suggests that they involve a weak kind of object topicalization. But such
sentences are invariably identified as 'passive' by the secondary
sources (e.g., MacDonald and Dardjowidjojo 1967, pp. 237–38; Kwee
1965, pp. 49–50). Since Indonesian already has one passive (see section
1.2), it would be typologically peculiar for the language to have another
construction of this type. Nonetheless there is evidence suggesting that
Object Preposing behaves more like a passive than like a topicalization.
One such piece of evidence is provided by the interaction of Object
Preposing and Equi.

Equi in Indonesian deletes the subject of an embedded clause under
identity with some NP in the higher clause. (A more detailed discussion
of the characteristics of Equi can be found in §1.5.) Consider (14), which
is related to (15) by Equi:

(14)   Dia datang sehingga dia dapat ber-tjakap2 dengan Ali.
       he come COMP   he can INTR-talk with   Ali
       'He came so that he could talk with Ali.'

(15)   Dia datang untuk ber-tjakap2 dengan Ali.
       he come for   INTR-talk with   Ali
       'He came to talk with Ali.'

Crucially, the deleted NP must be in subject position at the time when
Equi applies. Thus, in (17), deletion is ungrammatical because the
deleted NP is a direct object:

(16)   Saja mem-bawa   surat itu supaja teman saja dapat
       I   TRANS-bring letter the COMP friend my can
       mem-batja-nja.
       TRANS-read-it
       'I brought the letter so that my friends could read it.'

(17) ?*Saja mem-bawa   surat itu untuk teman saja (dapat)
       I   TRANS-bring letter the for   friend my can
       (mem)-batja.
       TRANS-read
       (I brought the letter for my friends to (be able to) read.)

But in (18), the direct object has been turned into a subject by Passive, and the deletion is allowed:

(18)   Saja mem-bawa   surat itu untuk (dapat) di-batja   oleh
       I   TRANS-bring letter the for   can   PASS-read by
       teman saja.
       friend my
       'I brought the letter to (be able to) be read by my friends.'

Now, when Object Preposing has applied to an embedded clause, it is the original direct object rather than the original subject that serves as the target for deletion. Thus, from (19) Equi deletes the original direct object to give (20):

(19)   Saja mem-bawa   surat itu supaja (surat itu) dapat kau
       I   TRANS-bring letter the COMP   letter the can   you
       batja.
       read
       'I brought the letter so that (the letter) you could read.'

(20)   Saja mem-bawa   surat itu untuk (dapat) kau batja.
       I   TRANS-bring letter the for   can   you read
       'I brought the letter to (be able to) be read by you.'

But the original subject may not be deleted from a sentence like (21) to give (22):

(21)   Saja pergi supaja mobil itu dapat kau perbaiki.
       I   go   COMP   car   the can   you repair
       'I left so that the car you could repair.'

(22)   *Saja pergi untuk mobil itu (dapat) perbaiki.
       I   go   for   car   the can   repair
       (I left to (be able to) repair the car.)

Notice the absence of the transitive prefix *meng-* and the inversion of subject and auxiliary, which show that Object Preposing has applied in the embedded clause in (19–22). Further evidence that Object Preposing has applied is provided by the fact that the underlying subject of the embedded clause must always be a pronoun (see (17)).

The contrast between (20) and (22) shows that Object Preposing in an embedded clause feeds Equi on the next higher clause. Since Equi in Indonesian is cyclic, it follows from this that Object Preposing is also cyclic. Further, if we assume that Equi deletes only subjects, then the ability of the original direct object to be deleted in (20) shows that Object Preposing turns the direct object into the subject of its clause.

In both of these respects, Object Preposing behaves like a canonical passive, not like a topicalization.

On the basis of this and other evidence (Chung 1976), I will assume that Object Preposing is a passive rule. This assumption will not substantially affect the arguments to be given below.

Object Preposing applies to direct objects, as in (13), but not to indirect objects or oblique NPs:

(23) a. Saja menj-erahkan   sendjata saja kepada polisi itu.
         I   TRANS-surrender weapon my to   police the
         'I surrendered my gun to the police.'
     b. Mereka sedang be-renang di danau itu.
         they   PROG INTR-swim in lake the
         'They were swimming in the lake.'

(24) a. *Polisi itu saja serahkan   sendjata saja (kepada).
          police the I   surrender weapon my   to
          (The police I surrendered my gun (to).)
     b. *Danau itu sedang mereka (be)-renang (di).
          lake   the PROG   they   INTR-swim in
          (The lake they were swimming (in).)

In this respect, its behavior is no different from that of Passive, as we saw in (5–6).

In addition to these syntactic operations, which are limited to direct objects, there are several processes that affect only subject or direct object NPs. The rules of this type that we will consider are Equi and Relative Clause Formation.

1.5   Equi

The Equi discussed here affects adverbial complements of purpose, which are typically introduced by the complementizers *sehingga* or *supaja* 'so that':

(25) a. Dia meng-endarai mobil itu supaja dia dapat
         he TRANS-drive   car   the COMP he can
         men-tjoba-nja.
         TRANS-try-it
         'He drove the car so that he could test it.'
     b. Mereka mem-beli ikan itu supaja (ikan itu) dapat
         they   TRANS-buy fish the COMP   fish the   can
         di-masak   saja.
         PASS-cook (by) me
         'They bought the fish so that it could be cooked by me.'

If the subject of such a complement is coreferential with the subject or direct object of the higher clause, it can optionally be deleted. A consequence of this deletion is that the complementizer is replaced by the preposition *untuk* 'for':

(26) a. Dia meng-endarai mobil itu untuk men-tjoba-nja.
         he TRANS-drive car   the for   TRANS-try-it
         'He drove the car to test it.'

     b. Mereka mem-beli ikan itu untuk dapat di-masak
         they   TRANS-buy fish the for   can   PASS-cook (by)
         saja.
         me
         'They bought the fish to (be able to) be cooked by me.'

In (26a), deletion is controlled by a higher subject; in (26b), it is controlled by a higher direct object. Notice that the deleted NP can be the derived or underlying subject of the embedded clause (see (14–22)).

Controllers of Equi can be underlying subjects or direct objects, but they cannot be underlying indirect objects or oblique NPs. Thus in (27–28), the underlying indirect object cannot trigger Equi in the embedded clause:

(27) Saja mem-bawa   surat itu kepada wanita itu supaja dia
      I   TRANS-bring letter the to   woman the COMP she
      dapat mem-batja-nja kepada anak2-nja.
      can   TRANS-read-it to   children-her
      'I brought the letter to the woman so that she could read it to her children.'

(28) *Saja mem-bawa   surat itu kepada wanita itu untuk (dapat)
       I   TRANS-bring letter the to   woman the for   can
       mem-batja-nja kepada anak2-nja.
       TRANS-read-it to   children-her
       (I brought the letter to the woman to (be able to) read it to her children.)

In (29–30), the underlying indirect object has been turned into a direct object by Dative (see §2), but it fails to control the deletion:

(29) Saja mem-bawa-kan   gadis itu seputjuk surat supaja dia
      I   TRANS-bring-BEN girl the a   letter COMP she
      bisa mem-batja-nja.
      can TRANS-read-it
      'I brought the girl a letter so that she could read it.'

(30) *Saja mem-bawa-kan   gadis itu seputjuk surat untuk (bisa)
     I   TRANS-bring-BEN girl   the a   letter for   can
     mem-batja-nja.
     TRANS-read-it
     (I brought the girl a letter to (be able to) read it.)

And in (31), the underlying indirect object has undergone Dative and then Passive, but it still cannot serve as the controller:

(31) *Gadis itu di-bawa-kan   seputjuk surat untuk
     girl   the PASS-bring-BEN a   letter for
     mem-batja-nja.
     TRANS-read-it
     (The girl was brought a letter to read it.)

Furthermore, it seems that controllers of Equi must be subjects or direct objects at the end of the cycle on that clause. Thus, in (32), the underlying subject has been removed to a prepositional phrase by Passive, and it can no longer control the deletion:[5]

(32) ??Mobil itu di-kendarai oleh Ahmad untuk men-tjoba-nja.
       car   the PASS-drive by   Ahmad for   TRANS-try-it
     (The car was driven by Ahmad to test it.)

The ungrammaticality of (32) cannot be attributed to the fact that the controller appears in a passive sentence; for (underlying) direct objects that have been turned into subjects by Passive are still allowed to control the deletion:

(33)   Buku itu di-beli   oleh Ali untuk di-batja   oleh kakak saja.
       book the PASS-buy by   Ali for   PASS-read by   sibling my
     'The book was bought by Ali to be read by my brother.'

Sentences (27–33) show that controllers of Equi must be subjects or direct objects in underlying structure, and subjects or direct objects at the end of the cycle on that clause. In order to account for this, the condition on controllers must be stated globally.

1.6   Relative Clause Formation

The major strategy for forming relative clauses in Bahasa Indonesia simply deletes the relativized noun.[6] The relative clause is introduced by the complementizer *jang,* which is invariant for person and number and occurs elsewhere only in focus constructions (topicalization and question movement):

(34) a. Orang jang datang itu adalah ajah saja.
          man   COMP come the be   father my
          'The man who came is my father.'

     b. Ikan jang tidak sehat   men-urunkan ikan jang tidak
          fish COMP not   healthy TRANS-beget fish COMP not
          sehat   pula.
          healthy again
          'Unhealthy fish beget more unhealthy fish.' (MacDonald and
          Dardjowidjojo 1967, p. 228)

The relativized noun may be a subject, as in (34), or a direct object, as in (35):

(35) a. Ikan jang saja masak untuk Ali tidak enak rasa-nja.
          fish COMP I   cook for   Ali not   good taste-its
          'The fish that I cooked for Ali didn't taste good.'

     b. Apa-kah kedjadian buku itu jang kamu sembunjikan?
          what?-Q fate   book the COMP you   hide
          'What happened to the book that you were hiding?'

One significant difference between the relative clauses of (34) and (35) concerns the distribution of the transitive prefix *meng-*: *meng-* can appear on the verb of the relative clause if the relativized noun is a subject, but it does not appear if the relativized noun is a direct object. The absence of *meng-* in relative clauses like (35) is exactly parallel to the absence of *meng-* in sentences to which Object Preposing has applied. This similarity might lead one to propose that Object Preposing has actually applied to all relative clauses of the type (35). Then the relativized noun would be a derived subject, rather than a direct object, at the time when Relative Clause Formation applies. Under such a proposal, the right generalization about the major strategy would be that it is only available to subjects; Relative Clause Formation would therefore not provide a test for direct objecthood at all.

However, several facts argue against this analysis of Relative Clause Formation. These facts suggest that the relative clauses of (35) and the Object Preposing sentences of (13) are produced by separate operations. First, there are poorly understood conditions under which *meng-* can appear on the verb of a relative clause like (35) (cf. Keenan 1972, pp. 183–84):

(36) a. Ada seorang anak perempuan jang saja ingin kamu
          there a   child female   COMP I   want you
          men-emui.
          TRANS-meet
          'There's a girl who I want you to meet.'

   b.   Anda me-lihat   orang jang saja men-tjoba bunuh?
       you TRANS-see man COMP I   TRANS-try kill
       'Has anyone seen the man who I tried to kill?'

But *meng-* can never appear on the verb if Object Preposing has applied:

(37) a. *Buku itu saja mem-batja.
         book the I   TRANS-read
         (That book I read.)
      b. *Orang itu kamu mem-bunuh.
         man the you TRANS-kill
         (That man you killed.)

Second, any NP can be the underlying subject of a relative clause like (35):

(38) a. Kau me-lihat   ikan jang anak itu masak?
         you TRANS-see fish COMP child the cook
         'Have you seen the fish that the child cooked?'
      b. Saja me-lihat   surat2 jang Ali kirim-kan kepada
         I   TRANS-see letters COMP Ali send-BEN to
         tahanan2 politik.
         prisoners political
         'I saw the letters which Ali sent to the political prisoners.'

But only a pronoun can be the underlying subject of a sentence to which Object Preposing has applied:

(39) a. *Ikan itu anak itu masak.
         fish the child the cook
         (The fish the child cooked.)
      b. *Buku itu Ali batja.
         book the Ali read
         (That book Ali read)

Compare:

(40) a. Ikan itu saja masak.
         fish the I   cook
         'The fish I cooked.'
      b. Buku itu dia batja.
         book the he read
         'The book he read.'

One might try to explain the ungrammaticality of (39) by claiming that Indonesian does not allow two full NPs to occur in preverbal position in surface structure. This explanation would attribute the difference between (38) and (39) to a relatively superficial fact; namely, that the preposed direct object in (38), but not in (39), has been deleted by a later rule. But this explanation fails, because it cannot account for the behavior of sentences like (41a, b) and (42a, b):

(41) a. Orang itu saja ingin kau temui.
         man   the I   want you meet
         'That person I want you to meet.'
     b. *Orang itu saja ingin laki2 itu temui.
         man   the I   want man the meet
         (That person I want the man to meet.)

(42) a. Buku ini di-anggap   (oleh Ali) sudah saja batja.
         book this PASS-believe by Ali PERF I   read
         'This book is believed (by Ali) to have been read by me.'
     b. *Buku ini di-anggap   (oleh Ali) (sudah) perempuan
         book this PASS-believe by Ali PERF   woman
         itu batja.
         the read
         (This book is believed (by Ali) to have been read by the woman.)

In (41–42), the direct objects *orang itu* 'the man' and *buku ini* 'this book' have undergone Object Preposing in the lower clause. They have then been raised to the higher clause, where they have undergone Passive (42) or Object Preposing (41).[7] Although the preposed direct objects have been moved away from their underlying subjects, the underlying subjects still cannot be full NPs. The fact that (41b) and (42b) satisfy the surface structure constraint, but are ungrammatical, shows that Object Preposing must be limited to sentences whose underlying subjects are pronouns. Obviously, the same restriction cannot be placed on Relative Clause Formation (38).

I conclude that relative clauses of the type (35) are produced by an operation different from Object Preposing. Therefore, the major strategy for Relative Clause Formation must apply to direct objects as well as to subject NPs. This conclusion, combined with the facts below, suggests that the major strategy does provide a test for direct objecthood.

NPs relativized by means of the major strategy can be subjects or direct objects (34–35), but they cannot be indirect objects or oblique NPs:

(43) a. *Saja ber-temu   dengan perempuan itu jang   kamu beli
I   INTR-meet with   woman   the COMP you   buy
badju   (untuk) kemarin.
clothes for   yesterday
(I met with the woman that you bought clothes (for) yesterday.)

b. *Siapa pemilik toko jang   kita pergi (ke) itu?
who? owner   store COMP we go   to the
(Who's the owner of the store that we went (to)?)

According to the secondary sources (e.g., Kwee 1965, p. 98), prepositional phrases like those in (43) can be relativized by means of a minor
strategy that involves movement rather than deletion. The relativized
noun is replaced by the appropriate form of the interrogative pronoun
and moved along with its preposition to the beginning of the relative
clause:

(44) a.   Siapa pemilik toko ke tempat mana   kita pergi?
who? owner   store to place   which? we go
'Who's the owner of the store to which we went?'

b.   Patjol dengan mana   ia meng-gali lubang itu adalah
spade with   which? he TRANS-dig hole   the be
punja saja. (Kwee 1965, p. 98)
thing my
'The spade with which he dug the hole is mine.'

Most native speakers, however, consider this type of relative clause
to be archaic and unacceptable in everyday speech. It seems more
common for prepositional phrases to be turned into direct objects
(where this is possible; see §2) and then relativized by means of the
major strategy.

1.7   Summary

To summarize, the five syntactic processes described above—Passive,
Reflexive, Object Preposing, control of Equi, Relative Clause Formation—are allowed for direct objects but not for indirect objects or
oblique NPs. They will therefore prove crucial to an understanding of
Dative, which is discussed in the following section.

2   **Dative**
2.1   General Description

The optional rule that I refer to as Dative applies to sentences with a
direct object (DO) and an indirect object or benefactive (IO). Indirect
objects in Bahasa Indonesia occur with the preposition *kepada* 'to';
benefactives with the preposition *untuk* 'for':

(45) a. Mereka mem-bawa   daging itu kepada dia.
        they   TRANS-bring meat   the to   him
        'They brought the meat to him.'
   b. Ali mem-beli   telefisi   untuk ibu-nja.
        Ali TRANS-buy television for   mother-his
        'Ali bought a television for his mother.'
   c. Saja bikin roti   untuk tetangga-ku.
        I   make bread for   neighbor-my
        'I made bread for my neighbors.'

Dative removes these prepositions and places the indirect object/benefactive between the underlying direct object and the verb, so that the word order is S V IO DO rather than S V DO Prep IO.[8] Applying Dative to (45) produces the synonymous (46):

(46) a. Mereka mem-bawa-kan   dia daging itu.
        they   TRANS-bring-BEN him meat   the
        'They brought him the meat.'
   b. Ali mem-beli-kan   ibu-nja   telefisi.
        Ali TRANS-buy-BEN mother-his television
        'Ali bought his mother a television.'
   c. Saja bikin-kan tetangga-ku roti.
        I   make-BEN neighbor-my bread
        'I made my neighbors bread.'

(To simplify matters, I will refer to NPs by their *underlying* grammatical relations except where specifically noted; thus *dia* is an (underlying) IO in (45a) as well as in (46a). We will see that the grammatical relations involved are in fact changed by the application of Dative.)

In addition, some form of the benefactive suffix must be attached to the verb. This suffix is normally realized as *-kan* (46), but it has the form *-i* or *-ø* for a handful of verbs whose indirect objects have undergone Dative:

(47) a. Laki2 itu meng-irim-i   wanita itu seputjuk surat.
        man   the TRANS-send-BEN woman the a   letter
        'The man sent the woman a letter.'
   b. Anak laki2 itu mem-bajar polisi itu lima dolar.
        child male the TRANS-pay police the five dollar
        'The boy paid the policeman five dollars.'

Although the choice of these forms varies slightly from speaker to speaker, there seems to be a general movement towards eliminating *-i* and *-ø* in favor of *-kan*. For many younger speakers, there are no verbs that take *-i* when Dative has applied, and only a few (including *beri* 'give', *kasih* 'give', *bajar* 'pay') that take -ø instead of -*kan*.

The behavior of the suffixes is complicated by the fact that -*kan* is sometimes attached to the verb when Dative has *not* applied. This attachment is always optional and intersects in an interesting way with the form of the benefactive suffix that is normally selected by the verb. Verbs that take -*i* or -ø when Dative has applied regularly allow -*kan* when the rule has not applied:

(48) a.   Laki2 itu meng-irim(-kan) surat kepada wanita itu.
          man   the TRANS-send-BEN letter to   woman the
          'The man sent a letter to the woman.'
     b.   Anak laki2 itu mem-bajar(-kan) lima dolar kepada
          child male the TRANS-pay-BEN five dollar to
          polisi itu.
          police the
          'The boy paid five dollars to the policeman.'

But verbs that take -*kan* when Dative has applied normally do not allow it otherwise (45).

Consistent with this description, the use of -*kan* in sentences like (48) has practically disappeared from the speech of younger Indonesians. It is exactly this group of speakers who have generalized -*kan* as the form of the benefactive suffix attached by Dative.

The distribution of the benefactive suffix can be summarized as follows:

(49)   Class I   Class II   Class III
     Before Dative   -ø   -kan/-ø   -kan/-ø
     After Dative   -kan   -i   -ø

For convenience, the Dative sentences in this section will only involve verbs taken from Class I (e.g., *masak* 'cook') or Class II (e.g., *kirim* 'send'). Verbs in Class II provide the clearest indication that Dative has applied, since they select -*i* as a result of Dative but -ø or -*kan* otherwise. Verbs of Class I also provide a reasonably clear indication, since they take -*kan* when Dative has applied but do not normally take it otherwise. It is assumed that arguments developed on the basis of these verbs can be naturally extended to verbs of Class III, where the interaction of Dative with the form of the benefactive suffix seems rather obscure.

Two general properties of Dative can be immediately established. First, a direct object as well as an indirect object/benefactive is required in order for Dative to apply. Sentences with an IO but no (overt) DO do not undergo the rule:[9]

(50) a. Ajah saja menj-umbang kepada rumah sakit.
         father my TRANS-donate to   house sick
         'My father donated to the hospital.'
     b. *Ajah saja menj-umbang(-kan) rumah sakit.
         father my TRANS-donate-BEN house sick
         (My father donated (to) the hospital.)

Second, related syntactic operations are responsible for the position
of the indirect object in (46) and the absence of its preposition. The
preposition cannot be omitted unless the IO is moved between the DO
and the verb:

(51) a. *Laki2 itu meng-irim(-i)   surat wanita itu.
          man   the TRANS-send-BEN letter woman the
          (The man sent a letter the woman)
     b. *Saja bikin(-kan) roti   tetangga-ku.
          I   make-BEN bread neighbor-my
          (I made bread my neighbors.)

Under normal circumstances, moreover, the IO cannot be moved between the DO and the verb unless its preposition is omitted:[10]

(52) a. Ali kasih (?*kepada) saja dia punja saputangan.
         Ali give   to   me his thing handkerchief
         'Ali gave (to) me his handkerchief.'
     b. Orang itu masak-kan (??untuk) perempuan itu ikan.
         man   the cook-BEN   for   woman   the fish
         'The man cooked (for) the woman fish.'

This behavior contrasts with the normal behavior of postverbal NPs,
which otherwise allow scrambling (§1.1). The close relationship of the
position of the IO and the appearance of its preposition suggests that
Dative involves more than a simple permutation of NPs.

   It is worth noting that Dative sentences of the type (46) cannot be
generated directly by the phrase structure rules. Such an approach
would be inadequate, because it would fail to account for the behavior
of the DO and IO in Dative sentences with respect to other syntactic
rules. In §1.5, for instance, I showed that the IO in Dative sentences
like (46) fails to control Equi, although it occupies the normal position
of a direct object NP. This fact can be explained by the global conditions
on Equi, if the sentences in (46) are syntactically derived from sentences in which the IO is a prepositional phrase. But it cannot be
accounted for if the IOs in (46) are generated in direct object position
by the phrase structure rules. Further, I will show in §4 that the original
DOs in (46) pattern with another type of NP that must have undergone

a syntactic rule. Without the assumption that (46) is syntactically derived from (45), this fact can only be accounted for in an ad hoc fashion.

Syntactic criteria like these show that the sentences in (46) must be
related to those in (45) by a syntactic rule. In the following sections,
I will establish that this rule, Dative, is an object-creating rule in the
sense described in the introduction.

2.2   Dative as an Object-Creating Rule

The argument that Dative is an object-creating rule is divided into two
parts. First, I will establish that it is the IO rather than the DO that
acts as the direct object after Dative has applied. This general syntactic
effect of Dative is amenable to several different analyses. In the rest
of §2, I will assume for the purposes of exposition that an analysis in
terms of grammatical relations is correct. Then, I will show that there
are properties of Dative that cannot be accounted for by the transformational notions of dominance and linear order. The evidence demonstrating that the rule must be stated in terms of grammatical relations
is presented in §§3 and 4.

2.3   Objecthood of IO

After Dative has applied, it is the underlying IO that acts as the direct
object NP. This is suggested first of all by its surface characteristics;
it immediately follows the verb and is not accompanied by a preposition
(see §1.1):

(53) a. Saja meng-irim-i   Hasan semua surat2.
          I   TRANS-send-BEN Hasan all   letters
          'I sent Hasan all of the letters.'
      b. Orang itu me-masak-kan   perempuan itu ikan.
          man the TRANS-cook-BEN woman   the fish
          'The man cooked the woman fish.'

Compare (53) with (54):

(54) a. Saja meng-irim-kan   semua surat2 kepada Hasan.
          I   TRANS-send-BEN all   letters to   Hasan
          'I sent all of the letters to Hasan.'
      b. Orang itu masak ikan untuk perempuan itu.
          man the cook fish for   woman   the
          'The man cooked fish for the woman.'

Furthermore, the IO can now undergo the syntactic processes described in §1, which apply to direct objects (and in some cases, to
subjects as well) but never to indirect objects or oblique NPs. The fact

that the IO is now available for these processes indicates that it has been turned into a direct object by Dative.

The IO can, for instance, be passivized:

(55) a. Wanita itu di-kirim-i   sebuah surat oleh laki2 itu.
         woman the PASS-send-BEN a   letter by   man the
         'The woman was sent a letter by the man.'
    b. Perempuan itu di-masak-kan   ikan oleh orang itu.
         woman   the PASS-cook-BEN fish by   man   the
         'The woman was cooked fish by the man.'

It can be replaced by the true reflexive, *diri* 'self':

(56) a. Kami meng-irim-i   diri kami surat.
         we   TRANS-send-BEN self our   letter
         'We sent ourselves a letter.'
    b. Kakak saja mem-beli-kan   diri-nja sepasang sepatu
         sibling my TRANS-buy-BEN self-his a pair   shoe
         merah.
         red
         'My brother bought himself a pair of red shoes.'

It can undergo Object Preposing, if the subject of the sentence is a pronoun.

(57) a. Wanita itu saja kirim-i   surat itu.
         woman the I   send-BEN letter the
         'That woman I sent the letter.'
    b. Perempuan itu saja masak-kan ikan.
         woman   the I   cook-BEN fish
         'That woman I cooked a fish.'
    c. Karena engkau sudah banjak men-olong John, *engkau*
         because you   PERF much TRANS-help John you
         akan saja beli-kan makan-siang di rumah-makan Tjina.
         FUT I   buy-BEN lunch   at restaurant   Chinese
         'Since you have helped John a lot, I will buy you lunch at a Chinese restaurant.' (Danoesoegondo 1971, p. 46)

And the original IO is subject to the major strategy, with *jang,* for Relative Clause Formation:[11]

(58) a. Tidak seorang pun suka kepada wanita jang ajah
         not   someone even like to   woman COMP father
         saja kirim-i   bunga.
         my   send-BEN flower
         'No one likes the woman who my father sent the flowers.'

b.   Orang jang   saja masak-kan daging itu adalah orang
     man   COMP I   cook-BEN   meat the be   man
     jang ber-topi merah.
     COMP INTR-hat red
     'The man who I cooked the meat is the man wearing the red
     hat.'

As illustrated by (59–62), none of these processes can affect an IO
that has not undergone Dative and which therefore occurs in a prepositional phrase. This is true regardless of whether the preposition is
stranded, deleted, or pied piped along with the IO. In (59), for instance,
an IO fails to undergo Passive:

(59) a.   *Wanita itu di-kirim   sebuah surat (kepada) oleh Ali.
          woman the PASS-send a   letter to   by Ali
          (The woman was sent a letter by Ali.)
     b.   *Perempuan itu di-masak ikan (untuk) oleh orang itu.
          woman   the PASS-cook fish for   by man the
          (The woman was cooked fish by the man.)

(Notice the absence of the benefactive suffix, which indicates that
Dative has not applied.) In (60), an IO fails to undergo Reflexive:

(60) a.   *Kami meng-irim(-kan) surat kepada diri kami.
          we   TRANS-send-BEN letter to   self our
          (We sent a letter to ourselves.)
     b.   *Kakak saja mem-beli   sepasang sepatu merah untuk
          sibling my TRANS-buy a pair   shoe   red   for
          diri-nja.
          self-his
          (My brother bought a pair of red shoes for himself.)

In (61), it fails to undergo Object Preposing:

(61) a.   *Wanita itu saja kirim surat itu (kepada).
          woman the I   send letter the to
          ('That woman I sent the letter to.')
     b.   *(Untuk) perempuan itu sudah saja masak ikan.
          for   woman   the PERF I   cook fish
          (That woman I already cooked a fish for.)

And in (62), it fails to undergo the major strategy for Relative Clause
Formation:

(62) a. *Tidak seorang pun suka kepada wanita jang ajah
　　　　not   someone even like to   woman COMP father
　　　　saja kirim surat (kepada).
　　　　my send letter to
　　　　(No one likes the woman who my father sent a letter to.)
　　　b. *Orang (untuk) jang saja masak daging itu adalah
　　　　man   for   COMP I   cook meat the be
　　　　orang jang ber-topi merah.
　　　　man   COMP INTR-hat red
　　　　(The man for whom I cooked the meat is the man wearing the
　　　　red hat.)

2.4 Nonobjecthood of DO

In contrast, the underlying DO no longer behaves like a direct object
after Dative has applied. It fails to undergo all of the syntactic processes
described in §1 as tests for direct objecthood.

　　Thus, the DO cannot be passivized:[12]

(63) a. *Surat itu di-kirim-i   wanita itu.
　　　　letter the PASS-send-BEN woman the
　　　　(The letter was sent the woman.)
　　　b. *Ikan di-masak-kan   perempuan itu oleh orang itu.
　　　　fish PASS-cook-BEN woman   the by man the
　　　　(A fish was cooked the woman by the man.)

(64) a. Surat itu di-kirim-kan   kepada wanita itu.
　　　　letter the PASS-send-BEN to   woman the
　　　　'The letter was sent to the woman.'
　　　b. Ikan di-masak   oleh orang itu untuk perempuan itu.
　　　　fish PASS-cook by man the for woman   the
　　　　'A fish was cooked by the man for the woman.'

Compare (63) with (64), which shows that the DO can undergo Passive
if Dative has not applied.

　　The DO cannot be replaced by the true reflexive, *diri:*[13]

(65) *Kami men-djual(-kan) pedagang itu diri kami.
　　　　we   TRANS-sell-BEN merchant the self our
　　　　(We sold the merchants ourselves.)

(66) Kami men-djual diri kami kepada pedagang itu.
　　　　we   TRANS-sell self our to   merchant the
　　　　'We sold ourselves to the merchants.'

Notice that the ungrammaticality of (65) cannot be attributed to the
presence of an NP intervening between the reflexive and its trigger. We

have seen in (8) that reflexive pronouns like *diri kami* need not occur in immediate postverbal position, but can be scrambled with other NPs.

The DO cannot undergo Object Preposing:

(67) a. *Buku itu saja kirim-i   kau.
          book the I   send-BEN you
          (That book I sent you.)

    b. *Ikan (itu) saja masak-kan perempuan itu.
          fish the I   cook-BEN woman   the
          (The fish I cooked the woman.)

(68) a. Buku itu saja kirim-kan kepada-mu.
          book the I   send-BEN to-you
          'That book I sent to you.'

    b. Ikan itu saja masak untuk perempuan itu.
          fish the I   cook for   woman   the
          'The fish I cooked for the woman.'

As (67a) shows, this cannot be explained by assuming that DOs that are moved by Object Preposing can only cross over pronominal NPs.

And the DO is no longer available for Relative Clause Formation:

(69) a. *Saja me-lihat   surat jang Ali kirim-i   kakak saja.
          I   TRANS-see letter COMP Ali send-BEN sibling my
          (I saw the letter that Ali sent my sister.)

    b. *Djaket jang saja djahit-kan Hasan ter-letak di atas
          coat   COMP I   sew-BEN   Hasan ACCID-lie on top
          medja.
          table
          (The coat that I sewed Hasan is lying on the table.)

(70) a. Saja me-lihat   surat jang Ali kirim-kan kepada kakak
          I   TRANS-see letter COMP Ali send-BEN to   sibling
          saja.
          my
          'I saw the letter that Ali sent to my sister.'

    b. Djaket jang saja djahit untuk Hasan ter-letak di
          coat   COMP I   sew   for   Hasan ACCID-lie on
          atas medja.
          top table
          'The coat that I sewed for Hasan is lying on the table.'

(The fact that (63), (65), (67), and (69) are ungrammatical shows that Passive, Reflexive, Object Preposing, and Relative Clause Formation cannot be stated so that they refer just to prepositionless NPs. Such a statement of the rules would wrongly predict that all of (63–70) would be grammatical. Sentences (63), (65), (67), and (69) therefore exclude the possibility, mentioned briefly in §1.2, that a general condition against stranding prepositions could account for the facts of §1.)

Finally, although the judgments involved are delicate, it seems that the DO can no longer serve as the controller for Equi after Dative has applied. Sentences like (71), where the DO triggers Equi, are ordinarily rejected by native speakers:

(71) a. ??Mereka meng-irim-i   wanita itu surat tersebut untuk
        they   TRANS-send-BEN woman the letter certain   for
        bisa di-batja-nja.
        can PASS-read-(by) her
        (They sent the woman a letter to be read by her.)
    b. ??Saja mem-bawa-kan   anak itu daging untuk
        I   TRANS-bring-BEN child the meat   for
        di-masak-nja.
        PASS-cook-(by) him
        (I brought the child the meat to be cooked by him.)

Compare (71) with (72), where Dative has not applied, and deletion can be legitimately controlled by the DO:

(72) a. Mereka meng-irim-kan   surat kepada wanita itu untuk
        they   TRANS-send-BEN letter to   woman the for
        bisa di-batja-nja.
        can PASS-read-(by) her
        'They sent a letter to the woman to be read by her.'
    b. Saja mem-bawa   daging kepada dia untuk
        I   TRANS-bring meat   to   him for
        di-masak-nja.
        PASS-cook-(by) him
        'I brought the meat to him to be cooked by him.'

In the few sentences of type (71) that were accepted by native speakers, the adverbial complement may have been intepreted as a modifier within the direct object NP (see English *water for drinking*). Such infinitival complements of nouns are fairly common in Bahasa Indonesia, and they have the same formal structure as complements to which Equi has applied.

(73)   Apakah daging ini   untuk di-simpan di lemari es?
        Q   meat this for   PASS-put in box   ice
        'Is this the meat to be put in the refrigerator?'

3   A Transformational Analysis
3.1   Two Transformational Alternatives

Within transformational grammar, there are two major alternatives for accounting for the syntactic facts discussed above. Both of these alternatives rely crucially on the relations of dominance and linear order described by Chomsky (1965).

Under the first alternative, one would assume that all of the syntactic processes of Bahasa Indonesia are stated in terms of linear order. The structural descriptions of Passive, Reflexive, and Object Preposing would refer to the NP immediately following the verb; the structural description of Relative Clause Formation (and perhaps Equi) would refer to the NP immediately preceding or following the verb. Similarly, Dative would be stated so that its principal effect would be to alter the linear order of the two postverbal NPs:

(74)   X NP V NP $\begin{Bmatrix} \text{kepada} \\ \text{untuk} \end{Bmatrix}$ NP Y

 1   2   3   4   5   6   7 $\longrightarrow$ 1 2 3 6 4 7

The effect of the rule sketched in (74) is to permute the DO and IO and to delete the preposition—in other words, to put the IO in a position immediately following the verb. In this position, it is the IO rather than the DO that would satisfy the structural description of later syntactic rules.

Under the second alternative, one would assume that the rules are stated in terms of dominance and linear order, but that they refer to prepositionless NPs regardless of their position in the sentence. One would assume further that there is some sort of no-ambiguity condition (in the sense of Hankamer 1973) governing the applicability of all movement and deletion transformations to the output of (74). (It is unimportant whether this condition would also account for Reflexive, which is neither a movement nor a deletion transformation.) This condition would allow only one interpretation for sentences in which one of two structurally identical NPs has been moved or deleted; namely, it would only allow the moved or deleted NP to be interpreted as the NP closest to the verb. For this condition to operate on the output of (74), Dative must leave the DO and IO in structurally similar positions:[14]

(75)

If Dative has the output sketched in (75), then movement or deletion of one of the two postverbal NPs would create a structural ambiguity—

just the sort of situation that is supposed to be handled by the no-ambiguity condition.

Both of these alternatives involve the assumption that the position of an NP determines whether or not syntactic processes will apply to it. Thus, it is the position of the IO in the output of Dative that enables it to undergo Passive, Reflexive, Object Preposing, and Relative Clause Formation; and it is *only* position that prevents a DO affected by Dative from undergoing the rules in exactly the same way.

Consequently, both alternatives make a clear prediction about the status of the DO with respect to later syntactic rules. This prediction follows from the fact that several rules are available to move or delete the IO in (74–75), leaving the DO as the NP closest to the verb. In such a position, the DO would have exactly the right relations of dominance and linear order to undergo Passive, Reflexive, Object Preposing, and Relative Clause Formation. The transformational alternatives would therefore have to predict that the DO could undergo all of these rules.

We can test this prediction—and the adequacy of the transformational alternatives—by examining the following sets of facts.

3.2   Interaction of Passive, Object Preposing, and Relative Clause Formation

First, consider the consequences of applying Passive to sentences that have undergone Dative, as in (76). Both the linear order hypothesis and the no-ambiguity hypothesis ensure that it is the IO rather than the DO that is turned into a subject by this rule:

(76) a.   Dia di-kirim-i   surat itu (oleh mereka).
           he PASS-send-BEN letter the by   them
           'He was sent the letter (by them).'
     b.   Saja di-bawa-kan   surat ini oleh Ali.
           I   PASS-bring-BEN letter this by   Ali
           'I was brought this letter by Ali.'
     c.   Saja di-masak-kan   ikan oleh perempuan itu.
           I   PASS-cook-BEN fish by   woman   the
           'I was cooked a fish by the woman.'

As a result of applying Passive, however, the original DO again occupies the position immediately after the verb. In this position it satisfies the structural descriptions for Object Preposing, Reflexive, and Relative Clause Formation.[15] It also satisfies the no-ambiguity condition, since the fact that the IO is a derived subject in (76) means that no structural ambiguity can be created by moving the DO.

Nonetheless, a DO in this position cannot undergo any of the rules whose structural description it satisfies. Thus the DOs of (76) cannot undergo Object Preposing:

(77) a. *Surat itu dia (di)-kirim-i   (oleh mereka).
        letter the he PASS-send-BEN by   them
        (That letter he was sent (by them).)
     b. *Surat ini   saja (di)-bawa-kan   oleh Ali.
        letter this I   PASS-bring-BEN by Ali
        (This letter I was brought by Ali.)
     c. *Ikan tersebut   saja (di)-masak-kan oleh perempuan
        fish aforementioned I   PASS-cook-BEN by   woman
        itu.
        the
        (The fish I was cooked by the woman.)

And they cannot be relativized by means of the major strategy:

(78) a. *Apakah kedjadian surat itu jang   kamu di-kirim-i
        Q   fate   letter the COMP you PASS-send-BEN
        oleh dia?
        by   him
        (What happened to the letter that you were sent by him?)
     b. *Ini-lah   surat jang gadis di-bawa-kan   oleh Ali.
        this-EMP letter COMP girl PASS-bring-BEN by   Ali
        (This is the letter that the girl was brought by Ali.)
     c. *Ikan jang   Ali di-masak-kan (oleh saja) tidak enak
        fish COMP Ali PASS-cook-BEN by   me   not   good
        rasa-nja.
        taste-its
        (The fish that Ali was cooked (by me) didn't taste good.)

The fact that the DO is inaccessible to Object Preposing and Relative Clause Formation after Passive has applied cannot be accounted for by either the linear order or the no-ambiguity hypothesis. Sentences (77–78) therefore provide a strong argument against the transformational alternatives for describing Dative.[16]

It might be objected that extrinsic rule ordering could account for the ungrammaticality of (77–78). For instance, if Object Preposing and Relative Clause Formation were extrinsically ordered before Passive, then they would be unable to operate on the original DO after Passive had applied in (76). This objection collapses, however, for the wrong results are produced no matter what order the rules apply in.

In (79), for instance, Object Preposing has applied to the output of the Dative rule:

(79) a.   Ali saja kirim-i   surat itu.
       Ali I   send-BEN letter the
       'Ali I sent the letter.'
  b.   Orang itu saja bawa-kan surat.
       man   the I   bring-BEN letter
       'That man I brought a letter.'
  c.   Perempuan itu saja masak-kan ikan.
       girl   the I   cook-BEN   fish
       'That girl I cooked the fish.'

But the DO of (79) cannot undergo Passive:[17]

(80) a.   *Ali surat itu di-kirim-i   oleh saja.
       Ali letter the PASS-send-BEN by   me
       (Ali that letter was sent by me.)
  b.   *Orang itu surat di-bawa-kan   oleh saja.
       man   the letter PASS-bring-BEN by   me
       (That man the letter was brought by me.)
  c.   *Perempuan itu ikan di-masak-kan   oleh saja.
       girl   the fish PASS-cook-BEN by   me
       (That girl a fish was cooked by me.)

And it cannot be relativized by means of the major strategy:

(81) a.   *Di mana   surat jang   Ali saja kirim-i?
       at where? letter COMP Ali I   send-BEN
       (Where is the letter that Ali I sent?)
  b.   *Ini-lah   surat jang   gadis itu saja bawa-kan.
       this-EMP letter COMP girl   the I   bring-BEN
       (This is the letter that the girl I brought.)
  c.   *Apa   jang   ter-djadi   terhadap ikan jang   Ali saja
       what? COMP ACCID-happen about   fish COMP Ali I
       masak-kan?
       cook-BEN
       (What happened to the fish that Ali I cooked?)

Similarly, in (82), Relative Clause Formation has applied to the output of Dative:

(82) a.   Tidak seorang pun suka kepada wanita jang   ajah
       not   someone even like to   woman COMP father
       saja (akan) kirim-i   bunga.
       my FUT send-BEN flower
       'No one likes the woman that my father (will) send the flowers.'

    b.   Ani adalah gadis jang saja bawa-kan surat ini.
         Ani be   girl COMP I   bring-BEN letter this
         'Ani is the girl that I brought this letter.'
    c.   Di mana   orang jang saja beli-kan badju   kemarin?
         at where? man COMP I   buy-BEN clothes yesterday
         'Where's the man that I bought clothes yesterday?'

But the DO of (82) cannot undergo Passive:

(83) a. *Tidak seorang pun suka kepada wanita jang bunga itu
        not   someone even like to   woman COMP flower the
        (akan) di-kirim-i   oleh ajah   saja.
        FUT PASS-send-BEN by   father my
      (No one likes the woman that the flowers (will) be sent by my
      father.)
    b. *Ani adalah gadis jang surat ini di-bawa-kan.
        Ani be   girl COMP letter this PASS-bring-BEN
      (Ani is the girl that this letter was brought.)
    c. *Di mana   orang jang badju   di-beli-kan   oleh saja
        at where? man COMP clothes PASS-buy-BEN by   me
        kemarin?
        yesterday
      (Where's the man that clothes were bought by me yesterday?)

And it never undergoes Object Preposing:

(84) a. *Tidak seorang pun suka kepada wanita jang bunga itu
        not   someone even like to   woman COMP flower the
        (akan) kau kirim-i.
        FUT you send-BEN
      (No one likes the woman that the flowers you (will) send.)
    b. *Ani adalah gadis jang surat ini saja bawa-kan.
        Ani be   girl COMP letter this I   bring-BEN
      (Ani is the girl that this letter I brought.)
    c. *Di mana   orang jang badju ini saja beli-kan kemarin?
        at where? man COMP clothes this I   buy-BEN yesterday
      (Where's the man that these clothes I bought yesterday?)

There is no extrinsic (or intrinsic) ordering of the rules that predicts
that all of (77–78), (80–81), and (83–84) will be ungrammatical.[18] Consequently, the transformational solution, even with the (ad hoc) addition
of extrinsic ordering, cannot account for the interaction of Passive,
Object Preposing, and Relative Clause Formation.

3.3   The *Meng*-Rule

A second argument against the transformational alternatives is provided by the rule that governs the distribution of the transitive prefix *meng-*. As mentioned in §1.2, this rule optionally attaches *meng-* to transitive verbs that are followed by their direct objects in surface structure:[19]

(85) a.   Mereka (me-)masak ikan untuk saja.
           they   TRANS-cook fish for   me
           'They cooked a fish for me.'
     b.   Saja (me-)lihat   diri saja dalam air.
           I   TRANS-see self my in   water
           'I saw myself in the water.'

However, it does not insert the prefix in sentences whose direct objects have been deleted by Relative Clause Formation or have been moved to the left by Passive, Object Preposing, Topicalization, or Question Movement:[20]

(86) a.   Dia (*men-)di-pukul oleh mereka.
           he TRANS-PASS-hit by   them
           'He was hit by them.'
     b.   Buku itu saja (*mem-)batja.
           book the I   TRANS-read
           'That book I read.'
     c.   Surat jang anak itu sedang (*men-)tulis   pandjang-nja
           letter COMP child the PROG   TRANS-write length-its
           tiga   halaman.
           three page
           'The letter that the child was writing is three pages long.'
     d.   Kamu-lah jang   saja (*men-)tunggu.
           you-EMP COMP I   TRANS-wait
           'It's you that I'm waiting for.'
     e.   Apa jang mereka (*me-)masak   untuk pesta?
           what? COMP they   TRANS-cook for   party
           'What are they cooking for the party?'

Within transformational grammar, the obvious formulation of the *meng*-rule is that it inserts *meng-* if the verb is immediately followed by an NP.[21] Such a formulation accounts for the fact that *meng-* does not occur in simple passive sentences or in relative clauses like (86c), but that it does occur in examples like the following:

(87) a.   Binatang jang menj-erang   saja adalah andjing.
           animal   COMP TRANS-attack me   be   dog
           'The animals that attacked me were dogs.'

b.   Di mana   orang untuk siapa Ali mem-beli   badju?
     at where? man for   who? Ali TRANS-buy clothes
     'Where's the man for whom Ali bought clothes?'

Example (87a) contains a relative clause in which the relativized noun is a subject; (87b) contains one (relativized by the minor strategy) in which the relativized noun is a benefactive. In both cases, *meng-* can be inserted because the verb is immediately followed by an NP.

Consider how this version of the *meng*-rule will interact with the formation of the relative clauses in (82). In these, the DO and IO have undergone Dative, and then the IO has been relativized by means of the major strategy:

(88) NP_i [NP_1 V NP_2 Prep NP_i]—(Dative)→

      NP_i [NP_1 V NP_i NP_2]—(Relative Clause Formation)→

      NP_i [NP_1 V NP_2]

Crucially, at every stage of the derivation, the verb of the relative clause is immediately followed by an NP. This means that the *meng*-rule ought to be able to apply in (88), regardless of how it is ordered with respect to Dative and Relative Clause Formation.

In fact, though, *meng-* can never be inserted in a relative clause like (88):

(89) a.   Kau me-lihat   wanita jang   Hasan (*meng)-kirim-i
          you TRANS-see woman COMP Hasan   TRANS-send-BEN
          surat?
          letter
          'Have you seen the woman that Hasan sent the letter?'
     b.   Di mana   orang jang   saja (*mem)-beli-kan   badju
          at where? man COMP I   TRANS-buy-BEN clothes
          kemarin?
          yesterday
          'Where's the man that I bought clothes yesterday?'

It seems clear that the ungrammaticality of *meng-* in these examples cannot be explained by any extrinsic (or intrinsic) ordering of the rules. Sentences like (89) therefore argue that, even with the addition of extrinsic ordering, the transformational solution for Dative cannot be correct.

3.4   Modifications of Transformational Solution

The arguments of §§3.2 and 3.3 indicate that the basic transformational alternatives for describing Dative must be rejected. Both alternatives predict that a DO that has been affected by Dative will be accessible to later syntactic rules. They are therefore unable to account for the actual behavior of the DO with respect to Passive, Object Preposing, Relative Clause Formation, and the *meng*-rule.

Despite this failure of the basic alternatives, the possibility remains that some alternative explanation could be found for the ungrammaticality of (77–78), (80–81), (83–84), and (89). If so, a modified transformational solution might be able to account for the facts of §§3.2 and 3.3. To show the lack of feasibility of such a project, I will now examine several modifications of the transformational solution. I will show that none of these solutions can account for the interaction of Dative with later syntactic rules.

3.5   Surface Structure Constraint

It might be proposed that sentences like (77–78), (80–81), and (83–84) are thrown out by a surface structure constraint in Indonesian. This constraint would state that the benefactive suffix -*kan* (or its variants -*i*, -*ø*) requires the presence of a prepositionless NP to the immediate right of the verb in surface structure. If such a constraint could be formulated to pick out the right forms of the benefactive suffix (see §2.1), it would guarantee that a DO that has been affected by Dative could never be touched by Passive, Object Preposing, or Relative Clause Formation.

However, a surface structure constraint could not account for the behavior of the DO with respect to the *meng*-rule. Although sentences like (89), where the DO has triggered the *meng*-rule, are ungrammatical, they have an NP (the DO) occurring to the immediate right of the verb on the surface. They would therefore not be thrown out by the surface structure constraint.

3.6   A Prohibition Condition

Alternatively, it might be proposed that some fact of derivational history is responsible for the ungrammaticality of (77–78), (80–81), (83–84), and (89). For instance, one might propose that there is a general condition in Indonesian preventing more than one of the syntactic processes of §§3.2 and 3.3 from applying within a single clause. This condition would throw out (77–78), (80–81), and (83–84) because these sentences have undergone both Passive and Object Preposing, or Passive and Relative Clause Formation, or Object Preposing and Relative Clause Formation; it would throw out (89) because the sentences in this example have undergone some combination of Dative, Relative Clause Formation, and the *meng*-rule.

A prohibition condition could conceivably account for sentences like (77) and (80), since Passive and Object Preposing in fact do not cooccur in Indonesian. However, such a condition would be unable to handle the ungrammaticality of (78), (81), or (83–84). In order to account for these sentences, the condition would have to block Relative Clause Formation from applying to any clause in which Passive or Object Preposing has also applied. But there are grammatical sentences of Indonesian in which these rules interact:

(90) a. Tidak seorang pun suka kepada wanita jang
         not   someone even like to   woman COMP
         di-kirim-i   bunga oleh ajah   saja.
         PASS-send-BEN flower by   father my
         'No one likes the woman that was sent flowers by my father.'

   b. Saja tidak suka kepada orang jang   di-masak-kan   ikan
       I   not like to   man COMP PASS-cook-BEN fish
       oleh anak itu.
       by   child the
       'I don't like the man who was cooked fish by the child.'

In (90), Passive has applied to the output of Dative, and then the derived subject (underlying IO) has undergone Relative Clause Formation.

(91) a. Tidak seorang pun suka kepada wanita jang   akan kau
         not   someone even like to   woman COMP FUT you
         kirim-i   bunga.
         send-BEN flower
         'No one likes the woman that you will send flowers.'

   b. Orang jang   sudah saja tulis-i   surat adalah paman-mu.
       man   COMP PERF I   write-BEN letter be   uncle-your
       'The man that I wrote a letter was your uncle.'

In (91), Object Preposing has applied to the output of Dative, as shown by the inversion of the pronominal subject with the auxiliary. The derived subject (underlying IO) has then undergone Relative Clause Formation.

Similarly, to account for (89), the prohibition condition would have to exclude all combinations of Dative, Relative Clause Formation, and the *meng*-rule. But, as (92) shows, there are sentences of Indonesian in which all of these rules operate within the same clause:

(92) a. Ajah   saja adalah orang jang   meng-irim-i   wanita
         father my be   man COMP TRANS-send-BEN woman
         itu surat.
         the letter
         'My father is the man who sent the woman a letter.'

  b. Di mana   orang jang me-masak-kan   perempuan itu
      at where? man COMP TRANS-cook-BEN woman   the
      ikan?
      fish
      'Where's the man who cooked the woman a fish?'

There seems to be no way to account for the grammaticality of
(90–92), but the ungrammaticality of (78), (81), (83–84), and (89), without complicating the statement of the prohibition condition in a hope-
lessly ad hoc way.[22] Sentences (90–92) therefore argue that the syntactic
character of Dative cannot be correctly described by a prohibition
condition.

3.7   Traces

Given the failure of the prohibition condition, one might try to account
for (77–78), (80–81), (83–84), and (89) by appealing to some other aspect
of derivational history. Thus one might propose, following Chomsky
(1973, note 49), that "every rule that moves an item from an obligatory
category (in the sense of Emonds (1970)) leaves a trace." Under such
a proposal, Passive would have the effect sketched in (93) (where the
trace t is controlled by the moved item, NP_j):[23]

(93) NP_i V NP_j—(Passive)⟶ NP_j di-V t_j oleh NP_i

Assuming that traces can function in subsequent syntactic operations, one might try to exclude (77–78), (80–81), (83–84), and (89) in
the following way. Sentences (77–78), (80–81), and (83–84) could be
thrown out by a surface structure constraint that excludes sequences
of the form: $*V\ t\ t$. This constraint would filter out Dative sentences
in which both DO and IO have subsequently undergone a movement
rule.[24] It would therefore account for the ungrammaticality of (77) and
(80), where both Passive and Object Preposing have applied:[25]

(94)   Derivation of (77) after Dative:
       NP_1 V NP_i NP_j—(Passive)⟶
       NP_i di-V t_i NP_j oleh NP_1—(Object Preposing)⟶
       NP_j NP_i (di)-V t_i t_j oleh NP_1

Further, if Relative Clause Formation were analyzed as involving movement rather than deletion, it would also leave behind a trace. The
constraint would then be able to account for the ungrammaticality of
(78), (81), and (83–84), as well.

Sentences like (89) could be excluded by assuming that the prefix
meng- is attached underlyingly to transitive verbs. (For an objection to
this, see the end of note 21.) The prefix could then be deleted by a late

rule of *meng*-Deletion, if the verb is immediately followed by a trace. Assuming, again, that Relative Clause Formation involves movement rather than deletion, the derivation of (88) would be:

(95) After Dative:
  NP_i [NP_1 meng-V NP_i NP_2]—(Relative Clause Formation)→
  NP_i [jang$_i$ NP_1 meng-V t_i NP_2]—(*meng*-Deletion)→
  NP_i [jang$_i$ NP_1 V t_i NP_2]

Here, the trace left by relativizing the IO would force *meng*- to be deleted, and sentences like the ungrammatical (89) would never be produced.

This sort of trace proposal appears to account for the ungrammaticality of (77–78), (80–81), (83–84), and (89). However, there is a large class of sentences in Indonesian that it cannot account for. In these sentences, the traces that would be left behind by various movement rules would occur in the configurations *V t t*, or *meng-V t*. Although these configurations would be excluded by the surface structure constraint or by application of *meng*-Deletion, the sentences are grammatical.

The sequence *V t t*, for instance, would appear in all of the following sentences:

(96) a. Apakah kamu me-lihat   orang kepada siapa$_j$ surat$_i$ telah
         Q   you TRANS-see man to   who? letter PERF
         di-beri-kan t_i t_j?
         PASS-give-BEN
         'Have you seen the man to whom the letter was given?'
     b. Tidak seorang pun suka kepada wanita kepada siapa$_j$
         not   someone even like to   woman to   who?
         bunga$_i$ itu saja beri-kan t_i t_j.
         flower the I   give-BEN
         'No one likes the woman to whom the flowers I gave.'

The examples in (96) are transitive sentences to which Dative has not applied.[26] The DO has been moved to the left by Passive/Object Preposing; the IO has been moved to the left by the minor strategy for Relative Clause Formation (§1.6).

(97) a. Kepada John$_j$, pajung$_i$ itu di-pindjam-kan t_i t_j oleh
         to   John   umbrella the PASS-lend-BEN   by
         perempuan itu.
         woman   the
         'To John, the umbrella was lent by the woman.'

    b. Kepada John$_j$, pajung$_i$ tersebut saja pindjam-kan t_i t_j.
       to   John umbrella certain I   lend-BEN
    'To John, the umbrella I lent.'

In (97), the DO has also been moved to the left by Passive/Object Preposing. The IO has been moved to the left by a topicalization rule that preposes prepositional phrases to the beginning of the sentence.

(98) a. Buku$_i$ ini di-beri-kan t_i t_j hari kamis   kepada orang$_j$
        book this PASS-give-BEN   day Thursday to   man
        jang baru datang dari Djakarta.
        COMP just come from Jakarta
        'This book was given on Thursday to the man who just came from Jakarta.'
    b. Buku$_i$ ini saja beri-kan t_i t_j pada hari kamis   kepada
        book this I   give-BEN   on   day Thursday to
        orang$_j$ jang baru datang dari Djakarta.
        man   COMP just come from Jakarta
        'This book I gave on Thursday to the man who just came from Jakarta.'

In (98), the DO has been moved to the left by Passive/Object Preposing; the IO has been moved to the right by Heavy NP Shift.[27]

(99) a. Ali$_i$ di-beri t_i t_j pada hari rabu   buku$_j$ jang ada
        Ali PASS-give   on   day Wednesday book COMP be
        di atas medja itu.
        on top table the
        'Ali was given on Wednesday the book that was lying on the table.'
    b. Orang$_i$ itu saja beri t_i t_j pada hari rabu   buku$_j$
        man   the I   give   on   day Wednesday book
        jang ada di atas medja.
        COMP be on top table
        'That man I gave on Wednesday the book that was lying on the table.'

And in (99), the DO and IO have undergone the Dative rule. The original IO has then been moved to the left by Passive/Object Preposing; the original DO has been moved to the right by Heavy NP Shift.

    Notice that both DO and IO in these examples should leave behind a trace, since both are obligatory categories (i.e., they are obligatory in the subcategorization of *beri* 'give' and *pindjam* 'lend, borrow') and the operations that affect them are movement rules. This means that, under a trace proposal, sentences (96–99) would have two traces immediately after the verb. They would therefore be wrongly thrown out by the surface structure constraint.

Similarly, the sequence *meng-V t* would appear in sentences like (100a, b):

(100) a.   Iwan me-masukkan t_i ke dalam truk   lima2 andjing$_i$
        Iwan TRANS-force   to inside truck five   dog
        jang ribut.
        COMP noisy
        'Iwan forced into the truck the five dogs who were barking loudly.'

     b.   Yati me-masak t_i untuk Ali ikan$_i$ jang di-tangkap oleh
        Yati TRANS-cook   for   Ali fish COMP PASS-catch by
        kakak-nja kemarin.
        sibling-her yesterday
        'Yati cooked for Ali the fish which were caught by her brother yesterday.'

In (100), the direct objects have been moved from immediate postverbal position by Heavy NP Shift. Since this movement would leave a trace, the sentences should undergo *meng*-Deletion—but *meng*-Deletion does not apply.

It is difficult to see how a trace proposal could account for (96–100), and the ungrammatical (77–78), (80–81), (83–84), and (89), without appealing to numerous and ad hoc complications.[28] Sentences (96–100), then, show that the trace proposal sketched above is inadequate as a description of Dative.

3.8   Restatement of Dative

The failure of the proposals sketched above makes it unlikely that any additional syntactic device could save the transformational solution for Dative. There is, however, another kind of alternative for accounting for the facts of §§3.2 and 3.3. The essence of this alternative is that, in addition to permuting DO and IO, Dative has the effect of turning the DO into a prepositional phrase:

(101) X NP V NP $\left\{ \begin{matrix} \text{kepada} \\ \text{untuk} \end{matrix} \right\}$ NP Y

    1 2 3 4   5   6 7 $\longrightarrow$ 1 2 3 6 [$_{PP}$P 4] 7

Whether the preposition in the output of (101) is phonologically null or deleted by a later rule is not crucial to this restatement of Dative.

What is crucial is that the preposition prevent the DO from undergoing any later syntactic rules, which are stated so that they apply only to prepositionless NPs.

Although the restatement of Dative in (101) is able to account for the facts of §§3.2 and 3.3, there is evidence in Indonesian that the original DO in (101) does not behave like a prepositional phrase. For instance, prepositional phrases in Indonesian can be relativized by means of a minor strategy that replaces the relativized noun with a *wh-*word and preposes the entire prepositional phrase (§1.6):

(102) a. Polisi itu men-tjoba meng-ambil kerandjang di mana
        police the TRANS-try TRANS-take basket   in which?
        kita me-letakkan sajur2-an.
        we TRANS-put   vegetables
        'The policeman tried to take the baskets in which we put the vegetables.'

    b. Di mana   orang untuk siapa badju ini saja beli
        at where? man   for   who? clothes this I   buy
        kemarin?
        yesterday
        'Where's the man for whom these clothes I bought yester-day?'

But this minor strategy is not allowed for DOs that have been affected by Dative:

(103) a. *Semua tahu   tentang lima ribu   dolar apa   mereka
        all   know about five thousand dollar what? they
        (men-)tawar-kan presiden.
        TRANS-offer-BEN president
        (Everyone knows about the five thousand dollars which they offered the president.)

    b. *Ikan apa   kami (me-)masak-kan   Ali hilang.
        fish what? we   TRANS-cook-BEN Ali disappear
        (The fish which we cooked Ali has disappeared.)

Similarly, prepositional phrases can be topicalized by a rule that simply preposes them to the beginning of the sentence:

(104) a. Kepada Ani, Hasan meng-irim-kan   surat itu.
        to   Ani   Hasan TRANS-send-BEN letter the
        'To Ani, Hasan sent the letter.'

    b. Di lapangan itu, kita ketemu Ahmad.
        in park   the we meet   Ahmad
        'In the park, we met Ahmad.'

But this type of topicalization is ungrammatical for DOs that have been affected by Dative:

(105) a. *Lima ribu   dolar, mereka (men-)tawar-kan presiden.
         five thousand dollar they   TRANS-offer-BEN president
         (Five thousand dollars, they offered the president.)
      b. *Ikan itu, kami (me)-masak-kan   Ali.
         fish the we   TRANS-cook-BEN Ali
         (That fish, we cooked Ali.)

It is important to note that the ungrammaticality of (103) and (105) cannot be attributed to the fact that the "preposition" preceding the DO is not overt in surface structure. This is because there are examples of Relative Clause Formation and Topicalization applying to prepositional phrases from which the preposition has been deleted. For instance, the minor strategy for Relative Clause Formation allows relativized nouns that are locatives to be optionally replaced by *tempat* 'place'. In such relative clauses, the locative preposition never appears in surface structure (see (102)):

(106)   Polisi itu men-tjoba meng-ambil kerandjang tempat kita
        police the TRANS-try TRANS-take basket   where we
        me-letakkan sajur2-an.
        TRANS-put   vegetables
        'The policemen tried to take the baskets where we put the vegetables.'

Similarly, the topicalization described above can be applied to NPs that describe time or extent of time. These NPs need not be accompanied by a preposition in their topicalized or untopicalized forms:

(107) a.   Setiap sore, saja batja buku.
           each   night I   read book
           'Each evening, I read a book.'
      b.   Sepandjang waktu, kami hanja ber-main2.
           length   time   we   only INTR-play
           'The whole time, we just played.'

When compared with (106–107), sentences (103) and (105) show conclusively that DOs that have been affected by Dative do not behave like prepositional phrases. We can conclude from this that the restatement in (101) must be rejected as an alternative explanation for Dative.

3.9   Summary

This section began with two of the basic alternatives for describing Dative within the framework of transformational grammar. After presenting these alternatives, I established that they could not by themselves account for the interaction of Dative with later syntactic rules. Then I presented four proposals for modifying the basic transformational solution so that it would produce the right results. I demonstrated that other facts of Indonesian force us to reject each of these proposals. The combination of arguments indicates that Dative cannot be formulated in transformational terms, i.e., in terms of constituent structure.

The possibility remains, of course, that some collection of purely transformational devices will be able to describe the syntactic properties of Dative. I suspect, though, that any solution of this type will not account for the facts in a unified fashion. Moreover, although ad hoc solutions can always be produced for (77–107), these solutions must be rejected if we can find an explanation that accounts for all of these sentences in a motivated way. In §4, I discuss such a solution and show that it makes the right predictions about the interaction of Dative with all other syntactic rules.

I conclude, then, that any attempt to state Dative in terms of dominance and linear order cannot account for all of the facts. The syntactic character of Dative can only be explained if the rules are stated in the grammar in some other way.

4   An Analysis in Terms of Grammatical Relations

An adequate solution for Dative will have to account for the fact that a DO affected by Dative is inaccessible to other syntactic rules. This is, essentially, why the transformational proposals of §3 had to be rejected; they failed to explain why an IO affected by Dative is accessible to later syntactic processes, while a DO affected by Dative is not. The failure of these proposals suggests that transformational grammar cannot adequately characterize the classes of NPs that can undergo particular syntactic rules. It should be obvious from the discussion of §3 that these classes of NPs cannot always be characterized in terms of dominance and linear order.

What is needed is a theory that will characterize the classes of available NPs in a different way, and which will be able to give a unified explanation for the properties of the Dative rule. A theory that seems to meet both of these criteria has recently been developed by Perlmutter and Postal (1974). In this theory of relational grammar, the basic syntactic notions for clause description are taken to be grammatical relations such as subject, direct object, indirect object (*terms*), and locative, benefactive, etc. (*nonterms*). In contrast, linear order is considered to be superficial and is specified relatively late in the grammar (after the end of the cycle). Consistent with the central position of grammatical relations, cyclic rules such as Dative[29] are stated directly in terms of grammatical relations, rather than in terms of dominance and linear order:

(108) $\left\{ \begin{array}{l} \text{Indirect Object} \\ \text{Benefactive} \end{array} \right\} \longrightarrow$ Direct Object

Compare this statement of Dative with a relational statement of Passive:

(109)   Direct Object $\longrightarrow$ Subject

A basic claim of Perlmutter and Postal with respect to relation-changing rules like Dative has to do with the status of the underlying direct object, once the rule has applied. This NP loses its original grammatical relation, according to their Relational Annihilation Law (RAL):

(110)   Relational Annihilation Law
If an NP_i assumes a grammatical relation previously borne by NP_j, then NP_j ceases to bear any term grammatical relation; it becomes a 'chômeur'.

The RAL states that an NP whose grammatical relation has been assumed by another NP will lose its original grammatical relation and become a particular kind of nonterm (a chômeur). It therefore claims that DOs that have been affected by Dative will differ significantly from term NPs—including DOs that have not undergone the rule.

Given the RAL, a relational theory is able to provide a far better account of Dative than any of the transformational solutions proposed in §3. Consider what a relational analysis of the facts of §§1–3 will look like. First, Passive, Reflexive, Object Preposing, Relative Clause Formation, and the *meng*-rule will be stated in terms of grammatical relations so that they apply to direct objects (and in the case of Relative Clause Formation, to subjects as well), but to no other types of NPs. Second, Dative will be stated so that it alters the grammatical relations of DO and IO, essentially as in (108) and in agreement with the RAL.

Such a formulation predicts that an IO affected by Dative will be able to undergo Passive, Reflexive, Object Preposing, Relative Clause Formation, and the *meng*-rule. This follows because Dative turns the IO into a direct object, and the other syntactic rules are stated so that they refer specifically to direct objecthood. Moreover, it predicts that a DO affected by Dative will be inaccessible to all of these rules. This follows because the direct objecthood of the DO has been removed in accordance with the RAL. What is crucial to this solution is that the availability of the DO for later syntactic rules is not determined by its position or syntactic bracketing. Since grammatical relations are the determining factor, the relational formulation correctly predicts that all of (77–78), (80–81), (83–84), and (89) will be ungrammatical.

Clearly, the RAL lies at the heart of this solution for Dative. Without this principle, there would be no reason to suppose that Dative deprives the original DO of its direct objecthood, and therefore no reason to suppose that the DO would be inaccessible to later syntactic rules. In view of the crucial nature of the RAL, it is significant that the category chômeur is supported by an independent set of facts in Indonesian. These facts involve the interaction of Dative and Passive with an optional rule that I call 'Quantifier Shift'.

Quantifiers in Indonesian usually occur to the left of their head noun. However, the quantifiers *seluruh* 'entire, all' and *semua* 'all' can be moved to the right of their NPs by an optional rule of Quantifier Shift:[30]

(111) a. Semua anak2   ber-larian pergi.
          all   children INTR-run go
          'All the children ran away.'
      b. Semua pemain musik pulang   pagi.
          all   player music go home early
          'All the musicians left early.'

(112) a. Anak2   semua ber-larian pergi.
          children all   INTR-run go
          'All the children ran away.'
      b. Pemain musik semua pulang   pagi.
          player music all   go home early
          'All the musicians left early.'

In addition to moving the quantifier, Quantifier Shift sometimes marks it with the pronominal copy *-nja*.

(113) a. Semua surat2 di-letakkan di atas medja.
          all   letters PASS-put   on top table
          'All the letters were put on the table.'
      b. Ia makan semua permen itu.
          he eat   all   candy the
          'He ate up all the candy.'

(114) a. Surat2 semua-nja di-letakkan di atas medja.
          letters all-PRO   PASS-put   on top table
          'All the letters were put on the table.'
      b. Ia makan permen itu semua-nja.
          he eat   candy   the all-PRO
          'He ate up all the candy.'

I do not understand the function of the copy, which is invariant for person and number.

Unlike other syntactic rules discussed here, Quantifier Shift is not restricted to subjects and direct objects, but applies to a wide syntactic range of NPs.[31] (In Perlmutter and Postal's terminology, it applies to terms and nonterms.) The rule affects subjects and direct objects:

(115) a. Semua serdadu itu meng-edjar   dia.
          all   soldier the TRANS-chase him
          'All the soldiers chased him.'
      b. Saja beri-kan   semua barang saja kepada Hasan.
          I   give-BEN   all   thing my   to   Hasan
          'I gave all of my things to Hasan.'

(116) a. Serdadu2 itu semua-nja meng-edjar   dia.
          soldiers the all-PRO   TRANS-chase him
          'All the soldiers chased him.'
      b. Saja beri-kan   barang saja semua-nja kepada Hasan.
          I   give-BEN   thing my   all-PRO   to   Hasan
          'I gave all of my things to Hasan.'

It likewise applies to indirect objects:

(117) Saja men-awar-kan   rokok   kepada semua anak2.
      I   TRANS-offer-BEN   tobacco to   all   children
      'I offered cigarettes to all the children.'

(118) Saja men-awar-kan   rokok   kepada anak2   semua-nja.
      I   TRANS-offer-BEN   tobacco to   children all-PRO
      'I offered cigarettes to all the children.'

And it affects a wide variety of oblique NPs:

(119) a. Saja me-masukkan sajur   ke dalam semua kerandjang2.
          I   TRANS-put   vegetable to inside all   baskets
          'I put vegetables into all the baskets.'
      b. Mereka pergi men-onton   filem dengan seluruh
          they   go   TRANS-watch   film with   all
          teman2-nja.
          friends-their
          'They went to watch the film with all their friends.'
      c. Dalam seluruh perdjalanan dari Boston ke New York, dia
          in   all   trip   from Boston to New York he
          men-anjakan matjam2-pertanjaan.
          TRANS-ask   sorts-questions
          'The whole trip from Boston to New York, he asked
          questions.'

(120) a.   Saja me-masukkan sajur   ke dalam kerandjang2
           I   TRANS-put   vegetable to inside baskets
           semua-nja.
           all-PRO
           'I put vegetables into all the baskets.'
     b.   Mereka pergi men-onton   filem dengan teman2
           they   go   TRANS-watch film with   friends
           seluruh-nja.
           all-PRO
           'They went to watch the film with all their friends.'
     c.   Dalam perdjalanan dari Boston ke New York, seluruh-nja,
           in   trip   from Boston to New York all- PRO
           dia men-anjakan matjam2-pertanjaan.
           he TRANS-ask   sorts-question
           'The whole trip from Boston to New York, he asked
           questions.'

In addition, Quantifier Shift can apply to IOs that have been turned
into DOs by Dative. The fact that the rule is allowed for these NPs is
consistent with the general observation that Quantifier Shift is blind to
the syntactic function of an NP:

(121) a.   Saja beri semua anak2   itu sebuah sepeda.
           I   give all   children the a   bicycle
           'I gave all the children a bicycle.'
     b.   Kami mem-beli-kan   seluruh anak2   suatu sepeda.
           we   TRANS-buy-BEN all   children a   bicycle
           'We bought all the children a bicycle.'

(122) a.   Saja beri anak2   itu semua-nja sebuah sepeda.
           I   give children the all-PRO   a   bicycle
           'I gave all the children a bicycle.'
     b.   Kami mem-beli-kan   anak2   seluruh-nja suatu sepeda.
           we   TRANS-buy-BEN children all-PRO   a   bicycle
           'We bought all the children a bicycle.'

Crucially, though, the rule is not allowed for original DOs that have
been displaced by Dative. In (124), Dative has applied, and application
of Quantifier Shift produces an ungrammatical sentence:

(123) a.   Saja meng-irim-i   Hasan semua surat2.
           I   TRANS-send-BEN Hasan all   letters
           'I sent Hasan all the letters.'
     b.   Saja beri saudara perempuan saja semua barang saja.
           I   give sibling female   my   all   thing   my
           'I gave my sister all of my things.'

(124) a. ?*Saja meng-irim-i   Hasan surat2 semua-nja.
          I   TRANS-send-BEN Hasan letters all-PRO
          (I sent Hasan all the letters.)

      b. ?*Saja beri saudara perempuan saja barang saja semua-nja.
          I   give sibling female   my   thing my all-PRO
          (I gave my sister all of my things.)

The fact that the DO fails to undergo a syntactic process that is available
to most other types of NPs suggests that it is substantively different
from these NPs once Dative has applied. The fact that the DO behaves
differently from all nonchômeurs is exactly what is predicted by the
RAL.

Within transformational grammar, the peculiar behavior of the DO
in (124) can only be attributed to some fact about dominance and linear
order. One would be forced to say that the DO fails to undergo Quantifier Shift because it is the second prepositionless NP after the verb
or because it does not take a preposition even though it occupies the
surface position of a prepositional phrase. Neither of these proposals
can be correct, though, because the DO does not undergo Quantifier
Shift even when it is the first NP after the verb:

(125) ?*Hasan di-kirim-i   surat2 semua-nja oleh saja.
         Hasan PASS-send-BEN letters all-PRO   by   me
       (Hasan was sent all the letters by me.)

In (125), the IO has undergone Passive, but Quantifier Shift is still
prevented from applying to the DO.

(126) ?*Hasan saja kirim-i   surat2 semua-nja.
         Hasan I   send-BEN letters all-PRO
       (Hasan I sent all the letters.)

In (126), the IO has undergone Object Preposing, but Quantifier Shift
is still prevented from applying to the DO.

The ungrammaticality of (125–126) shows that the behavior of the
DO with respect to Quantifier Shift is independent of its position in the
sentence.

Further, the DOs displaced by Dative are not the only NPs that fail
to undergo the rule. In addition, the underlying subjects of passive
sentences do not allow their quantifiers to be shifted:[32]

(127) a. Kami di-serang   oleh semua pradjurit.
           we   PASS-attack by   all   soldier
          'We were attacked by all the soldiers.'

      b. Ikan di-makan oleh semua anak2   itu.
           fish PASS-eat by   all   children the
          'The fish was eaten by all the children.'

(128) a. *Kami di-serang   oleh pradjurit semua-nja.
         we   PASS-attack by   soldier   all-PRO
         (We were attacked by all the soldiers.)
      b. *Ikan di-makan oleh anak2   (itu) semua-nja.
         fish PASS-eat by   children the all-PRO
         (The fish was eaten by all the children.)

Compare (128) with (129), where Passive has not applied and Quantifier
Shift produces a grammatical sentence:

(129) a. Pradjurit semua menj-erang   kita.
         soldier   all   TRANS-attack us
         'All the soldiers attacked us.'
      b. Anak2 (itu) semua-nja makan ikan.
         children the all-PRO   eat   fish
         'All the children ate the fish.'

The underlying subject of a passive sentence has all the surface characteristics of a prepositional phrase, but most prepositional phrases
permit Quantifier Shift (120). This makes sentences like (128) extremely
difficult to account for in terms of dominance and linear order. Moreover, even if a transformational solution could be given for (128), it is
hard to see how it could be extended to cover sentences like (124–126).
This is because there are almost no characteristics of constituent structure shared by underlying subjects of passive sentences and DOs that
have been affected by Dative.[33]

In relational grammar, however, the RAL provides the means to
characterize the ungrammaticality of (128) and (124–126). The RAL
claims that the underlying subjects in (128) and the DOs in (124–126)
are alike in that they have had their original grammatical relations
removed, i.e., they are chômeurs; they can therefore be expected to
pattern together as opposed to all other types of NPs. The fact that
these NPs differ from other NPs in their failure to undergo Quantifier
Shift provides syntactic evidence for the category chômeur. It also
suggests that the correct formulation of Quantifier Shift is that it applies
to nonchômeurs. In order for this formulation to work, Dative and
Passive must crucially be stated so that they alter the grammatical
relations of particular NPs.

5   Conclusions

Two specific conclusions can be drawn from the interaction of Dative
with other syntactic rules. First, in order to account for Dative, an
adequate theory of grammar must allow syntactic rules to have access
to grammatical relations such as subject, direct object, and indirect
object. Second, the theory must also provide some way of character-

izing the similarity between underlying DOs of Dative sentences and underlying subjects of Passive sentences; in other words, it must be able to identify those NPs whose original grammatical relations have been removed. Only a theory that satisfies both of these criteria will be able to explain the behavior of Dative with respect to Passive, Object Preposing, and Relative Clause Formation; the interaction of Dative with the *meng*-rule; and the interaction of Dative and Passive with Quantifier Shift.

In summary, the facts presented in this article argue that grammatical relations are relevant for the operation of syntactic rules. They therefore argue in favor of a theory of grammar that allows rules to refer directly to grammatical relations.

Notes

1. According to many of the secondary sources, this rule is limited to sentences whose underlying subjects are third person; sentences with first or second person subjects are passivized by means of a different rule (see section §1.4). There may be some historical basis for this restriction, but it is no longer operative in the contemporary language; see MacDonald and Dardjowidjojo (1967, 235) for a discussion.

In passive sentences like (4), the preposition *oleh* is optional if the underlying subject occurs to the immediate right of the verb. The optionality of this preposition does not affect the arguments of this article.

2. The scrambling of postverbal NPs is illustrated by examples like (i) and (ii):

(i)   Iwan me-masukkan andjing itu ke truk.
       Iwan TRANS-force dog   the to truck
       'Iwan forced the dogs into the truck.'
(ii)   Iwan me-masukkan ke truk andjing itu.
       Iwan TRANS-force to truck dog   the
       'Iwan forced the dogs into the truck.'

3. I have found some speakers who allow indirect objects and oblique NPs to be reflexivized with a true reflexive plus *sendiri*. This construction is less preferred than the one in (10), and it is ungrammatical if *sendiri* is omitted as in (11):

(i)   Kakak saja mem-beli   sepasang sepatu merah untuk diri-nja sendiri.
       sibling my TRANS-buy a pair   shoe   red   for   self-his EMP
       'My brother bought a pair of red shoes for himself.'

Speakers who accept (i) still form reflexive direct objects as in (7). For these speakers, then, the occurrence of a reflexive pronoun without *sendiri* constitutes a test for direct objecthood.

4. Some native speakers allow the direct object to be preposed only if the subject is a first or second person pronoun. (These same speakers allow Passive for subjects of all persons; see note 1.) This additional restriction on the Object Preposing rule does not affect the arguments of this article.

5. Native speakers vary somewhat in their judgments of (32). However, all

native speakers I have talked to find such sentences noticeably worse than the sentences in (26).

6. *Major strategy* is used by Keenan and Comrie (1972) to refer to types of relativization that apply to subject (and possibly other) NPs; *minor strategy* is used to refer to types of relativization that are not available for subjects.

It might be possible to analyze the major strategy described here as involving movement rather than deletion of the relativized noun. This alternative analysis has no real effect on the arguments of this article (however, see §3.7).

7. The preposed direct objects (= derived subjects) in (41–42) have been transported to the higher clause by a rule of Subject-to-Object Raising. This is not the place for a general discussion of the existence or nonexistence of Subject-to-Object Raising rules. I assume that Postal (1974) has established the existence of Subject-to-Object Raising for English. In Indonesian, the evidence for a similar rule is that: (i) NPs like *orang itu* and *buku ini* in (41–42) act as matrix direct objects rather than embedded subjects for the purposes of Passive, Object Preposing, Reflexive, etc. (ii) These NPs cannot be directly passivized, etc., from their underlying position as embedded subjects, because Passive and the other rules cannot be stated so that they operate blindly on the first NP after the verb. The demonstration that Passive, etc., cannot be stated this way is independent of (41–42); this demonstration is given in §3.

8. This description of Dative in terms of movement and deletion is used for convenience. In the analysis that I propose in §4, neither movement nor deletion is a part of the Dative rule; rather, the position of the IO and its prepositional marking are determined by relatively late operations.

9. Some condition on structural recoverability (see Hankamer 1973) seems to be involved here, since Dative is not allowed for: (i) sentences with a deleted, generic direct object, as in (50); (ii) sentences in which the direct object is deleted through the ordinary rules of pronominalization; and (iii) sentences in which either DO or IO has undergone Topicalization, Question Movement, Scrambling, or Heavy NP Shift.

10. However, permutation of DO and IO is allowed if the DO is a heavy NP:

(i)   Saja mem-beri   kepada Ali semua uang   jang   kamu kasih.
      I   TRANS-give to   Ali all   money COMP you   give
      'I gave to Ali all the money that you gave (to me).'

11. Sentences like (58) are also cited by Kwee (1965, p. 98) and Sarumpaet (1967) for Bahasa Indonesia. Compare Keenan (1972, p. 184), where it is reported that indirect objects in Malay can never be relativized by means of the major strategy.

In general, it seems that relative clauses involving indirect objects (58a) are more common than those involving benefactives (58b). A few native speakers I have talked to stated that examples like (58b) are grammatical, but unpopular in everyday speech.

12. The ungrammaticality of (63) is confirmed by MacDonald and Dardjowidjojo (1967, p. 244), who state that sentences of this type "simply do not occur." However, there seem to be a few native speakers who allow sentences like (i):

(i)   ?Pisau-nja Ahmad di-kasih   Ida (oleh mereka).
      knife-his Ahmad PASS-give Ida by   them
      'Ahmad's knife was given Ida (by them).'

Sentences like (i) are extremely restricted. They are only allowed when the IO is a pronoun or short proper name and the verb is *beri* or *kasih* 'give'; even then they are not always accepted by the people who claim that they are allowed. These restrictions suggest that (i) is derived by a low-level cliticization of the IO, rather than by application of Dative. Such a conjecture is supported by the distribution of the benefactive suffix *-kan* for those speakers who allow *-kan* to appear on *beri* or *kasih* at all. (Recall that *beri* and *kasih* are Class III; this means that they never take *-kan* if Dative has applied, but sometimes allow it if Dative has not applied.) These speakers will accept (i) when the verb takes *-kan,* but not otherwise, arguing that Dative has in fact failed to apply (see Dardjowidjojo 1974).

13. I have not managed to construct an example like this with a benefactive NP.

14. The presence of the VP in (75) is irrelevant for the proposal. I know of no evidence supporting the existence of a VP in Indonesian.

15. Although the DO also satisfies the structural description of Passive, I do not consider this possibility, since Passive has already applied once in (76).

16. In addition, the DO cannot undergo Reflexive after any of Passive, Object Preposing, or Relative Clause Formation have applied to the IO. This fact is inconclusive, though, because it is impossible to construct derivations in which Reflexive (on the IO) precedes Passive, Object Preposing, or Relative Clause Formation (on the DO). Given the lack of these derivations, the explanation for the behavior of Reflexive might be simply that it is extrinsically ordered before Passive, Object Preposing, and Relative Clause Formation.

17. In applying Passive to (80), I have assumed that it takes the NP immediately preceding the verb. If Passive is formulated to take the first NP in the sentence, then applying it to the output of Object Preposing will produce ungrammatical sentences like those in (77).

18. This situation cannot be changed by appealing to the notion of the cycle. For instance, if Passive is cyclic and Relative Clause Formation postcyclic, then ungrammatical sentences of the type (78) will be produced. If Relative Clause Formation is cyclic and Passive postcyclic, then ungrammatical sentences of the type (83) will be produced. If Passive is cyclic, Relative Clause Formation is successive cyclic, and the two rules are unordered with respect to each other, sentences like (78) and (83) will result. And so on. The possible orderings involving the cycle are, clearly, subcases of the orderings illlustrated in (77–78), (80–81), and (83–84).

19. The *meng*-rule must be formulated to apply before generic direct objects are deleted and before direct objects are deleted by pronominalization-by-deletion. It must also be formulated so that it does not apply to imperative sentences, which do not take the transitive prefix:

(i)   Lihat-lah bodoh-nja harimau itu!
      see-EMP stupid-its tiger   the
      'Look at the stupidity of that tiger!' (MacDonald and Dardjowidjojo 1967, p. 262)

Under conditions that are ill-defined, *meng-* can sometimes be attached to nouns and intransitive verbs. Attachment of *meng-* to a noun turns it into a verb (e.g., *pekik* 'a scream', *me-mekik* 'utter a scream'); attachment of *meng-* to an intransitive usually adds a sense of continuity or duration (e.g., *turun* 'go down', *men-urun* 'decline'). Since these uses of *meng-* involve some change in meaning and are lexically rather restricted, I do not consider them here.

20. Although Topicalization (86d) and Question Movement (86e) are formally similar to Relative Clause Formation (86c), they are produced by separate operations. That they do not involve Relative Clause Formation is indicated most clearly by their interaction with Dative. While the IO (but not the DO) in the output of Dative can undergo Relative Clause Formation, neither NP can be affected by Topicalization or Question Movement. See note 9.

21. Conceivably, one could propose that the transitive prefix is not inserted by a late rule, but is present at some deeper level of structure. Under this proposal, *meng-* would be deleted whenever the NP following the verb is removed by Passive, Object Preposing, Relative Clause Formation, Topicalization, or Question Movement. There are, however, two objections to stating the distribution of *meng-* in this way. First, incorporating the deletion of *meng-* into the statement of Passive, Object Preposing, etc., would result in redundant complication of these rules. Second, a deletion hypothesis could not account for the fact that there are some sentences in Indonesian into which *meng-* must be inserted in derived structure. Such sentences are produced by a syntactic rule of Locative, which turns a Locative NP into a direct object if it is attached to an (underlying) intransitive verb:

(i)   Mereka sedang be-renang di danau itu.
      they   PROG   INTR-swim in lake   the
      'They were swimming in the lake.'
(ii) Mereka sedang me-renang-i   danau itu.
      they   PROG   TRANS-swim-LOC lake   the
      'They were swimming in the lake.'

After Locative has derived (ii) from (i), the transitive prefix can be attached to the verb, because the verb is followed by a derived direct object. While the presence of the transitive prefix in (ii) can be handled easily by the *meng*-rule, it cannot be accounted for by a deletion hypothesis in any motivated way.

22. One way of getting around this argument would be to claim that subjects and direct objects are relativized by different operations. Since sentences (90–92) involve relativization of subjects, but (78), (81), (83–84), and (89) involve relativization of direct objects, the prohibition condition would be stated so as to refer only to the latter operation. It should be obvious that this division of Relative Clause Formation would result in great loss of generality.

23. I use *t* for the trace that Chomsky (1973, p. 269) identifies as "a controlled PRO . . . or a null symbol dominated by its former categories."

Notice that the postposed agent in (93) does not leave behind a trace *t*. This is because, according to Chomsky (1973, note 49), it leaves behind a different kind of trace, *, whose position must be filled by some subsequent rule. (In (93), this rule is the part of Passive that moves the direct object to subject position.) Because * traces are not relevant for the discussion below, only *t* traces are represented in the examples.

The definition of *obligatory category* will be of some interest to the discussion below. According to Emonds (1970, chap. 3), an obligatory node (apparently the equivalent of Chomsky's obligatory category) is one that must be present and nonempty at some point in a transformational derivation. From the discussion surrounding this definition, it seems clear that Emonds intends the class of obligatory nodes to include (i) nodes that are obligatory in the expansion of the phrase structure rules, and (ii) nodes that are obligatory in the subcategorization of a particular lexical item. For instance, Emonds asserts that the verb *brace* is obligatorily subcategorized for a following NP. This NP is then obligatory in derivations involving *brace,* and it must be filled at some point in the derivation.

24. The statement of the surface structure constraint is complicated by the fact that the DO and IO in (77–78), (80–81), (83–84), and (89) have also undergone Dative. There are several possibilities for dealing with this. It could be assumed that Dative is a structure-preserving rule that exchanges the positions of DO and IO (essentially as proposed by Emonds 1970); if so, the rule will leave behind * traces, and the surface structure constraint can be stated as in the text. Or, it could be assumed that Dative only involves movement of the IO, and that this movement leaves behind a trace *t*. Under this assumption, the surface structure constraint can be reformulated as: *$V\ t\ t\ t$ (with one trace left by Dative, and the other two by subsequent movement rules). In (99), I give examples showing that this alternative statement cannot be correct.

It is worth noting that the assumption that Dative is a syntactic rule causes problems for a trace proposal. If Dative is a syntactic rule, than all sentences of the type (46) must be derived from sentences of the type (45). But not all sentences of the type (45) are obligatorily subcategorized for an IO. For these sentences, movement of the IO will not leave behind a trace (because the IO will not be an obligatory category in the sense of Emonds 1970). Therefore, illegal derivations like (77c) will not be thrown out by the surface structure constraint. In order to correct this, it must either be assumed that Dative sentences are generated directly by the phrase structure rules, or that all NPs that have undergone movement rules—even NPs in optional categories—leave behind a trace. For some arguments against the former option, see §2.1.

25. In applying Object Preposing to (94), I have assumed that the trace left by Passive does not undergo subsequent syntactic rules (Chomsky (1973, p. 280)). Conceivably, it could be assumed that traces do undergo later rules. Under this assumption, the original DO of (94) could not be touched by Object Preposing, since this rule would be forced to operate instead on the trace left by the IO. Sentences like (i) could then be excluded by positing a general convention that would throw out sentences in which a trace t_i both precedes and commands its antecedent, NP_i:

(i)   Alternative to (77), after Dative:
       $NP_1\ V\ NP_i\ NP_2$—(Passive)$\longrightarrow$
       NP_i di-V $t_i\ NP_2$ oleh NP_1—(Object Preposing)$\longrightarrow$
       $t_i\ NP_i$ (di)-V $(t_i)\ NP_2$ oleh NP_1

A general convention like this seems to account for (77–78), (80–81), and (83–84), but it does not account for (89). Moreover, it is hard to see how such a convention can be maintained if all rules that move items from obligatory categories are to leave a trace. This combination of assumptions would exclude sentences like (100), where Heavy NP Shift leaves a trace that precedes and commands its antecedent.

There are doubtless other ways of trying to use traces to describe the facts of §§3.2–3.3. Clearly, an examination of all possible trace proposals is beyond the scope of this article.

26. The verbs used in these examples are *beri* 'give', from Class III, and *pindjam* 'lend, borrow', from Class II.

27. Heavy NP Shift relates (98a) to the extremely awkward (i):

(i) Buku ini di-beri-kan   kepada orang jang baru datang dari
    book this PASS-give-BEN to   man COMP just come from
    Djakarta, hari kamis.
    Jakarta   day Thursday
    'This book was given to the man who just came from Jakarta, on Thursday.'

Example (i) illustrates the normal position of time expressions, which ordinarily come at the end of the sentence.

In note 9, I noted that Heavy NP Shift is not allowed for the DO or IO of a Dative sentence. This restriction no longer holds if the IO has been turned into a subject by Passive; so (99) is grammatical. The fact that the restriction operates only when DO and IO are next to each other provides more evidence for the structural recoverability condition mentioned in note 9.

28. One could try to claim, for instance, that *meng*-Deletion is extrinsically ordered before Heavy NP Shift. This extrinsic ordering would be able to describe the fact that *meng-* is allowed in (100), but not in relative clauses like (89). In a similar fashion, one could account for (96–98) by claiming that prepositional phrases do not leave traces; and for (99), by claiming that traces are only left by leftward movement rules. The problem with these modifications is that there is no reason, apart from (96–100), for incorporating them into the theory of grammar. They only serve to disguise the fact that (96–100) cannot be accounted for by a trace proposal.

29. Perlmutter and Postal (1974) propose that all term-creating rules are cyclic rules. Although Dative in Indonesian can be shown to be cyclic, I will not demonstrate this here.

30. Quantifier Shift is to be distinguished from a rule of Quantifier Float, which moves the quantifier all the way to the end of the sentence:

(i) Pertahanan2 telah kabur seluruh-nja.
    prisoners   PERF flee all-PRO
    'The prisoners all ran away.'

Unlike Quantifier Shift, Quantifier Float seems to be limited to subject and direct object NPs. (For oblique NPs, the two constructions can be disambiguated by placing some other constituent between the shifted quantifier and the rest of the NP.) Both constructions are mentioned briefly by Dyen (1964, 22b.8).

Although it seems clear that Quantifier Shift and Quantifier Float are both associated with some difference in meaning, I have not been able to determine the exact nature of this difference.

31. I have found a few native speakers who allow quantifiers to shift from subjects and direct objects, but no other NPs. For these speakers, the restrictions on Quantifier Float and Quantifier Shift appear to be the same. Such speakers judge (118) and (120) to be ungrammatical, but agree with all the other grammaticality judgments given in this section. Their judgments therefore provide an argument for the nonobjecthood of the original DO after Dative has applied (124–126), although they do not provide evidence for the syntactic category chômeur.

32. Sentence (128b) is grammatical if the quantifier is interpreted as having floated off the derived subject NP (see note 30), as in 'The whole fish was eaten by the children.' Notice that derived subjects can also undergo Quantifier Shift; (114a) gives an example.

33. A conceivable explanation for the inaccessibility of these NPs might be that both of them have been moved to the right by a syntactic rule. Under the assumption that Dative involves rightward movement of the DO, this proposal could describe the behavior of original DOs in (124–126) and the behavior of underlying subjects in (128). However, it could not account for the fact that an NP can undergo Quantifier Shift even if it has been moved to the right by Heavy NP Shift:

(i)   Kami masak untuk Ali ikan itu semua-nja.
      we   cook   for   Ali fish the all-PRO
      'We cooked for Ali all of the fish.'
(ii) Kami masak untuk Ali ikan jang   ber-warna biru semua-nja.
      we   cook   for   Ali fish COMP INTR-color blue all-PRO
      'We cooked for Ali all of the blue fish.'

(Sentence (ii) also has a reading on which the quantifier *semua* originates in the relative clause.)

References

Anderson, S., and Kiparsky, P., eds. 1973. *A Festschrift for Morris Halle*. New York: Holt, Rinehart, & Winston.

Chomsky, N. 1965. *Aspects of the Theory of Syntax*. Cambridge, Mass.: MIT Press.

———. 1973. "Conditions on Transformations." In S. Anderson and P. Kiparsky, 1973.

Chung, S. 1976. "On the Subject of Two Passives in Indonesian." In C. Li, 1976.

Danoesoegondo, P. 1971. *Bahasa Indonesia for Beginners*, Book 2. Sydney, Australia: Sydney University Press.

Dardjowidjojo, S. 1974. "The Role of Overt Markers in Some Indonesian and Javanese Passive Sentences." Paper read at the First International Conference on Comparative Austronesian Linguistics, January 2–7, 1974, Honolulu.

Dyen, I. 1964. *Beginning Indonesian, Lessons 1–24*. 4 vols. Washington, D.C.: U.S. Department of Health, Education, and Welfare, Office of Education (Language Development Program, NDEA).

Echols, J., and Shadily, H. 1963. *An Indonesian-English Dictionary*. Ithaca, N.Y.: Cornell University Press.

Emonds, J. 1970. "Root and Structure-Preserving Transformations." Ph.D. diss., MIT.

Hankamer, J. 1973. "Unacceptable Ambiguity." *Linguistic Inquiry* 4:17–68.

Keenan, E. 1972. "Relative Clause Formation in Malagasy." In Peranteau et al. 1972.

Keenan, E., and Comrie, B. 1972. "NP Accessibility and Universal Grammar." Mimeograph.

Kwee, J. 1965. *Teach Yourself Indonesian*. London: English Universities Press.

Li, C., ed. 1976. *Subject and Topic*. New York: Academic Press.

MacDonald, R., and Dardjowidjojo, S. 1967. *A Student's Reference Grammar of Modern Formal Indonesian*. Washington, D.C.: Georgetown University Press.

Peranteau, P.; Levi, J.; and Phares, G.; eds. 1972. *The Chicago Which Hunt*. Chicago Linguistic Society, University of Chicago.

Perlmutter, D., and Postal, P. 1974. Lectures on Relational Grammar. Summer Linguistic Institute of the LSA, University of Massachusetts, Amherst.

Postal, P. 1974. *On Raising*. Cambridge, Mass.: MIT Press.

Sarumpaet, J. 1967. *The Structure of Bahasa Indonesia*. Melbourne, Australia: University of Melbourne.

7 Indirect Object Advancement in Tzotzil

Judith L. Aissen

Introduction

The subject of this paper is the advancement of indirect object to direct object in Tzotzil, a Mayan language of Mexico.[1] One reason this phenomenon is interesting is that the effects of the rule are somewhat camouflaged. As a result, a number of earlier studies have assumed that no such advancement rule exists and have assumed that in sentences like the following, in which we will argue that *li Šune* is the final direct object, *li Šune* is both initial and final indirect object.[2]

(1) ʔI-ø-h-čon-be   čitom li Šune.
     ASP-A3-E1-sell-BE pig   the Šun
     'I sold (the) pigs to Šun.'

Two facts about Tzotzil obscure the existence of Indirect Object Advancement. First is the fact that (1) is the only way to say 'I sold pigs to Šun.' That is, there are no sentences in which the indirect object has not advanced to direct object. In fact, there are *no* final indirect objects in Tzotzil. There being no other obvious candidates for indirect object in Tzotzil (obvious by case marking or as part of a prepositional phrase), *li Šune* in (1) has been analyzed as a final indirect object essentially because it is assumed to be an initial indirect object to which nothing relevant has happened.

This work was supported in part by the Radcliffe Institute and in part by the American Council of Learned Societies. Support in the form of hospitality during the time I was in Chiapas was extended by Evon and Nan Vogt and by Richard Gonzalez, to whom I am grateful.

I wish to thank Sandra Chung, Jorge Hankamer, and especially David Perlmutter for reading an earlier draft and suggesting various improvements; and Will Norman for discussion of many of the issues in this paper. I owe a special debt to John Burstein, who checked some of the data for me after I had left Chiapas. This paper was completed in 1977.

Second, *čitom* 'pig' in (1) is, it will be claimed, initial direct object, but not final direct object, this relation being held by *li Šune*. *Čitom* is a final direct object chômeur. However, neither final direct object nor final direct object chômeur is morphologically marked in any way. *Čitom* in (1) has the same surface form that it has in (2) where it is final direct object. (The presence of *li* and *-e* in (2) and their absence in (1) have nothing to do with the grammatical relation of *čitom* in either sentence. These morphemes are discussed below.)

(2) ʔI-ø-h-čon   li   čitome.
     ASP-A3-E1-sell the pig
     'I sold the pig(s).'

Thus, there is nothing in the nominal morphology that would lead one to conclude that *čitom* and *Šun* have final grammatical relations different from their initial grammatical relations.

Nonetheless, it is clear that *Šun* in (1) is the final direct object of the clause while *čitom* is not, and we will argue for this here.

Aside from its relevance to the understanding of Tzotzil syntax, this analysis has an interesting consequence for syntactic theory. Accounting for the nonexistence of final indirect objects is of interest since the most obvious solution—making the rule of Indirect Object Advancement obligatory—appears to be incorrect. It is argued here that the nonexistence of indirect objects in final structure must be accounted for by a constraint on final structure itself or on derivations.

The first sections of this paper deal with some general facts about Tzotzil syntax, the argument that initial indirect objects are final direct objects, and the argument that these nominals are in fact initial indirect objects. The final section posits a constraint on the rule of Indirect Object Advancement and argues against making it obligatory.

1 The Theoretical Framework

The theoretical framework in which this analysis is presented shares certain features with the theory of relational grammar as articulated in Postal 1977 and Perlmutter and Postal 1977, and diverges from it in other respects.

The theory of relational grammar (as presented in the above references) assumes that the grammatical relations subject, direct object, and indirect object which a nominal may bear to a verb are defined at all levels of structure and that syntactic rules may refer directly to these relations. Like transformational grammar, relational grammar characterizes the syntactic structure of a sentence in terms of a number of distinct levels of structure. In relational grammar, these are relational structures—structures which, among other things, associate a verb with a set of nominals and specify the relations borne by those nominals to the clause at that level of structure. While some levels of structure may specify how particular elements are ordered linearly with respect to others, it is claimed that this is not a property of all levels of structure. The structures of transformational grammar are phrase markers which specify constituency and linear order at all levels of structure. Transformational rules may not refer directly to grammatical relations. In Chomsky 1965 grammatical relations are defined in terms of deep structure configurations.

Unlike transformational grammar, at least some versions of relational grammar (e.g., Postal 1977) claim that the levels of structure associated with a sentence do not constitute a derivation in the sense of transformational grammar. While my conception of sentence structure follows that of relational grammar in its essentials, I assume that these levels of relational structure do constitute a derivation, roughly in the spirit of transformational grammar.

Specific levels of structure are referred to here. By 'initial' structure, I refer to a level of structure which is determined by the lexical entry of a verb. This entry specifies what underlying syntactic relations may be associated with a verb; further, it associates each of these initial syntactic relations with a notional relation (e.g., agent, instrument, recipient) which is relevant to the meaning of the sentence. By 'final' structure, I mean the last configuration of grammatical relations associated with a verb. This is distinct from surface structure, which I take to be characterized not only by certain grammatical relations but also by linear order.

2   Background
2.1   Pronouns

Though there are independent pronominal forms in Tzotzil, these are frequently omitted in surface structure. The following examples illustrate sentences both with (3b) and without (3a, c) independent pronominal subjects. As will be seen in subsequent examples, this phenomenon is not restricted to subjects. The following examples are all from a single text:

(3) a.   K'usi š-a-naʔ-ø?
         what ASP-E2-know-A3
         'What do you know?'
    b.   Mi ʔu   k'u š-a-naʔ-ø   li voʔote?
         ? exists what ASP-E2-know-A3 the you
         'Is there anything you know?'

    c. Mu?yuk mu k'u h-na?-ø.
        nothing NEG what E1-know-A3
        'Nothing, I don't know anything.'

As will be seen shortly, the person of both subject and object is marked on the verb in Tzotzil by a set of verbal affixes. Thus, the omission of independent pronouns does not result in ambiguity.

2.2 Word Order

Unmarked word order in Tzotzil is VOS. Nominals are not marked for case.

(4)   Tal-ø   li   viniketik ?une.
       come-A3 the men   PTS
       'The men came.' (Laughlin, p. 339)
(5)   ?Ayan-ø š-č'amal   ?un.
       born-A3 his-children PTS
       'His children were born.' (Laughlin, p. 291)
(6)   ?I-ø-s-pet   lok'el ?an¢   ti t'ule.
       ASP-A3-E3-carry away woman the rabbit
       'The rabbit carried away the woman.' (Laughlin, p. 47)
(7)   S-hipan-ø la ta   ?ora ti ?ok'il ti t'ul ?une.
       E3-tie-A3 PT right away the coyote the rabbit PTS
       'The rabbit tied up the coyote right away.' (Laughlin, p. 160)

In examples (4–7), *ti* and *li* function somewhat like definite articles and differ in proximateness, *ti* being the less proximate.[3] *?Un* and *-e* are particles which occur in phrase-final position; *la* follows the first major constituent of a sentence and indicates that the speaker does not have firsthand knowledge of the situation he is describing.[4]

In general, a nominal dependent of the verb may occur in preverbal position if it is definite. Topicalized nominals frequently occur in the frame: ?A li ——e . . . :

(8)   ?A li   vo?one h-na?-ø   sutum ?ik.
       the I   E1-know-A3 whirlwind
       'I know the whirlwind.' (Laughlin, p. 328)
(9)   ?A li   s-tot   tah ¢eb ?une ba   la s-mel¢an-be-ø
       the her-father that girl PTS   went PT E3-make-BE-A3
       s-vayeb   ?un.
       their-sleeping place PT
       'The father of that girl went to make them their sleeping place.'
       (Laughlin, p. 361)

2.3   Person Agreement

Intransitive verbs agree obligatorily with their final subjects in person and transitive verbs obligatorily with both final subject and final direct object. The agreement system is morphologically ergative in that for any given person, the agreement markers for intransitive subject and transitive object are the same (called absolutive) and differ from that of transitive subject (called ergative). In (10), the intransitive subject is first person and the verb bears the affix -*i*- in agreement with it. The same affix refers to first person transitive object in (11). But in (12), the transitive subject is first person and the verb bears the affix -*h*- in agreement with it. In the glosses to these examples, A or E followed by 1, 2, or 3 (pl) indicate whether the affix is absolutive or ergative and what the grammatical person and number are.

(10)   Č-i-bat.
      ASP-A1-go
      'I'm going.'

(11)   L-i-s-mah.
      ASP-A1-E3-hit
      'He hit me.'

(12)   Ta-ø-h-mah.
      ASP-A3-E1-hit
      'I'm going to hit him.'

Note that the absolutive prefix precedes the ergative (11). It is possible to read off from the glosses a substantial amount of information regarding the final grammatical relations of a clause. If the verb has only one agreement affix (always absolutive), it is finally intransitive, and the nominal cross-referenced by that affix is its final subject. If the verb has two agreement affixes, the nominal cross-referenced by the ergative is final subject and the one cross-referenced by the absolutive is final direct object.

The morphology of the agreement system is complicated by two factors. First, as in many other Mayan languages, the ergative prefixes come in two sets, one which is used with consonant-initial stems and one which is used with 'vowel'-initial stems.[5] Thus, *h*- appears in (12) because *mah*- 'hit' is consonant-initial; *k*- occurs in 'vowel'-initial stems like *ʔil*- 'see':

(13)   ʔI-ø-k-il   li   ¢ebetike.
      ASP-A3-E1-see the girls
      'I saw the girls.'

Second, the absolutive forms also come in two sets, one a set of prefixes, the other a set of suffixes. Corresponding to the prefix -*i*- (first person) is the suffix *-on* (first person). In the dialect of Tzotzil described here, that of Zinacantán, any given verb form occurs with only one absolutive agreement marker, either suffix or prefix.[6] It appears that forms with an overt aspectual prefix take the prefixed absolutive form while forms without (adjectives, nominals, forms with no overt aspectual prefix) take the suffixed absolutive form:

(14)   Vinik-on.
       man-A1
       'I am a man.'

(15)   Kolta-o-[o]tik.
       help-IMP-A1PL
       'Help us!' (Laughlin, p. 38)

There is one exception to this characterization of the distribution of absolutive prefixes and suffixes. One situation in which a verb with an aspectual prefix must take the absolutive suffix is when the subject is second person and the object first person:

(16)   ?A li ha? no ?oš č-a-kolta-on   ?o komel.
       if   only   ASP-E2-let loose-A1
       'Only if you will let me go free.' (Laughlin, p. 64)

(17)   Mi č-a-mah-on.
        ?   ASP-E2-hit-A1
       'Are you going to hit me?'

(18)   Ta to š-a-k'opon-on.
       ASP PT ASP-E2-speak-A1
       'You are still speaking to me.' (Laughlin, p. 66)

The chart below indicates the person agreement markers in Zinacantán Tzotzil:[7]

(19)   Ergative   Absolutive
        prevocalic   preconsonantal   prefix   suffix
   1   k-   h-   -i-   -on
   2   av-   a-   -a-   -ot
   3   y-   s-   -ø-   -ø

In the following examples, the third person absolutive marker -ø- is represented as a suffix when the verb bears no aspectual prefix or when the second person ergative marker occurs; otherwise it is represented as a prefix.

2.4   Number Agreement

There is a set of plural morphemes which optionally occur with the ergative and absolutive *prefixes* to mark plurality of the subject or object. These morphemes are suffixes:[8]

(20)   *with ergative prefix*   *with absolutive prefix*

	with ergative prefix	with absolutive prefix
1pl inclusive	-tik	-otik
1pl exclusive	-tikótik	-otikótik
2pl	-ik	-ik
3pl	-ik	-ik

While these suffixes may indicate plurality of either subject or object, no more than one suffix from (20) may occur in any given form. Agreement with the subject is illustrated in (21) and with object in (22):[9]

(21) a.   Ha? to te   h-¢ak-tik-ø   i   h-či?iltike.
          then   there E1-seize-1PL-A3 the our-friend
          'Then we'll seize our friend there.' (Laughlin, p. 287)

     b.   Ta la š-čik'-ik-ø   pat čenek' ?un.
          ASP PT E3-burn-3PL-A3 bean pods   PT
          'They were burning bean pods.' (Laughlin, p. 356)

(22)   Č-a-h-kolta-ik.
       ASP-A2-E1-help-2PL
       'We'll help you.' (Laughlin, p. 61)

Note that in (22), the subject as well as the object is plural (this is clear from the text), but the plural marker on the verb is that of second person, not first person.

   Number agreement is distinct from person agreement because it is controlled only by animate nominals, while person agreement is not so restricted. Thus, while the verb *p'ah-* 'fall' can have either an animate or inanimate subject, but if the verb is plural, the subject must be animate:

(23)   ?I-ø-p'ah   yalel ta lum   li   ¢ebetike /li pulatuetike.
       ASP-A3-fall down to ground the girls   /the bowls
       'The girls/the bowls fell on the ground.'

(24)   ?I-ø-p'ah-ik   yalel ta lum   li   ¢ebetike /*li pulatuetike.
       ASP-A3-fall-3PL down to ground the girls   /the bowls
       'The girls/*the bowls fell on the ground.'

Similarly, if the subject is pronominal and does not appear in surface structure, a plural verb is understood as having an animate subject:

(25) ?I-ø-p'ah-ik   yalel ta lum.
      ASP-A3-fall-3PL down to ground
      'They (animate) fell on the ground.'

Likewise, a verb agrees in number with a plural object only if it is animate. The following sentences are ungrammatical, in contrast to (21–22) above:

(26) *Ta-ø-h-lo?-ik.
      ASP-A3-E1-eat-3PL
      (I'll eat them.)

Example (26) cannot refer to eating animate things because the verb *lo?-* is restricted to objects which are soft and somewhat runny, e.g., egg, honeycomb, excrement (Laughlin 1975, p. 214).

(27) *Ta-ø-h-mel¢an-ik.
      ASP-A3-E1-make-3PL
      (I'll make them.)

The verb does agree in person with an inanimate subject:

(28) Ta-ø-s-k'an   taš-ø-[y]-ič'   ho¢'-el.
      ASP-A3-E3-want ASP-A3-[E3]-receive dig-nom
      'It [the floor of the valley] needs to be dug out.' (Laughlin, p. 128)

Here, the ergative third person marker in both *ta sk'an* and *ta šič'* cross-references 'the floor of the valley'.

2.5   Passive

The object of a transitive verb may be the subject of a corresponding intransitive 'passive' verb. This is accounted for by assuming a rule of Passive in Tzotzil which advances a direct object to subject. The resulting verb, lacking a direct object, is intransitive and takes one of two passive suffixes *-e* or *-at*. Subject to conditions which are not understood, the subject-chômeur may be the object of the preposition *ta* or it may function as possessor of the obligatorily possessed noun stem *-u?un*. Some examples of passive sentences:

(29) L-i-¢ak-e,   l-i-čuk-e.
      ASP-A1-catch-PASS ASP-A1-tie-PASS
      'I was caught, I was tied up.' (Laughlin, p. 66)

(30) Č-a-k'opon-at.
      ASP-A2-speak-PASS
      'You will be spoken to.' (Laughlin, p. 38)

(31) Te   la ʔi-ø-¢'ot-e-ik.
      there PT ASP-A3-entangle-PASS-3PL
      'There they got entangled.' (Laughlin, p. 39)

(32) . . . ti š-ø-tiʔ-at   ta čon   ʔune.
          that ASP-A3-eat-PASS by animal PTS
      '. . . that he would be eaten by animals.' (Laughlin, p. 81)

Like other intransitive verbs, passive verbs take only one set of agreement affixes: the absolutive set.

Three facts show that the initial direct object of a transitive verb is
subject of the corresponding passive. First, this nominal controls person agreement (see (29–30)). Second, it controls number agreement
(31). Third, it occurs in sentence-final position, the position that subjects occur in:

(33) a. ʔI-ø-ʔil-at   yuʔun Šun li Maruče.
         ASP-A3-see-PASS by   Šun the Maruč
         'Maruč was seen by Šun.'
     b. ʔI-ø-k'opon-at   yuʔun Petul li ¢ebe.
         ASP-A3-speak-PASS by   Petul the girl
         'The girl was spoken to by Petul.'

3 Indirect Object Advancement

Consider the following pairs of sentences. Sentences (34a) and (35a)
have two nominal (or pronominal) dependents, subject and object.
Sentences (34b) and (35b) have an additional dependent, understood
as recipient (in all these examples, pronominal dependents do not appear in the sentence). Morphologically, the verbs of the (a) and (b)
sentences differ, in that those of (b) are suffixed with the morpheme
-*be,* glossed here simply as -BE.

(34) a. Ba y-ak'-ø   ʔune.
         go E3-give-A3 PTS
         'He went to give it.' (Laughlin, p. 337)
     b. Ti mi č-av-ak'-b-on   ʔep tak'ine.
         if   ASP-E2-give-BE-A1 much money
         'If you will give me a lot of money.' (Laughlin, p. 75)

(35) a. Ba š-čon-ø   li nukul ʔune.
         go E3-sell-A3 the skin   PTS
         'He went to sell the skin.' (Laughlin, p. 336)
     b. Mi mu š-a-čon-b-on   l-a-čitome.
         ? NEG ASP-E2-sell-BE-A1 the-your-pig
         'Won't you sell me your pigs?' (Laughlin, p. 86)

In (34a) and (35a), the notional object is final direct object. In this section, we show that in (34b) and (35b), the notional recipient and not the notional object is final direct object.

It is assumed here that the notional recipients of (34b) and (35b) are initial indirect objects and the notional objects initial direct objects. The fact that initial indirect objects are final direct objects will be accounted for by positing a rule which advances indirect object to direct object. In this analysis, -be is a morphological reflex of the advancement of indirect object to direct object. In *all* sentences containing a notional recipient, the verb bears the suffix -be. Thus, apparently all structures with initial indirect objects which underlie grammatical surface structures undergo Indirect Object Advancement.

As noted above, several previous accounts of Tzotzil posit no rule of Indirect Object Advancement (or the equivalent), but instead describe -be as a morpheme which attaches to the verb when the clause contains an indirect object. Under such analyses, -be registers the presence of an indirect object in the clause. This will be referred to as the registration analysis.

3.1   Direct Object Behavior of the Initial Indirect Object

Three properties of direct objects in Tzotzil have been discussed in previous sections:

(36) a.   A transitive verb agrees in person with a final direct object.
     b.   A transitive verb may agree in number with a final direct object.
     c.   A direct object may advance to subject by Passive.

In sentences whose verb is augmented with -be, the initial indirect object, and not the initial direct object, has the three properties ascribed to direct objects in (36).

3.1.1   *Person Agreement*

In sentences with an initial indirect object, the verb agrees in person with the indirect object and not the direct object. This is evident in (34b) and (35b) where the indirect object is first person and the verb agrees with a first person object.

In such sentences, the verb does *not* agree in person with the initial direct object. Sentences like the following where the verb agrees with a third person direct object are grammatical but are interpreted as having initial third person indirect objects, not initial first person indirect objects:[10]

(37) Ti mi č-av-ak'-be-ø   ʔep tak'ine.
      if   ASP-E2-give-BE-A3 much money
      'If you will give him plenty of money.'
      [Not: 'If you will give me plenty of money.']

(38) Mi mu š-a-čon-be-ø   l-a-čitome.
      ?   NEG ASP-E2-sell-BE-A3 the-your-pig
      'Won't you sell him your pigs?'
      [Not: 'Won't you sell me your pigs?']

That is, it is the initial indirect object that the verb agrees with in such
sentences.

3.1.2   *Number Agreement*

In §2.4, it was shown that a transitive verb may agree in number with
an animate direct object. This is illustrated in the following sentences
which have underlying direct objects but no indirect object:

(39) ʔA li Šune ʔi-ø-s-k'el-ik   s-kremtak.
       the Šun ASP-A3-E3-look-3PL his-sons
      'Šun was looking at his sons.'

(40) Š-i-s-mil-otik   ʔun.
      ASP-A1-E3-kill-1PL PT
      'He'd killed us.' (Laughlin, p. 317)

But in sentences containing both an initial indirect and direct object,
the verb agrees in number with the initial indirect object:

(41) Č-a-k-ak'-be-ik.
      ASP-A2-E1-give-BE-2PL
      'I'm giving it [the bell] to you (pl.) [children] (Laughlin, p. 95)

(42) ʔI-ø-k-ak'-be-ik   li Šune.
      ASP-A3-E1-give-BE-3PL the Šun
      'I gave Šun to them.'

The verb may not agree with the underlying direct object. Thus, (42)
cannot be interpreted to mean 'I gave them to Šun,' where the plural
morpheme -*ik* refers to the initial direct object.

3.1.3   *Passive*

In sentences with both an initial direct object and an initial indirect object, it is the initial indirect object which advances to subject in passive
sentences. The initial direct object does not. There are three kinds of
evidence that the initial indirect object is the final subject of the passive
sentence: evidence from person agreement, number agreement, and

word order. In the following sentences, note that the passive suffix is always *-at* after *-be,* (never *-e*), and that the final *-e* of *-be* elides.

In the passive versions of sentences with an underlying indirect object, the verb agrees with this indirect object. Since intransitive verbs agree in person uniquely with their final subjects, the initial indirect objects of (43–45) must be the final subjects of the passive verbs:

(43) Č-i-ʔak'-b-at   hun ¢eb.
       ASP-A1-give-BE-PASS a   girl
       'I am being given a girl.' (Laughlin, p. 66)

(44) Mi 1-a-ʔak'-b-at   ʔa-veʔel?
       ?   ASP-A2-give-BE-PASS your-meal
       'Were you given your meal?'

(45) Č-ø-ʔak'-b-at   s-loʔbol.
       ASP-A3-give-BE-PASS his-fruit
       'He is given fruit.' (Laughlin, p. 351)

In passive versions of sentences with an initial indirect object, the verb may agree in number with this indirect object, but not with the initial direct object:

(46) Te   ʔak'-b-at-ik-ø   ʔun.
       there give-BE-PASS-3PL-A3 PT
       'There they were attacked.' (Lit.: 'There they were given it.')
       (Laughlin, p. 342)

(47) Poh-b-at-ik-ø   ʔun yuʔun tah pukuh ʔune.
       take-BE-PASS-3PL-A3 PT by   that devil PTS
       'It was taken away from them by that devil.' (Laughlin, p. 355)

Example (46) cannot mean 'They were given to him,' where the initial indirect object is interpreted as singular and the initial direct object as plural; nor can (47) mean 'They were taken away from him.'

Finally, the sentence-final position of the initial indirect object in passive sentences indicates that it is the final subject:

(48) ʔI-ø-ʔak'-b-at   libro li Šune.
       ASP-A3-give-BE-PASS book the Šun
       'Šun was given the book.'

(49) ʔI-ø-toh-b-at   s-tohol li   Petule.
       ASP-A3-pay-BE-PASS its-price the Petul
       'Petul was paid its price.'

(50) ʔAk'-b-at-ø   hun syen soltaro li hčamuʔ   preserente
give-BE-PASS-A3 one 100   soldiers the Chamulan magistrate
ʔune.
PTS
'The magistrate of Chamula was given a hundred soldiers.'
(Laughlin, p. 103)

The final subject cannot precede the final direct object chômeur:

(51) *Mi ʔi-ø-ʔak'-b-at   Šun li   čitome?
? ASP-A3-give-BE-PASS Šun the pig
(Was Šun given the pig(s)?)

(52) *Mi l-a-čon-b-at   voʔot li   kašlane?
? ASP-A2-sell-BE-PASS you   the chicken
(Were you sold the chicken(s)?)

In passive sentences, then, the verb agrees with the initial indirect
object in person and number; further it is the underlying indirect object
which occurs sentence-finally. Since intransitive verbs otherwise agree
in person and number with their final subjects and since the position
for final subjects is sentence-final, we conclude that the initial indirect
object is the final subject of the passive sentence.

3.2   The Argument for Indirect Object Advancement

The argument for Indirect Object Advancement can now be made explicitly. In transitive sentences without an initial indirect object, it is
the direct object with which the verb agrees in both person and number
and the direct object which advances to subject by Passive. In transitive
sentences with an initial indirect object, it is the indirect object and
not the direct object with which the verb agrees and which advances
to subject by Passive.

Two accounts of these facts can be contrasted. The first, which we
refer to as the advancement analysis, posits a rule which advances
indirect object to direct object. The advancement analysis has one
person agreement rule, one number agreement rule, and one passive
rule:

(53) a. Person Agreement
A verb agrees in person with its final subject and final direct
object.
b. Number Agreement
A verb may agree in number with either its final subject or
final direct object.
c. Passive
Direct object advances to subject.

The underlying indirect object is the derived direct object of its clause. As direct object, it may advance by Passive. If it does not advance to subject, it is final direct object of its clause and as final direct object, the verb agrees with it in person and number.

One additional assumption within the advancement analysis explains the fact that the verb may *not* agree with the initial direct object of these clauses. This is the assumption that at any particular level no more than one nominal may bear a given grammatical relation to the verb (the Stratal Uniqueness Law proposed by Perlmutter and Postal (1977)). Thus, one consequence of the advancement of indirect object to direct object in this theory is that the initial direct object ceases to bear that relation to the verb. In the terms of relational grammar (as in Perlmutter and Postal (1977)), the initial direct object is put 'en chômage' as a result of Indirect Object Advancement and is final direct object chômeur (the Chômeur Law proposed by Perlmutter and Postal (1977)).

The advancement analysis contrasts with the registration analysis. The registration analysis posits no advancement of indirect object to direct object. The initial indirect object is assumed to be final indirect object and -*be* is analyzed as a suffix which registers the presence of an indirect object in the clause.

The problem with the registration analysis is that it fails to explain why in sentences containing an indirect object, the indirect object and not the direct object behaves like the direct object of a transitive clause. Thus, in the registration analysis, Person Agreement, Number Agreement, and Passive must each be formulated in two parts: one statement relevant for transitive clauses without an indirect object and one relevant for transitive clauses with an indirect object:

(54) a. Person Agreement
   i. In clauses containing a final indirect object, the verb agrees in person with the final subject and final indirect object.
   ii. Otherwise, the verb agrees in person with final subject and final direct object.
   b. Number Agreement
   i. In clauses containing a final indirect object, the verb may agree in number with the final subject or the final indirect object.
   ii. Otherwise, the verb may agree in number with the final subject or the final direct object.
   c. Passive
   i. In clauses containing an indirect object, the indirect object may advance to subject by Passive.

       ii.   Otherwise, the direct object may advance to subject by Passive.

It is clear that the registration analysis, as outlined here, is inadequate since it fails to account for the fact that in Tzotzil the initial indirect object of a clause behaves like the direct object with respect to any rule which refers to noninitial direct objects. This follows directly under the advancement analysis since the initial indirect object *is* the derived direct object of the clause.

3.3   Word Order

The surface word order of sentences in which Indirect Object Advancement has applied is:

(55)   Verb—final direct object chômeur—final direct object—final subject

(Final direct object chômeur and final direct object in a transitive clause correspond to initial direct object and initial indirect object, respectively.) In fact, it seems that no more than two of the three nominals of (55) ever occur postverbally. If all three occur in a sentence, one (generally the subject) occurs preverbally. But the schema in (55) correctly describes the relative order of any combination of postverbal nominals. Note that (55) holds both for final transitive clauses in which there is a final direct object and final intransitive (e.g., passive) clauses in which there is not.[11]

(56)   Taš-ø-k-ak'-be   ʔok'ob   tak'in li Šune.
      ASP-A3-E1-give-BE tomorrow money the Šun
      'I'm going to give money to Šun tomorrow.'

(57)   L-i-y-ak'-be   tak'in li Šune.
      ASP-A1-E3-give-BE money the Šun
      'Šun gave me the money.'

(58)   ʔAk'-b-at-ø   nan   mi čaʔ-mil mi ʔoš-mil tak'in
      give-BE-PASS-A3 maybe ? 2   000 ? 3   000 money
      ti   Pégro ʔune.
      the Pegro PTS
      'Pegro was given maybe two or three thousand pesos.' (Laughlin, p. 87)

In terms of the schema in (55), the word orders of (56–58) are:

(56')   Verb—direct object chômeur—direct object
(57')   Verb—direct object chômeur—subject
(58')   Verb—direct object chômeur—subject

3.4   The NonExistence of Paraphrases

As conclusion to this section on Indirect Object Advancement, it needs to be pointed out that there is no way to express sentences like (34b) and (35b) *without* advancement. The following sentence types exhaust, as far as is known, the possible alternatives for paraphrase. These sentences are ungrammatical. In (59), the pronoun *vo?on* 'I' is simply added to the sentence without suffixing *-be* to the verb. In (60), the phrase *ta vo?on* 'to me' is added; *ta* is the only preposition in Tzotzil and functions variously to introduce locative, temporal, and instrumental phrases. In (61), the obligatorily possessed nominal *-u?un* which is used to express various concepts including benefactive and possessor has a first person possessor.

(59) *Mi mu š-a-čon-ø   ?a-čitom li   vo?one?
     ?   NEG ASP-E2-sell-A3 your-pig the I
     (Won't you sell me your pigs?)

(60) *Mi mu š-a-čon-ø   ?a-čitom ta vo?on?
     ?   NEG ASP-E2-sell-A3 your-pig to I

(61) *Mi mu š-a-čon-ø   ?a-čitom k-u?un?
     ?   NEG ASP-E2-sell-A3 your-pig my-u?UN

In order to express the reading of sentences like (34b) and (35b), the verb must be suffixed with *-be* and made to agree with its initial indirect object. Apparently no indirect objects occur in final structure in Tzotzil. Possible accounts of this fact are discussed in §5.2.

4   Evidence for Initial Indirect Objects
4.1   Introduction

It is clear from the preceding sections that the nominals we understand to be recipients are the final direct objects of their clauses.

In the preceding discussion, we have assumed that such nominals are initial indirect objects and that therefore they must advance to direct object. However, we might alternatively propose that notional recipients are initial direct objects. This would eliminate the rule of Indirect Object Advancement. Instead, a semantic rule would be needed to associate some initial direct objects with notional recipients.

Two sets of facts are presented here which suggest that there are initial indirect objects in Tzotzil and that therefore a rule advancing them is required.

4.2   Interaction of Indirect Object Advancement
with Clause Union

A causative construction has been described for numerous languages in which nominals associated in initial structure with a clause dependent on a causative verb are made dependents of the causative verb according to the following schema:

(62) a. The complement subject of a transitive clause is indirect object of the matrix clause.
  b. The complement subject of an intransitive clause and complement object of a transitive clause are direct object of the matrix clause.

We will term the rule which makes complement nominals dependents of the matrix clause according to (62) 'Clause Union'. This construction is illustrated by the following sentences of Turkish (from Lewis 1953, pp. 107–8):

(63) Ben daktilo-ya mektub-u yaz-dɨr-dɨ-m.
   I   typist-DAT letter-ACC write-CAUS-PAST-1SG
   'I got the typist to write the letter.'

(64) Onu   söyle-t-me-di-ler.
   her-ACC speak-CAUS-NEG-PAST-3PL
   'They didn't let her speak.'

Let us consider what Tzotzil would look like if it had Clause Union (as described above) and Indirect Object Advancement. It is crucial that Clause Union creates matrix indirect objects when the complement clause is transitive but not if it is intransitive. Thus, in Tzotzil, Indirect Object Advancement would apply to the output of Clause Union when the complement is transitive, resulting in -be appearing on the causative verb. When the complement clause is intransitive, no indirect object is created by Clause Union. Thus, Indirect Object Advancement is inapplicable and -be will not appear on the causative verb.

There are two causative constructions in Tzotzil, both periphrastic and both formed with the matrix verb ʔak'-. It is assumed here that these two constructions share a common underlying structure in which ʔak'- takes a sentential direct object. The basic meaning of ʔak'- is 'give', but when it governs a complement clause, it means 'cause, make, let'. In the first construction, the complement clause is final direct object of ʔak'- (as well as initial direct object) regardless of the transitivity of the complement clause:[12]

(65) Muk' buč'u ʔi-ø-y-ak'   k-il-ø   ti boh-ʔosile.
   NEG who ASP-A3-E3-let E1-see-A3 the clearing of the land
   'There was no one who let me see the clearing of the land.'
   (Laughlin, p. 289)

(66) K'u yuʔun mu š-av-ak'-ø   k-uč'-ø   voʔe.
      why   NEG ASP-E2-let-A3 E1-drink-A3 water
      'Why don't you let me drink water?' (Laughlin, p. 45)

(67) Mu š-ø-[y]-ak'   lok'-ik-on.
      NEG ASP-A3-[E3]-let leave-UK-A1
      'He doesn't let me leave.' (Laughlin 1975, p. 40)

In all these cases, ʔak'- is transitive, as shown by the ergative prefix
on the verb. The object in each case is third person; thus it cannot be
that the complement subject (in all these sentences first person) is
object of the matrix clause. The complement clause itself is matrix
direct object.

There is a second construction, in which the complement subject
and direct object are final dependents of the matrix verb. The properties
of this construction follow automatically if it is derived by Clause Union
and if Tzotzil has Indirect Object Advancement.[13] In this construction,
the subject of the complement clause is final direct object of ʔak'-
whether the complement is transitive or intransitive. However, when
the complement clause is transitive, the suffix -be appears on ʔak'-
(68–70). This is not the case when the complement clause is intransitive
(71–72):

(68) ʔAk'-b-o-ø   s-melʦan-ø.
      let-BE-IMP-A3 E3-make-A3
      'Let them prepare it.' (Laughlin, p. 361)

(69) Č-av-ak'-be-ø   s-tiʔ-ø   čoy.
      ASP-E2-let-BE-A3 E3-eat-A3 fish
      'You are letting them eat fish.' (Laughlin, p. 315)

(70) ʔI-ø-y-ak'-be-ik   s-kuč-ø   krus.
      ASP-A3-E3-let-BE-3PL E3-carry-A3 cross
      'They made him carry the cross.' (Laughlin, p. 26)

(71) a. L-i-y-ak'   kom-ik-on.
         ASP-A1-E3-let stay-UK-A1
         'He let me stay.'
     b. *L-i-y-ak'-be   kom-ik-on.
         ASP-A1-E3-let-BE stay-UK-A1

(72) a. Mi č-av-ak'-ø   kom-uk-ø li kreme?
         ? ASP-E2-let-A3 stay-UK-A3 the boy
         'Are you going to let the boy stay?'
     b. *Mi č-av-ak'-be-ø   kom-uk-ø li kreme?
         ? ASP-E2-let-BE-A3 stay-UK-A3 the boy

Furthermore, if a transitive subject becomes a dependent of the matrix verb, *-be* must appear on the matrix verb. When the complement subject is third person, it is not obvious that it is matrix object because the agreement marker is zero; with first and second person subject, it is clear:

(73) a. ʔA li Šune l-i-y-ak'-be   h-tuč'-ø   turasnu.
          the Šun ASP-A1-E3-let-BE E1-pick-A3 peach
          'Šun let me pick peaches.'
     b. *ʔA li Šune l-i-y-ak'   h-tuč'-ø   turasnu.
          the Šun ASP-A1-E3-let E1-pick-A3 peach

(74) a. Č-a-y-ak'-be   ʔa-kuč-ø   krus.
          ASP-A2-E3-let-BE E2-carry-A3 cross
          'They'll let you carry the cross.'
     b. *Č-a-y-ak'   ʔa-kuč-ø   krus.
          ASP-A2-E3-let E2-carry-A3 cross

These facts follow if Clause Union derives these sentences and if Indirect Object Advancement applies on its output. When the complement verb is transitive, as in (68–70), Clause Union makes the complement subject indirect object of *ʔak'-*. This indirect object advances to direct object of *ʔak'-* by Indirect Object Advancement and *ʔak'-* is suffixed with *-be*. When the complement clause is intransitive, as in (71–72), Clause Union makes the complement subject direct object of *ʔak'-* and Indirect Object Advancement is inapplicable. Thus, the verb is not marked with *-be*.

This analysis depends on there being indirect objects in Tzotzil, for the rule of Clause Union is formulated to create indirect objects. It also depends on there being a rule which advances indirect objects to direct object. Thus, if this analysis for the causative construction is correct, there must exist in Tzotzil an Indirect Object Advancement rule like the one proposed earlier. With this rule posited for the causative construction, no additional complication is entailed if notional recipients are initial indirect objects. Their advancement is accounted for by the same rule, and the rule required to relate initial indirect objects to notional recipients is well-motivated cross-linguistically.

4.3   The Interaction of Indirect Object Advancement
with *-van*

There is a second set of facts which suggests that notional recipients are not initial direct objects.

A final transitive clause has both a subject and a direct object. Tzotzil has a derivational suffix, *-van,* which derives intransitive stems from transitive stems. Verbs suffixed with -*van* have a reading like 'to do *x* to *y,* or with respect to *y*' where *y* must be human, either a nonspecific human or a discourse referent. In either case, verbs suffixed with -*van* never occur with an overt object:[14]

(75) a. Muk' bu š-ï-mil-van.
    never   ASP-A1-kill-VAN
    'I never killed anyone.' (Laughlin, p. 286)

   b. . . . š-k'ot   sibtas-van-uk-ø.
     ASP-come frighten-VAN-UK-A3
    '. . . he came to frighten [people].' (Laughlin, p. 190)

   c. Mi ʔo   buč'u n-a-s-k'el   ti   mil-van-em-ot.
    ?   exist who   ASP-A2-E3-watch the kill-VAN-PERF-A2
    'If there was someone who watched you kill. . . ' (Laughlin, p. 287)

   d. ʔAk'-b-at-ø   s-veʔel, ʔi-ø-veʔ   lek. Ta ša   la
    give-BE-PASS-A3 his-meal ASP-A3-eat well ASP now PT
    š-ø-mey-van,   ta ša   la š-ø-buȼ'-van   ti
    ASP-A3-embrace-VAN ASP now PT ASP-A3-kiss-VAN the
    kriarailetike.
    maids
    'He was given his meal, he ate well. The maids embraced [him] and kissed [him].' (Laughlin, p. 75)

The morphology of the verbs in (75a–d) shows that verbs suffixed with -*van* are intransitive. First, the subject is cross-referenced on the verb by the absolute prefixes and suffixes—those which cross-reference intransitive subjects. Second, intransitive verbs are distinguished in Tzotzil from transitive verbs by the occurrence of the suffix -*(u)k,* or -*(i)k-* word-internally, on intransitive but not transitive verbs in certain environments. One of these is as main verb of an auxiliary construction. In this construction, exemplified in (75b), the auxiliary bears the aspectual prefix and main verb bears the person agreement markers. Note that in (75b), the main verb *sibtasvan* is suffixed with -*uk,* showing that it is intransitive. Compare (76) and (77) where the main verb is transitive:

(76) Ba y-ak'-ø   ʔune.
   go E3-give-A3 PTS
   'He went to give it.' (Laughlin, p. 337)

(77) *Ba y-ak'-uk-ø   ʔune.
   go E3-give-UK-A3 PTS

Third, there are perfective verb forms whose morphology distinguishes transitive from intransitive stems. -*Em* is suffixed to intransitive stems and -*oh* to transitive stems. The verb of (75c) is a perfective form; suffixation by -*em* shows that the verb is intransitive. Compare the transitive perfective form:

(78)   ?A li   vo?on h-mil-oh-ø.
       the I   E1-kill-PERF-A3
       'I killed him.'

For the sake of discussion, I propose that derivatives in -*van* are derived by a rule which eliminates a direct object which is human and either unspecified or discourse referential. This leaves the verb with no direct object—an intransitive verb. Whether the initial direct object is an 'invisible direct object chômeur' in final structure (as proposed for similar constructions in Postal 1977) or not present in final structure is not relevant.

Derivation by -*van* is quite regular and apparently unrestricted in the sense that there appear to be no lexical exceptions to it, given the restriction to human direct objects.[15] However, two verbal constructions have been identified which do not form derivatives in -*van* despite the fact that the verbs are transitive and take human objects. One of these constructions is the verb suffixed with -*be*. Examples (79b) and (80b) cannot be derived from (79a) and (80a), despite the fact that the derived direct object is human:

(79) a.   Ta-ø-š-čon-be   čitom li   Maruče.
          ASP-A3-E3-sell-BE pig   the Maruč
          'He's selling pigs to Maruč.'
     b.   *Taš-ø-čon-be-van   čitom.
          ASP-A3-sell-BE-VAN pig
          (He's selling pigs [to people].)

(80) a.   Ta-ø-s-heč'-be   machita li   kremotike.
          ASP-A3-E3-hit-BE machete the boys
          'He's hitting the boys with a machete.'
     b.   *Taš-ø-heč'-be-van machita.
          ASP-A3-hit-BE-VAN machete
          (He's hitting [people] with a machete.)

Similarly with ?*ak'*-. Examples (81a), (82a), and (83a) are grammatical sentences in which Clause Union has applied making the complement subject direct object of ?*ak'*-. If the complement subject is unspecified instead, then when it is raised by Clause Union, ?*ak'*- has a direct object which is human and unspecified. The ungrammaticality of (81b),

(82b), and (83b) shows that it is nonetheless not possible to derive
ʔak'van from ʔak'- in this construction:

(81) a. Taš-tal   y-ak'-ø   ʔabteh-uk-ø.
         ASP-come E3-make-A3 work-UK-A3
         'He's coming to make him/them/her work.'

     b. *Taš-tal   ʔak'-van-uk-ø   ʔabteh-uk-ø.
         ASP-come make-VAN-UK-A3 work-UK-A3
         (He's coming to make [people] work.)

(82) a. L-i-y-ak'   lok'-ik-on.
         ASP-A1-E3-let leave-UK-A1
         'He let me leave.'

     b. *ʔI-ø-ʔak'-van   lok'-uk-ø.
         ASP-A3-let-VAN leave-UK-A3
         (He let there be leaving/he let [people] leave.)

(83) a. Mu š-i-y-ak'   vay-k-otik.
         NEG ASP-A1-E3-let sleep-UK-A1PL
         'He won't let us sleep.'

     b. *Mu š-ø-ʔak'-van   vay-uk-ø.
         NEG ASP-A3-let-VAN sleep-UK-A3
         (He won't let there be sleeping.)

The impossibility of deriving -van stems from verbs suffixed with -be
and from causative ʔak'- requires explanation. The explanation proposed here is that the rule which derives -van forms takes as input
initial structure. Thus, -van stems are only derived from verbs whose
initial direct object is human and it is this direct object which is eliminated by the rule. How do the facts support this? As far as can be
determined, any verb which takes an initial direct object which is human can form a derivative in -van. However, in the analysis proposed
here for causative ʔak'-, the direct object created by Clause Union is
not the initial direct object of ʔak'-. Causative ʔak'- governs an initial
clausal direct object; thus, it has no derived form in -van. This bears
on the question of whether direct objects to verbs suffixed with -be are
initial direct objects or initial indirect objects as follows. If it is initial
direct objects which are eliminated by the rule, the indirect object
advancement analysis predicts that direct objects which have advanced
from indirect object will not be subject to the -van rule. That is, it
predicts the nonexistence of verbs of the form V-be-van. This prediction
is correct; the nonexistence of such verbs is therefore evidence that
the final direct objects of verbs suffixed with -be are initial indirect
objects which advance to direct object.

5   Two Conditions on Indirect Object Advancement
5.1   Transitivity Condition

It is necessary to restrict the application of Indirect Object Advancement to transitive clauses, i.e., clauses with a direct object. This restriction has a morphological correlate: *-be* may be suffixed only to transitive stems. This restriction is needed for a number of different cases.[16]

5.1.1   *Benefactives*

There are two ways to express a notional benefactive in Tzotzil. One way is as possessor of the obligatorily possessed noun stem *-uʔun:*

(84)   ʔI-ø-s-komȼan   hun kampana y-uʔun   hč'ultottik
        ASP-A3-E3-leave a   bell   his-UʔUN Our Holy Father
        San-torenso.
        San Lorenzo
        'They left a bell for Our Holy Father St. Lawrence.' (Laughlin, p. 132)

The second way is as final direct object to a verb suffixed with *-be:*

(85)   ʔI-ø-s-mil-be-ik   čih.
        ASP-A3-E3-kill-BE-3PL sheep
        'They killed sheep for him.' (Laughlin, p. 110)

(86)   Mi mu š-a-saʔ-b-on   tal   ti   bu   batem
        ?   NEG ASP-E2-look-BE-A1 coming the   where went
        ti   čihe.
        the sheep
        'Won't you bring the sheep for me from where they went?'
        (Laughlin, p. 340)

(87)   Č-a-h-mil-be-ik.
        ASP-A2-E1-kill-BE-2PL
        'I'll kill it/them for you(pl).'

That the notional benefactives are final direct objects of these verbs is shown by the fact that the verb agrees with them in number (87) and person (86–87).

I assume here that notional benefactives may occur in two distinct underlying syntactic relations. Those that surface as possessors of *-uʔun* I assume to be underlying possessors of oblique nominal phrases; i.e., the underlying and surface relations are assumed to be essentially the same. Those that function as final direct objects to verbs suffixed with -*be* I assume to be underlying indirect objects which advance to direct object by the rule of Indirect Object Advancement.[17] In addition to the fact that these nominals control number and person agreement, as direct objects they may advance to subject by Passive:

(88) ?I-ø-mil-b-at   čon   li   ¢ebetike.
      ASP-A3-kill-BE-PASS animal the girls
      'The animal was killed for the girls.

Sentence-final position of *li ¢ebetike* shows that it is the final subject of (88).

While a benefactive may be initial indirect and final direct object in a transitive clause, this is not possible with a verb which is intransitive. Thus, compare (85–87) above with the following pairs (89–91). In each pair, both sentences have intransitive verbs. In the grammatical sentences, the benefactive is expressed as possessor of -*u?un* (which can be translated not only 'for' but also 'on account of'). In the ungrammatical sentences, the verb is suffixed with -*be* and the benefactive treated as direct object of the verb.

(89) a.   ?A li   na   le?e ?i-ø-mel¢ah   ša   y-u?un
          the house that ASP-A3-make   now his-U?UN
          li   Petule.
          the Petul
          'That house was made for/because of Petul.'
    b. *?A li   na   le?e ?i-ø-s-mel¢ah-be   li   Petule.
          the house that ASP-A3-E3-make-BE   the Petul
          (That house was made for Petul.)

(90) a.   ?A li   Petule ?i-ø-tal   y-u?un   li   Maruče.
          the Petul ASP-A3-come her-U?UN the Maruč
          'Petul came for/on account of Maruč.'
    b. *?A li   Petule ?i-ø-s-tal-be   li   Maruče.
          the Petul ASP-A3-E3-come-BE   the Maruč
          (Petul came on account of/for Maruč.)

(91) a.   Ta-ø-h-k'el   kik mi š-ø-lok'   ?av-u?un   ta ?ak'in
          ASP-A3-E1-look PT ? ASP-A3-leave your-U?UN at weeding
          i   h-čob   ?une.
          the my-cornfield PTS
          'I'll see if my cornfield turns out well for you after the weeding.'
          (Laughlin, p. 292)

b. *Ta-ø-h-k'el   kik mi š-a-s-lok'-be   ta ʔak'in   i
   ASP-A3-E1-look PT ? ASP-A2-E3-leave-BE at weeding the
   h-čob   ʔune.
   my-cornfield PTS
   (I'll see if my cornfield turns out well for you after the weeding.)

In each of the ungrammatical sentences, the verb is inflected as transitive, as any verb augmented with -*be* must be (as long as Passive has not applied subsequently). However, in Tzotzil, there is a sharp morphological distinction between transitive and intransitive stems. Transitive stems take transitive inflection, but not intransitive inflection and vice versa. Some stems are 'bivalent' and occur with both transitive and intransitive inflection. I assume that we are dealing with two stems in such cases. The stems of (89–90) are strictly intransitive and as such, the verb forms of (89) and (90) are alone enough to render the sentences ungrammatical. *Ismelȼahbe* and *istalbe* are not Tzotzil words. *Lok'*, however, is 'bivalent' and occurs with both intransitive inflection, as in (91a) 'turn out' and with transitive inflection meaning 'remove' or 'cut off'. Thus, the form *šaslok'be* is a possible verb form. However, (91b) makes no sense and in any case cannot mean anything like (91a).

There are (at least) two ways to interpret these facts. First, they might be taken to indicate that a notional benefactive may not be indirect object to an intransitive verb (either because of a restriction on initial subcategorization or because of a restriction on a rule advancing benefactives to indirect object, depending on one's account). If a benefactive cannot be indirect object in some environment, it clearly cannot advance to direct object by Indirect Object Advancement.

But it might be that a notional benefactive can be indirect object to any verb, transitive or intransitive, but that there is a restriction on Indirect Object Advancement which permits its application only in transitive clauses.

I argue here for the second alternative on the grounds that this restriction is independently required.

5.1.2   *Passives*

It is a fact that Indirect Object Advancement cannot apply on the output of Passive. That is, it is not possible to advance the initial direct object to subject by Passive and then advance the initial indirect object to direct object.

The verbs which would result from such derivations are inevitably morphologically anomalous, for passive verbs are intransitive and therefore cannot form the bases for derivatives in -*be:*

(92) *I-ø-y-ak'-at/e-be   Šun li   libroe.
     ASP-A3-E3-give-PASS-BE Šun the book
     (The book was given to Šun.)

(93) *ʔI-ø-s-toh-at/e-be   Petul li   s-tohole.
     ASP-A3-E3-pay-PASS-BE Petul the its-price
     (Its price was paid to Petul.)

Such sentences are totally impossible by virtue of the verb forms alone.

These sentences will be characterized as ungrammatical if Indirect Object Advancement is constrained to applying only in transitive clauses. The other constraint considered above, namely, restricting benefactive indirect objects to transitive clauses, is irrelevant here since these sentences do not involve benefactives.

An alternative account of the facts of this section would be to restrict Passive to advancing the *last* direct object of its clause (i.e., the last nominal to bear the relation direct object to the verb). This is adequate here, but irrelevant to the case discussed above and the one to be discussed below.

5.1.3   *-van*

There is a third class of intransitive verbs in which Indirect Object Advancement does not apply, although it might be expected to. This is with verbs suffixed with *-van*. See §4.3 for evidence that these verbs are intransitive. Semantically, there seems to be nothing to prevent verbs suffixed with *-van* from taking initial indirect objects since in their unsuffixed form such verbs take indirect objects. Yet sentences like (94b) and (95b) do not exist in Tzotzil:[18]

(94) a. Č-i-ʔak'-van.
         ASP-A1-give-VAN
         'I'm giving' [my daughter] [in marriage].
     b. *Taš-ø-k-ak'-van-be   li   Šune.
         ASP-A3-E1-give-VAN-BE the Šun
         (I'm giving [my daughter] to Šun [in marriage].)

(95) a. ʔI-ø-man-van   ta   tak'in.
         ASP-A3-buy-VAN with money
         'He bought [someone] with money.' (I.e., 'He paid the bride price in one lump sum.')
     b. *ʔI-ø-s-man-van-be   ta   tak'in li   s-huntot
         ASP-A3-E3-buy-VAN-BE with money the her-uncle
         ti   ¢ebe.
         the girl
         (He paid the bride price to the girl's uncle (in one lump sum).)

Restricting Indirect Object Advancement to transitive clauses explains these facts as well.

Within a theory which allowed extrinsic ordering statements to govern order of rule application, one might propose an alternative account of these facts in which Indirect Object Advancement was extrinsically ordered before the rule which derives intransitive stems in -*van*. However, if this ordering restriction makes any claim at all about Tzotzil, it is that there *are* derivations in which Indirect Object Advancement applies before the -*van* rule. In §4.3, however, it was shown that there are no such derivations and it was claimed that the -*van* rule applies to initial structure and therefore not to structures in which Indirect Object Advancement has applied. If this is correct, Indirect Object Advancement cannot be ordered before the -*van* rule without making it a lexical rule, thus leaving unexplained, once again, the nonexistence of verbs with the form *V + *be* + *van*-.

Furthermore, constraining detransitivization rules like Passive and the -*van* rule to affect only the last direct object of the clause is ineffectual for the same reason. The -*van* rule does not apply to the output of Indirect Object Advancement.

We conclude, then, that Indirect Object Advancement is restricted to transitive clauses. This conclusion is crucial to the following section.

5.2   The Nonexistence of Final Indirect Objects

We now turn to the question of how to account for the nonexistence of final indirect objects in Tzotzil. We distinguish here between two kinds of formal accounts of this fact. One possible solution is to restrict the rule of Indirect Object Advancement in some way which will result in there being no final indirect objects. The most plausible and most obvious solution of this type is to make the rule obligatory:

(96)   Constraint on Rule:
        Indirect Object Advancement is obligatory.

An alternative class of solutions involves conditions on other aspects of derivations. Two possible solutions are:

(97) a.   Constraint on final structure:
           Any derivation in which the final level of structure contains an indirect object is ill-formed.
     b.   Derivational constraint:
           Any derivation containing an indirect object at one level which does not advance to direct object at some later level is ill-formed.

What we can do here is show that making Indirect Object Advancement obligatory is the wrong solution. Since this appears to be the only plausible solution which constrains the rule itself, the conclusion is that these facts cannot be accounted for by constraining the advancement rule itself.

It is fairly easy to see why making Indirect Object Advancement obligatory cannot account for the nonexistence of indirect objects in final structure, given the constraint on transitivity discussed in the preceding section. The effect of making a rule obligatory is that any structure that meets the conditions for the rule's application and fails to undergo it is characterized as ungrammatical. What is crucial is that a rule can be characterized as obligatory only relative to structures which meet the conditions for the rule's application. For there may be an infinite number of structures which do not undergo an obligatory rule, yet underlie grammatical sentences—namely, structures which do not meet the conditions of the rule.

There are abstract structures in Tzotzil which are hypothesized to contain indirect objects in which Indirect Object Advancement is inapplicable. These are structures with intransitive verbs like the ones discussed in §§5.1.1–5.1.3. The indirect objects in such structures cannot advance, yet they cannot remain indirect objects. Because these structures do not meet the conditions for Indirect Object Advancement, failure to undergo the rule, obligatory though it may be, cannot characterize these structures as ill-formed. Thus, making the advancement rule obligatory fails to account for the nonexistence of final indirect objects. Once it is concluded that making the rule obligatory fails to account for the ungrammaticality of some sentences containing indirect objects, there is no reason to make the rule obligatory at all. It can apply optionally in all structures; whatever rules out intransitive clauses with final indirect objects can rule out transitive clauses with final indirect objects.

Two alternative accounts for the nonexistence of final indirect objects are given in (97a, b). Neither involves constraining the rule itself. The facts of Tzotzil do not choose between these, as far as I know.

Notes

1. Tzotzil is spoken in the state of Chiapas, southernmost state of Mexico. The number of speakers is reported by Laughlin (1975) at around 120,000. Five dialect areas of Tzotzil can be distinguished; the speakers I worked with are all from the municipality of Zinacantán, in the central area. As far as I know, the advancement phenomenon described here is found in the other dialects, as well as in the sister language Tzeltal. Recently published works on Tzotzil

include a grammar (Cowan 1965), a dictionary (Laughlin 1975), and texts (Laughlin 1977). I have profited greatly from unpublished notes by John Haviland (1972) which he kindly lent me. The examples here come from Laughlin 1977 and from my own field notes. I worked principally with Maryan Lopis Čikuʔ, to whom I am indebted. Two other speakers were consulted on certain points.

2. Examples of earlier works which have analyzed -*be* as a marker of the presence of an indirect object in the clause include Cowan 1965, Haviland 1972, and Laughlin 1975—the last reference (a dictionary) more implicitly than explicitly.

The orthography used here is that of Laughlin 1975. The symbol *č* represents the palatal affricate and *ȼ* the alveolar affricate; *C'* represent the glottalized consonants. The symbol *b* represents a variety of sounds: it is a preglottalized voiced labial stop in prevocalic position, a preglottalized voiced labial nasal stop preconsonantally, and a preglottalized voiceless bilabial nasal stop word-finally. The orthography used here differs from that of Laughlin 1977.

The abbreviations used in the glosses are: 'ASP', aspectual prefix; 'E1' (2, 3) (PL), ergative first (second, third) person (plural); 'A1' (etc.), absolutive first (etc.) person; 'PT(s)' particle(s); 'PASS' passive; 'NEG' negative; '?' yes/no question particle; 'PERF' perfective; 'IMP' imperative; 'DAT' dative; 'ACC' accusative; 'CAUS' causative. Four morphemes are glossed as -BE, -VAN, -UK, -UʔUN. These are explained in the text.

Elements in the English translation that correspond to nothing overt in the Tzotzil are enclosed in square brackets.

3. In general, only the last nominal in the sentence occurs with the article *li* (see (1–2)). *Ti* often occurs with more than one postverbal nominal (see (7)).

4. Three aspects may be marked on the verb. Perfective aspect is derivationally marked; these forms are discussed in §4.3. Incompletive and completive aspects are marked by prefixes and clitics. Incompletive aspect is marked by two generally cooccurring morphemes *ta* and *š*. There are certain environments in which one or the other of these is omitted. *Š* is a prefix; *ta* is a cliticlike element that occurs as first element of a sentence. If nothing intervenes between *ta* and *š*, they frequently contract to *č* in this dialect. Completive aspect is indicated by a number of different allomorphs (all prefixes) conditioned by the person(s) of the verb. The forms are: ø when the verb has a second person transitive subject; *l-* when the verb has a first or second person intransitive subject or transitive object; *ʔi-* elsewhere. There are also forms with no overt aspect marking where *ʔi-* would be expected. In such examples no aspect prefix is indicated.

5. Actually, all 'vowel'-initial stems have underlying representations with an initial glottal stop which deletes after the ergative prefixes.

6. This is not true of all dialects of Tzotzil. In the dialect of Huistán described in Cowan 1965, both prefix and suffix occur in certain cases.

7. This chart is incomplete and misleading in one respect. Alone among the four columns, the absolutive suffixes are marked for number. -*On* and -*ot* are used only for first and second person singular, distinct suffixes being used for the plurals. Thus, -*on*, -*ot*, and -ø are part of a larger paradigm while the other three classes are not.

8. In cases where overt absolutive *suffixes* are used, the number of the person cross-referenced by the absolutive is obligatorily marked. As pointed out in the previous note, -*on* and -*ot* are first person and second person singular; the

plural forms are *-otik* first person inclusive, *otikótik* first person exclusive, *-ošuk* second person plural.

9. The third person ergative prefix *s-* has the form *š-* before *č*.

10. Adding the full pronominal form *vo?on* 'I' to these sentences only renders them ungrammatical. It does not force the desired reading:

(i) *Ti mi čavak'be ?ep tak'in li vo?one.
(ii) *Mi mu šačonbe ?ačitom li vo?one?

11. The position for subject-chômeur is not fixed. Thus, it has been omitted from (55). This freedom is probably due to the fact that, unlike subjects, direct objects, and direct object-chômeurs, subject-chômeurs are overtly marked as such being either object of the preposition *ta* or possessor of the noun stem *-u?un*.

12. In the complement to *?ak'-*, intransitive verbs occur with the suffix *-(u)k* (*-(i)k* word-internally). Because the complement verb bears no aspectual prefix, the absolutive suffixes, not prefixes, are used for both intransitive subject and transitive object.

With respect to (67), *y* is deleted after *š* by a regular phonological rule. The same rule applies in (28).

13. There are many aspects of this causative construction which are not understood at present. Among these are the conditions which govern the alternation between the Clause Union construction and the other construction discussed above. For a description of the clause union construction in Jacaltec, a fairly close relative of Tzotzil, see Craig 1977.

14. Laughlin (1975, p. 26) describes this construction as follows: "Transitive verb stems may take an intransitivizing suffix *-van*. In nearly all instances, it denotes that the action is directed towards, on behalf of, or in relation to people (people in general)."

A class of constructions of which this is probably a member is called 'absolutive antipassive' and discussed in reference to Mayan languages in general in Smith-Stark (n.d.).

15. There are some verbs which do not take human direct objects but which have derivatives in *-van* meaning something like 'to do *x* with respect to people in general, or a particular person'. For example, according to entries in Laughlin 1975 *mel¢an* (transitive verb) which means among other things 'settle, set one's affairs in order' and apparently does not take a human direct object, has a *-van* derivative *mel¢anvan,* meaning 'settle case for a person'. At present, I do not know how general a phenomenon this is and whether derivatives like *mel¢anvan* should be derived like other forms with *-van*.

16. Note that this restriction is independent of the restriction discussed in §4.3, where it was shown that verbs derived with the suffix *-van* cannot be derived from verb stems already suffixed with *-be*. In that case an intransitive verb could not be derived from a transitive stem with *-be*. Here, we show that a transitive verb with *-be* cannot be derived from *any* intransitive stem (including stems suffixed with *-van*).

17. Another possibility is that notional benefactives are initial benefactives which advance to indirect object by a rule specifically so formulated. I know of no evidence from Tzotzil which bears on this.

18. These examples illustrate the fact that the reading of a particular verb suffixed with *-van* may be somewhat narrower than the reading of the base verb.

References

Chomsky, N. 1965. *Aspects of the Theory of Syntax*. Cambridge, Mass.: MIT Press.

Cowan, M. 1965. *Tzotzil Grammar*. Summer Institute of Linguistics, Santa Ana, California.

Craig, C. 1977. *The Structure of Jacaltec*. Austin: University of Texas Press.

Haviland, J. 1972. "Notes on Zinacantan Tzotzil Syntax." manuscript.

Laughlin, R. 1975. *The Great Tzotzil Dictionary of San Lorenzo Zinacantán*. Washington, D.C.: Smithsonian Institution Press.

————. 1977. *Of Cabbages and Kings: Tales from Zinacantán*. Washington, D.C.: Smithsonian Institution Press.

Lewis, G. 1953. *Teach Yourself Turkish*. London: English Universities Press.

Perlmutter, D., and Postal, P. 1977. "Toward a Universal Characterization of Passive." *Proceedings of the Third Annual Meeting of the Berkeley Linguistic Society* (Berkeley Linguistic Society: Berkeley). Reprinted in this volume.

Postal, P. 1977. "Antipassive in French." *Proceedings of the Seventh Annual Meeting of the North Eastern Linguistics Society*. MIT Linguistics Department, Cambridge, Mass.

Smith-Stark, T. (n.d.) "Mayan Antipassive: Some Facts and Fictions."

8 Advancements and Verb Agreement in Southern Tiwa

Barbara J. Allen and Donald G. Frantz

1 Introduction

The purpose of this paper is to demonstrate, as straightforwardly as possible, given the complexity of certain details of morphology, that verb prefixes of Southern Tiwa reflect features of the *initial* direct object (DO) as well as the *final* DO and subject (SU). Before demonstrating this, however, we must present the clearest facts about agreement in intransitive and transitive clauses so that these facts can enter into the arguments for our main claim.[1]

2 Background Facts

Intransitive verb agreement reflects person and number of SU, including a distinction between dual and plural in all persons (this latter fact is a useful test for final SU), as illustrated in (1–3):

(1) te-'aru-we.
     1SG-cry-PRES
     'I'm crying.'
(2) in-'aru-we.
     1DU-
     'We [2] are crying.'
(3) i-'aru-we.
     1PL-
     'We [>2] are crying.'

This is a slightly revised version of "Verb Agreement in Southern Tiwa," which appeared in *Proceedings of the Fourth Annual Meeting of the Berkeley Linguistics Society* (Berkeley: University of California, 1978).

The following chart shows the full paradigm of prefixes:

	sg	du	pl
1st	te	in	i
2d	a	men	ma
3d	ø	in	i

Transitive verb agreement reflects person and number of both SU and DO; in addition, noun class of third person DO is indicated. There are three noun classes, which we will designate as i, ii, and iii; the first includes all and only animate nouns. Examples (4–13) illustrate these facts:

(4) bey-mu-ban.
     2SG:1SG-see-PAST
     'You saw me.'
(5) a-mu-ban.
     2SG:3iSG-
     'You saw him.'
(6) i-mu-ban.
     1SG:2SG-
     'I saw you.'
(7) ti-mu-ban.
     1SG:3iSG-
     'I saw him.'
(8) ti-seuan-mu-ban.
     1SG:3iSG-man-
     'I saw the man.'
(9) men-seuan-mu-ban.
     2DU:3iSG-
     'You [2] saw the man.'
(10) ma-seuan-mu-ban.
      2PL:3iSG-
      'You [>2] saw the man.'
(11) ti-shut-pe-ban.
      1SG:3iiSG-shirt-make-
      'I made a shirt.'
(12) te-shut-pe-ban.
      1SG:3iiPL-
      'I made shirts.'
(13) bi-mukhin-tuwi-ban.
      1SG:3iiiSG-hat-buy-
      'I bought a hat.'

As stated earlier, the dual-plural distinction is reflected in verb agreement for SU only. The lone exception to this is with first person SU and second person DO, in which case there is a three-way contrast for number of the DO rather than for the SU.[2]

There is a good deal of homophony or overlap or both in the use of prefixes between and within paradigms,[3] but comparison of full paradigms leads to the statements we have made above.

As illustrated in (8–13), the noun head of a DO is usually incorporated into the verb. Details of the constraints on this incorporation are beyond the scope of this paper (see Allen and Gardiner 1977 for a preliminary treatment).

3   Passive

Certain constraints in Southern Tiwa constrain passivization. These include:

1. No rule may put first or second person en chômage.[4]
2. The final DO must not outrank the final SU on a hierarchy in which first and second person outrank animate third person which in turn outranks inanimate third person.[5]

Examples (14) and (15) are passive because of constraint 2.[6] Example (17) illustrates the only circumstance in which Passive is possible but not necessary; compare (16). And (18) and (19) violate constraint 1.

(14)   seuanide-ba te-mu-che-ban.
       man-INSTR   1SG-see-PASS-PAST
       'The man saw me' (I was seen by the man).
(15)   seuanide-ba a-mu-che-ban.
       man-INSTR   2SG-see-PASS-PAST
       'The man saw you' (You were seen by the man).
(16)   seuanide ø-liora-mu-ban.
       man   3:3ISG-lady-see-PAST
       'The man saw the lady.'
(17)   liorade ø-mu-che-ban   seuanide-ba.
       lady   3-see-PASS-PAST man-INSTR
       'The lady was seen by the man.'
(18) *te-mu-che-ban   'ï-ba.
       1SG-see-PASS-PAST 2-INSTR
       (I was seen by you.)
(19) *a-mu-che-ban   na-ba.
       2SG-see-PASS-PAST 1-INSTR
       (You were seen by me.)

As evidence that a sentence such as (14) is truly passive as characterized within relational grammar (chap. 1), observe that the verb prefix is from the intransitive paradigm given earlier and agrees only with the putative final SU (initial DO). Further evidence that first person is final SU of (14) is seen in (20) and (21), for, as stated earlier, the dual-plural distinction is made only for (final) subjects:

(20)   seuanide-ba in-mu-che-ban.
　　　　　　　　　1DU
　　　'The man saw us [2]' (We were seen by the man).
(21)   seuanide-ba i-mu-che-ban.
　　　　　　　　　1PL-
　　　'The man saw us [>2]' (We [>2] were seen by the man).

Observe also that the initial SU of the putative passives is marked with the same postposition which otherwise marks instrument and means; this in itself is so extremely common with passives in languages around the world that it constitutes circumstantial evidence for the passive analysis of these sentences.

　　　Noun incorporation offers further support for the claim that the initial DO is not a final DO in the putatively passive cases. As Allen and Gardiner (1977) show, DO incorporation is possible, and usually necessary, depending upon various factors. Yet just in the cases we are claiming are passive, incorporation of the noun head of the initial DO is not possible. Thus *liorade* 'lady' could not be incorporated in (17). This is exactly what the passive analysis predicts, given Allen and Gardiner's findings that animate final SU's are never incorporated.

4　IO Advancement

We have now presented sufficient background to enable us to demonstrate that indirect objects (IO) in Southern Tiwa may be advanced to DO, after which we will demonstrate the main thesis of this paper: that verbs in such clauses agree with the initial DO as well as the final DO and final SU.

　　　Compare (23) with (22), (25) with (24), and (27) with (26):

(22)   ti-khwien-wia-ban　　　　'ī-'ay.
　　　 1SG:3iSG-dog-give-PAST 2-to
　　　 'I gave the dog to you.'
(23)   ka-khwien-wia-ban.
　　　 1SG:2SG:3iSG-
　　　 'I gave you the dog.'
(24)   ti-khwien-wia-ban seuanide-'ay.
　　　 1SG:3iSG-　　　　　man-to
　　　 'I gave the dog to the man.'

(25) ta-khwien-wia-ban seuanide.
  1SG:3iSG:3iSG-
  'I gave the man the dog.'

(26) a-khwien-wia-ban na-'ay.
  2SG:3iSG-   1-to
  'You gave the dog to me.'

(27) ben-khwien-wia-ban.
  2SG:1SG:3iSG-
  'You gave me the dog.'

Observe first of all that the verbs of (22), (24), and (26) have prefixes which are a function of first or second person SU and third person animate DO ('dog'), as seen earlier in (8) and (5). These even-numbered examples have a final SU, DO, and IO, the latter marked by postposition -'ay. Compare now the odd-numbered examples that follow each of (22), (24), and (26); these differ in at least two ways: the IO's of the even-numbered examples are not postpositional phrases in the corresponding odd-numbered examples, and the verb prefixes are different. Both of these differences are accounted for by an analysis involving advancement of IO to DO, and hence enter into arguments for this analysis.

First, if the initial IO is final DO, it should not be marked by the postposition which marks final IOs (because pronouns in Southern Tiwa do not appear unless emphatic or supporting postpositions, (23) and (27) display no pronouns).[7] This we have seen to be true in the odd-numbered examples.

Second, as we showed above, verb prefixes are a function of both SU and DO. If the initial IO is final DO, varying this putative DO should vary the prefix. Comparing (23) with (25) and (28), we see that the prefix shape *is* a function of the putative final DO. (The prefixes are not from the same set seen earlier on transitive verbs; see §7).

(28) mim-khwien-wia-ban seuanin
  1SG:3iPL:3iSG-   men
  'I gave the men the dog'.

Third, we saw earlier that Southern Tiwa sanctions advancement of DO to SU. If the initial IO is final DO in sentences such as (23), (25), (27), and (28), then we should expect advancement of the DO to SU under the same conditions outlined for advancement of initial DOs. These conditions were as follows:

(*a*) Passive is possible only if the initial SU is a third person; thus the passive counterparts to (23) and (27) should be bad, and they are:

(29) *ka-khwien-wia-che-ban   na-ba.
    2sg:3isg-dog-give-PASS-PAST 1-INSTR
    (You were given the dog by me.)
(30) *in-khwien-wia-che-ban 'ī-ba.
    1sg:3isg-
    (I was given the dog by you.)

(b) Passive is necessary if the DO outranks the SU; thus if an initial IO is first or second person, and the initial SU is third person, advancement of the initial IO to DO would require its further advancement to SU. This we see in (32) and (34); compare (31) and (33) which involve no advancement:[8]

(31)   liorade ø-khwien-wia-ban na-'ay.
       lady   3isg:3isg-   1-to
       'The lady gave a dog to me.'
(32)   liorade-ba in-khwien-wia-che-ban.
       lady-INSTR 1sg:3isg-dog-give-PASS-PAST
       'The lady gave me a dog' (I was given a dog by the lady).
(33)   liorade ø-khwien-wia-ban ī-'ay.
                                      2-to
       'The lady gave a dog to you.'
(34)   liorade-ba ka-khwien-wia-che-ban.
              2sg:3isg-
       'The lady gave you a dog' (You were given a dog by the lady).

(c) If the DO does not outrank a third person SU, then Passive is possible but not necessary. Thus we would expect a sentence such as (35) to have two paraphrases involving advancement of the initial IO, one in which the initial IO is final DO, and another in which the initial IO advances to DO and then to SU. But we find only the latter, as illustrated in (36):

(35)   liorade ø-khwien-wia-ban 'u'ude-'ay.
                                      child-to
       'The lady gave the dog to the child.'
(36)   liorade-ba a-khwien-wia-che-ban 'u'ude.
              3isg:3isg-   child
       'The child was given the dog by the lady.'

This state of affairs can be accounted for in conjunction with the IO-to-DO advancement hypothesis by adding the additional constraint that if an IO advances, it must advance as high as possible on the term hierarchy. We will call this the 'all-the-way' constraint. And since DO-to-SU advancement is possible only when the initial SU is third person, it is just in cases like (35) and (36) that this all-the-way constraint comes into play.

We should briefly consider the possibility that the 'all-the-way' constraint requires direct IO-to-SU advancement (rather than IO-to-DO, then to SU), subject of course to constraint 1. This would give no explanation for the passive morphology of such sentences, unless we require such morphology for any advancement to SU which puts a former SU en chômage. This latter requirement can be shown to be wrong. Allen 1978 has recently discovered cases in which an IO or Goal of an intransitive verb advances to SU, and such sentences do *not* show passive morphology. Furthermore, direct IO-to-SU advancement would not put the initial DO en chômage, eliminating the only feasible explanation for its incorporation behavior, as will be discussed in §6.

5   Agreement with Initial DO

In (22–36) we were concerned with demonstrating advancement of IO to DO, and therefore held the initial DO constant. But now we are ready to demonstrate that verb agreement must make reference to features of the initial DO in such cases, as well as to features of the final SU and final DO. These affixes are a function of three variables in the transitive cases and of two variables in the passive cases. We now look again at cases where an IO has advanced to DO (and no higher), but this time we will hold the final DO constant and vary the initial DO as in (37–42). Prefixes are glossed 'final SU:final DO:initial DO-'.

(37)   ka-'u'u-wia-ban.
       1SG:2SG:3iSG-baby-give-PAST
       'I gave you the baby.'
(38)   kam-'u'u-wia-ban.
       1SG:2SG:3iPL-
       'I gave you the babies.'
(39)   ka-shut-wia-ban.
       1SG:2SG:3iiSG-shirt-
       'I gave you the shirt.'
(40)   kow-shut-wia-ban.
       1SG:2SG:3iiPL-
       'I gave you the shirts.'
(41)   kam-keuap-wia-ban.
       1SG:2SG:3iiiSG-shoe-
       'I gave you the shoe.'
(42)   kow-keuap-wia-ban.
       1SG:2SG:3iiiPL-
       'I gave you the shoes.'

It is clear that the verb prefix shape is a function of the class and number of the initial DO.[9]

Perhaps even more impressive are the cases with third person initial SU. Recall that in these cases an advanced IO must be final SU, and so the clause has no final DO. (See §6.) Yet even these passive verbs are marked for number and class of the initial DO as well as the final SU. To make this clear, we will hold the final SU (initial IO) constant and vary only the initial DO in (43–45). The prefixes will be glossed 'final SU:initial DO-'.

(43)   'u'ude a-shut-wia-che-ban   seuanide-ba.
       child   3SG:3iiSG-shirt-give-PASS-PAST man-iNSTR
       'The child was given the shirt by the man.'
(44)   'u'ude ow-shut-wia-che-ban seuanide-ba.
              3SG:3iiPL-
       'The child was given the shirts by the man.'
(45)   'u'ude am-keuap-wia-che-ban seuanide-ba.
              3SG:3iiiSG-
       'The child was given the shoe by the man.'

Compare these examples to a passive which involves no IO advancement and thus is inflected like an "ordinary" intransitive verb:

(46)   'u'ude ø-mu-che-ban   seuanide-ba.
       child   3-see-PASS-PAST
       'The child was seen by the man.'

In (43–45) observe that the verb prefix varied as the class and number of the initial DO varied. Note the obvious relationship to the affixes in (37–42). This relationship is not so obvious with first person as final SU, but the verb prefix shape is still a function of the initial DO, as (47–49) show:

(47)   in-'u'u-wia-che-ban seuanide-ba.
       1SG:3iSG-child-
       'I was given the child by the man.'
(48)   im-'u'u-wia-che-ban seuanide-ba.
       1SG:3iPL-
       'I was given the children by the man.'
(49)   iw-shut-wia-che-ban seuanide-ba.
       1SG:3iiPL-shirt-
       'I was given the shirts by the man.'

6   Final Status of Initial DO

Our argument that verb agreement makes reference to features of the initial DO as well as the final SU and final DO was based in part on the assumption that in sentences where the initial IO advances to DO, the initial DO is a final chômeur, in accordance with the Chômeur Condition of Perlmutter and Postal 1977, which states that if any rule of grammar assigns a given term relation R to some nominal N_b in stratum S_i, and some other nominal N_a bears R in stratum S_{i-1}, then N_a bears the chômeur relation in stratum S_i. An alternative hypothesis might be advanced, under which verb agreement is stated exclusively in terms of final grammatical relations, the verb agreeing with the final SU and DO or DOs. Under this analysis, which we will call the "two-DO hypothesis," advancement of an IO to DO results in two DOs in a single stratum. This analysis also violates the Stratal Uniqueness Law of Perlmutter and Postal 1977, which states that no more than one nominal can bear a given term relation in a given stratum. Under the two-DO hypothesis, when an IO advances to DO, the verb agrees with the initial DO not because it is initial DO, but because it is also a final DO. The theoretical issue posed by the two-DO hypothesis is whether verb agreement can be stated so that it refers only to final grammatical relations, rather than with respect to both initial and final relations, as we propose.

We give two arguments here against the two-DO hypothesis, and thus in support of our claim that verb agreement refers to initial DO-hood. Since the two-DO hypothesis violates the Stratal Uniqueness Law and the Chômeur Condition, the arguments against the two-DO hypothesis are also arguments against a version of relational grammar without these principles.

The first argument against the two-DO hypothesis is based on passivization. We have already shown that an IO which has advanced to DO will be further advanced to SU if the initial SU is third person. But we cannot have, in a single clause, both advancement of the initial IO to DO and advancement of the initial DO to SU. Thus, it is the IO advanced to DO, and not the initial DO, that behaves like a DO with respect to passivization. This is exactly what the Stratal Uniqueness Law and the Chômeur Condition predict, while the two-DO hypothesis makes the incorrect prediction that both will behave like DOs with respect to passivization.

The second argument is based on incorporation. Allen and Gardiner (1977) demonstrate that incorporation of the head noun of a DO is very common in Southern Tiwa. Yet in cases of IO advancement, it is only the initial DO that is incorporated, never the advanced IO. Furthermore, IO advancement makes incorporation of the initial DO necessary, whereas without IO advancement, there are certain circumstances in which DO incorporation is otherwise optional, e.g., if the DO is human and singular, as shown in (51):

(50)   ti-'u'u-mu-ban.
       1SG:3isG-child-see-PAST
       'I saw the child.'
(51)   'u'ude ti-mu-ban.
       child   1SG:3isG-see-PÅST
       'I saw the child.'

Compare (52) and (53), which show that in the IO advancement cases, incorporation of the initial DO is *necessary:*

(52)   mim-'u'u-wia-ban   seuanin.
       1SG:3iPL:3isG-child-give-PAST men
       'I gave the men the child.'
(53)   *'u'ude mim-wia-ban seuanin

Thus, the conditions on incorporation differ for an initial DO which is final DO and an initial DO which is final DO chômeur according to the Chômeur Condition. Under the single-DO hypothesis, necessary incorporation of the initial DO (final DO chômeur) can be accounted for by an independently motivated constraint (see Allen and Gardiner 1977) against unincorporated DO chômeurs.

In summary, then, the two-DO hypothesis does not account for which of the two putative DOs advances to SU, nor does it give any reason to expect that advancement of an IO should make incorporation of the initial DO necessary. The single-DO hypothesis dictated by the Stratal Uniqueness Law and the Chômeur Condition makes the passivization data follow from the universal characterization of passivization, and the incorporation data from an independently motivated constraint in Southern Tiwa. We therefore reject the two-DO hypothesis for Southern Tiwa. Its inadequacy for this language provides some support for the Stratal Uniqueness Law and the Chômeur Condition as linguistic universals. Most important for the present paper, however, the inadequacy of the two-DO hypothesis means that verb agreement in Southern Tiwa cannot be stated solely in terms of final grammatical relations, but must refer to initial DO-hood as well.

7   Conclusion

Southern Tiwa rules of verb agreement must make reference to person, number, and class of final SU, final DO, and where it is distinct from either of those, the initial DO: in just this latter case, the prefixes will be drawn from a different set.[10]

Notes

1. Southern Tiwa is a Tanoan language spoken in Isleta and Sandia pueblos in New Mexico. Data are exclusively from the Isleta pueblo and were gathered by Barbara Allen and Donna Gardiner in conjunction with their assignment with S.I.L. from October 1973 until 1978. We are greatly indebted to David Perlmutter for his encouragement and insights during later stages of the analysis and for comments on an earlier draft of this paper. We also appreciate the contribution of David McNiel, who worked with us in the early analysis of these prefixes.

Abbreviations used in glosses include: 1 = first person; 2 = second person; sg = singular; du = dual; pl = plural; 3i = animate third person; 3ii and 3iii designate the other two noun classes; pass = passive; instr = instrument. Colons in glosses separate sets of features of terms reflected in verb prefixes, e.g., '1sg: 2sg' means 1sg SU, 2sg DO.

2. These cases are definitely not passive, however, for the following reasons: (a) the verb does not have passive morphology; (b) if present for emphasis, the first person pronoun cannot be marked with -ba as a subject chômeur (see below).

3. The most notorious examples of overlap follow a pattern referred to as "number reversal" by Tanoan scholars: iiisg = ipl, iiipl = iipl, while isg = iisg.

4. This constraint was formulated after discussion with Terry Klokeid of his work on Nitinaht.

5. There also may be a constraint against final inanimate ergatives no matter what the semantic class of the DO, but the facts are not yet clear.

6. It is not possible to present ungrammatical sentences in which constraint 2 is violated because there are no transitive verb prefixes for these person combinations.

7. If emphatic, the pronouns will be used and, like other final DOs, occur either before or after the verb:

(i) $\begin{Bmatrix} \text{kakhwienwiaban} & \text{'ï} \\ \text{'ï} & \text{kakhwienwiaban} \end{Bmatrix}$

'I gave *you* the dog.'

(ii) $\begin{Bmatrix} \text{benkhwienwiaban} & \text{na} \\ \text{na} & \text{benkhwienwiaban} \end{Bmatrix}$

'You gave *me* the dog.'

Note that like other final DOs, 'ï and na in these examples are not accompanied by postpositions.

8. Here again, we are unable to present ungrammatical sentences which violate constraint 2, because there are no verb prefixes for the resultant combinations of persons as SU and DO.

9. See note 3 for the appearance of the same prefix in more than one of these examples; also, some analysis of these prefixes is possible. In the set appearing in (37–42) it is possible to segment off a k- indicating that final SU and SO are first and second person, respectively, while the remainder of each prefix indicates class and number of the initial DO. Such segmentation has no real bearing on the claims of this paper, however.

10. As mentioned earlier, this statement will probably have to make reference

to the initial absolutive rather than initial DO. This is seen to be necessary when cases of ascension of a possessor from initial subject are taken into account. Research is in progress on this, as well as many other aspects of Southern Tiwa grammar.

References

Allen, B. 1978. "Goal Advancement in Southern Tiwa." Work Papers of the Summer Institute of Linguistics, North Dakota Session, Vol. 22.

Allen, B. and Gardiner, B. 1977. "Noun Incorporation in Isleta." Work Papers of the Summer Institute of Linguistics, North Dakota Session, Vol. 21.

Part 3

9 Subject–Direct Object Raising in Niuean

William J. Seiter

Introduction

In this paper, I argue for Raising in Niuean, a Polynesian language.[1] The rule operates on the subject or direct object of complements of a small class of higher governing verbs. A raised NP becomes the subject of the governing verb.[2] Of central interest is the fact that Niuean Raising operates on complement direct objects as well as subjects. My goal here is to show that aside from that feature, Niuean Raising is fundamentally like versions of Subject Raising in other languages (e.g., English) in that it effects the same change in grammatical relations.

The issues dealt with here are framed in a linguistic theory that captures cross-linguistic syntactic generalizations by positing an inventory of universal rules or rule schemata.[3] In such a theory, particular languages select items from the inventory in a largely predictable fashion and may contribute a language-specific component to at least some of the rules. The most coherent theory of this sort to date has been Perlmutter and Postal's relational grammar,[4] in which a significant class of syntactic rules is represented in universal grammar in terms of grammatical relations. For this reason, my discussion of Niuean Raising will likewise be in terms of grammatical relations.

I will argue that Niuean Raising should be regarded as an instance

A much abbreviated version of this paper appeared in K. Whistler, et al., *Proceedings of the Fourth Annual Meeting of the Berkeley Linguistics Society* (Berkeley: University of California, 1978).

This paper is based on my field research in New Zealand and Niue Island from January through May 1976, which was supported by NSF grant SOC-76-02030.

I wish to thank Ligipati Wea, Marion McQuoid, Sione Otia, and Tale and Nogi Pulevaka of Auckland, Leslie Rex of Avatele, Pitasoni tanaki of Hakupu, Tale Pita, and Lemani, Lefu, and Ieni Tafatu of Alofi, for providing their judgments on the Niuean sentences. I am grateful to Sandra Chung, Pamela Munro, David Perlmutter, and Alan Timberlake for many helpful comments on earler versions of this paper.

of a universal rule of Raising. Such a demonstration is of theoretical interest because Niuean Raising is typologically unusual: since it applies freely to complement direct objects as well as subjects, it violates Postal's (1974) suggestion that Raising should be restricted universally to complement subjects.[5] What I hope to establish is that the identification of Niuean Raising as an instance of universal Raising makes interesting predictions about its interaction with other features of Niuean syntax, but that no other analysis makes all of the same predictions. The arguments against the conceivable non-Raising analyses will establish that: (i) a raised NP in Niuean originates as a complement subject or direct object; (ii) it also acts as the subject of the higher, governing verb; and (iii) it cannot have originated in the higher clause and triggered deletion of a coreferential NP in the complement clause.

The discussion is organized as follows. In §1, I present a brief sketch of basic facts about Niuean case marking and word order. In §2, I introduce my analysis of the Niuean Raising phenomenon. The next three sections argue against several types of alternative analyses. In §3, I argue against an analysis which would treat raised NPs as higher subjects at all levels of structure. I show that instead a raised NP is a complement subject or direct object at some level. In §4, I argue that Niuean Raising sentences must not be derived by a rule which merely reorders a complement NP, because a raised NP is clearly the subject of its governing verb. And in §5, I argue that an analysis which would posit underlying occurrences of a raised NP in both the higher and lower clauses is untenable, since the evidence rules out the possibility that Raising sentences in Niuean are derived through some version of Equi-NP Deletion. Finally, §6 comments on the theoretical implications of Niuean Raising and suggests how Raising might be represented in universal grammar in order to accommodate the Niuean facts.

1   Case Marking and Word Order

Niuean is a strict VSO language with an ergative system of case marking. This type of system treats intransitive subjects (SUs) and direct objects (DOs) as a unified category which excludes transitive subjects. Case is indicated by two series of prepositional particles, one for common nouns, the other for pronouns and proper nouns.

SUs of intransitive sentences occur in the absolute case, which is marked with *e* on common nouns and *a* on pronouns and proper nouns:[6]

(1) a.   Ne   fano e   tehina   haaku ke he fale   koloa.
         PAST go   ABS brother my   to   house goods
     'My little brother went to the store.'

b.   Mitaki lahi a   Niuē.
good   very ABS Niue
'Niue Island is very nice.'

SUs of transitive sentences occur in the ergative case, marked with *he* on common nouns and *e* on pronouns and proper nouns; DOs, like intransitive SUs, occur in the absolutive:

(2) a.   Ne   kai he   pusi ia   e   moa.
PAST eat ERG cat   that ABS chicken
'That cat ate the chicken.'
  b.   To   lagomatai he   ekekafo a   ia.
FUT help   ERG doctor   ABS him
'The doctor will help him.'
  c.   To   tunu e   au e   moa.
FUT cook ERG I   ABS chicken
'I'll cook the chicken.'

A variety of oblique nominals, including locatives and agents of stative verbs, are marked with *he* for common nouns and *i* for pronouns and proper nouns:

(3) a.   Nofo e   taokete haana he māga   ha mautolu.
live ABS brother his   in village of US-PL-EX
'His big brother lives in our village.'
  b.   Matakutaku a   ia i   a   Pita.
frightened   ABS he AGT PERS Pita
'He's frightened of Pita.'

Several other types of oblique nominals, including goals, indirect objects (IOs), and objects of most verbs of perception, are marked with *ke he* for common nouns and *ki* for pronouns and proper nouns:

(4) a.   Hake a   Tofua ki Makefu.
go-up ABS Tofua to Makefu
'Tofua's going up to Makefu (village).'
  b.   Ne   fakahū e   au e   tohi ke he kapitiga haaku.
PAST send   ERG I   ABS letter to   friend my
'I sent a letter to my friend.'
  c.   Onoono e   tama nā ke he tau gata   gagau kona.
look-at ABS child that to   PL snake bite   poison
'That child is looking at the poisonous snakes.' ·

Benefactives are marked with *ma*. Common noun benefactives also bear the absolutive particle *e,* which immediately follows *ma,* while benefactive pronouns are formed with possessive stems, optionally including the possessive marker *ha:*

(5) a. Gahua a   au ma e   tagata kō.
       work ABS I for ABS man that
       'I work for that man there.'

   b. Ne taute e   au e   pasikala afi ma (ha-)ana.
       PAST fix   ERG I ABS bicycle fire for of-him
       'I fixed the motorbike for him.'

Finally, instruments bear the preposition *aki,* which is immediately followed by an absolutive particle:

(6) Kua hele tuai e   Sione e   falaoa aki e   titipi haana.
     PERF cut PERF ERG Sione ABS bread with ABS knife his
     'Sione has cut the bread with his knife.'

The chart below summarizes the facts about Niuean case marking which I have just outlined:

(7) Case Particles

	Abs	Erg	Loc	Goal	Ben	Instr
Common	e	he	he	ke he	ma e	aki e
Proper/Pro	a	e	i	ki	ma	aki a

With several minor exceptions which need not concern us here,[7] the order of NPs in a Niuean clause is invariably:

(8) V − S − DO − IO − other oblique NPs.

2 The Raising Proposal

The discussion in this paper is limited to two of the verbs which I claim govern Raising in Niuean, the epistemic modal *maeke* 'can, be possible' and the aspectual *kamata* 'begin'. Other verbs that govern Niuean Raising include an emphatic negative *fakaai* 'not', *mahani* 'usual, customary', *teitei* 'almost', and *fetamakina* 'nearly'. The arguments in this paper involving *maeke* and *kamata* may be made in essentially the same form for the other Raising governors as well. Raising operates on sentential complements introduced by the subjunctive marker *ke* and embedded in one of these verbs. Consider (9a–b), for example:

(9) a. Maeke ke nofo a   Pita i Tuapa.
       possible SBJ stay ABS Pita at Tuapa
       'Pita can stay at Tuapa (village).'

   b. Ne   kamata ke uku hifo e   tama ke he toka.
       PAST begin SBJ dive down ABS child to   bottom
       'The child began to dive down to the bottom.'

I claim that Raising relates the sentences in (9) to those in (10):

(10) a.   Maeke   a   Pita ke nofo i Tuapa.
          possible ABS Pita SBJ stay at Tuapa
          'Pita can stay at Tuapa.'

    b.   Ne   kamata e   tama ke uku hifo ke he toka.
         PAST begin   ABS child SBJ dive down to   bottom
         'The child began to dive down to the bottom.'

Raising may apply to SUs of intransitive complements, as in (10), and to SUs of transitive complements. Thus, Raising relates the sentences in (11) to those in (12):

(11) a.   To   maeke   ke lagomatai he ekekafo e   tama ē.
          FUT possible SBJ help   ERG doctor ABS child this
          'The doctor could help this child.'

    b.   Kua kamata ke hala he   tama e   akau.
         PERF begin   SBJ cut ERG child ABS tree
         'The boy has begun to cut down the tree.'

(12) a.   To   maeke   e   ekekafo ke lagomatai e   tama ē.
          FUT possible ABS doctor SBJ help   ABS child this
          'The doctor could help this child.'

    b.   Kua kamata e   tama ke hala e   akau.
         PERF begin   ABS child SBJ cut ABS tree
         'The child has begun to cut down the tree.'

Furthermore, Raising may apply to complement DOs, relating, for example, the sentences in (11) to those in (13):[8]

(13) a.   To   maeke   e   tama ē   ke lagomatai he   ekekafo.
          FUT possible ABS child this SBJ help   ERG doctor
          'This child could be helped by the doctor.'

    b.   Kua kamata e   akau ke hala he   tama.
         PERF begin   ABS tree SBJ cut ERG child
         'The tree has begun to be cut down by the child.'

The analysis of Niuean Raising which I am going to propose in this section presupposes a version of Perlmutter and Postal's relational grammar which includes the notion of syntactic derivation. In this theory, a significant class of syntactic rules, including Raising, are formulated directly in terms of grammatical relations (GRs) such as SU, DO, IO ('terms'), and benefactive, instrumental, locative, and so on ('nonterms'). I will refer to IOs and nonterms as 'oblique NPs'. Rules that alter the GR held by an NP are called 'relation-changing rules'. The GR held by an NP before any relation-changing rules have applied in its clause.is called its 'initial GR'. Perlmutter and Postal claim that the assignment of initial GRs is universally determined by principles referring to the semantic roles of NPs. Of course, an NP's initial GR may be different from the 'derived GR' it holds once relation-changing rules have applied. The GR held by an NP after all relation-changing rules have applied to a sentence I will call its 'final GR'. I will assume here that syntactic rules apply cyclically but that within the cycle no rules are extrinsically ordered.

With these background assumptions, I now outline my analysis of Raising sentences, e.g., those in (10), (12), and (13). I propose that Niuean Raising accepts as input a biclausal structure involving a Raising governor as the higher verb taking a sentential SU. In the output structure produced by Raising, the former complement SU or DO bears the GR previously held by the sentential complement; this is predicted by Perlmutter and Postal's (this volume) Relational Succession Law. In other words, Niuean Raising turns a complement SU or DO into the SU of the next highest clause. Moreover, the remnant of the sentential complement then bears the nonterm chômeur relation as a consequence of Perlmutter and Postal's Relational Annihilation Law:[9]

(14)   Relational Annihilation Law
       If an NP_i assumes a grammatical relation previously borne by NP_j, then NP_j ceases to bear any *term* grammatical relation; it becomes a chômeur.

So consider, for example, the derivation of (10a). Its initial structure may be represented in an oversimplified and informal fashion as (15), which is also the initial structure of (9a):[10]

(15)

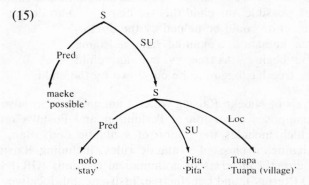

Raising operates optionally on (15), creating the derived structure (16), which is the final structure of (10a):

(16)

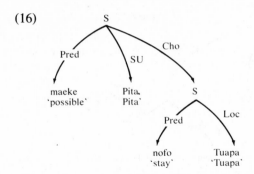

Likewise, (11a), (12a), and (13a) all have the same initial structure, represented in (17), which is also the final structure of (11a):

(17)

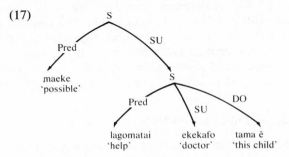

In this structure, the complement SU and complement DO are both eligible for Raising. Thus, Raising may turn (17) into (18), which is the final structure of (12a):

(18)

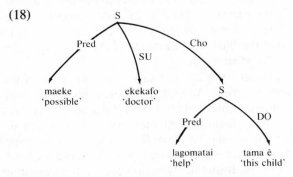

Or Raising may turn (17) into (19), which is the final structure of (13a):

(19)

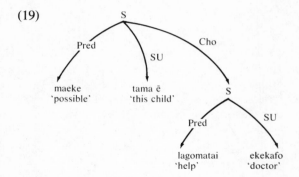

In the next three sections, I will defend the Raising analysis which I have just outlined. The evidence presented against several alternative analyses will establish that Niuean Raising promotes a complement SU or DO to become the derived SU of the higher governing verb. Since the arguments do not depend crucially on syntactic rules referring directly to GRs, they could also be taken to establish the existence of a Raising rule in a transformational framework.

3   Downstairs Subjecthood or Direct Objecthood

The simplest alternative to the Raising analysis, which I will call the Initial analysis, would claim that there is no rule which turns raised NPs into upstairs (i.e., higher) SUs. Rather, each raised NP would be an initial upstairs SU and would not bear a GR in the complement clause at any stage of derivation. According to the Initial analysis, (17), which is the initial structure of (11a), (12a), and (13a) under the Raising analysis, would be the initial structure only of (11a). And (18) and (19) would be not only the final structures of (12a) and (13a), respectively, but also their initial structures.

In §3, I argue against the Initial analysis on the basis of four other rules, Case Marking, Verb Agreement, Quantifier Float, and Instrumental Advancement, which interact with Raising. The arguments are each of the following form. I first motivate a rule which is clause-internal and crucially involves a SU or DO. Then I show that application of the rule in the complement clause of a Raising sentence may involve the raised NP. For the Initial analysis to account for this, undesirable complications would have to be made in the statement of the rule in question. Hence, the Initial analysis is inferior to the Raising analysis, which automatically accounts for the rule's effects in Raising complements.

3.1   Case Marking

The basic facts of case marking in Niuean have been outlined in §1. One argument against the Initial analysis concerns case marking in complement clauses from which a DO has been raised. Consider, for example, the sentences in (13). Under the Initial analysis, *e tama ē* 'this child' and *e akau* 'the tree' would be initial upstairs subjects and would bear no complement GRs at any level. This means that the complement clauses in (13) would be intransitive at all levels of structure. To account for the ergative complement SUs in (13), the Initial analysis would have to resort to an ad hoc condition on the rule assigning ergative case marking: the condition would make an intransitive SU undergo ergative marking just in case the next highest clause contained *maeke* or *kamata* taking a lexical SU.

Under the Raising analysis, *e tama ē* and *e akau* in (13) are initial complement DOs. Assuming Case Marking to be cyclic, it must apply in the complement clauses in (13) before Raising, which can apply only on the higher cycle. This insures that the complement SUs in (13) are placed in the ergative, since prior to Raising these complement clauses contain a DO.[11]

3.2   Verb Agreement
3.2.1   *Subject-Verb Agreement*

Certain verbs in Niuean agree in number with their SUs, the plural form being obligatorily triggered by a dual or plural SU. Intransitive verbs of motion have plurals formed on the suppletive verb stem *ō*. For example, compare the singular verb in (20a) with the plural in (20b):

(20) a. To   fano a   au apogipogi ki Queen Street.
         FUT go   ABS I   tomorrow to Queen Street
         'I'm going to Queen Street tomorrow.'

     b. To ō   a   tautolu   apogipogi ki Queen Street.
         FUT go-PL ABS we-PL-INC tomorrow to Queen Street
         'We're going to Queen Street tomorrow.'

Many other intransitive verbs have plurals formed by reduplicating the first syllable of their singular form:

(21) a. Nofo agaia nakai e   matua fifine   haau i Mutalau?
         live still Q   ABS parent female your at Mutalau
         'Does your mother still live at Mutalau (village)?'

     b. Nonofo agaia nakai e   tau mamatua haau i Mutalau?
         live-PL still Q   ABS PL parents   your at Mutalau
         'Do your parents still live at Mutalau?'

Several intransitive verbs also occur as syntactic transitives with a location as absolutive-marked DO; semantically, the event described is viewed as having a direct effect on the location. In this use, these verbs obligatorily agree with the transitive, ergative-marked SU:

(22) a. Ai lā nofo ia e   ia e   nofoa nei.
not yet sit   yet ERG he ABS chair this
'He has never sat in this chair.'

b. Ai lā nonofo ia e   laua   e   nofoa nei.
not yet sit-PL   yet ERG they-DU ABS chair this
'They've never sat in this chair.'

For our discussion, the important generalization is that with all of these verbs, agreement is triggered only by the SU of the agreeing verb, so that agreement is clause-internal.

Now, under the initial analysis, the raised NPs *e tau tagata nā* 'those people' in (23b) and *a laua* 'they' in (24b) would be initial SUs of the Raising verbs *kamata* 'begin' and *maeke* 'be possible', respectively; at no stage of derivation would they bear any relation to the complement verbs *ō hake* 'go up-PL' and *nonofo* 'sit-PL':

(23) a. Kua kamata tuai e   tagata nā ke hake motokā.
PERF begin   PERF ABS person that SBJ go-up car
'That person has begun to go up by car.'

b. Kua kamata tuai e   tau tagata nā ke ō hake
PERF begin   PERF ABS PL person that SBJ go-up-PL
motokā.
car
'Those people have begun to go up by car.'

(24) a. Ai maeke a   ia ke nofo e   nofoa nei.
not possible ABS he SBJ sit   ABS chair this
'He can't sit on this chair.'

b. Ai maeke a   laua   ke nonofo e   nofoa nei.
not possible ABS they-DU SBJ sit-PL   ABS chair this
'They can't sit on this chair.'

Since Verb Agreement is clause-internal, the Initial analysis could not account for (23b) and (24b). At no level would these sentences have a complement SU, so nothing would be able to trigger the plural forms *ō hake* and *nonofo*. To maintain the Initial analysis, then, the statement of Verb Agreement would have to be complicated to treat (23) and (24) as a special case: lexical SUs of *maeke* and *kamata* would trigger plural agreement down into immediately embedded clauses on subjectless verbs which otherwise agree with their own SUs. This amended Verb

Agreement rule would be undesirable because it entails significant loss of generality and destroys the generalization that agreement is clause-internal.

In contrast, the Raising analysis treats *e tau tagata nā* in (23b) and *a laua* in (24b) as initial complement SUs. Given the assumption that Verb Agreement applies cyclically, it must apply in the complements of (23b) and (24b) before Raising, which can apply only on the higher cycle. This accounts for the plural verb forms *ō hake* and *nonofo*. Thus, the Raising analysis accounts for (23) and (24) without ad hoc complications in the statement of Verb Agreement.

3.2.2   *Direct Object-Verb Agreement*

Several transitive verbs obligatorily agree in number with their DOs. Compare the singular verb in (25a) to the plural in (25b):

(25) a.   Kua hala e   ia e   lā   akau.
        PERF cut   ERG he ABS branch tree
        'He cut down the branch.'
    b.   Kua hahala e   ia e   tau lā   akau.
        PERF cut-PL ERG he ABS PL branch tree
        'He cut down the branches.'

According to the Initial analysis, *e tau akau* 'the trees' in (26b) would be the initial SU of *kamata;* it would bear no relation at any level to complement verb *hahala* 'cut-PL':

(26) a.   Kua kamata e   akau ke hala e   Pita.
        PERF begin   ABS tree SBJ cut   ERG Pita
        'The tree had begun to be cut down by Pita.'
    b.   Kua kamata e   tau akau ke hahala e   Pita.
        PERF begin   ABS PL tree SBJ cut-PL ERG Pita
        'The trees had begun to be cut down by Pita.'

To account for (26), the Initial analysis would again have to claim that Verb Agreement was not always clause-internal. Instead, lexical SUs of *maeke* and *kamata* would have to trigger agreement down into immediately embedded clauses on DO-less verbs which normally agree with their own DOs. The Raising analysis requires no such complication, since it treats *e tau akau* in (26b) as an initial complement DO which triggers the plural *hahala* prior to Raising.

3.3   Quantifier Float

The Niuean version of Quantifier Float applies to the quantifier *oti* 'all', which immediately follows the noun it modifies:

(27) Kua fia-momohe tuai e   tau tagata oti nā.
       PERF want-sleep-PL PERF ABS PL person all that
       'All of those people have gotten sleepy.'

Through Quantifier Float, *oti* is optionally removed from an NP and cliticized to the verb in the same clause. Thus, the rule relates (27) to (28):

(28) Kua fia-momohe oti tuai e   tau tagata nā.
       PERF want-sleep-PL all PERF ABS PL person that
       'Those people have all gotten sleepy.'

   Quantifier Float may apply to intransitive SUs, as in (28), and to transitive SUs and DOs:

(29) a. Kua tele tuai e   lautolu oti a   au.
          PERF kick PERF ERG they   all ABS me
          'All of them have kicked me.'
     b. Kua tele oti tuai e   lautolu a   au.
          PERF kick all PERF ERG they   ABS me
          'They've all kicked me.'

(30) a. Moua e   maua   mo Sione e   tau mata afi oti.
          get ERG we-DU-EX with Sione ABS PL match   all
          'Sione and I have already won all the matches.'
     b. Moua oti e   maua   mo Sione e   tau mata afi.
          get all ERG we-DU-EX with Sione ABS PL match
          'Sione and I have already won all the matches.'

But oblique NPs cannot undergo Quantifier Float. For instance, *oti* may not be removed from an IO:

(31) a. Ne   tutala a   au ke he tau momotua oti.
          PAST talk ABS I   to   PL elders   all
          'I talked to all the elders.'
     b. *Ne   tutala oti a   au ke he tau momotua.
          PAST talk all ABS I   to   PL elders
          (I talked to all the elders.)

   In addition to being limited to SUs and DOs, Quantifier Float is clause-internal, i.e., an NP always launches *oti* to the verb in the same clause, never to a verb in a higher or lower clause. In particular, note that an NP cannot launch *oti* down into a *ke-* complement:

(32) a. Kua manako a   lautolu oti ke mohe a   Pita.
          PERF want   ABS they   all SBJ sleep ABS Pita
          'All of them want Pita to sleep.'

b. *Kua manako a   lautolu ke mohe oti a   Pita.
   PERF want   ABS they   SBJ sleep all ABS Pita
   (All of them want Pita to sleep.)

The Initial analysis would make two predictions about the operation of Quantifier Float in Raising sentences. First of all, since raised NPs would be initial upstairs SUs, they should be able to undergo Quantifier Float upstairs. This prediction is correct, as (33b) attests:

(33) a.   Kua kamata tuai e   tau tagata oti nā   ke
          PERF begin   PERF ABS PL person all that SBJ
          fia-momohe.
          want-sleep-PL
          'All of those people have begun to get sleepy.'
     b.   Kua kamata oti tuai e   tau tagata nā ke
          PERF begin   all PERF ABS PL person that SBJ
          fia-momohe.
          want-sleep-PL
          'Those people have all gotten sleepy.'

However, the Initial analysis would also predict that *oti* should never float from a raised NP to the complement verb, since at no level would the raised NP belong to the complement clause. This prediction is incorrect though, because (34a), related to (33a) through Quantifier Float, and (34b) are grammatical:

(34) a.   Kua kamata tuai e   tau tagata nā ke fia-momohe
          PERF begin   PERF ABS PL person that SBJ want-sleep-PL
          oti.
          all
          'Those people have all begun to get sleepy.'
     b.   Maeke e   tau talo nā ke kai oti he faiaoga.
          possible ABS PL taro that SBJ eat all ERG teacher
          'Those taros can all be eaten by the teacher.'

To maintain the Initial analysis in light of (34), we would have to complicate the statement of Quantifier Float. The rule would usually be clause-internal, with the sole exception that it could operate on lexical SUs of *maeke* and *kamata* with two outcomes: *oti* could either cliticize to the Raising verb or sink into the immediately embedded clause and cliticize to the complement verb. Such an amended rule would be less general than the original and would destroy the generalization that Quantifier Float is a clause-internal phenomenon. A stronger objection is that not only would the complication of this rule under the Initial analysis be ad hoc, but it is ad hoc in precisely the same fashion as Verb Agreement would be. The problem is that it would be an accidental feature of the Initial analysis that its peculiar amendment of Quantifier Float parallels its peculiar amendment of Verb Agreement.

But the Raising analysis automatically predicts the grammaticality of (34a) and (34b), given the independently motivated assumption that Quantifier Float is clause-internal and limited to SUs and DOs. Since the raised NP in (34a) originates as complement SU, and that in (34b) originates as complement DO, both are eligible to launch *oti* to the complement verb prior to Raising.

3.4   Instrumental Advancement

My third argument against the Initial analysis involves a clause-internal advancement rule established in Seiter 1979:

(35)   Instrumental $\longrightarrow$ Direct Object

As a result of (35) instruments in transitive clauses become eligible to undergo Relative Deletion, Raising, and Quantifier Float, each of which is limited to SUs and DOs. For example, (35) turns the complement instrument *e toki* 'the axe' in (36a) into a derived complement DO, so that it is eligible to undergo Raising, giving (36b):

(36) a. Kua kamata ke hio aki e   Sefa e   toki
         PERF begin   SBJ chop with ERG Sefa ABS axe
         e   akau motua.
         ABS tree old
         'Sefa had begun to chop down the old tree with the axe.'
     b. Kua kamata e   toki ke hio aki e   Sefa
         PERF begin   ABS axe SBJ chop with ERG Sefa
         e   akau motua.
         ABS tree old
         'Sefa had begun to chop down the old tree with the axe.'

Likewise, *aki e tau mena gahua oti nā* 'with all those tools' in (37a) may become a derived DO through (35) and is therefore able to launch *oti,* giving (37b):

(37) a. To tā   e   ia e   fale haana aki e   tau
         FUT build ERG he ABS house his   with ABS PL
         mena gahua oti nā.
         thing work all that
         'He's going to build his house with all those tools.'

    b. To tā   oti e   ia e   fale   haana aki e
        FUT build all ERG he ABS house his   with ABS
        tau mena gahua nā.
        PL thing work that
        'He's going to build his house with all those tools.'

What is of interest to us here is that Instrumental Advancement (35) can apply only in clauses which already have a DO. This accounts for the fact that instruments in intransitive clauses never become derived DOs and are thus unable to undergo Relative Deletion, Raising, or Quantifier Float, e.g.:

(38) a. Kua tohitohi e   tama aki e   tau pene oti.
        PERF write   ABS child with ABS PL pen all
        'The child is writing with all of the pens.'
    b. *Kua tohitohi oti e   tama aki e   tau pene.
        PERF write   all ABS child with ABS PL pen
        (The child is writing with all of the pens.)

Now consider sentences like (39), involving a raised NP and an instrument in the complement clause. The Initial analysis would claim that (39) has an initial structure essentially like (40):

(39) Maeke e   fakatino ke tā   aki e   Lemani e
     possible ABS picture SBJ draw with ERG Lemani ABS
     tau malala   oti.
     PL charcoal all
     'The picture might be drawn by Lemani with all the charcoals.'

(40)

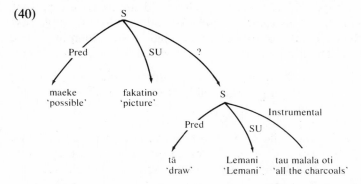

Since the complement clause in (40) has no DO, the instrument should be unable to become a derived DO through Instrumental Advancement. In particular, then, the Initial analysis would predict that the complement instrument in (39) should be unable to undergo Quantifier Float.

However, (41) shows that the prediction is incorrect:

(41) Maeke e   fakatino ke tā   aki oti e   Lemani
      possible ABS picture SBJ draw with all ERG Lemani
      e   tau malala.
      ABS PL charcoal
      'The picture might be drawn by Lemani with all the charcoals.'

Likewise, the Initial analysis would predict, incorrectly, that the complement instrument in (42a) cannot undergo Relative Deletion to produce the relative clause in (42b):[12]

(42) a. Kua maeke   e   tau fakatino mitaki ke tā   aki
         PERF possible ABS PL picture good SBJ draw with
         e   pene haaku.
         ABS pen my
         'Good pictures can be drawn with my pen.'
     b. Kua taha nī hāku a pene ne   kua maeke e
         PERF one just my   pen NONFUT PERF possible ABS
         tau fakatino mitaki ke tā   aki.
         PL picture good SBJ draw with
         'I have only one pen which good pictures can be drawn with.'

It would be no use to reformulate Instrumental Advancement to apply to (i) clauses containing a DO or (ii) DO-less complements of *maeke* and *kamata* when those verbs have a lexical SU. Even if we ignore the objection that condition (ii) replicates the ad hoc complications which the Initial analysis required for Verb Agreement and Quantifier Float, this approach would unfortunately predict that the complement instrument in (43a) should be able to undergo Instrumental Advancement and therefore be eligible for Quantifier Float, giving (43b). The prediction is incorrect, since (43b) is ungrammatical:

(43) a. To kamata e   tama ke tohitohi aki e   tau
         FUT begin ABS child SBJ write   with ABS PL
         pene oti.
         pen all
         'The child's going to begin to write with all the pens.'
     b. *To kamata e   tama ke tohitohi aki oti e
         FUT begin ABS child SBJ write   with all ABS
         tau pene.
         PL pen
         (The child's going to begin to write with all the pens.)

The Raising analysis accounts automatically for the grammaticality of (41) and (42b) and the ungrammaticality of (43b), assuming that

Instrumental Advancement applies only in clauses containing a DO.
For sentences (39) and (41), the Raising analysis posits an initial structure like:

(44)

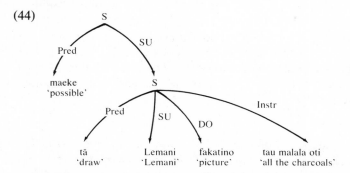

The complement clause in (44) meets the conditions for Instrumental
Advancement, since it contains an instrumental NP and a DO. If the
rule applies, it creates the derived structure:[13]

(45)

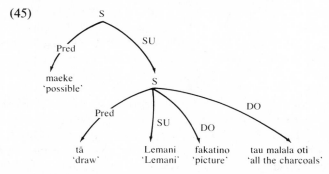

Both DOs in (45) are eligible for Raising, and the derived DO is also
eligible for Quantifier Float. If Quantifier Float applies and the initial
DO undergoes Raising, we get (46), which is the final structure of (41):

(46)

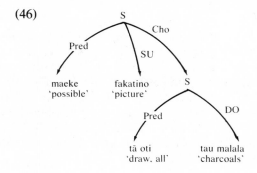

Similarly, the Raising analysis claims that the complement clause in (42a) is eligible for Instrumental Advancement prior to Raising, since it contains an instrumental NP and an initial DO. Thus, the complement instrument may become a derived DO and undergo Relative Deletion, giving (42b). But in the initial structure of (43a), the complement contains a SU, but at no level does it contain a DO. Therefore, conditions are never met for Instrumental Advancement, so the complement instrument cannot become a derived DO. This accounts for the ungrammaticality of (43b), in which the instrument has undergone Quantifier Float.

3.5   Summary

In this section, I considered an analysis which would have dispensed with Raising by treating raised NPs as initial upstairs SUs. Since raised NPs would bear no complement GR at any level, the Initial analysis could not straightforwardly account for the fact that raised NPs are involved in applications of clause-internal rules in Raising complements. In particular, the Initial analysis would have entailed undesirable complications in the statements of Case Marking, Verb Agreement, and Quantifier Float, and could not have provided a correct account of applications of Instrumental Advancement in Raising complements. I conclude that the Initial analysis is inferior to the Raising analysis, which correctly predicts the applications of those four rules in Raising complements.

The reason the Raising analysis accounts for the facts presented in §§3.1–3.4 is that it claims that raised NPs originate as complement SUs or DOs. But there are two other types of analyses which treat raised NPs as initial complement SUs or DOs, and thus account for the facts presented so far. Therefore, I will show in §§4 and 5 that there are other facts about Niuean which are predicted by the Raising analysis, but which could not be accounted for under the two other types of alternatives.

4   Upstairs Subjecthood

One of the remaining alternatives to the Raising analysis would claim that raised NPs are initial complement SUs or DOs, so that, for example, (11a), (12a), and (13a) would all have the same initial structure (17). Unlike the Raising analysis, however, this alternative would derive sentences like (12a) and (13a) through application of a superficial, non-relation-changing, movement transformation: this rule would optionally shift a complement SU or DO to a position immediately before the subjunctive marker *ke*, without affecting the NP's clause membership.[14] I will call this the NP Shift analysis.

Notice that absolute case marking would somehow have to be assigned to the shifted NP after the operation of the NP Shift transformation, since even a shifted transitive complement SU, e.g., *e eke-kafo* 'the doctor' in (12a), must appear in the absolutive, not the ergative case. Under the Raising analysis, the fact that all NPs raised to *maeke* or *kamata* appear in the absolutive follows from the fact that they are derived intransitive SUs.

In §§4.1–4.3, I will demonstrate that raised NPs are derived upstairs SUs, based on their ability to undergo Quantifier Float, Equi, and Possessive Marking in nominalizations. I will argue, therefore, that the NP Shift analysis is inadequate for Niuean, because it would not assign the 'shifted' NP subjecthood in the upstairs clause. In contrast, the Raising analysis correctly predicts that raised NPs should undergo SU-referring rules in upstairs clauses.

4.1   Quantifier Float

Recall from §3.2 that Quantifier Float in Niuean is limited to SUs and DOs, and only applies clause-internally. Therefore, the NP Shift analysis would predict that a raised NP containing *oti* 'all', though it might launch the quantifier to the complement verb, could not do so to the higher verb, since it would not belong to the higher clause at any level. The prediction is incorrect, though, as shown by:

(47) a.   Maeke oti a   tautolu   ke vagahau fakapālagi mo e
          possible all ABS we-PL-INC SBJ speak   English   and
          fakaniuē.
          Niuean
          'We can all speak English and Niuean.'
     b.   Kua kamata oti tuai e   tau fuakau ke fakagoagoa
          PERF begin all PERF ABS PL old-men SBJ fool
          e   ia.
          ERG he
          'The old men have all begun to be fooled by him.'

The Raising analysis claims that *a tautolu* 'we' in (47a), which is an initial complement SU, and *e tau fuakau* 'the old men' in (47b), which is an initial complement DO, are derived SUs of *maeke* and *kamata,* respectively. This makes them eligible to launch *oti* in the upstairs clause, once Raising has applied. Thus, the Raising analysis predicts the grammaticality of (47a) and (47b).

Strictly speaking, the sentences in (47) only argue that raised NPs are either derived SUs or derived DOs of *maeke* and *kamata*. I will now show that raised NPs undergo rules in upstairs clauses which apply exclusively to SUs.

4.2   Equi

Niuean has a rule of Equi, described in §5.2, which obligatorily deletes
a complement SU under conreference with an upstairs controlling NP.
Whenever an upstairs Equi controller is coreferential with an NP other
than the SU of the Equi complement, the complement NP cannot even
optionally be deleted. So the NP Shift analysis would claim that if a
Raising sentence, such as (48a), is embedded under an Equi verb, the
raised NP should not delete under coreference with a controlling NP,
since the raised NP would not be SU of the embedded sentence. This
would predict that (48b) is ungrammatical and (48c) is grammatical. In
fact, though, the reverse is the case:

(48) a.   Kamata a   Sione ke fakapuke e   tau lupo.
          begin   ABS Sione SBJ fill   ABS PL bottle
          'Sione's beginning to fill the bottles.'
     b.   Kua lali a   Sione ke kamata ke fakapuke e
          PERF try ABS Sione SBJ begin   SBJ fill   ABS
          tau lupo.
          PL bottle
          'Sione has tried to begin filling the bottles.'
     c. *Kua lali a   Sione ke kamata a   ia ke fakapuke
          PERF try ABS Sione SBJ begin   ABS he SBJ fill
          e   tau lupo.
          ABS PL bottle
          (Sione has tried to begin filling the bottles.)

Under the Raising analysis, *a Sione* in (48a) is the derived SU of
kamata. In (48b), in which (48a) has been embedded under an Equi
verb, the derived SU of *kamata* undergoes Equi as expected of an Equi
complement. The fact that Equi is an obligatory rule accounts for the
ungrammaticality of (48c).

4.3   Possessive Preposing in Nominalizations

Sentence nominalizations in Niuean are introduced by a case marker
from the common noun series. For example, (49b) is a nominalization
related to the simple sentence (49a). One NP in the nominalization may
optionally become a possessive modifier of the nominalized verb
through a rule of Possessive Marking, which relates (49b) to (49c):

(49) a.   Kua pākia tuai a   au he pilu nā.
          PERF injured PERF ABS I   on knife that
          'I've been injured on that bush knife.'
     b.   e   pākia a   au he pilu nā
          ABS injured ABS I   on knife that
          'my being injured on that bush knife'

c. e   pākia haaku he pilu nā
    ABS injured my   on knife that
    'my being injured on that bush knife'

Possessive Marking may apply to an intransitive SU, as in (49c), a transitive SU, or a DO:[15]

(50) a. e   uta haana i a   au ki Alofi
         ABS take his   PERS me to Alofi
         'his taking me to Alofi'
     b. e   kotofa haaku (e   lautolu) ke fakamatala
         ABS choose my   ERG they   SBJ speak
         'my being chosen (by them) to make a speech'

A rule of Possessive Preposing shifts a pronominal or proper possessive NP in front of the noun it modifies; the preposed possessive is separated from the noun by a particle *a*. Note that when this rule has applied, rearticulated *aa* in the singular possessive pronouns becomes long *ā* and the absolutive marker *e* may fail to appear:

(51) a. e   kulī haaku
         ABS dog my
         'my dog'
     b. hāku a kulī
         my   dog
         'my dog'

In nominalizations, intransitive or transitive SUs which have been placed in the possessive may undergo Possessive Preposing, as in (52a) and (52b), which are related to (49c) and (50a), respectively:

(52) a. hāku a pākia he pilu nā
         my   injured on knife that
         'my being injured on that bush knife'
     b. hāna a uta i a   au ki Alofi
         his   take PERS me to Alofi
         'his taking me to Alofi'

However, possessivized DOs may not undergo Possessive Preposing, as shown by (53), which corresponds to (50b):

(53) *hāku a kotofa (e   lautolu) ke fakamatala
       my   choose ERG they   SBJ speak
      (my being chosen (by them) to speak)

Notice that stating Possessive Preposing solely in terms of linear order cannot produce the right results, since the possessivized NP in a nominalization, whether a SU or DO, is always immediately following the nominalized verb. This argues that Possessive Preposing must be limited to the SU of the nominalized verb.

Now the NP Shift analysis would claim that when a Raising sentence, such as (54a), is turned into a nominalization, the raised NP should undergo neither Possessive Marking nor Possessive Preposing, since it would not be the SU or DO of the Raising verb at any level. The facts contradict such a claim, though, because the raised NP may become a possessive modifier of the Raising verb, as in (54b), and may be preposed, as in (54c):

(54) a. To maeke a   au ke āhi he   kapitiga haaku.
         FUT possible ABS I SBJ visit ERG friend   my
         'It will be possible for me to be visited by my friend.'

     b. Kua oti   tei   e   maeke haaku ke āhi he
         PERF finish PERF ABS possible my   SBJ visit ERG
         kapitiga haaku.
         friend   my
         'The possibility of me being visited by my friend is through.'

     c. Kua oti   tei   hāku a maeke   ke āhi he   kapitiga
         PERF finish PERF my   possible SBJ visit ERG friend
         haaku.
         my
         'The possibility of me being visited by my friend is through.'

The Raising analysis treats *a au* 'I' in (54a) as the derived SU of *maeke*. Therefore, in the related nominalization, it is eligible to undergo both Possessive Marking, which is limited to SUs and DOs, and Possessive Preposing, which is limited to SUs.

4.4   Summary

The NP Shift analysis would have claimed that raised NPs precede the subjunctive marker *ke* as a result of a superficial movement rule which would not affect their clause membership and grammatical relations. It therefore would have excluded the possibility that a raised NP might undergo rules limited to upstairs NPs. In fact, though, raised NPs behave as SUs of *maeke* and *kamata* in undergoing Quantifier Float, Equi, and Possessive Preposing in nominalizations. The NP Shift analysis is incompatible with these facts. In contrast, the Raising analysis predicts the facts presented in §§4.1–4.3, since Raising turns NPs into derived SUs of *maeke* and *kamata*.

5   Change in Grammatical Relations

In §3 it was argued that (i) a raised NP in Niuean is an initial complement SU or DO and in §4 that (ii) a raised NP is also an upstairs SU at some level. Analyses which fail to accommodate (i) or (ii) were rejected. The Raising analysis predicts (i) and (ii), but so does an analysis which would posit two coreferential occurrences of each raised NP in initial structure, one the upstairs SU, the other the complement SU or DO. According to this Two-NP analysis, the Raising sentence (13a) would have an initial structure like (55):

(55)

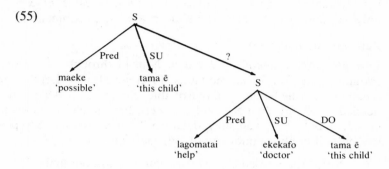

Positing two initial occurrences of the raised NP in a Raising sentence would trivially insure that (i) and (ii) were both the case in a single derivation. Under this analysis, the derivation of a Raising sentence would have to involve deletion of the downstairs occurrence of the raised NP, after such rules as Verb Agreement, Quantifier Float, and Instrumental Advancement had had an opportunity to apply to the complement clause. It follows, then, that the Two-NP analysis can be maintained only if some deletion rule can be claimed to derive Niuean Raising sentences.

In the rest of this section, I will argue that the Two-NP analysis is untenable, because there can be no deletion rule through which the full range of Raising sentences is derived. In §5.1, I point out that the appropriate deletion rule could not simply be Zero Pronominalization. Instead, it would have to be some obligatory version of Equi, which I call 'R-equi'. Briefly in §5.2 I describe the genuine rule of Equi in Niuean, not involved in Raising sentences. In §§5.3–5.6, I examine four properties which R-equi would have to have under the Two-NP analysis and contrast these with properties of genuine Niuean Equi. The differences argue that the Two-NP analysis would require two totally distinct rules of Equi in Niuean. While genuine Niuean Equi deletes only complement SUs and no like-NP constraint is imposed on Equi configurations, R-equi would delete complement SUs and DOs and a Like-Subject-or-Direct-Object Constraint would have to be imposed on R-equi configurations. Both characteristics of the latter, I argue, are highly improbable for any variety of Equi. §5.5 argues that

R-equi could not be a coreferential deletion and §5.6 shows that in its interaction with reflexive and reciprocal clauses, R-equi would not behave the way obligatory deletion rules are expected to behave in Niuean. Since the assumption that a version of Equi derives Niuean Raising sentences is completely undermined by the facts presented, I conclude that the Two-NP analysis must be rejected. The Raising analysis, which automatically predicts all of the same facts, emerges as the only adequate treatment of the Niuean Raising phenomenon.

5.1   Zero Pronominalization

Pronouns are frequently deleted in Niuean through a rule of 'Zero Pronominalization' (also known as 'Pronoun Drop'). Let us consider whether this rule would be a reasonable candidate for the deletion rule needed under the Two-NP analysis. Zero Pronominalization is ungoverned, unbounded, and may delete NPs of all syntactic types. For example, it applies optionally in (56), deleting *a ia* 'he':

(56)   Ne   kitia e   au a   Maka neafi.   Malōlō lahi
       PAST see   ERG I ABS Maka yesterday strong very
       (a   ia).
       ABS he
       'I saw Maka yesterday. He's feeling very well.'

If Zero Pronominalization were responsible for deriving (13a) from (55), then (57) would, incorrectly, be expected to be grammatical, since Zero Pronominalization is optional:

(57)   *To maeke   e   tama ē   ke lagomatai he   ekekafo
        FUT possible ABS child this SBJ help   ERG doctor
        a   ia.
        ABS him
        (This child could be helped by the doctor.)

The fact is that raised NPs can never be resumed by a downstairs pronoun copy:

(58) a.   To maeke   e   ekekafo ke lagomatai (*e   ia) e
          FUT possible ABS doctor SBJ help   ERG he ABS
          tama ē.
          child this
          'The doctor could help this child.'
     b.   Ne   kamata e   tama ke uku hifo (*a   ia)
          PAST begin ABS child SBJ dive down ABS he
          ke he toka.
          to   bottom
          'The child began to dive down to the bottom.'

This means that for the Two-NP analysis to account for Raising sentences, it would have to posit a rule which obligatorily deleted downstairs NPs under coreference with an upstairs one. This rule would be governed by *maeke* and *kamata,* and would be bounded, since it could only delete SUs and DOs of the verb immediately embedded in a governing verb. In sum, the appropriate rule would be some obligatory version of Equi. Following a brief description of geniune Niuean Equi, I will examine the possibility that a version of Equi derives Niuean Raising sentences.

5.2   Genuine Equi

Equi in Niuean is governed by verbs of intention, volition, desire, and command which take sentential complements introduced by the subjunctive marker *ke*. The rule obligatorily deletes the SU of a *ke*-complement under coreference with an upstairs controlling NP. Depending on the governing verb, the deletion is controlled by an upstairs SU, DO, or IO:

(59) a.   Kua lali a   au ke tā   e   fāloku.
           PERF try ABS I   SBJ play ABS flute
           'I've tried to play the flute.'
     b.   Kotofa tuai e   lautolu a   au ke holoholo e
           choose PERF ERG they   ABS me SBJ wash   ABS
           tau kapiniu.
           PL dish
           'They chose me to wash the dishes.'
     c.   Tala age   ke he tugane haau ke fano ke he fale
           tell thither to   brother your SBJ go   to   house
           koloa.
           goods
           'Tell your brother to go to the store.'

Niuean Equi deletes all types of complement SUs, including those of transitive verbs, as in (59a) and (59b), those of active intransitive verbs, as in (59c), and those of stative verbs:

(60)   Ne   manako a   laua   ke mamate.
        PAST want   ABS they-DU SBJ die-PL
        'They wanted to die.'

However, Niuean Equi never deletes coreferential complement nonsubjects. Instead, complement nonsubjects in Equi configurations which are coreferential with an Equi controller must undergo personal pronominalization, not deletion:[16]

(61) a. Kua lali lahi   e   kapitiga haau ke sake e
PERF try really ABS friend   your SBJ sack ERG
au a   ia.
I   ABS him
'Your friend is really trying to get me to sack him.'

b. *Kua lali lahi   e   kapitiga haau ke sake e
PERF try really ABS friend   your SBJ sack ERG
au.
I
(Your friend is really trying to get me to sack him.)

(62) a. Kua tala age   e   au ke he tama ke age
PERF tell thither ERG I   to   child SBJ give
he faiaoga e   malala ki a   ia.
ERG teacher ABS charcoal to PERS him
'I told the child to have the teacher give him the charcoal.'

b. *Kua tala age   e   au ke he tama ke age
PERF tell thither ERG I   to   child SBJ give
he faiaoga e   malala
ERG teacher ABS charcoal
(I told the child to have the teacher give him the charcoal.)

Several verbs, including *maeke* and *kamata,* govern Equi controlled by an oblique-case-marked NP, which I refer to as a 'dative of interest'. In Equi sentences involving such a controller, the governing verb predicates ability, volition, or obligation on the part of the dative-of-interest NP. With *maeke,* dative-of-interest NPs are marked with *i* for pronouns and proper nouns and *he* for common nouns. For example, Equi in (63) is controlled by *i a au* 'at me':

(63)   Maeke vave   i a   au ke maama   e   tau
possible quickly at PERS me SBJ understand ABS PL
mena ne   tohi e   koe.
thing NONFUT write ERG you
'I'm easily able to understand what you write.'

With *kamata,* datives of interest may be marked either with *i* or *ki* for pronouns and proper nouns, and with *he* or *ke he* on common nouns. For example, *ki a Sione* 'to Sione' controls Equi in:

(64)   Kua kamata tuai ki a   Sione ke maama   e
PERF begin   PERF to PERS Sione SBJ understand ABS
tau mena mogonei.
PL thing now
'Sione has begun understanding things now.'

In §5.6, I will use examples of the dative-of-interest construction to make a critical, near-minimal contrast between Equi and Raising in Niuean.

5.3   Coreferential Complement Subject or Direct Object Deletion

Under the Two-NP analysis, the downstairs occurrences of raised NPs would be deleted by R-equi, an obligatory version of Equi. R-equi would have to delete complement SUs to derive sentences like (12a) and complement DOs to derive sentences like (13a). Although R-equi would apply to complement DOs as well as SUs, geniune Niuean Equi applies only to complement SUs. Recall that a complement DO co-referential with a controller must undergo personal pronominalization, not Equi, as in (61a).

This means that if the Two-NP analysis were correct, Niuean would have two distinct versions of Equi. The first, governed by verbs of intention, volition, desire, and command, deletes coreferential complement SUs. The second, R-equi, would be governed by verbs such as *maeke* and *kamata,* and would delete coreferential complement SUs and DOs.

5.4   A Like-Subject-or-Direct-Object Constraint

Given two occurrences of a raised NP in initial structure, nothing about the Two-NP analysis as it stands would prevent the downstairs NP from bearing a complement GR other than SU or DO. Those downstairs occurrences which were IOs or nonterms would simply fail to undergo R-equi, so that there would be grammatical sentences featuring a lexical SU of *maeke* or *kamata* coreferential with an oblique complement NP.

The fact is, however, that no such sentences exist. Instead, raised NPs must be initial complement SUs or DOs. For instance, the result of raising the oblique object of a verb of emotion, such as *ke he tehina haau* 'to your little brother' in (65a), is ungrammatical, with or without a downstairs pronoun copy, as (65b) attests:

(65) a.   Maeke   nakai ke falanaki a   mautolu ke he tehina
          possible Q   SBJ trust   ABS we-PL-EX to   brother
          pau?
          your
          'Can we trust your little brother?'
     b. *Maeke   nakai e   tehina haau ke falanaki a   mautolu
          possible Q   ABS brother your SBJ trust   ABS we-PL-EX
          (ki ai)?
          to him
          (Can your little brother be trusted by us?)

Likewise, (66b) shows that raising the oblique agent of a stative verb, such as *he tagata ia* 'on account of that man' in (66a), cannot result in a grammatical sentence:

(66) a. Ne   kamata ke matematekelea a   Tale he   tagata ia.
          PAST begin SBJ be-in-trouble ABS Tale AGT man   that
          'Tale began to get in trouble on account of that man.'

    b. *Ne   kamata e   tagata ia   ke matematekelea (ai) a
          PAST begin ABS person that SBJ be-in-trouble PRO ABS
          Tale.
          Tale
          (That man began to get Tale in trouble.)

To rule out sentences like (65b) and (66b), the Two-NP analysis would have to impose a constraint, somewhat reminiscent of Perlmutter's (1971) Like-Subject Constraint, on the initial structure of R-equi configurations:

(67)   Like Subject-or-Direct-Object Constraint
       An R-equi controller (i.e., lexical SU of *maeke* or *kamata*) must be coreferential with the initial complement SU or DO.

In contrast to R-equi, notice that genuine Niuean Equi configurations are not subject to any like-NP constraint. With genuine Equi verbs, the would-be controller may be coreferential with a complement SU, DO, or any type of oblique NP. For example, the Equi controllers *ke he tama* 'to the child' in (68a) and *a mautolu* 'we' in (68b) are coreferential with the complement IO and complement stative agent, respectively:

(68) a. Kua tala age   e   au ke he tama ke age
          PERF tell thither ERG I to   child SBJ give
          he   faiaoga e   malala ki a   ia.
          ERG teacher ABS charcoal to PERS him
          'I told the child to have the teacher give him the charcoal.'

    b. Kua manako a   mautolu ke matakutaku a   Pule i
          PERF want   ABS we-PL-EX SBJ frightened ABS Pule AGT
          a   mautolu.
          PERS us-PL-EX
          'We want Pule to be frightened of us.'

For that matter, an Equi controller need not be coreferential with any complement NP in initial structure:

(69)   Kua lali a   mautolu ke tokologa e   tau tagata
       PERF try ABS we-PL-EX SBJ many   ABS PL person
       ka   ō mai   ke he fonoaga apogipogi.
       FUT come-PL to   meeting tomorrow
       'We are trying to have plenty of people come to the meeting
       tomorrow.'

We can see now that genuine Niuean Equi and R-equi would be distinct in two significant ways. First, the former deletes only complement SUs, while the latter would delete complement DOs as well as SUs. Second, although there is no coreference constraint on initial configurations involving Equi governors, those involving R-equi governors would be subject to a Like Subject or Direct Object Constraint (67). Notice that the constraint does not follow from any intrinsic feature of the Two-NP analysis, but rather is motivated exclusively to account for the ungrammaticality of sentences like (65b) and (66b). Here the Raising analyis becomes more interesting than the Two-NP analysis, since the ungrammaticality of those sentences follows immediately from positing a Raising rule which operates only on SUs and DOs.

Furthermore, it is highly improbable that syntactic theory should allow a constraint like (67). Perlmutter's Like-Subject Constraint is apparently a constraint on agency or controllability: the would-be target for deletion must be able to control the event described by the embedded verb. But semantically, DOs are the least likely NPs to control acts. So it is implausible that a controllability constraint would identify SUs and DOs, to the exclusion of all other types of NPs. Since the Two-NP analysis would impose such a constraint on R-equi configurations, it is quite suspect as a possible analysis. Therefore, we are led to prefer the Raising analysis, which calls for no coreference constraint.

5.5   Idiom Chunks

The behavior of idioms in Raising sentences argues in two ways against the Two-NP analysis. Consider first the expression *pouli a fafo* 'it's dark', as in:

(70)   Kua teitei pouli tei   a   fafo.
       PERF nearly dark PERF ABS outside
       'It's nearly dark.'

Pouli 'dark' is the only verb in Niuean which allows *a fafo* 'outside' to appear as its SU, except that when this idiom is embedded in a Raising verb, *a fafo* optionally appears as the upstairs SU:

(71) Hāne kamata a   fafo   ke pouli.
     PROG begin   ABS outside SBJ dark
     'It's beginning to get dark.'

The Two-NP analysis would treat *a fafo* as the initial SU of *kamata* in (71), complicating selectional restrictions in an ad hoc way: *a fafo* could be an initial SU of *pouli* or any Raising verb, but not of any other verbs. Under the Raising analysis, *a fafo* in (71) is the derived SU of *kamata,* so the restriction that it be an initial SU only of *pouli* is maintained.

Now consider the idiom *oeli e tau matahui* 'get drunk' (lit., 'oil the knees'), as in:

(72) Loto a   au ke oeli e   tau matahui, ti   koli.
     like ABS I   SBJ oil ABS PL knee   then dance
     'I like to get a little drunk, then dance.'

The DO in this idiom *e tau matahui* 'the knees' optionally appears as the SU of a Raising verb. Thus, (73) has a figurative sense:

(73) Kua kamata tei   e   tau matahui ke oeli e   lautolu.
     PERF begin   PERF ABS PL knee   SBJ oil ERG THEY
     'They've begun to get a little drunk.'

The Two-NP analysis would claim that the initial structure of (73) contained two occurrences of *e tau matahui.* But on the idiomatic reading of (73), *e tau matahui* is nonreferential. Therefore, R-equi could not delete the downstairs occurrence under coreference. Since R-equi cannot be used to account for sentences like (73), the Two-NP analysis is inadequate. The Raising analysis accounts for (73) by claiming that *e tau matahui* originates in the complement clause and is the derived SU of *kamata.*

5.6   Reflexives and Reciprocals

A final argument against positing a version of Equi, R-equi, to derive Niuean Raising sentences involves reflexive and reciprocal clauses, which I describe briefly here. Reflexive in Niuean operates clause-internally, optionally marking a nonsubject with the postnominal particle *nī* under coreference with the SU. For example, *nī* may mark the reflexive DO in (74a) and the reflexive IO in (74b):

(74) a. Kitia he   tama fifine   a   ia   (nī)   he fakaata.
        see   ERG child female ABS her   REFL in mirror
        'The girl sees herself in the mirror.'

b. Ne fakafano mai e   au e   tohi ki a   au (nī).
PAST send   hither ERG I ABS letter to PERS me REFL
'I sent a letter to myself.'

Subjects may never be marked with reflexive *nī* under coreference with any clausemate.

Morphological reciprocal verbs are productively formed with the prefix *fe-* and the suffix *-aki:*

(75) Kua fe-kitia-aki   e   Lemani mo Maka a   laua.
PERF RECIP-see-RECIP ERG Lemani with Maka ABS them-DU
'Lemani and Maka see each other.'

Surprisingly, an oblique NP related reciprocally to its SU must not appear in surface structure. For example, the reciprocal IO is missing in:

(76) Kua fe-fakafano-aki   e   maua   e   tau tohi.
PERF RECIP-send-RECIP ERG we-DU-EX ABS PL letter
'We send each other letters.'

What is of interest here is the way reflexive and reciprocal clauses are treated by obligatory deletion rules in Niuean. Although Niuean Equi is in general obligatory, complement SUs related reflexively or reciprocally to a clausemate (i.e., are coreferential with a clausemate) are only optionally deleted when the conditions for Equi are met. Thus, the reflexive complement SU *e koe* 'you' in (77a) and the reciprocal complement SU *a laua* 'they' in (77b) may or may not be deleted under coreference with equi controllers:

(77) a. Fia manako nakai a   koe ke kitia (e   koe) a koe
want want   Q   ABS you SBJ see ERG you ABS you
i loto   he vai?
in middle of water
'Would you like to see yourself in the water?'

b. Kua amaamanaki e   nā   tama ke fe-tohitohi-aki
PERF hope   ABS pair boy SBJ RECIP-write-RECIP
hololoa (a   laua).
frequently ABS they-DU
'The two boys are hoping to write to each other frequently.'

When SUs or DOs are relativized in Niuean, they undergo a rule of Relative Deletion, which obligatorily deletes the relative noun under coreference with the head. Thus, the relative clause in (78) is ungrammatical if it includes a pronoun copy of the relativized SU:

(78) e   tagata ne   hoka (*e   ia) a   Maka
      ABS man [NONFUT stab   ERG he ABS Maka]
      'the man who stabbed Maka'

However, if a reflexive or reciprocal SU is relativized, Relative Deletion
applies only optionally. For example, the reflexive relative clause in
(79a) may include the SU pronoun *e ia* 'he', and the reciprocal relative
clause in (79b) may include the SU pronoun *a laua* 'they':

(79) a. e   tagata ne   hoka (e   ia) a   ia
         ABS man [NONFUT stab   ERG he ABS him]
         'the man who stabbed himself'
     b. e   nā fifine   ne   fe-ita-aki   (a   laua)
         ABS pair woman [NONFUT RECIP-angry-RECIP ABS they-DU]
         'the women who are angry at each other'

Although I cannot offer a satisfying explanation for the resistance
of Niuean reflexive and reciprocal SUs to deletion, the generalization
to be made based on (77) and (79) seems clear enough. Reflexive and
reciprocal SUs in Niuean optionally undergo deletion rules which are
otherwise obligatory.

Now the rule required under the Two-NP analysis to derive Raising
sentences, R-equi, would be an obligatory deletion rule. So the generalization which I have just motivated would predict that reflexive
and reciprocal SUs should undergo R-equi only optionally. Therefore,
from an initial structure like (80), the Two-NP analysis would derive
both (81a) and (81b), depending on whether or not R-equi applied. This
would produce the wrong result, however, because (81b) is ungrammatical:

(80)

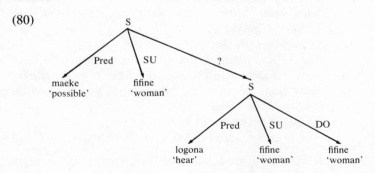

(81) a. Liga ai maeke e   fifine   ke logona a   ia (nī).
         likely not possible ABS woman SBJ hear   ABS her REFL
         'The woman couldn't hear herself.'

    b. *Liga ai   maeke   e   fifine   ke logona e   ia   a
       likely not possible ABS woman SBJ hear   ERG she ABS
       ia   (nī).
       her REFL
       (The woman couldn't hear herself.)

Compare the ungrammatical (81b) with the analogous dative-of-interest sentence (82). The complement reflexive SU *e ia* 'she' may appear in (82), since it only optionally undergoes genuine Equi controlled by *he fifine* 'at the woman':

(82) Liga ai   maeke   he fifine   ke logona e   ia   a
       likely not possible at woman SBJ hear   ERG she ABS
       ia   (nī).
       her REFL
       'The woman was unable to hear herself.'

Similarly, R-equi would need to apply obligatorily to the complement reciprocal SU *e laua* 'they' in the Raising sentence (83a), since (83b) is ungrammatical. In contrast, genuine Equi, which is generally obligatory, only optionally deletes *e laua* in a dative-of-interest sentence like (83c):

(83) a. Kua nākai maeke a   Lemani mo Maka ke
       PERF not   possible ABS Lemani with Maka SBJ
       fe-kitia-aki   a   laua.
       RECIP-see-RECIP ABS them-DU
       'Lemani and Maka cannot see each other.'
   b. *Kua nākai maeke a   Lemani mo Maka ke
       PERF not   possible ABS Lemani with Maka SBJ
       fe-kitia-aki   e   laua   a   laua.
       RECIP-see-RECIP ERG they-DU ABS them-DU
       (Lemani and Maka cannot see each other.)
   c. Kua nākai maeke i a   Lemani mo Maka ke
       PERF not   possible at PERS Lemani with Maka SBJ
       fe-kitia-aki   e   laua   a   laua.
       RECIP-see-RECIP ERG they-DU ABS them-DU
       'Lemani and Maka are unable to see each other.'

The facts in this section constitute an interesting syntactic argument against the Two-NP analysis. It was established in §§5.1–5.5 that R-equi would have to be an obligatory deletion rule. But, as we see here, obligatory deletion rules are optional in reflexive and reciprocal clauses in Niuean. R-equi would thus be anomalous in having to be obligatory in an environment in which other usually obligatory deletion rules are optional. What the facts presented here suggest is that Niuean Raising sentences simply do not involve deletion.

The ungrammaticality of (81b) and (83b) follows immediately from the Raising analysis. A reflexive or reciprocal SU which undergoes Raising is removed from the complement clause in which it originates, so it automatically cannot surface in that clause as a pronoun copy.

6   Conclusion

It has been shown that Niuean has a version of Raising which operates on complement subjects and direct objects. A variety of syntactic facts about Niuean indicated that the Raising analysis sketched in §2 is superior to the alternative analyses considered. In §§3 and 4 it was established that a raised NP originates as a complement subject or direct object, but also acts as the subject of the higher, governing verb. And §5 argued that a raised NP must not originate in the higher clause and trigger deletion of a coreferential NP in the complement clause. In particular, the facts ruled out an analysis of Niuean Raising as a version of Equi-NP Deletion. Since §§3–5 collectively show that Niuean Raising promotes an NP from a complement clause to the higher clause, it is desirable to identify the rule as a version of Raising.

Because Niuean Raising applies to complement direct objects as well as subjects, it violates Postal's (1974) suggestion that Raising should be restricted universally to complement subjects, a view which has been implicit in most work on Raising in both transformational and relational frameworks. Thus, Raising cannot be represented in universal grammar simply as:[17]

(84)   Raise the subject of a complement.

The failure of (84) raises the question of how universal grammar may be made flexible enough to recognize the Niuean rule as an instance of universal Raising. Apparently, the representation of Raising in universal grammar should indicate that it must operate on complement subjects and may operate on complement direct objects, as in the following statement, where the parenthesized condition is optionally included on a language-particular basis:

(85)   Raise the subject (or direct object) of a complement.

The prediction made by (85) is that while there are languages in which Raising applies only to complement subjects, e.g., English, and ones in which Raising applies only to complement subjects and direct objects, e.g., Niuean, in no language will Raising apply to complement direct objects but not subjects. Of course, the claim made by (85) can be maintained only if a principled distinction may be drawn universally between Raising and Tough Movement, since Tough Movement is allowed to raise complement direct objects but not subjects. I suspect that the two rules can ultimately be distinguished in universal grammar in terms of the semantics of possible governing predicates for each rule, although the issue of such a semantic characterization is clearly beyond the scope of this paper.

Appendix: Niuean Raising, Case Marking, and the Cycle

Presupposing a derivational theory of syntax, the interaction of Raising with Case Marking in Niuean provides an interesting argument for the notion of cyclic rule application. Consider case marking in complement clauses from which a DO has been raised, as in (13). In order to account for the ergative complement SUs in (13), Case Marking must apply in the complement before Raising, because only prior to Raising does the complement clause contain a DO. If Case Marking were to apply in the complement clause after raising of the complement DO, the complement SU would appear in the absolutive. But the result of such a derivation is ungrammatical, as shown by:

(86) a. *To   maeke   e   tama ē   ke lagomatai e   ekekafo.
         FUT possible ABS child this SBJ help   ABS doctor
         (This child could be helped by the doctor.)
     b. *Kua kamata e   akau ke hala e   tama.
         PERF begin ABS tree SBJ cut ABS child
         (The tree has begun to be cut down by the child.)

Given the above facts, it is clear that Raising and Case Marking cannot simply apply freely with respect to each other. Instead, the interaction of the two rules must be constrained to insure that Case Marking in a complement clause always precedes and never follows Raising from the complement.

Let us consider briefly various noncyclical theories of rule interaction to see how they might account for the facts above. First, consider a theory with no cycle which allows pairs of rules to be extrinsically ordered. One might propose for Niuean that Case Marking is ordered before Raising, to account for the sentences in (13) while blocking the derivation of the ungrammatical ones in (86). However, this ordering constraint would produce incorrect results in derivations involving raising of a transitive complement SU. Case Marking would only be able to apply to the transitive complement SU before Raising, placing it in the ergative. This would predict, for example, that (87b) but not (87a) is grammatical, when in fact the reverse is the case. Compare (87a) and (87b) with (87c), in which Raising has not applied:

(87) a. To   maeke   e   ekekafo ke lagomatai e   tama ē.
         FUT possible ABS doctor   SBJ help   ABS child this
         'The doctor could help this child.'

     b. *To   maeke   he   ekekafo ke lagomatai e   tama ē.
         FUT possible ERG doctor   SBJ help   ABS child this
         (The doctor could help this child.)

     c. To   maeke   ke lagomatai he   ekekafo e   tama ē.
         FUT possible SBJ help   ERG doctor   ABS child this
         'The doctor could help this child.'

In the derivation of (87a), Case Marking must place *ekekafo* 'doctor' in the absolute after Raising has already applied, since prior to Raising *ekekafo* is a transitive SU. This argues that in a noncyclical theory extrinsic rule ordering cannot account for the interaction of Niuean Raising and Case Marking.

Since Case Marking is an obligatory rule but Raising is an optional one, it is worth considering whether their interaction could be accounted for by Ringen's (1972) Obligatory-Optional Precedence principle:

(88)   If a representation meets the structural description of both an obligatory and an optional rule, the obligatory rule must apply to the representation. (Ringen 1972, p. 272)

This principle would have to be able to account for both (13a) and (87a), which have the same initial structure:

(89)

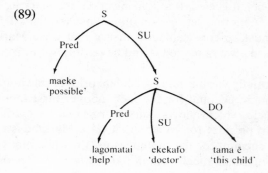

The conditions for Case Marking and Raising are both met in (89), so Obligatory-Optional Precedence would dictate that Case Marking, the obligatory rule, must apply giving the derived structure:[18]

(90)

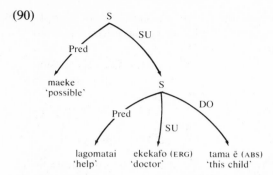

Raising the complement DO in (90) would produce:

(91)

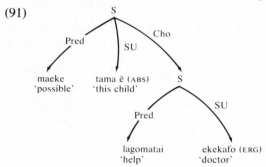

However, Obligatory-Optional Precedence would not prevent Case Marking from applying again to (91), this time placing *ekekafo* in the absolutive and producing the ungrammatical (86a) instead of (13a). One might avoid this result by claiming that Case Marking cannot reapply to NPs which have already undergone it, but then sentences like (87a) could not be accounted for. The initial structure of (86a) is represented above in (89). As before, Obligatory-Optional Precedence would dictate that Case Marking must apply giving (90). Raising the complement SU in (90) would produce:

(92)

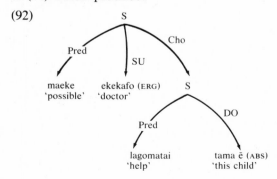

Under the assumption that Case Marking cannot reapply to NPs that have already undergone it, (92) would have to surface as the ungrammatical (87b), and (87a) could not be generated. To summarize, Ringen's Obligatory-Optional Precedence principle cannot explain the interaction of Case Marking and Raising in Niuean, since it would fail to account either for (13a) or for (87a).

Finally, let us consider a theory with no cycle in which rule interaction is constrained by an antibleeding principle such as (93), which I have taken from Breckenridge and Hakulinen (1976):

(93)   No rule can apply so as to destroy the environment for an obligatory rule which would otherwise have been able to apply. (Breckenridge and Hakulinen 1976, p. 58)

Notice that such a theory would account for sentences like those in (13), in which obligatory Case Marking applies in the complement before Raising applies to the complement DO. Obviously, such derivations conform to constraint (93). But we must also determine whether (93) would block the derivation of ungrammatical sentences like those in (86). Consider once again the initial structure represented in (89). Applying Raising to the complement DO would produce:

(94)

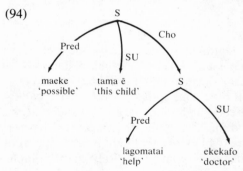

But this structure may still undergo Case Marking to produce:

(95)

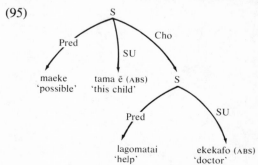

The derivation sketched above would not be blocked by the antibleed-ing principle in (93), because Raising does not destroy the environment for the obligatory rule of Case Marking. This means that in a noncyclical theory (93) cannot account for the ungrammaticality of sentences like those in (86). Therefore, an antibleeding principle like (93) fails to explain the interaction of Case Marking and Raising in Niuean.

Having reviewed the inadequacies of several noncyclical approaches to the Niuean data above, let us turn to consider how a theory incor-porating the cycle and the principle of Strict Cyclicity accounts for the same facts. Starting with the initial structure represented in (89), the conditions for Case Marking are met on the lower cycle, so it must apply, giving:

(96)

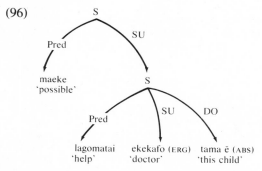

On the next cycle, Raising may operate on the complement DO, pro-ducing (91). Following Raising, Case Marking applies on the higher cycle, placing *tama ē* 'this child', which is an intransitive SU in the higher clause, once again in the absolutive. Strict Cyclicity prevents Case Marking on the higher cycle from reapplying to the complement SU, which must therefore remain in the ergative. This accounts both for the grammaticality of (13a) and for the ungrammaticality of (87a). Returning to the structure in (96), Raising on the higher cycle may also operate on the complement SU, giving (92). As before, the conditions for Case Marking are met on the higher cycle after Raising has applied. Since *ekekafo* is a derived intransitive SU, it must be placed in the absolutive. This predicts correctly that (87a) but not (87b) is gram-matical. So the cyclic principle and Strict Cyclicity account for the full range of facts about the interaction of Raising with Case Marking in Niuean.

I have just shown that a noncyclical theory of rule interaction cannot explain certain facts about Raising and Case Marking in Niuean by appealing to extrinsic rule ordering, a obligatory-optional precedence principle, or an antibleeding principle. Since the obligatory-optional and antibleeding principles each deal adequately with a wide range of

rule interactions which originally motivated the cycle in transformational literature, their failure to account for the Niuean facts is significant. In contrast, the cyclic principle and Strict Cyclicity straightforwardly explain the facts presented above. Therefore, assuming a derivational theory of syntax, the interaction of Raising with Case Marking
in Niuean should be taken to argue in favor of the notions of cyclic
rule application and Strict Cyclicity.

Notes

1. Niuean, which is closely related to Tongan, is the first language of roughly
3,500 people on Niue Island and another 7,000 of the Niueans now living in
New Zealand.
2. This paper is concerned only with Raising to Subject, though there are
several verbs in Niuean which govern Raising to Object. Chap. 3 of Seiter 1980
presents a unified treatment of Raising to Subject and Raising to Object in
Niuean. I show there that Raising to Object also operates on complement direct
objects as well as complement subjects.
3. Bach (1971), Postal (1970), and Ross (1970), among others, advocated a
theory of this sort in a transformational framework.
4. The analysis I forward here will be based on a derivational version of
relational grammar essentially like that represented in Johnson 1977 and Perlmutter and Postal 1974. Relational grammar as currently conceived by Perlmutter, Postal, and Johnson rejects the notion of syntactic derivation (see
Perlmutter and Postal 1977). The conclusions I reach here would, I believe,
have analogous implications in current nonderivational relational grammar.
5. Niuean Raising is, to my knowledge, the only clearly attested instance of
its type. Trithart (1976) reports sentences in Chichewa which appear to involve
raising of a complement object to the verb -ganiz- 'think'. She notes, however,
that the acceptability of such sentences is subject to a good deal of variation
among her consultants. Furthermore, the sentences convey a special contras-
tive emphasis which is not typical of Raising sentences. So it is unclear whether
the Chichewa rule can be shown to be an instance of Raising. Chung (1978)
argues that in Samoan, while some verbs govern Subject Raising, others govern
a type of Raising which is available to complement NPs regardless of syntactic
type, and which under certain conditions results in a complement pronoun
copy coreferential with the raised NP.
6. In the Niuean orthography g = [ŋ], and before front vowels t = [s]. The
orthography distinguishes long vowels (e.g., $\bar{a}$) from rearticulated like vowels
(e.g., aa). Word stress is penultimate.
   The glosses include the following abbreviations:

Abs	absolutive	Pers	personal article
Agt	oblique agent	Pl	plural
Du	dual	Pro	pronoun copy
Erg	ergative	Prog	progressive
Ex	exclusive	Q	question particle
Fut	future	Recip	reciprocal
Inc	inclusive	Refl	reflexive
Nonfut	nonfuture	Sbj	subjunctive
Perf	perfect		

7. There are three types of occasional exceptions to the scheme in (8). Locative or time NPs sometimes precede a SU or DO:

(i) Ne fakamau he aho faiumu   a   Ray mo Lee.
     PAST marry   on day Saturday ABS Ray with Lee
     'Ray and Lee were married on Saturday.'

Indirect objects, usually pronominal, and benefactive pronouns may precede a DO, but never a SU:

(ii) Ne age e   au ki a   ia   e   tohi haau.
      PAST give ERG I to PERS him ABS letter your
      'I gave him your letter.'

And goals taken from a small class of pronominally case-marked local nouns optionally precede an intransitive SU:

(iii) Ne hake ki uta   au mo e nofo ai   he māla.
       PAST go-up to inland I and stay then on plantation
       'I landed and stayed on the plantation.'

8. Sentences with a raised DO differ subtly from their nonraising counterparts in topicality, emphasis, and so forth. This semantic difference is approximated by the English translations, which involve a raised passive SU.

9. The Relational Annihilation Law was replaced by a nonderivational analogue, the Chômeur Condition, in Perlmutter and Postal 1977.

Nothing in the discussion that follows hinges on the grammatical status of the clausal complement after Raising has applied.

10. Structures (15–19) are only intended to indicate clause membership and GRs. The branches of each structure are unordered, and the labels Pred, SU, etc., indicating relations borne by verbal and nominal dependents to a clause node S, are not supposed to be category labels, so these informal representations should not be interpreted as phrase markers.

11. In the appendix to this paper, I argue that the interaction of Raising with Case Marking in Niuean provides evidence for the notions of cyclic rule application and Strict Cyclicity.

12. The structure of (42b) involves a predicate adjective *taha* 'one' whose SU is the relative clause *hāku a pene ne kua maeke e tau fakatino mitaki ke tā aki* 'the pen of mine which good pictures can be drawn with'.

13. Seiter (1979) argues that Niuean Instrumental Advancement violates Perlmutter and Postal's Relational Annihilation and Stratal Uniqueness Laws. Thus, the initial DO in the complement of (44) continues to bear the DO relation, even after its clausemate has become a derived DO.

14. Reordering rules which create sentences superficially resembling Raising sentences, without changing the clause membership of an NP, are actually attested in some verb-initial languages. For instance, Sandra Chung (personal communication) claims that certain sentential adverbs in Maori govern such a rule, while Maori negative verbs govern genuine Raising. And Stenson (1976, pp. 115–23) argues that sentences in Modern Irish which appear to involve Raising to Object actually involve reordering of an NP within a complement clause.

15. Once a transitive SU has been placed in the possessive, the DO in a nominalization may not appear in the absolutive, but is instead case marked with *i* for pronouns and proper nouns and *he* for common nouns, as in (50a). A possessivized DO must immediately follow the nominalized verb, as in (50b),

whether the SU appears overtly or is unspecified. See Seiter (1980) for a more detailed description of Niuean nominalizations.

16. It is interesting that Zero Pronominalization, which is generally optional, cannot optionally delete complement nonsubjects under coreference with Equi controllers.

17. Specifically, Postal (1974) proposed that Raising might be represented in universal grammar simply as:

(i)   Promote the subject of a complement. (Postal 1974, p. 288)

Postal's use of the term 'promotion' here includes both 'ascensions', some of which assign an NP a GR in a higher clause, and 'advancements', which assign an NP a higher rank within a clause along the relational hierarchy:

(ii)   Subject > Direct Object > Indirect Object > nonterms.

Given the statement of Raising as a promotion in (i), the fact that it is an ascension rather than an advancement is predicted by specifying which nominal is to be promoted: for a complement SU to be promoted, it must ascend to the higher clause, since it cannot advance within the complement clause.

However, stating Niuean Raising along the lines of (i) will not work:

(iii)   Promote the subject or direct object of a complement.

The trouble is that through (iii), a SU would ascend to the higher clause, but a DO might, incorrectly, only advance to SU in the complement clause. So Postal's representation of Raising in (i), even when extended to DOs, is incorrect because it is too general. Instead, the statement of Raising in universal grammar must explicitly mention that the complement NP it operates on is promoted to the higher clause, i.e., that it is an ascension rule.

18. In the representations below, the assignment of a nominal to a case category is indicated informally by (ERG) and (ABS).

References

Bach, E. 1971. "Questions." *Linguistic Inquiry* 2:153–66.
Breckenridge, J., and Hakulinen, A. 1976. "Cycle and After." In S. Steever et al., eds. *Papers from the Parasession on Diachronic Syntax*. Chicago Linguistics Society, Chicago, Illinois.
Chung, S. L. 1978. *Case Marking and Grammatical Relations in Polynesian*. Austin and London: University of Texas Press.
Chung, S., and Seiter, W. 1977. "On the Passive-to-Ergative Reanalysis and the History of Relativization and Raising in Polynesian." Mimeo, University of California, San Diego.
Johnson, D. E. 1977. "On Relational Constraints on Grammars." In P. Cole and J. Sadock, eds. *Syntax and Semantics: Grammatical Relations*. New York: Academic Press.
Perlmutter, D. M. 1971. *Deep and Surface Structure Constraints in Syntax*. New York: Holt, Rinehart & Winston.
Perlmutter, D., and Postal, P. 1974. Linguistic Institute Lectures, University of Massachusetts, Amherst.
Perlmutter, D., and Postal, P. 1977. "Toward a Universal Characterization of Passivization," in K. Whistler, et al., eds. *Proceedings of the Third Annual Meeting of the Berkeley Linguistics Society,* Berkeley, California. Reprinted in this volume.

Perlmutter, D., and Postal, P. (this volume) "The Relational Succession Law."

Postal, P. M. 1970. "The Method of Universal Grammar." In P. Garvin, ed. *Method and Theory in Linguistics*. The Hague: Mouton.

Postal, P. M. 1974. *On Raising: One Rule of English Grammar and Its Theoretical Implications*. Cambridge, Mass.: MIT Press.

Ringen, C. 1972. "On Arguments for Rule Ordering." *Foundations of Language* 8:266–73.

Ross, J. R. 1970. "Gapping and the Order of Constituents." In M. Bierwisch and K. Heidolph, eds. *Progress in Linguistics*. The Hague: Mouton.

Seiter, W. J. 1979. "Instrumental Advancement in Niuean." *Linguistic Inquiry* 10:595–621.

Seiter, W. J. 1980. *Studies in Niuean Syntax*. New York: Garland Publishing Co.

Stenson, N. J. 1976. "Topics in Irish Syntax and Semantics." Ph.D. diss., University of California, San Diego.

Trithart, M. L. 1976. "Relational Grammar and Chichewa Subjectivization Rules." Masters thesis, UCLA.

Whistler, K., et al., eds. 1978. *Proceedings of the Fourth Annual Meeting of the Berkeley Linguistics Society*. Berkeley: University of California.

10 Clause Reduction in Spanish

Judith L. Aissen and David M. Perlmutter

Introduction

This paper is a report of work on a number of syntactic phenomena in Spanish that we seek to explain by positing a rule of Clause Reduction that makes dependents of a complement verb dependents of the matrix verb. Here we confine ourselves to data from Spanish though similar arguments can generally be made for Italian.

Most of the discussion in this paper is couched in terms of the theoretical framework of relational grammar proposed by Perlmutter and Postal. In this framework, the structure of a sentence is regarded as a network of grammatical relations or, more simply, as a 'relational network'. For the purposes of this paper, we need only be concerned about a proper subset of the grammatical relations posited in that theory: the relations 'subject of', 'direct object of', and 'indirect object of'. Following Perlmutter and Postal, we will refer to these grammatical relations as '1', '2', and '3', respectively, and represent sentence structures as relational networks. For example, the structure underlying the sentence

(1)   Pablo le dio un regalo a Mercedes.
      'Pablo gave a gift to Mercedes.'

is represented as:[1]

(2)

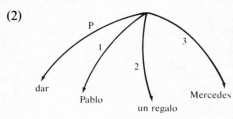

360

This clause consists of a predicate and three 'nominal dependents'. The 'arc' headed by each nominal dependent indicates that the nominal in question bears a grammatical relation to the clause and the numeral on each arc indicates *which* grammatical relation it is. The relative order of the 1, the 2, and the 3 in (2) is arbitrary, since the relational network represents grammatical relations and not the linear order of elements in surface structure.

In certain cases, it is necessary to make further distinctions. For example, consider the sentence:

(3)   Los ministros fueron criticados por la prensa.
      'The ministers were criticized by the press.'

Traditional grammarians would have said that in (3) *la prensa* is the 'logical subject' of *criticar* and *los ministros* is the 'grammatical subject'. Transformational grammarians would say that in (3), *la prensa* is the 'deep (structure) subject' and *los ministros* is the 'derived subject'. In Perlmutter and Postal's theory of relational grammar, in (3) *la prensa* is the 'initial 1' of *criticar* and *los ministros* is the final 1. [Editor's note: For a definition of these terms see Chapter 3.]

1   Two Rules of Spanish
1.1   Clitic Placement

A nonpronominal final 2 or 3 of a verb generally follows its verb in surface structure, as does *el edificio nuevo* in:

(4)   Eduardo vio el edificio nuevo.
      'Eduardo saw the new building.'

A pronominal object is in the strong form when it occurs under emphasis and in positions of contrast. In such cases, it is subject to the same word order rules as nonpronominal objects.

(5)   Eduardo no la vio a *ella* sino a *él*.
      'Eduardo didn't see *her* but *him*.'

Noncontrastive and nonemphatic object pronouns are represented by clitics. Spanish has a rule of Clitic Placement that attaches a clitic

This work was supported in part by the National Science Foundation through Grant No. BNS 76-00764 to the Massachusetts Institute of Technology. We are indebted to Paul Postal for comments on an earlier version of this paper and to the native speakers of Spanish who put their intuitions at our disposal, especially David Nasjleti, María Graña, Bárbara Cigarroa, Marisa Escribano Clements, and Luis Restrepo.

An earlier version of this paper appeared in the *Proceedings of the Second Annual Meeting of the Berkeley Linguistics Society*.

This paper owes much to Rivas 1974. Rivas saw that the verbs allowing 'clitic climbing' also manifest agreement with complement objects in *se*-constructions and allow what in our terms is Reflexive Passive with complement objects.

to the verb of which it is a dependent. When a clitic is attached to a finite verb, it precedes the verb:

(6)   Eduardo *la* vio.
      'Eduardo saw her.'

When a clitic is attached to a nonfinite verb form (either an infinitive or a gerund), it follows the verb:

(7) a.   Quiere ver*la*.
         'He wants to see her.'
    b.   Sigue viéndo*la*.
         'He continues seeing her.'

Since this contrast in clitic position is predictable from the finiteness of the verb, we will not be concerned with it further here. When clitics are attached to verbs, the combination of clitic plus verb forms a single phonological word. This is reflected in Spanish orthography when the clitic follows the verb, but not when it precedes it.

1.2   Subject Pronoun Drop

In general, nonemphatic and noncontrastive subject pronouns do not occur in surface structure in Spanish. They are deleted by a rule we call 'Subject Pronoun Drop'. In the sentences in (7), the third person singular subject pronoun has been deleted by Subject Pronoun Drop.

2   Two Classes of Verbs in Spanish

The matrix verbs in (8) contrast systematically with those in (9).

(8) a.   Luis quiere comer las manzanas amarillas.
         'Luis wants to eat the yellow apples.'
    b.   Luis trató de comer las manzanas amarillas.
         'Luis tried to eat the yellow apples.'
    c.   Luis suele comer las manzanas amarillas.
         'Luis tends to eat (the) yellow apples.'

(9) a.   Luis insistió en comer las manzanas amarillas.
         'Luis insisted on eating the yellow apples.'
    b.   Luis soñó con comer las manzanas amarillas.
         'Luis dreamed of eating the yellow apples.'
    c.   Luis parece haber comido las manzanas amarillas.
         'Luis seems to have eaten the yellow apples.'

Without attempting to justify it here, we assume that (8a, b) and (9a, b) involve Equi controlled by the matrix subject, while (8c) and (9c) involve Subject-to-Subject Raising. A pronominal object of the infinitive cliticizes to the verb.

(10) a. Luis quiere comer*las*.
         'Luis wants to eat them.'
     b. Luis trató de comer*las*.
         'Luis tried to eat them.'
     c. Luis suele comer*las*.
         'Luis tends to eat them.'

(11) a. Luis insistió en comer*las*.
         'Luis insisted on eating them.'
     b. Luis soñó con comer*las*.
         'Luis dreamed of eating them.'
     c. Luis parece haber*las* comido.
         'Luis seems to have eaten them.'

The point of prime importance for us here is that, alongside (10), the following sentences are also grammatical:

(12) a. Luis *las* quiere comer.
         'Luis wants to eat them.'
     b. Luis *las* trató de comer.
         'Luis tried to eat them.'
     c. Luis *las* suele comer.
         'Luis tends to eat them.'

In (12) the pronominal clitic that is the initial 2 of the complement verb appears on the finite matrix verb. If the matrix verb is one of the matrix verbs in (9), however, this is not possible. Thus, alongside (11), the following examples are ungrammatical:

(13) a. *Luis *las* insistió en comer.
     b. *Luis *las* soñó con comer.
     c. *Luis *las* parece haber comido.

In brief, two classes of verbs must be distinguished in Spanish according to whether or not they can support a clitic pronoun that originates as a dependent of a complement verb (henceforth 'complement clitic'). We will refer to verbs that can support complement clitics as 'trigger verbs' and to those that cannot as 'nontrigger verbs'. Thus, the matrix verbs of (8) are trigger verbs while those of (9) are nontrigger verbs.

For a given speaker, most verbs that govern infinitival or gerund complements fall clearly into one class or the other. However, the membership of each class varies somewhat from speaker to speaker. In this paper we present a hypothesis to account for the difference in syntactic behavior between trigger verbs and nontrigger verbs. This hypothesis does not predict the class any particular verb will belong to for any individual speaker. However, it does offer a means of testing the class membership of a particular verb for any speaker and makes certain predictions about the syntactic behavior of the verb once its class membership is known.[2]

Below is an illustrative list of trigger and nontrigger verbs.

Trigger Verbs	Nontrigger Verbs
soler 'tend'	*parecer* 'seem'
acabar (*de*) 'have just'	*deber* (*de*) 'must (epistemic)'
querer 'want'	*insistir* (*en*) 'insist'
tratar (*de*) 'try'	*soñar* (*con*) 'dream (of)'
poder 'can, be able'	*decidirse* (*a*) 'decide (to)'
deber 'ought, should'	*evitar* 'avoid'
empezar (*a*) 'begin'	*sugerir* 'suggest'
terminar (*de*) 'finish'	*pedir* 'ask'
continuar 'continue'	*decir* 'say'
seguir 'keep on'	*afirmar* 'affirm'
dejar (*de*) 'stop'	
volver (*a*) 're-, again'	
ordenar 'order'	
permitir 'permit'	

3   Two Hypotheses Concerning the Difference between Trigger Verbs and Nontrigger Verbs

3.1   The Clitic Climbing Hypothesis

Under the Clitic Climbing Hypothesis, the grammar of Spanish contains a rule of Clitic Climbing that optionally moves clitics from a subordinate clause into a higher clause (under conditions that need not concern us here), accounting for the position of the clitic pronouns in (12). Under this hypothesis, trigger verbs are characterized as triggering Clitic Climbing, while nontrigger verbs do not trigger this rule.

3.2   The Clause Reduction Hypothesis

Under the Clause Reduction hypothesis, trigger verbs differ from nontrigger verbs in that they trigger a rule of Clause Reduction that makes dependents of the complement verb dependents of the matrix verb. Consider (8a). Without Clause Reduction, *las manzanas amarillas* is the direct object of only *comer*. With Clause Reduction, however, this nominal is also the direct object of *querer*.

Under the Clause Reduction hypothesis, there is no need for a rule of Clitic Climbing. The rule of Clitic Placement attaches each clitic to the verb in the highest clause of which it is a dependent. Thus, if instead of *las manzanas amarillas* the initial 2 of *comer* is pronominal, and if

Clause Reduction is not triggered, the pronoun is a dependent only of *comer* and therefore is attached to *comer;* the resulting sentence is (10a). If, however, Clause Reduction makes it a dependent of *querer,* Clitic Placement attaches it to *querer,* and (12a) results.

Under the Clause Reduction hypothesis, trigger verbs are characterized as permitting Clause Reduction, while nontrigger verbs do not allow this rule. Since both the sentences in (10) and those in (12) are grammatical, Clause Reduction is an optional rule.

4   Evidence for Clause Reduction: Constraints on Clitic Climbing

In §4 we show that the Clause Reduction hypothesis immediately makes two predictions that the Clitic Climbing hypothesis does not make. In each case a grammar that incorporates a rule of Clitic Climbing will be forced to postulate an additional constraint that is unnecessary in a grammar with Clause Reduction. We conclude that the data in §4 constitutes evidence for rejecting the Clitic Climbing hypothesis in favor of the Clause Reduction hypothesis.

4.1   Multiple Clitic Dependents of a Single Embedded Verb

Consider first the case of a complement verb that has more than one clitic dependent, as in

(14)   Quiero mostrár*telos.*
        I + want show + you + them
        'I want to show them to you.'

In (14), both *te* and *los* are clitic dependents of the complement verb *mostrar.* Under the Clause Reduction hypothesis, (14) results from a structure that has not undergone Clause Reduction. If the underlying structure undergoes Clause Reduction, *te* and *los* will become dependents of *querer* and Clitic Placement will consequently attach them to that verb, producing the sentence

(15)   *Te los* quiero mostrar.
        'I want to show them to you.'

Under the Clause Reduction hypothesis, there are only two possibilities: either the structure undergoes Clause Reduction or it does not. The former produces (14), while the latter produces (15); no other sentences can arise from the structure in question.

Under the Clitic Climbing hypothesis, however, there are additional possibilities. Since Clitic Climbing is an optional rule, there is nothing to prevent one complement clitic from moving to the matrix verb while the other stays behind. This would produce the following ungrammatical sentences:

(16) **Te* quiero mostrar*los*.
(17) **Los* quiero mostrar*te*.

A grammar that incorporates a rule of Clitic Climbing therefore needs an additional constraint:[3]

(18)   The Multiple Clitic Constraint
        If a verb has more than one clitic dependent, then either all clitic dependents of that verb undergo Clitic Climbing or none do.

A grammar that accounts for the phenomenon by means of a rule of Clause Reduction, however, cannot generate *(16–17) and thereby automatically predicts that these sentences will be ungrammatical. In other words, the Clause Reduction hypothesis explains why these sentences are ungrammatical. The ungrammaticality of sentences like *(16–17) constitutes evidence for rejecting the Clitic Climbing hypothesis, which needs an additional device to account for them, in favor of the Clause Reduction hypothesis, which explains them.

4.2   Intersecting Clitic Climbing

Now consider a three-storey structure such as (19) in which the second and third verbs each have a pronominal dependent, and the two higher verbs both optionally trigger Clause Reduction.[4]

(19)   Quiero permitir*te* hacer*lo*.
        'I want to allow you to do it.'

In (19), without Clause Reduction, *te* is the 3 only of *permitir* and *lo* is the 2 only of *hacer;* as a result, *te* is attached to *permitir* and *lo* is attached to *hacer* in the surface structure of (19).

Consider what can happen to the structure underlying (19) under the Clause Reduction hypothesis. In a structure in which only *permitir* triggers Clause Reduction, *lo* will become a dependent of *permitir,* producing the sentence

(20)   Quiero permitír*telo* hacer.
        'I want to allow you to do it.'

In a structure in which both *querer* and *permitir* trigger Clause Reduction, both *te* and *lo* will become dependents of *querer,* producing the sentence

(21)   *Te lo* quiero permitir hacer.
        'I want to allow you to do it.'

In a structure in which *querer* triggers Clause Reduction but *permitir* does not, *te* will become a dependent of *querer* but *lo* will remain a dependent of *hacer*. The result will be the sentence

(22)   *Te* quiero permitir hacer*lo*.
       'I want to allow you to do it.'

Finally, if neither *querer* nor *permitir* triggers Clause Reduction, *te* will remain a dependent of *permitir* and *lo* will remain a dependent of *hacer,* resulting in (19). Under the Clause Reduction hypothesis, this exhausts the possibilities.

Under the Clitic Climbing hypothesis, however, there is still another possibility. Since Clitic Climbing is optional, there is nothing to prevent *te* from moving to *querer* and *lo* from moving to *permitir* in the same structure. The result, however, is ungrammatical:

(23)   **Te* quiero permitir*lo* hacer.

A grammar that incorporates an optional rule of Clitic Climbing thus needs some device to prevent sentences like *(23) from being generated. But under the Clause Reduction hypothesis, the ungrammaticality of sentences like *(23) follows automatically, without any additional devices. Thus, unless it can be shown that the additional device or devices needed by the Clitic Climbing hypothesis to prevent sentences like *(23) are motivated independently,[5] the ungrammaticality of such sentences constitutes grounds for rejecting the Clitic Climbing hypothesis in favor of the Clause Reduction hypothesis.[6]

5   Second Type of Evidence for Clause Reduction: Reflexive Passive
5.1   Reflexive Passive

Sentences (24–26) are produced by the rule we call 'Reflexive Passive', which advances a 2 to 1. This advancement produces sentences in which the clitic *se* (the third person reflexive pronoun) accompanies the verb. We therefore call this construction by the traditional name of 'Reflexive Passive'.

(24)   Las propiedades se vendieron ayer.
       'The pieces of property were sold yesterday.'
(25)   Estas canciones se cantan siempre primero.
       'These songs are always sung first.'
(26)   Esta construcción se emplea con toda clase de sujetos.
       'This construction is used with all kinds of subjects.'

In each case, the initial 2 of the verb has advanced to 1. In these examples, *las propiedades, estas canciones,* and *esta construcción* are the final 1s of their respective verbs.

Spanish thus has two distinct rules that advance a 2 to 1. Example (24), produced by Reflexive Passive, contrasts with (27), produced by Passive.

(27)   Las propiedades fueron vendidas ayer.
        'The pieces of property were sold yesterday.'

In both (24) and (27), *las propiedades,* the initial 2 of *vender,* has advanced to 1. However, (27) has passive morphology, with *fueron* (a form of the auxiliary verb *ser*) and *vendidas* (the past passive participle of *vender*). In both (24) and (27), the finite verb is plural in agreement with its final 1, *las propiedades.* The two constructions differ in another way. In an ordinary passive, the initial 1 can appear as the object of the preposition *por* 'by' while this is impossible in the reflexive passive:

(28)   Las propiedades fueron vendidas por los dueños ayer.
        'The pieces of property were sold by the owners yesterday.'
(29)   *Las propiedades se vendieron por los dueños ayer.

The initial 1 of the construction illustrated by (24–26) is understood to be human. It never appears in surface structure in Spanish. We will refer to it as PRO. It is probably the entity that is realized as *on* in French and *man* in German.

The initial 2 that advances to 1 in sentences like (24–26) we will call the 'pivot nominal'.

In §5.2 we briefly sketch four arguments that the pivot nominals in (24–26) are final 1s. In §5.3 we show that Reflexive Passive operates on the output of Clause Reduction, thus providing further evidence for Clause Reduction in Spanish.

5.2   The Subjecthood of the Pivot Nominal in Reflexive Passives

We now briefly sketch three pieces of evidence that the pivot nominal in reflexive passives in the final 1 of the verb and not its final 2.

The first piece of evidence comes from word order. Spanish has considerable freedom of word order, but in the natural order used in many situations the final 1 precedes the verb. The fact that the pivot nominal precedes the verb in (24–26) is thus evidence that it is the final 1.

The second piece of evidence comes from the pronominal form of the pivot nominal in reflexive passives. Final 2s appear as accusative pronouns, as in

(30)   *Las* vendimos ayer.
        'We sold them yesterday.'

But replacement of the pivot nominals in reflexive passives by accusative pronouns results in ungrammaticality:[7]

(31) *Se *las* vendieron ayer.

(32) *Se *las* cantan siempre primero.

Replacement of the pivot nominals in reflexive passives by their pronominal counterparts requires nominative pronominal forms, which are generally deleted by the rule of Subject Pronoun Drop. The resulting sentences are:[8]

(33) Se vendieron ayer.
      'They were sold yesterday.'

(34) Se cantan siempre primero.
      'They are always sung first.'

The pronominal form of the pivot nominal in reflexive passives is deleted by Subject Pronoun Drop, just as the pronominal forms of other final 1s are. This is further evidence that they are final 1s.

   Third, 1s produced by Reflexive Passive undergo Subject-to-Subject Raising. Thus, the structure that underlies (35) can also be realized as (36):

(35) Parece que las propiedades se vendieron ayer.
      'It seems that the pieces of property were sold yesterday.'

(36) Las propiedades parecen haberse vendido ayer.
      'The pieces of property seem to have been sold yesterday.'

In (36) *las propiedades,* the 1 produced by Reflexive Passive, has become the 1 of *parecer,* triggering the Verb Agreement rule that results in the plural form *parecen.* Since only final 1s undergo Subject-to-Subject Raising, this is evidence that the pivot nominal of a Reflexive Passive is a final 1.

5.3   Interaction of Clause Reduction and Reflexive Passive

We have already shown that certain verbs of Spanish, which we call 'trigger verbs', trigger Clause Reduction, which makes dependents of the complement verb dependents of the trigger verb; this accounts for complement clitics showing up on the trigger verb in surface structure. In §5 we have shown that Spanish has a rule of Reflexive Passive that advances the 2 of the verb to 1. Taken together, our rule of Clause Reduction and our rule of Reflexive Passive make further predictions. Under Clause Reduction, dependents of a complement verb become dependents of the trigger verb, the 2 of the complement of a trigger verb becoming the 2 of the trigger verb itself. And since Reflexive Passive advances the 2 of a verb to 1, it should advance the original complement 2 (the derived 2 of the trigger verb) to *1 of the trigger verb*. We will now show that this prediction is correct.[9]

Consider the trigger verbs *empezar* 'begin', *tratar* 'try', and *querer* 'want'. If the prediction made jointly by Clause Reduction and Reflexive Passive is correct, there should be grammatical sentences in which the initial 2 of a verb embedded beneath one of the trigger verbs *empezar, tratar,* or *querer* undergoes Reflexive Passive and thus becomes the 1 of the trigger verb. The correctness of this prediction is indicated by the following examples:

(37)   Los mapas ya se empezaron a preparar.
       'The maps have already begun to be prepared.'
(38)   Las canciones cortas se tratan de cantar siempre primero.
       'The short songs are always tried to be sung first.'
(39)   Estas secciones de la ciudad se quieren eliminar sin que nadie
       lo sepa.
       'These sections of the city are wanted to be eliminated without
       anyone knowing it.'

In these examples, *los mapas, las canciones cortas,* and *estas secciones de la ciudad* are the final 1s of the verbs *empezaron, tratan,* and *quieren,* respectively. Each of these nominals precedes the verb of which it is the final 1, and in each case the verb is plural in agreement with its final 1. Further, the pronominal forms that replace these nominals are nominative pronouns that undergo Subject Pronoun Drop, producing the following sentences:

(40) a.   Ya se empezaron a preparar.
          'They have already begun to be prepared.'
     b.   Se tratan de cantar siempre primero.
          'They are always tried to be sung first.'
     c.   Se quieren eliminar sin que nadie lo sepa.
          'They are wanted to be eliminated without anyone knowing it.'

In addition, *los mapas, las canciones cortas,* and *estas secciones de la ciudad* can be shown to be final 1s in (37–39) by virtue of the fact that they undergo Subject-to-Subject Raising.

(41) a.   Los mapas parecen haberse empezado a preparar.
          'The maps seem to have begun to be prepared.'
     b.   Las canciones cortas parecen haberse tratado de cantar
          primero.
          'The short songs seem to have been tried to be sung first.'

    c. Estas secciones de la ciudad parecen quererse eliminar sin que nadie lo sepa.
       'These sections of the city seem to be wanted to be eliminated without anyone knowing it.'

Our hypothesis makes another prediction: if the matrix verbs in (37–39) are replaced by verbs that do not trigger Clause Reduction, then such sentences will be ungrammatical. This prediction is also correct. We illustrate this with the verbs *insistir en* 'insist on' and *soñar con* 'dream of', shown in §2 to be nontrigger verbs.

Consider the sentences

(42) Los turistas insistieron en visitar las pirámides.
      'The tourists insisted on visiting the pyramids.'
(43) Sueño con solucionar esos problemas.
      'I dream of solving those problems.'

If the subjects of (42–43) are replaced by PRO, the sentences that would be produced by Reflexive Passive are ungrammatical:

(44) *Las pirámides se insistieron en visitar.
(45) *Esos problemas se sueñan con solucionar.

The ungrammaticality of these examples follows automatically under our hypothesis, under which only the 2 of a verb can undergo Reflexive Passive. Since *insistir en* and *soñar con* do not trigger Clause Reduction, there is no way that *las pirámides* and *esos problemas* can become 2s of these verbs. Hence they cannot undergo Reflexive Passive and *(44–45) are ungrammatical.

Finally, note that if several verbs that trigger Clause Reduction are embedded one beneath the other, the initial 2 of a verb several storeys down can become the 2 of a trigger verb several storeys up and can therefore undergo Reflexive Passive. This results in sentences like

(46) Estas secciones de la ciudad se quieren tratar de eliminar sin que nadie lo sepa.
      'These sections of the city are wanted to try to be eliminated without anyone knowing it.'

Estas secciones de la ciudad, the initial 2 of *eliminar,* becomes the 2 of *querer* (two storeys up) by Clause Reduction, and thus becomes the 1 of *querer* by Reflexive Passive. The result is (46). But if a verb that does not trigger Clause Reduction intervenes, there is no way that the initial 2 of *eliminar* can become the 2, and hence (by Reflexive Passive) the 1, of *querer*. As a result, the following sentence is ungrammatical:

(47) *Estas secciones de la ciudad se quieren insistir en eliminar sin
    que nadie lo sepa.
    (These sections of the city are wanted to insist on being eliminated
    without anyone knowing it.)

In sum, in §5.3 we have shown that the initial 2 of a complement
verb can become the 1 of a matrix verb by Reflexive Passive in those
cases, and only in those cases, where it can become the 2 of that matrix
verb by Clause Reduction. This is exactly what our hypothesis predicts.

6   **Third Type of Evidence for Clause Reduction:
    Object Raising**
6.1   Object Raising

Predicates like *fácil* 'easy', *difícil* 'difficult', and *imposible* 'impossible'
take clausal 1s that can be extraposed, producing sentences like the
following:

(48)   Será difícil componer estas radios.
       'It will be difficult to fix these radios.'
(49)   Es fácil entender los resultados.
       'It is easy to understand the results.'
(50)   Fue imposible comer el postre.
       'It was impossible to eat the dessert.'

Spanish has a rule of Object Raising that raises the 2 of a verb
embedded immediately beneath one of these predicates to 1 of the
matrix predicate. Object Raising produces sentences like the following:

(51)   Estas radios serán difíciles de componer.
       'These radios will be difficult to fix.'
(52)   Los resultados son fáciles de entender.
       'The results are easy to understand.'
(53)   El postre fue imposible de comer.
       'The dessert was impossible to eat.'

In each of these sentences, the initial 2 of the complement is the final
1 of the matrix clause, triggering agreement of the matrix verb and
adjective. Thus, in (51) *serán* and *difíciles* are plural in agreement with
estas radios, and in (52) *son* and *fáciles* are plural in agreement with
los resultados. Note also that in Object Raising sentences the preposition *de* appears between the Object Raising trigger and the complement.
    In all of the above examples, the 3 of the matrix clause (which is
coreferential with the 1 of the embedded clause) is understood as PRO.
Non-PRO 3s of the matrix clause appear in surface structure, preferably
in clause-initial position:[10]

(54)   A Francisco le será difícil componer estas radios.
       'For Francisco it will be difficult to fix these radios.'
(55)   A Francisco estas radios le serán difíciles de componer.
       'For Francisco these radios will be difficult to fix.'

In §6.2 we briefly sketch the evidence that the nominals raised by Object Raising are matrix 1s. In §6.3 we show that Object Raising operates on structures produced by Clause Reduction, providing further evidence for Clause Reduction in Spanish.

6.2   The Subjecthood of the Promoted Nominal in Object Raising Sentences

The raised nominal in Object Raising sentences is the final 1 of the matrix verb and adjective.

In §6.1 we pointed out that the raised nominal in Object Raising sentences triggers agreement on the matrix verb and adjective. This is one piece of evidence that it is the matrix 1.

In addition, the kinds of evidence used to show that the pivot nominal in Reflexive Passive sentences is the final 1 of the verb can also be used to argue for the final 1-hood of the raised nominal in Object Raising sentences.

First, the fact that it generally appears in preverbal position in surface structure follows automatically if it is the final 1.

Second, if the raised nominals are pronominal, they are nominative and undergo Subject Pronoun Drop:

(56)   Serán difíciles de componer.
       'They will be difficult to fix.'
(57)   Son fáciles de entender.
       'They are easy to understand.'

Since only final 1s undergo Subject Pronoun Drop, this is evidence that the raised nominal is the matrix 1.

Third, the raised nominals undergo Subject-to-Subject Raising, which produces (58b) and (59b) below from the structures underlying (58a) and (59a):

(58) a.   Parece que estas radios son difíciles de componer.
          'It seems that these radios are difficult to fix.'
     b.   Estas radios parecen ser difíciles de componer.
          'These radios seem to be difficult to fix.'
(59) a.   Parece que los resultados son fáciles de entender.
          'It seems that the results are easy to understand.'
     b.   Los resultados parecen ser fáciles de entender.
          'The results seem to be easy to understand.'

6.3   Interaction of Clause Reduction and Object Raising

We have shown that Spanish has a rule of Object Raising that raises the 2 of verbs embedded beneath Object Raising triggers to 1. The rule of Clause Reduction and the rule of Object Raising, taken together, make further predictions. Under Clause Reduction, dependents of a complement verb become dependents of the trigger verb, the 2 of the complement of a trigger verb becoming the 2 of the trigger verb. And since Object Raising raises the 2 of a verb, it should be able to raise the original complement 2 (the derived 2 of the trigger verb). We will now show that this prediction is correct.

Consider a structure in which *difícil* has a clausal 1 containing a Clause Reduction trigger and a complement embedded beneath it. One such structure can be realized, with Extraposition, as:

(60)   Será difícil empezar a hacer estos mapas.
       'It will be difficult to begin to make these maps.'

Since Clause Reduction makes the 2 of *hacer* the 2 of *empezar,* Object Raising should be able to make it the 1 of *difícil.* We observe in (61) that it can:

(61)   Estos mapas serán difíciles de empezar a hacer.
       'These maps will be difficult to begin to make.'

Similarly, if we substitute the trigger verb *dejar* (*de*) 'stop' for *empezar,* the initial 2 of the verb embedded beneath it can be raised by Object Raising:

(62)   Es casi imposible dejar de comer estas galletas.
       'It's almost impossible to stop eating these cookies.'
(63)   Estas galletas son casi imposibles de dejar de comer.
       'These cookies are almost impossible to stop eating.'

Clause Reduction makes *estas galletas* the 2 of *dejar,* and Object Raising makes it the 1 of *imposible.*

The Clause Reduction hypothesis, together with the rule of Object Raising, further predicts that if a verb that does not trigger Clause Reduction is embedded beneath an Object Raising trigger, then the 2 of an embedded verb will not be able to undergo Object Raising. We will illustrate this with the verbs *insistir* (*en*) and *soñar* (*con*), which do not trigger Clause Reduction. These verbs can be embedded beneath *difícil,* as the following sentences show:

(64)   Es difícil insistir en hacer tales cosas.
       'It is difficult to insist on doing such things.'
(65)   Es fácil soñar con componer sinfonías como esa.
       'It is easy to dream of composing symphonies like that one.'

But, exactly as our hypothesis predicts, the corresponding Object Raising sentences are ungrammatical:

(66) *Tales cosas son difíciles de insistir en hacer.
(Such things are difficult to insist on doing.)
(67) *Sinfonías como esa son fáciles de soñar con componer.
(Symphonies like that one are easy to dream of composing.)

Our hypothesis likewise predicts that a nominal initially embedded several storeys down can become the 1 of an Object Raising trigger as long as all the intervening verbs are Clause Reduction triggers. And this is correct:

(68)   Errores como esos son difíciles de seguir tratando de corregir.
'Mistakes like those are difficult to keep on trying to correct.'

But if one of the intervening verbs is not a Clause Reduction trigger, there will be no way for the embedded nominal to become the 2 of the verb embedded immediately beneath the Object Raising trigger, and the resulting sentence with Object Raising will be ungrammatical:

(69) *Errores como esos son imposibles de seguir insistiendo en
corregir.
(Mistakes like those are impossible to keep on insisting on correcting.)

The ungrammaticality of *(69) follows from the fact that *insistir* does not trigger Clause Reduction.

In sum, in §6.3 we have shown that in structures in which Clause Reduction has made the 2 of a verb embedded two storeys below an Object Raising trigger the 2 of the verb immediately beneath the Object Raising trigger, this 2 can become the matrix 1 by Object Raising. But in structures without Clause Reduction this is impossible. This is exactly what the Clause Reduction hypothesis predicts.

7   Further Evidence for Clause Reduction: Interaction of Reflexive Passive and Object Raising with Clitic Placement

In §5–6, we argued for Clause Reduction by showing that initial downstairs 2s behave like upstairs 2s by undergoing Reflexive Passive and Object Raising as 2s of the upstairs verb. Our formulation of Clause Reduction, however, makes not only the downstairs 2 but any dependent of the complement verb a dependent of the matrix verb. In this section we provide evidence that 3s of the complement become dependents of the matrix verb.

Crucial to the discussion is the assumption made explicit in §3.3 that a pronominal dependent cliticizes to the verb in the highest clause of which it is a dependent. Our argument focuses on the position of clitics corresponding to initial downstairs 3s in sentences with Clause Reduction. The Clause Reduction hypothesis predicts that in a Clause Reduction structure the initial downstairs 3 will cliticize only to the upper verb and not to the lower verb. Here we will show that this prediction is correct.

7.1   Clitic Placement and Reflexive Passive

Consider the sentences:

(70) a.   Los dueños quieren alquilar*les* estas casas a los generales.
     b.   Los dueños *les* quieren alquilar estas casas a los generales.
          'The owners want to rent these houses to the generals.'

The *les* in (70) is a clitic copy of the 3 *los generales*. Since Clause Reduction is optional, there are two grammatical outputs. In (70a), without Clause Reduction, *los generales* is the final 3 of *alquilar* and not of *querer,* and *les* consequently cliticizes to *alquilar.* In (70b), with Clause Reduction, *los generales* is the final 3 of *querer* as well, and consequently *les* cliticizes to *querer.*

Now consider the structure that is like that of (70) except that the initial 1 of *querer* is PRO instead of *los dueños.* The structure to be considered allows Clause Reduction and Reflexive Passive, with the result that the initial 2 of the complement can be the final 1 of *querer.* Now, our hypothesis that in sentences with Clause Reduction *all* dependents of the lower verb become dependents of the upper verb predicts that, in this case, *los generales,* the initial 3 of *alquilar,* will also be a dependent of the upstairs verb and consequently that *les* will cliticize to *querer,* the upstairs verb. And this is correct:

(71)   Estas casas se *les* quieren alquilar a los generales.
        'These houses are wanted to be rented to the generals.'

The fact that under Clause Reduction *los generales* must become a dependent of *querer* can be seen in the fact that its clitic copy, *les,* cannot cliticize to the lower verb:

(72) *Estas casas se quieren alquilar*les* a los generales.

The ungrammaticality of *(72) is an automatic consequence of our hypothesis. The fact that *las casas* is advanced to 1 of *querer* by Reflexive Passive shows that this is a structure with Clause Reduction. This being the case, *los generales* must be the 3 of *querer,* and as a result its clitic copy *les* must cliticize to the matrix verb *querer* rather than to *alquilar.*

The same thing can be seen in the following examples. Since Clause Reduction is optional, *los estudiantes* can be the 3 either of just *vender* or of *empezar* as well, with corresponding differences in the placement of its clitic copy *les:*

(73) a. Esa compañía empezó a vender*les* estos libros a los
      estudiantes.
   b. Esa compañía *les* empezó a vender estos libros a los
      estudiantes.
     'That company began to sell these books to the students.'

But in a structure in which Reflexive Passive makes the initial 2 of *vender* the 1 of *empezar,* Clause Reduction must have made all dependents of *vender* dependents of *empezar,* with the result that the clitic copy of *los estudiantes* must cliticize to *empezar* and cannot cliticize to *vender:*[11]

(74) a. Estos libros se *les* empezaron a vender a los estudiantes.
     'The books were begun to be sold to the students.'
   b. *Estos libros se empezaron a vender*les* a los estudiantes.

Thus, the Clause Reduction hypothesis explains why the advancement of an initial complement 2 by Reflexive Passive in the upper clause restricts the placement of an initial complement clitic to the upper verb.

7.2 A Contrast Explained

We have seen that Equi triggers such as *querer* 'want' and Subject-to-Subject Raising triggers such as *soler* 'tend', both of which trigger Clause Reduction, make it possible for the initial downstairs 2 to become the 1 of the upstairs verb by Reflexive Passive, as in the following examples:

(75) Secciones de la ciudad como esas se suelen eliminar sin que nadie
     lo sepa.
     'Sections of the city like those tend to be eliminated without
     anyone knowing it.'
(76) Secciones de la ciudad como esas se quieren eliminar sin que
     nadie lo sepa.
     'Sections of the city like those are wanted to be eliminated without
     anyone knowing it.'

However, there is an interesting contrast between these two classes of verbs. In the case of Subject-to-Subject Raising triggers, the clitic *se* that results from Reflexive Passive can also appear on the downstairs verb, while in the case of Equi triggers this is not possible:

(77) Secciones de la ciudad como esas suelen eliminar*se* sin que nadie
     lo sepa.
     'Sections of the city like those tend to be eliminated without
     anyone knowing it.'

(78) *Secciones de la ciudad como esas quieren eliminar*se* sin que nadie lo sepa.

At first glance, the contrast between (77) and *(78) might seem mysterious. This contrast, however, follows automatically from our hypothesis. In the case of Subject-to-Subject Raising triggers like *soler,* Reflexive Passive in the complement can make the initial 2 of the complement the 1 of the complement. As a result of Subject-to-Subject Raising, the 1 of the complement becomes the 1 of the matrix verb. All of this happens in a sentence *without* Clause Reduction (which is optional). As a result, the initial 2 of the complement is the 1 of the matrix verb, but the *se* that results from Reflexive Passive in the complement is still in the complement.[12] Consequently it cliticizes to the complement verb, and sentences like (77) result. With an Equi trigger like *querer,* however, this is impossible. With such verbs, the only way that the initial 2 of the complement can become the 1 of the matrix verb is as a result of the combination of Clause Reduction and Reflexive Passive. And in such cases, since the resulting structure has only one clause, no clitics can appear on the complement verb. Thus sentences like *(78) are ungrammatical.

Thus, contrasts like that between (77) and *(78) are an automatic consequence of our hypothesis. At the same time, they provide an additional piece of evidence for the syntactic difference between Equi triggers and Subject-to-Subject Raising triggers that is quite unlike any of the arguments offered in support of the distinction between these two classes of verbs in English.

7.3   Clitic Placement and Object Raising

Consider the structure that is actualized as:

(79) a.   Va a ser difícil empezar a hacer*les* estos mapas a los profesores.
   b.   Va a ser difícil empezar*les* a hacer estos mapas a los profesores.
       'It's going to be difficult to begin to make these maps for the professors.'

If *empezar* does not trigger Clause Reduction, *estos mapas* and *los profesores* are dependents of *hacer,* and consequently *les* (the clitic copy of *los profesores*) cliticizes to *hacer,* as in (79a). But if *empezar* triggers Clause Reduction, *estos mapas* and *los profesores* are also dependents of *empezar,* and *les* then cliticizes to the higher verb, *empezar,* as in (79b).

If *empezar* triggers Clause Reduction, *estos mapas* (as the 2 of *empezar*) can undergo Object Raising, becoming the 1 of *difícil.* Since this can happen only in a sentence with Clause Reduction, and since Clause Reduction makes both *estos mapas* and *los profesores* dependents of *empezar,* our hypothesis automatically predicts that the clitic copy *les* of *los profesores* cannot cliticize to *hacer.* And this is correct:

(80) *Estos mapas van a ser difíciles de empezar a hacer*les* a los profesores.
      (These maps are going to be difficult to begin to make for the professors.)

Thus, our hypothesis automatically explains why, in Object Raising sentences like *(80), a clitic corresponding to the initial complement 3 cannot appear on the complement verb.

   In Object Raising sentences, most speakers relax the requirement that the 3 have a clitic copy. Thus the structure underlying *(80) is realized as:

(81) Estos mapas van a ser difíciles de empezar a hacer a los profesores.
      'These maps are going to be difficult to begin to make for the professors.'

In sentences that are like (81) except that *los profesores* has a clitic copy, the clitic should attach to *empezar* because *los profesores* is a dependent of *empezar.* However, the resulting sentence is ungrammatical:

(82) *Estos mapas van a ser difíciles de empezar*les* a hacer a los profesores.

The ungrammaticality of sentences like *(82) is left unexplained by our hypothesis.

8   Clause Union in Causatives and Clause Reduction

The causative construction in a number of different languages has been the subject of considerable study in recent years. In Spanish, this construction is found with the verbs *hacer* 'make' and *dejar* 'let'.[13] In the framework of relational grammar, this construction is produced by the rule of Clause Union, which makes all dependents of the embedded verb into dependents of the matrix verb. Clause Union is universally characterized by the following:

(83) a.   If the complement is intransitive, the 1 of the complement verb becomes the 2 of the matrix verb.
     b.   If the complement is transitive, the 2 of the complement verb becomes the 2 of the matrix verb and the 1 of the complement verb becomes the 3 of the matrix verb.

Clause Union produces sentences like the following:

(84) *Los* hice caminar toda la noche.
      'I made them walk all night.'
(85) *Les* hice poner sus nombres en la lista.
      'I made them put their names on the list.'

The complement 1s are the accusative pronoun *los* in (84) and the dative pronoun *les* in (85), indicating their status as a 2 and a 3 of *hacer,* respectively. With *dejar,* Clause Union is optional. In sentences with Clause Union, the complement 1 is the 2 or 3 of the matrix verb, as in (84–85). Sentences without Clause Union may undergo Subject-to-Object Raising, which makes the complement 1 the 2 of *dejar* (regardless of the transitivity of the complement).

The question naturally arises as to the relationship between Clause Union in the causative construction and the process of Clause Reduction that is the topic of this paper. We characterized Clause Reduction by saying that dependents of the complement verb become dependents of the matrix verb. That is also the characterization of Clause Union in the causative construction. Viewed in the framework of relational grammar, the two must be the same rule. We will consequently begin to use 'Clause Union' to refer to the process studied in this paper.

The trigger verbs considered in this paper trigger Clause Union *optionally.* In this respect, they are like *dejar* rather than like *hacer.*

There is another respect in which the trigger verbs studied in this paper differ from both *dejar* and *hacer.* Consider what happens with *querer.* There are grammatical sentences of Spanish in which the 1 of the complement of *querer* is distinct from the 1 of *querer:*

(86) Pilar quiere que mis primos pongan sus nombres en la lista.
      'Pilar wants my cousins to put their names on the list.'

In (86), the complement is introduced by *que,* which is found in sentences with *querer* in which the complement and matrix 1s are distinct. But in sentences with *querer* that undergo Clause Union, the complement 1 has been deleted by Equi. Clause Union with *querer* is thus subject to the condition that the complement 1 must be deleted in order for Clause Union to be possible. This condition differentiates *querer* from *dejar* and *hacer,* accounting for the fact that sentences like (85) with *hacer* are not possible with *querer:*[14]

(87) *Pilar les quiere poner sus nombres en la lista a mis primos.

The other Equi triggers that trigger Clause Union that we have discussed in this paper are subject to the same conditions as *querer.*

Since Clause Union is possible with these verbs only if the complement 1 is the victim of Equi, (83) holds with these verbs. Since the complement 1 is out of the picture, the only part of (83) that is relevant is that the complement 2 becomes the 2 of the matrix verb. Evidence that this is correct has already been presented in §5.6.

It remains to consider the Subject-to-Subject Raising triggers that trigger Clause Union.

We could say that the following characterizes Clause Union with these verbs:

(88)   The 1 of the complement verb becomes the 1 of the matrix verb and the 2 of the complement verb becomes the 2 of the matrix verb.

This characterization does describe the data. But even if we adopt (88), we still need (83).

Since (83b) makes the complement 2 the 2 of the matrix verb, (88) is not needed for that; it is needed only to make the 1 of the complement the 1 of the matrix verb. But we already have a device that makes the 1 of the complement into the 1 of the matrix verb: Subject-to-Subject Raising, which these verbs trigger. Thus, if we say that Clause Union operates on structures produced by Subject-to-Subject Raising, (88) can be eliminated. Then we can say that Equi triggers such as *querer* 'want' and Subject-to-Subject Raising triggers such as *soler* 'tend' allow Clause Union under exactly the same condition:

(89)   Clause Union is possible with these verbs only if the complement has no 1.

Thus Clause Union will be possible with Equi triggers like *querer* only upon deletion of the complement 1 by Equi and with Subject-to-Subject Raising triggers like *soler* only upon raising of the complement 1 to become the 1 of the matrix verb. Condition (89) governs Clause Union with both of these verb classes. And the fact that they are subject to this condition is what differentiates the behavior of these verbs with respect to Clause Union from that of *hacer* and *dejar*, which are not subject to (89).

9   A Proposed Universal of Grammar

We began this study with the observation that with certain matrix verbs, clitics that originate in the complement can appear on the matrix verb. We considered two hypotheses to account for this phenomenon of clitic climbing—one that posited a rule of Clitic Climbing and one that posited a rule of Clause Union. We have given evidence that in Spanish, the clitic-climbing phenomenon is due to Clause Union and not to a rule of Clitic Climbing. We now wish to make an additional claim:

(90)   There is no language whose grammar contains a rule of Clitic Climbing that moves clitics from a complement clause into the matrix clause.

We claim that the clitic-climbing phenomenon in any language is due to Clause Union, which unites the two clauses into a single clause. Clitic Placement then places a clitic on the highest verb of which it is a dependent.[15] The fact that this happens in Spanish, we claim, is not an accident of Spanish grammar, but the only possibility.

In (90) we claim that Clitic Climbing is not a possible rule of human language. We thus adopt the view that the inventory of possible rules is a restricted set specified by universal grammar.[16]

Our claim that the clitic-climbing phenomenon is universally due to Clause Union makes certain testable predictions.

First, recall the constraints on placement of more than one clitic dependent of the same verb that were discussed in §4.1, and the ungrammaticality of sentences with intersecting clitic climbing of the kind that were discussed in §4.2. Our hypothesis that the clitic-climbing phenomenon is universally due to Clause Union predicts that these phenomena will be universal. More specifically, in no language will sentences like those starred in §4 be grammatical.

Our hypothesis that the clitic-climbing phenomenon is universally due to Clause Union has two sides to it. On the one hand, we claim that no language can have a rule of Clitic Climbing. On the other, we propose that in languages in which clitics are placed on the verb, a clitic is placed on the highest verb of which it is a dependent. This makes predictions about the placement of clitics in sentences in which initial dependents of a complement verb become dependents of the matrix verb.

In relational grammar, there are only two ways that dependents of a complement verb can become dependents of the matrix verb—by raising rules and by Clause Union. Our hypothesis about Clitic Placement predicts that in cases in which complement dependents become matrix verb dependents by a raising rule, the raised nominal, if pronominal, will cliticize in the matrix clause. Other dependents of the complement verb, which do not become dependents of the matrix verb, will cliticize in the complement.

In cases where a given verb triggers Clause Union, however, all dependents of the complement verb will become dependents of the matrix verb. Thus, if they are pronominal, they will cliticize in the matrix clause. There are two aspects of this prediction.

First, our hypothesis predicts that in a language with the clitic-climbing phenomenon, the class of verbs that can be shown on other grounds to trigger Clause Union will be the same class of verbs that accepts complement clitics, while those verbs that do not trigger Clause Union will be the verbs that do not accept complement clitics.

Second, our hypothesis predicts that in a given sentence that can be accounted for only on the assumption that Clause Union has been triggered (such as the reflexive passives in Spanish discussed in §5 and the Object Raising sentences discussed in §6), clitics originating in a complement that has merged with the matrix clause can be placed only on the matrix verb and not on the complement verb. Any deviations from this will be due to rules or constraints for which there is independent evidence in the language in question.

Stated in the most general terms, our hypothesis predicts that whatever evidence there may be in a particular language to decide between the Clitic Climbing hypothesis and the Clause Union hypothesis will in fact decide in favor of the Clause Union hypothesis.

Postscript

In this paper, we argued that certain verbs in Spanish occur in structures in which dependents of the complement are also dependents of the matrix clause. In §8 we claimed that this is but a special case of Clause Union, a widely recognized rule in causative constructions. The difference is that, with certain verbs, Clause Union is possible only in structures involving Equi or Raising. The latter verbs are called 'Clause Reduction triggers'. Since Clause Union is involved with both classes of verbs, we use the term 'Clause Union' in this Postscript both for Clause Union in structures involving Equi or Raising (called 'Clause Reduction' earlier), and for Clause Union in causative constructions. We depart from this only in §P1, where we again call the former 'Clause Reduction' to distinguish it from the latter.

In §§P1–P2, we give two additional arguments for Clause Union in structures involving Equi or Raising in Spanish. In §P3 we make explicit one of our results, which has the consequence that clitic placement is a diagnostic for clause membership. A relational analysis in terms of Clause Union is contrasted in §P4 with transformational proposals in terms of adjunction or 'restructuring'.

P1   Evidence for Clause Reduction Based on Interaction with Clause Union in Causatives

Aissen (1977) presents an additional argument for Clause Union in Equi and Raising structures (i.e., 'Clause Reduction') in Spanish based on its interaction with Clause Union in causative constructions. Spanish

Perlmutter's work on the postscript was supported in part by the National Science Foundation through Grant No. BNS 78-17498 to the University of California, San Diego, and an I. W. Killam Senior Fellowship at the University of British Columbia.

has Clause Union with the causative verbs *hacer* 'make' and *dejar* 'let', among others.[17] Clause Union in Spanish conforms to the scheme proposed as universal in Perlmutter and Postal 1974, given in (83) and restated here in terms of RNs:

(P1) a.   The final 1 of a finally intransitive complement heads a 2-arc in the matrix clause.

     b.   The final 1 of a finally transitive complement heads a 3-arc in the matrix clause.

Since the complement in (P2) is intransitive, its final 1 is a matrix 2 and is therefore in the accusative case. In (P3) the complement is transitive, so its final 1 is a 3 of the matrix clause and is therefore in the dative case:[18]

(P2) a.   *La*   hice   correr.
        her-ACC I-made run
        'I made her run.'

     b.   *Le hice correr.

     c.

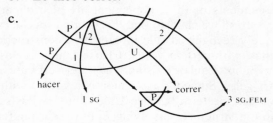

(P3) a.   *Le*   hice   buscar las herramientas.
        her-DAT I-made seek   the tools
        'I made her look for the tools.'

     b.   *La hice buscar las herramientas.

     c.

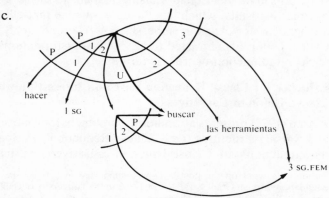

Evidence that the complement 2 *las herramientas* in (P3) heads an arc in the matrix clause comes from the fact that its pronominal clitic appears on the matrix verb:

(P4) a.   Se *las* hice buscar.[19]
          'I made her look for them.'
      b.   *Le hice buscar*las*.[20]

Finally, in the Clause Union construction the final 1 of the complement cannot appear between the matrix and complement verbs:[21]

(P5) a.   *Le* hice *a Pilar* buscar las herramientas.
      b.   *Le* hice buscar las herramientas *a Pilar*.
          'I had Pilar look for the tools.'

Descriptively then, we can isolate three properties of causative Clause Union in Spanish. First, the grammatical relation borne by the complement 1 to the matrix clause depends on the final transitivity of the complement, as indicated in (P1). Second, clitics corresponding to complement nominals appear in the matrix clause. Third, the complement 1 cannot appear between the Clause Union trigger and the complement infinitive.

Dejar 'let' occurs in two constructions:

(P6) *Les*   dejamos ganar la   partida *a los extranjeros*.
      them-DAT we-let   win   the game   to the foreigners
      'We let the foreigners win the game.'
(P7) Dejamos *a los extranjeros* ganar la partida.
      'We let the foreigners win the game.'

Sentence (P6) is an example of Clause Union, with the final 1 of a transitive complement the 3 of the matrix clause:

(P8)

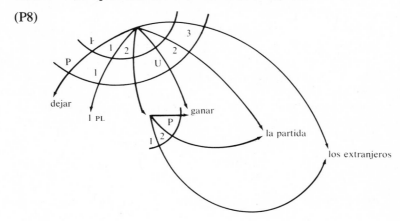

We assume (P7) to be a case of Subject-to-Object Raising, the final 1 of the complement heading a 2-arc in the matrix clause.[22]

(P9)

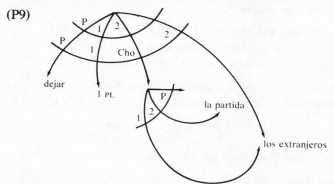

In the Clause Union construction, *all* elements heading arcs in the complement also head arcs in the main clause, while in the Subject-to-Object Raising construction, only the final 1 of the complement does.

There are three pieces of evidence for the contrasting analyses of (P6) and (P7) given in (P8) and (P9). First, a pronoun corresponding to *los extranjeros* in (P6) will be in the dative case, while one corresponding to *los extranjeros* in (P7) will be accusative. Thus, the clitic copy *les* of *los extranjeros* in (P6) is dative, but in dialects in which final 2s also have clitic copies, the copy of *los extranjeros* in (P8) is accusative and not dative:

(P10) a.   *Los* dejamos *a los extranjeros* ganar la partida.
          'We let the foreigners win the game.'
      b. **Les* dejamos *a los extranjeros* ganar la partida.

Second, the linear position of *los extranjeros* is different in the two cases. In (P6) it has the position that *Pilar* has in the Clause Union construction in (P5). The fact that *los extranjeros* intervenes between the matrix verb and the infinitive in (P7) shows that this cannot be Clause Union. Third, the position of a clitic corresponding to the complement 2 *la partida* in (P6) and (P7) reflects the differences in structure posited in (P8) and (P9). As (P9) indicates, *la partida* heads a 2-arc only in the complement. A clitic corresponding to it therefore must appear in the complement:

(P11) a.   Dejamos a los extranjeros ganar*la*.
          'We let the foreigners win it.'
      b. **La* dejamos a los extranjeros ganar.[24]

In (P6, P8), however, *la partida* heads a 2-arc in the matrix clause, and so a clitic corresponding to it appears with the matrix verb:

(P12) a.   Se *la* dejamos ganar a los extranjeros.[25]
          'We let the foreigners win it.'
      b.   *Les dejamos ganar*la* a los extranjeros.

Now that the structures corresponding to (P6) and (P7) have been established, consider the situation where the complement C_1 in a Clause Union construction itself has an infinitival complement C_2. The final 1 of C_1 can only be accusative:

(P13) a.   *La* dejé empezar a bailar.
          'I let her begin to dance.'
      b.   **Le* dejé empezar a bailar.

Presumably, (P13a) could be the result of either Clause Union or Subject-to-Object Raising. The sentence *(P13b) would result under Clause Union if the complement of *empezar* were a *final 2* of *empezar*. If that were the case, the complement would be transitive in the final stratum, its final 1 would head a 3-arc in the matrix clause, and a pronoun corresponding to it would be in the dative case, as in *(P13b). The ungrammaticality of *(P13b) thus shows that the complements of infinitival Clause Union complements are not final 2s of those complement clauses.[26]

It is the final transitivity of the clause *immediately below* the Clause Union trigger that is decisive for Clause Union. The transitivity of the clause beneath that one is irrelevant.

(P14) a.   Vamos a dejar*la* perseverar en buscar la respuesta.
          'We're going to let her persevere in looking for the answer.'
      b.   *Vamos a dejar*le* perseverar en buscar la respuesta.
(P15) a.   *La* dejamos soñar con ganar el premio.
          'We let her dream of winning the prize.'
      b.   **Le* dejamos soñar con ganar el premio.

The fact that *buscar la respuesta* and *ganar el premio* are transitive clauses makes no difference; the complements of *dejar* whose transitivity determines the fate of the complement 1 under Clause Union are the clauses whose predicates are *perseverar* and *soñar*. Examples *(P14b) and *(P15b) therefore have the same status as *(P13b).[27]

It is crucial that *perseverar* and *soñar* do *not* govern Clause Reduction. For sentences with Clause Reduction triggers in their place, the Clause Reduction hypothesis makes a prediction:

(P16)   There are well-formed structures in which the 2 of the *complement* of a Clause Reduction trigger is a 2 of the reduction trigger's clause. If such a structure is embedded beneath *dejar,* its final 1 will be a 3 of the *dejar* clause under Clause Union.

This prediction is confirmed, as can be seen in the dative form *le* of the pronominal clitic:

(P17)   Van a dejar*le* empezar a sacar las fotografías *a Pilar*.
        'They're going to let Pilar start to take the pictures.'
(P18)   *Al niño le* dejaron tratar de hacer los deberes solo.
        'They let the child try to do his homework by himself.'

With Clause Reduction triggers such as *empezar* 'begin' and *tratar* 'try' instead of nontriggers such as *perseverar* 'persevere' and *soñar* 'dream', the 2s of the complements of these clauses also head 2-arcs in these clauses, which makes them finally transitive. As a consequence, the complement 1 is a 3 of the *dejar* clause under Clause Union.

Examples (P17–P18) contrast with (P14–P15). They confirm the prediction of the Clause Reduction hypothesis, providing additional evidence that it is correct.

This argument rests on the claim that (P17–P18) involve Clause Union in addition to Clause Reduction. Three facts support this.

First, if the most deeply embedded clause is finally intransitive rather than transitive, the final 1 of the Clause Reduction trigger will be the 2 and not the 3 of *dejar*. The contrast between (P13) and (P17–P18) confirms this.

Second, if the 2 of the most deeply embedded clause is pronominal, it will attach to the Clause Union trigger and not to either of the two embedded verbs. This is because under Clause Union it heads an arc in the clause of the Clause Union trigger, the highest clause in which it heads an arc. This too is confirmed:

(P19) a.   Van a dejár*selas* empezar a sacar.
           'They're going to let her start taking them.'
      b.   *Van a dejar*le* empezar a sacar*las*.
      c.   *Van a dejar*le* empezar*las* a sacar.

Third, the 3 of *dejar* (the final 1 of its complement) cannot separate *dejar* and the complement verb:

(P20) a.   *Le* dejamos *a Pilar* empezar a sacar las fotos.
      b.   *A Pilar le* dejamos empezar a sacar las fotos.
           'We let Pilar start taking the pictures.'
(P21) a.   *Le* dejaron *al niño* tratar de hacer los deberes solo.
      b.   *Al niño le* dejaron tratar de hacer los deberes solo.
           'They let the child try to do his homework alone.'

Since *dejar* also governs Subject-to-Object Raising, there are grammatical sentences in which the final 1 of the complement of *dejar* is the 2 of the *dejar* clause (and is consequently accusative) regardless of the transitivity of the complement:

(P22) a.   Van a dejar*la* empezar a sacar las fotos.
           'They're going to let her start taking the pictures.'
      b.   *Lo* dejaron tratar de hacer los deberes solo.
           'They let him try to do his homework alone.'

Since in this construction the 2 of the most deeply embedded clause does not head an arc in the *dejar* clause, its clitic cannot appear in the *dejar* clause. Two positions are possible for clitics here, depending on whether or not the *empezar* clause and its complement are united by Clause Reduction. If they are, then *las fotos* heads a 2-arc in both the *sacar* clause and the *empezar* clause; its clitic then attaches to *empezar:*

(P23)   Van a dejarla empezar*las* a sacar.
        'They're going to let her start taking them.'

Without Clause Reduction, the 2 of the *sacar* clause does not head any arcs in any other clauses, and consequently attaches to *sacar:*

(P24)   Van a dejarla empezar a sacar*las*.
        'They're going to let her start taking them.'

Finally, with Subject-to-Object Raising, the final 2 of *dejar* (the final 1 of its complement) may separate *dejar* from the complement infinitive:

(P25) a.   Van a dejar *a Pilar* empezar a sacarlas.
           'They're going to let Pilar begin to take them.'
      b.   Dejaron *al niño* tratar de hacerlos solo.
           'They let the child try to do it alone.'

Embedding Clause Reduction triggers beneath *dejar* thus allows the full range of sentences our analysis predicts. The crucial point concerns the contrast between (P14–P15) and (P17–P18), which provides further evidence for Clause Reduction, that is, for Clause Union in structures involving Raising or Equi.

P2   Interaction of Clause Union with Passive
P2.1   Passive

It was noted in §5.1 that Spanish has both (Plain) Passive and Reflexive Passive, both of which involve advancement of a 2 to 1.[28] In (Plain) Passive sentences, the verb appears in the past participial form with the auxiliary verb *ser* 'be', and the Passive chômeur is marked with the preposition *por:*

(P26)   Las cartas le fueron devueltas.
        'The letters were returned to him.'
(P27)   El maestro es respetado por todos.
        'The teacher is respected by everyone.'
(P28)   El secreto me fue revelado por su esposa.
        'The secret was revealed to me by his wife.'

The advancees in (P26–28) (*las cartas, el maestro,* and *el secreto*) can be shown to be final-stratum 1s by the same arguments that were used in Reflexive Passive and Object Raising sentences. First, they occur in immediate preverbal position, which is the natural position for final 1s in Spanish. Second, if they are replaced by pronouns, the subject pronominal forms must be used; use of the object pronoun forms results in ungrammaticality. As noted in §1.2, no subject pronouns corresponding to inanimate final 1s appear overtly:

(P29)   a.   Le fueron devueltas.
             'They were returned to him.'
        b.   *Se *las* fueron devueltas.[29]
(P30)   a.   (El) es respetado por todos.
             'He is respected by everyone.'
        b.   *Lo* es respetado por todos.

Third, the advancee to 1 in Passive clauses can be the final 1 of a matrix clause in the Subject-to-Subject Raising construction:

(P31)   Las cartas parecen haberle sido devueltas.
        'The letters seem to have been returned to him.'

In (P31), *las cartas* is the final 1 of the matrix clause, causing the verb *parecen* to appear in the plural form. This indicates that it is the final 1 of the complement, since Subject-to-Subject Raising is restricted to final 1s in Spanish.

P2.2   Interaction of Passive and Clause Union

We have hypothesized that in sentences involving Clause Union the final 2 of the complement is a 2 of the matrix clause. Passivization of such nominals should be possible in the matrix clause, as in (P32b) and (P33b):

(P32)   a.   Los obreros están terminando de pintar estas paredes.
             'The workers are finishing painting these walls.'
        b.   Estas paredes están siendo terminadas de pintar (por los
             obreros).
             (Lit.: 'These walls are being finished to paint (by the
             workers).')

(P33) a.   Los obreros acabaron de pintar las casas ayer.
          'The workers finished painting the houses yesterday.'
     b.   Las casas fueron acabadas de pintar (por los obreros)
          ayer.
          (Lit.: 'The houses were finished to paint (by the workers)
          yesterday.')

These pairs of sentences have the same type of rough synonymy exhibited by other active-passive pairs. In each case, the *matrix* verb is in the participial form (*terminadas, acabadas,* etc.) characteristic of passive clauses. This makes these sentences unlike anything in English.

The possibility of such sentences follows from the Clause Union hypothesis. Since the matrix verbs in (P32–P33) trigger Clause Union, it is possible for a final 2 of the complement to be a 2 of the matrix clause and advance to 1 in the passive construction.

Our hypothesis further predicts that if the matrix verb is *not* a Clause Union trigger, a final 2 of the complement cannot be a 2 of the matrix clause and therefore cannot passivize there:

(P34) a.   Insistieron en pintar las paredes.
          'They insisted on painting the walls.'
     b. *Las paredes fueron insistidas en pintar.
          (Lit.: The walls were insisted on to paint.)

(P35) a.   Soñaron con construir edificios como ese.
          'They dreamed of building buildings like that one.'
     b. *Edificios como ese fueron soñados con construir.
          (Lit.: Buildings like that one were dreamt of building.)

The contrast of sentences (P32b) and (P33b) with sentences (P34b) and (P35b) follows from the Clause Union hypothesis.

Unsupplemented by any further devices, the Clause Union hypothesis predicts that *all* Clause Union triggers will occur in grammatical passives like (P32–P33). However, this is not the case; some Clause Union triggers allow this, but the majority do not. Thus, *(P36b) and *(P37b) are ungrammatical:

(P36) a.   Trataron de pintar las paredes ayer.
          'They tried to paint the walls yesterday.'
     b. *Las paredes fueron tratadas de pintar ayer.
          (Lit.: The walls were tried to paint yesterday.)
(P37) a.   Quieren cortar esta madera.
          'They want to cut this wood.'
     b. *Esta madera es querida cortar.
          (Lit.: This wood is wanted to cut.)

The subclass of Clause Union triggers that allow passives like (P32b) and (P33b) seems to be roughly the class that specifies the end point of an action. We have no explanation for this, which we assume to be a language-particular fact that needs to be stated in the grammar of Spanish. Thus we assume that there are languages in which Passive in Clause Union structures is not limited to a small subclass of Clause Union triggers.

P2.3   Interaction of Passive and Clitic Placement

Our hypothesis makes the following claims:

(P38) a.   Passive sentences like (P32–P33) in which the *matrix* clause is passive, are possible only in sentences involving Clause Union.
     b.   In sentences involving Clause Union, any clitics from the complement appear on the matrix verb.

From (P38a–b) it follows that in sentences like (P32–P33) involving both Clause Union and Passive, a clitic from the complement can appear on the matrix verb but not on the complement verb. To test this prediction, consider an example in which the complement clause has a clitic:

(P39)   *Les* pintan las paredes a los dueños.
     'They paint the walls for the landlords.'

Les is the required clitic copy of the final 3, *los dueños*. To test the prediction of (P38a–b), consider an example in which (P39) is embedded beneath *terminar*. Our prediction is correct, as can be seen in the contrast between (P40b) and *(P41b).

(P40) a.   *Les* están terminando de pintar estas paredes a los dueños.
     b.   Están terminando de pintar*les* estas paredes a los dueños.
     'They are finishing painting these walls for the landlords.'

(P41) a.   Estas paredes *les* están siendo terminadas de pintar a los dueños.
     (Lit.: 'These walls are being finished to paint for the landlords.')
     b.   *Estas paredes están siendo terminadas de pintar*les* a los dueños.

Examples (P40a–b) are not passives. Example (P40a) involves Clause Union while (P40b) does not; the clitic appears on the matrix verb in (P40a) and on the complement verb in (P40b). Example (P41a) involves Clause Union and Passive, with the matrix verb *terminadas* in the past participial form. Since this sentence involves Clause Union, the clitic *les* necessarily appears on the matrix verb, as in (P41a). Example *(P41b) illustrates the fact that a clitic from the complement cannot appear on the complement verb, as (P38a–b) together predict. The ungrammaticality of *(P41b) thus provides additional evidence for (P38a–b), and hence for the Clause Union hypothesis.

P3   Clitic Placement in a Universal Perspective

In §9 we claimed that no language can have a rule of Clitic Climbing that moves clitics from a lower clause to a higher clause. This claim can be stated in terms of RNs as follows:

(P42)   A clitic cannot appear in a clause unless the nominal in question heads an arc in that clause.

Thus, unless a nominal heading an arc in a complement also heads an arc in the matrix clause (as in Raising and Clause Union constructions), its clitic cannot appear in the matrix clause. However, nothing excludes cases in which the clitic of a nominal heading arcs in both the complement and matrix clauses appears in the complement.

It is necessary to distinguish clearly between a principle like (P42), which restricts the clause in which clitics can appear, and a language-particular clitic placement rule, as in Spanish:

(P43)   Clitic Placement in Spanish
Clitics are proclitic on a finite verb and enclitic on a nonfinite verb.

Together with appropriate definitions of 'finite' and 'nonfinite', (P43) will account for the position of Spanish clitics within the clause.[30] For languages in which clitics occupy different positions in the clause, different language-particular clitic placement rules will be needed.

The interesting claim that clitic placement provides a diagnostic of clause membership is made in (P42); if a clitic ostensibly from a complement appears in the matrix clause, the only possibilities are Raising and Clause Union. In the case of Raising, on the one hand, only the raised nominal can cliticize in the matrix clause; all other dependents of the complement must cliticize in the complement. In the case of Clause Union, on the other hand, all dependents of the complement can cliticize in the matrix clause (unless there is a language-particular rule specifying that they cliticize in the complement).

P4   Clause Union Contrasted with Adjunction or Restructuring

The arguments for Clause Union (Clause Reduction) show dependents of a complement behaving like dependents of the matrix clause. We conceive of this phenomenon in terms of grammatical relations, proposing that in this construction nominals that bear grammatical relations to the complement clause also bear relations to the matrix clause. This is the essence of the Clause Union proposal. The formal device to accomplish this consists of assigning the relevant sentences RNs in which nominals heading arcs in the complement also head arcs in the matrix clause.

Rivas (1974) and Rizzi (1976, 1978),[31] working in a transformational framework, conceive of sentence structure not in terms of grammatical relations, but rather in terms of structures representing linear order and dominance relations. Their conception of syntactic rules is that of operations on the linear order or dominance relations among elements of a sentence or both. Consequently they account for data like that discussed here in these terms. Rizzi (1978, pp. 117–18) states:

> The hypothesis for which I would like to argue is the following: there exists a restructuring rule in Italian syntax, governed by modals, aspectuals, and motion verbs . . . which optionally re-analyzes a terminal substring V_x (P) V as a single verbal complex, hence automatically transforming the underlying bisentential structure into a simple sentence. . . . Consider an intermediate structure such as (16), successive to the application of Equi or Subject Raising; Restructuring can reanalyze the terminal substring included in the braces as a single verbal complex . . . :

(16)

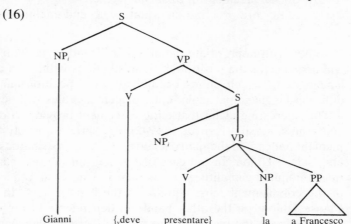

If Restructuring has applied to (16), yielding the simple structure (17a), nothing can not prevent the clitic from moving to the "main verb" *dovere* . . . and further application of C[litic] P[lacement] will yield (17b):

(17) a.   Gianni [$_V$ deve presentare] la a Francesco.
  b.   Gianni la deve presentare a Francesco.

If Restructuring has not applied to (16), the structure remains bisentential.[32]

The basic idea of Rizzi's proposal is clear:

(P44)   Restructuring
   A rule is posited which creates a single node dominating both the matrix verb and the embedded verb. Other devices (the formulation of other rules, universal constraints, etc.) are appealed to to yield the correct outputs.

Clause Union in a relational framework and Restructuring in a transformational framework are both trying to account for the same phenomenon:

(P45)   Elements of the complement behave like elements of the matrix clause.

Both proposals seek to collapse two clauses into one in order to account for (P45). The question is which is the appropriate device to account for (P45)—Clause Union or Restructuring? At issue in a larger sense are the relational and transformational frameworks themselves: which provides the right concepts to account for (P45)?

Although there are many differences in detail, it is unlikely that there is evidence in Italian or Spanish to decide between the two proposals (see note 35). The significant difference between them concerns the different predictions the two devices make about the class of natural languages:

(P46) a.   Restructuring predicts that (P45) will be found only in languages where a single node can be posited dominating the verbs of the complement and the matrix clause.
  b.   Clause Union predicts that (P45) can be found in languages regardless of whether or not the complement and matrix verbs form a single constituent.

For example, under the Clause Union proposal, the complement verb heads a Union arc in the matrix clause[33] and can be assigned linear precedence relations in that clause as a function of its heading a Union arc in that clause; it therefore need not be adjacent to the matrix verb.

The question, then, is whether there are languages with (P45), where the matrix and complement verbs are not even adjacent. In fact, such languages are attested.

First, Cole (to appear) argues convincingly that Ancash Quechua has

Clause Union in Equi (and perhaps Raising) constructions,[34] just as in the Spanish cases called Clause Reduction. One argument for this is based on the fact that the validator $m(i)$, which can attach only to elements of the matrix clause, can attach to elements of the complement in the Clause Union construction, thus providing evidence that in this construction they are dependents of the matrix clause:

(P47) a.   *Qalla-rqo-o* kechwa-ta-*m*   *yachatsi-r.*
             begin-PAST-1 Quechua-ACC-VAL teach-INFIN
             'I began to teach Quechua.'
       b.   Noqa *muna-a* Lima-chaw-*mi yacha-y-ta.*
             I   want-1 Lima-in-VAL   live-INFIN-ACC
             'I want to live in Lima.'
       c.   Noqa kay wata *qalla-rqo-o* Lima-chaw-*mi yacha-r.*
             I   this year begin-PAST-1 Lima-in-VAL   live-INFIN
             'I began to live in Lima this year.'

Of primary interest here is the fact that the matrix and complement verbs, italicized in (P47), are not adjacent in the string.[35] Ancash Quechua is thus a language with (P45) in sentences where the matrix and complement verbs are not adjacent.

Second, there are cases of Clause Union in *causative* constructions in which the matrix and complement verbs are not adjacent. Toman (1976) argues for Clause Union in Czech sentences like:

(P48)   Jana se   nechala Karlovi   vyfotografovat.
         Jana REFL let   Karel/DAT photograph
         'Jana_i let Karel photograph her_i.'

Here the matrix and complement verbs *nechala* and *vyfotografovat* are not adjacent. In the same vein, Craig (1977) argues for Clause Union in Jacaltec sentences like

(P49)   Ch-oň   y-a'   naj munlahoj.
         ASP-A1PL E3-make he to-work
         'He makes us work.'

Here the matrix and complement verbs *y-a'* and *munlahoj* are not adjacent.

Cases like those cited from Ancash Quechua, Czech, and Jacaltec can be characterized in terms of Clause Union, with the complement predicate heading a Union arc and the other complement dependents heading arcs in the matrix clause, but not in terms of adjunction or restructuring.

Notes

1. This structure ignores a number of things, such as the tense of the verb, the internal structure of the nominal *un regalo,* and the clitic copy *le* of the 3 *Mercedes.* Spanish has a rule that creates pronominal copies of 3s. These pronominal copies appear as clitics attached to the verb in surface structure. This copying rule is generally obligatory. It produces the clitics that are crucial to the argument in §7.

2. The class membership of verbs whose indirect objects control Equi is subject to extreme variation from speaker to speaker. For example, for many speakers *ordenar* 'order' is a trigger verb, while *sugerir* is a nontrigger verb. But there are many speakers for whom *sugerir* is a trigger verb, and some speakers for whom *ordenar* is a nontrigger verb.

We have noticed that for many speakers there are certain verbs whose class membership is not clear. In such cases, the speaker may have difficulty deciding whether a particular verb behaves like a trigger verb or a nontrigger verb, or may change his or her mind from week to week.

3. The Multiple Clitic Constraint is not the only device one might use to rule out sentences like *(16–17) in the framework of transformational grammar. For example, one might postulate a structure in which all clitic dependents of a verb are dominated by a single node and then make Clitic Climbing move that node rather than moving the clitics individually. The point is that under the Clitic Climbing hypothesis, the ungrammaticality of *(16–17) does not follow automatically. Under the Clause Reduction hypothesis, however, it does.

4. As was indicated in §2, there is a great deal of variation from speaker to speaker with respect to which verbs are trigger verbs, especially in the case of verbs that take an initial 3. Thus, while *permitir* is a trigger verb for many speakers, there are also speakers for whom it is not. For such speakers, our argument can be reconstructed using a different verb in the examples.

5. It might be thought that the ungrammaticality of such sentences would follow from the conjunction of the following three things: (a) a cyclical theory of grammar; (b) a statement that the rule of Clitic Climbing is cyclical; and (c) whatever device is used to account for the ungrammaticality of sentences like *(16–17) in §4.1. Thus, it might be thought that once *lo* moves to *permitir* on the second cycle, the requirement that *te* and *lo* have to move together or not move at all would be sufficient to insure that *(23) would not be generated. To see that this will not be sufficient to prevent the generation of ungrammatical sentences, consider:

(i) *Jorge dijo que *te* quiero permitir*lo* hacer.
    (Jorge said that . . .)

Even with (a–c), under the Clitic Climbing hypothesis ungrammatical sentences like *(i) can be generated if on the *querer*-cycle, *te* attaches to *quiero* and on the cycle of *dijo, lo* attaches to *permitir.* Thus, even with (a–c), it would still be necessary to posit something to prevent sentences like *(i) from being generated. To accomplish this, one could add yet another condition, one like the Strict Cycle Condition proposed by Chomsky (1973, p. 243).

However, this proposal is still untenable because in a cyclical theory of grammar, Clitic Climbing cannot be a cyclical rule. This conclusion was reached by Perlmutter (1973). We give here only one of his arguments, which is based on the Platense dialect of Spanish spoken in the Río de la Plata basin of Argentina and Uruguay.

The Platense dialect has an obligatory rule of Clitic Doubling that creates a pronominal copy of a definite animate 2; as a result of Clitic Placement, the pronominal copy appears on the verb in surface structure. This dialect thus has sentences like

(ii)   *Los* vi a los chicos ayer.
'I saw the children yesterday.'

In (ii) the *los* preceding the verb is a clitic copy of the 2, *los chicos*. Clitic Doubling in the complement of an Object Raising trigger can be seen in the sentence

(iii)   Es difícil convencer*los* a los chicos.
'It is difficult to convince the children.'

In (iii) the clitic copy *los* of the 2 of *convencer* appears on *convencer*. Now, if Clitic Doubling were a cyclical rule, it would apply in the complement of sentences like (iii) on the first cycle. However, Object Raising could apply on the second cycle, producing the ungrammatical sentence

(iv)   *Los chicos son difíciles de convencer*los*.

The grammatical sentence that should result is one without a clitic copy:

(v)   Los chicos son difíciles de convencer.
'The children are difficult to convince.'

One could propose adding an ad hoc constraint to the grammar preventing Object Raising from applying if Clitic Doubling has applied in the complement, but even that would not work in dialects such as the Platense dialect in which Clitic Doubling is obligatory; with such a constraint in the grammar, (v) could not be generated. It is therefore necessary to conclude that in a cyclical theory of grammar, Clitic Doubling is a postcyclical rule.

To show that Clitic Climbing cannot be a cyclical rule, it suffices to show that it applies to clitics produced by Clitic Doubling, as in:

(vi) a.   Quiero seguir criticándo*los* a los candidatos.
'I want to continue criticizing the candidates.'
b.   Quiero seguir*los* criticando a los candidatos.
c.   *Los* quiero seguir criticando a los candidatos.

Since Clitic Climbing cannot be a cyclical rule and (b) states that it is, any account of the ungrammaticality of sentences like *(23) that depends on (b) must be spurious.

For dialects of Spanish that do not have the rule of Clitic Doubling, the interaction of Clitic Placement and Object Raising can be used to show that Clitic Placement must be postcyclical in a cyclical theory of grammar. It then follows that Clitic Climbing cannot be cyclical because it applies to clitics produced by Clitic Placement.

6. Note that the Clause Reduction hypothesis also correctly predicts the ungrammaticality of the sentence

(i)   *Lo* quiero permitir*te* hacer.

In *(i) *lo,* the initial dependent of *hacer,* appears on the matrix verb *querer,* while *te,* the initial dependent of *permitir,* remains on *permitir.* Under the Clause Reduction hypothesis, the only way that *lo* can appear on *querer* in surface structure is if both *querer* and *permitir* trigger Clause Reduction. But then *te* would appear on *querer* as well, and the result would be (21).

7. Sentences (31–32) are actually generated by the grammar as grammatical sentences as a result of the application of the spurious *se* rule discussed by Perlmutter (1971, pp. 20–25) and Aissen and Rivas (1975). This rule produces (31–32) from sentences with the clitic sequences *le las* or *les las* by changing the third person dative pronoun *le* or *les* to *se*. Thus (31–32) are grammatical with the meanings 'They sold them to him/her/them yesterday' and 'They always sing them to him/her/them first.' But the *se* in (31–32) cannot be the *se* found in reflexive passives, and as a result (31–32) do not have the meanings they would have if they were reflexive passives. Because they are ungrammatical as reflexive passives, we have starred them.

8. Subject pronouns can remain in surface structure only if they are animate and under emphasis or contrast. Since the pivot nominals in the sentences under discussion are inanimate, the nominative pronominal forms they would have cannot appear in surface structure, but rather must be deleted by Subject Pronoun Drop.

9. Arguments similar to these are offered by Rivas (1974) in support of a rule of Verb Adjunction formulated in the transformational framework.

10. Spanish has a rule doubling a 3 as a clitic pronoun. In most instances, this rule is obligatory. The *le* in (54–55) is the clitic copy of the 3 (*Francisco*).

11. Some speakers accept sentences such as

(i)   Estos libros se empezaron a vender a los estudiantes.
       'These books were begun to be sold to the students.'

In (i) the 3 *los estudiantes* lacks a clitic copy. In this construction these speakers relax the requirement that the 3 have a clitic copy.

12. In using the phrase "is still in the complement" we are deliberately being imprecise because a discussion of the nature of Reflexive Passive in Spanish lies beyond the scope of this paper. Given our assumption that Clitic Placement places a clitic on the highest verb of which it is a dependent, it would have to be the case that the *se* that results from Reflexive Passive is a dependent of the verb. In fact, we claim that this is the case, since we maintain that Reflexive Passive advances the 2 of a verb to 1, leaving behind a copy as 2, which reflexivizes. As a result, we get the reflexive pronoun *se,* which is a dependent of the verb and cliticizes to it. Spanish Reflexive Passive is thus a member of the class of 'copy advancements' postulated by Perlmutter and Postal. To justify that here, however, would take us beyond the scope of this paper.

13. For studies of this construction in Spanish, see Aissen 1974a, 1974b and Bordelois 1974.

14. Sentence *(87) might be grammatical for some speakers with the meaning 'Pilar wants to put their names on the list for my cousins', but regardless of whether or not it can have this meaning, it definitely is not grammatical with a meaning synonymous with (86). Since this is the only point of relevance here, we have starred it.

15. In languages in which the clitic appears not on the verb itself, but rather in second position in the clause, the clitic will appear in second position in the clause defined by the verb of which it is a classic dependent. In the discussion that follows, we will speak loosely of Clitic Placement as placing clitics "on the verb," not bothering to repeat each time that in some languages clitics actually appear in second position in the clause in surface structure, rather than attached to the verb.

16. On this view of the nature of the options open to particular languages, see Postal 1970, Ross 1970, Bach 1971, Hankamer 1971, and Perlmutter and Orešnik 1973.

17. For many speakers, *mandar* 'have' is also a Clause Union trigger. Among the verbs of perception, at least *ver* 'see' and *oir* 'hear' govern Clause Union. Some properties of this construction are subject to dialectal and idiolectal variation which makes it impossible to draw any conclusions from the grammaticality or ungrammaticality of isolated sentences. Claims can only be made in the context of analyses of other classes of sentences in a given dialect or idiolect.

18. For many speakers, *hacer* also governs Subject-to-Object Raising, as noted for *dejar* 'let' below.

19. The clitic sequence *se las* occurs instead of the expected *le las*. This is due to the previously mentioned 'Spurious *se*' rule.

20. Some speakers accept sentences like *(P4b). A sentence like it is cited by Roldán (1974, p. 135), presumably as grammatical. One of our informants also accepts *(P4b).

21. This is a special case of a broader generalization: no nominals (and little else) can appear between the Clause Union trigger and the complement infinitive.

22. The clitic *le* in (P5) is a copy of the final 3 *Pilar*.

23. Another possibility is that (P7) is an Equi construction, with *los extranjeros* the initial 2 of the matrix clause. If this were the case, our argument would not be affected.

The *a* preceding *los extranjeros* in (P7) appears with certain final 2s. Since final 3s are regularly marked with *a* in Spanish, the contrast between dative and accusative case of pronominal clitics (*not* the presence of *a*) must be used to distinguish final 2s from final 3s (though even this is subject to some dialectal variation).

24. Various scholars, including Bordelois (1974), Rivas (1974), and Roldán (1974) attribute the ungrammaticality of sentences like *(P11b) to the putative inability of clitics to "cross" a nominal (or most adverbs) between the main and embedded verbs. This has no bearing on our argument.

Some speakers may accept the sentence *La dejamos ganar a los extranjeros.* This is a less preferred variant of (P12a) (without a clitic copy of the final 3).

25. The clitic sequence *se la* in (P12) is due to the 'Spurious *se*' rule.

26. We offer no principled account of this fact. Since *empezar* governs Raising, Raising out of its complement would make the complement a chômeur, which would account for the fact that it is not a final 2. However, such an account will not work in all cases because the facts are the same if the complement verb governs not Raising but Equi.

27. Under our assumptions, (P13a), (P14a), and (P15a) should be structurally ambiguous, having both Clause Union and Subject-to-Object Raising (or, as discussed in note 23, Equi) structures.

28. For discussion of Plain Passive and Reflexive Passive, and a proposal concerning the structure of these two constructions, see Perlmutter and Postal (to appear).

29. This is the form (P29a) would have if the accusative pronoun *las* were used for *las cartas*. The third person singular dative pronoun *le* would then be realized as *se* because of the 'Spurious *se*' rule.

30. In order for (P43) to be sufficient to account for the details of clitic

placement in Spanish, it is necessary to group the indicative and subjunctive verb forms together as finite and the infinitive, gerund, and imperative as nonfinite. The fact that clitics precede the verb in negative imperatives will follow from the fact that subjunctive forms are used in negative imperatives.

While this solution works for Spanish, it would not work for French or Italian, where clitics precede the verb in negative imperatives, and where negative imperatives use verb forms that elsewhere require clitics to follow them. However, the question of how these details of clitic placement in French and Italian are to be handled is beyond the scope of this paper.

31. Rizzi's 1976 paper on Italian and ours on Spanish were written at the same time, independently of each other. The parallels between the two papers with respect to their conclusions and the argumentation used to support them are striking. Although our paper began with a reference to our work on Italian, Rizzi's paper made publication of that work superfluous.

Rizzi (1978, n. 31) refers to our paper as follows: Rivas (1974) "has been reconsidered in a relational framework by Aissen and Perlmutter (1976)." This statement is misleading in several respects.

Rivas made the fundamental observation that the verbs allowing so-called clitic climbing and those allowing what we analyze as Reflexive Passive are the same. However, our paper pursued the consequences of this observation and consequently contains a number of arguments based on areas of data that Rivas did not consider: 1) the argument for what we called 'Clause Reduction' based on its interaction with Object Raising; 2) the arguments based on the fact that complement clitics cannot appear on the complement verb in clauses with Reflexive Passive involving the complement 2 and in clauses with Object Raising involving the complement 2; 3) the argument for the distinction between Equi and Raising structures based on the placement of *se* in impersonal constructions; 4) the uniting of the phenomena in Equi and Raising structures with causative constructions.

Rizzi's statement also ignores the different predictions verb adjunction and Clause Union make about the class of natural languages. One of the goals of §P4 is to make these different predictions explicit.

32. Rizzi 1978, pp. 117–18. Like Quicoli (1980), Rizzi appeals to Chomsky's (1973, 1977) Specified Subject Condition to block clitic movement in structures to which Restructuring has not applied. For a critique of Quicoli's treatment, see Postal 1981.

33. The Union relation, which characterizes Clause Union constructions, is the relation the predicate of the complement bears to the main clause in such constructions.

34. Cole explicitly claims that Ancash Quechua has Clause Union in Equi constructions, but makes no claims about Raising constructions. Some of his examples (such as those with *qalla* 'begin') suggest that Clause Union may also be found in Raising constructions in this language. Pursuit of this question would require tests distinguishing between Equi and Raising structures in Ancash Quechua.

35. Since Ancash Quechua has considerable freedom of word order, it also has Clause Union in sentences where the matrix and complement verbs *are* adjacent.

Even Italian and Spanish may provide an argument like that based on Ancash Quechua, since in these languages adverbs can intervene between the two verbs in the construction we treat by Clause Union and Rizzi by Restructuring.

From this, Rizzi (1978, p. 154) concludes that the node he posits as dominating the matrix and complement verbs together cannot simply be a *V*-node. He seems to regard this as a detail about the derived structure produced by Restructuring. However, it can also be interpreted as evidence that (P45) is possible even in cases where the two verbs are not adjacent (as in (P47) in Ancash Quechua, and in the Czech and Jacaltec examples cited below), and hence that the Restructuring approach to the phenomenon is inferior to a Clause Union and relational approach to clause structure.

References

Aissen, Judith L. 1974a. "The Syntax of Causative Constructions." Ph.D. diss., Harvard University.

————. 1974b. "Verb Raising." *Linguistic Inquiry* 5:325–66.

————. 1977. "The Interaction of Clause Reduction and Causative Clause Union in Spanish." In *Proceedings of the Seventh Annual Meeting of the North Eastern Linguistic Society.* Cambridge, Mass.: MIT Press.

Aissen, Judith L., and Rivas, Alberto. 1975. "The Proper Formulation of the Spurious-*se* Rule in Spanish." In *Proceedings of the First Annual Meeting of the Berkeley Linguistics Society.* Berkeley: University of California.

Anderson, Stephen and Kiparsky, Paul, eds. 1973. *A Festschrift for Morris Halle.* New York: Holt, Rinehart & Winston.

Bach, Emmon. 1971. "Questions." *Linguistic Inquiry* 2:153–66.

Bordelois, Ivonne. 1974. "The Grammar of Spanish Causative Complements." Ph.D. diss., MIT.

Chomsky, Noam. 1973. "Conditions on Transformations." In Anderson and Kiparsky 1973.

Chomsky, Noam. 1977. "On WH-Movement," in Peter Culicover, Thomas Wasow and Adrian Akmajian, eds. *Formal Syntax.* New York: Academic Press.

Cole, Peter (to appear) "Clause Reduction in Ancash Quechua."

Craig, Colette G. 1977. *The Structure of Jacaltec.* Austin and London: University of Texas Press.

Hankamer, Jorge. 1971. "Constraints on Deletion in Syntax." Ph.D. diss., Yale University.

Perlmutter, David M. 1971. *Deep and Surface Structure Constraints in Syntax.* New York: Holt, Rinehart & Winston.

————. 1973. "Evidence for a Post-Cycle in Syntax." Paper presented at the annual meeting of the Linguistic Society of America, San Diego.

————. 1976. "Evidence for Subject Downgrading in Portuguese." In J. Schmidt-Radefeldt, ed., *Readings in Portuguese Linguistics.* Amsterdam: North-Holland Publishing Co.

————. 1979. *'Predicate': A Grammatical Relation.* In *Linguistic Notes from La Jolla,* 6. (University of California, San Diego).

Perlmutter, David M., and Orešnik, Janez. 1973. "Language-Particular Rules and Explanation in Syntax." In Anderson and Kiparsky 1973.

Perlmutter, David M., and Postal, Paul M. 1974. Lectures on Relational Grammar, Summer Linguistic Institute of the Linguistic Society of America, University of Massachusetts at Amherst.

————. 1977. "Toward a Universal Characterization of Passivization." In *Pro-*

ceedings of the Third Annual Meeting of the Berkeley Linguistics Society (University of California, Berkeley). Reprinted in this volume.

————. This volume. "Some Proposed Laws of Basic Clause Structure."

————. To appear. "Impersonal Passives and Some Relational Laws."

Postal, Paul M. 1970. "The Method of Universal Grammar." In Paul Garvin, ed., *Method and Theory in Linguistics*. The Hague: Mouton & Co.

————. 1981. "A Failed Analysis of the French Cohesive Infinitive Construction." *Linguistic Analysis* 8.3:281–323.

Quícoli, Antonio Carlos. 1980. "Clitic Movement in French Causatives." *Linguistic Analysis* 6:131–85.

Rivas, Alberto. 1974. "Impersonal Sentences and Their Interaction with Clitic Movement in Spanish." Unpublished paper, MIT.

Rizzi, Luigi. 1976. "Ristrutturazione." *Rivista di Grammatica Generativa* 1:1–54.

————. 1978. "A Restructuring Rule in Italian Syntax." In S. Jay Keyser, ed. *Recent Transformational Studies in European Languages*. Cambridge, Mass.: MIT Press.

Roldán, Mercedes. 1974. "Constraints on Clitic Insertion in Spanish." In R. J. Campbell et al., eds. *Linguistic Studies in Romance Languages*. Washington, D.C.: Georgetown University Press.

Ross, John R. 1970. "Gapping and the Order of Constituents." In Manfred Bierwisch and Karl Erich Heidolph, eds. *Progress in Linguistics*. The Hague: Mouton & Co.

Toman, Jindřich. 1976. "Clause Union in Czech: Some Implications for the Study of Causatives in Universal Grammar." In *Papers from the Sixth Meeting of the North Eastern Linguistic Society*. Montreal: McGill University, Université de Montréal, and Université du Québec à Montréal.

Index